# Lecture Notes in Artificial Inte

T0259900

## Subseries of Lecture Notes in Computer Science

### LNAI Series Editors

Randy Goebel
*University of Alberta, Edmonton, Canada*
Yuzuru Tanaka
*Hokkaido University, Sapporo, Japan*
Wolfgang Wahlster
*DFKI and Saarland University, Saarbrücken, Germany*

### LNAI Founding Series Editor

Joerg Siekmann
*DFKI and Saarland University, Saarbrücken, Germany*

Massimo Cossentino   Michael Kaisers
Karl Tuyls   Gerhard Weiss (Eds.)

# Multi-Agent Systems

9th European Workshop, EUMAS 2011
Maastricht, The Netherlands, November 14-15, 2011
Revised Selected Papers

 Springer

Series Editors

Randy Goebel, University of Alberta, Edmonton, Canada
Jörg Siekmann, University of Saarland, Saarbrücken, Germany
Wolfgang Wahlster, DFKI and University of Saarland, Saarbrücken, Germany

Volume Editors

Massimo Cossentino
ICAR-CNR, Palermo, Italy
E-mail: cossentino@pa.icar.cnr.it

Michael Kaisers
Maastricht University, Department of Knowledge Engineering
Maastricht, The Netherlands
E-mail: michaelkaisers@googlemail.com

Karl Tuyls
Maastricht University, Department of Knowledge Engineering
Maastricht, The Netherlands
E-mail: k.tuyls@maastrichtuniversity.nl

Gerhard Weiss
Maastricht University, Department of Knowledge Engineering
Maastricht, The Netherlands
E-mail: gerhard.weiss@maastrichtuniversity.nl

ISSN 0302-9743                       e-ISSN 1611-3349
ISBN 978-3-642-34798-6       e-ISBN 978-3-642-34799-3
DOI 10.1007/978-3-642-34799-3
Springer Heidelberg Dordrecht London New York

Library of Congress Control Number: 2012951794

CR Subject Classification (1998): I.2.11, I.2, H.3, H.4, C.2.4, D.2

LNCS Sublibrary: SL 7 – Artificial Intelligence

© Springer-Verlag Berlin Heidelberg 2012
This work is subject to copyright. All rights reserved, whether the whole or part of the material is
concerned, specifically the rights of translation, reprinting, re-use of illustrations, recitation, broadcasting,
reproduction on microfilms or in any other way, and storage in data banks. Duplication of this publication
or parts thereof is permitted only under the provisions of the German Copyright Law of September 9, 1965,
in its current version, and permission for use must always be obtained from Springer. Violations are liable
to prosecution under the German Copyright Law.
The use of general descriptive names, registered names, trademarks, etc. in this publication does not imply,
even in the absence of a specific statement, that such names are exempt from the relevant protective laws
and regulations and therefore free for general use.

*Typesetting:* Camera-ready by author, data conversion by Scientific Publishing Services, Chennai, India

Printed on acid-free paper

Springer is part of Springer Science+Business Media (www.springer.com)

# Preface

In the last two decades, we have seen a significant increase of interest in agent-based computing. This field is now set to become one of the key technologies in the twenty-first century. It is crucial that both academics and industrialists within Europe have access to a forum at which current research and application issues are presented and discussed.

In December 2003, the First European Workshop on Multi-Agent Systems (EUMAS) was held at the University of Oxford, UK. This workshop emerged from a number of related workshops and other scholarly activities that were taking place at both national and European levels, and was intended to provide a single recognized forum at which researchers and those interested in activities relating to research in the area of autonomous agents and multi-agent systems could meet, present research results, problems, and issues in an open and informal but academic environment. This set-up allows for discussions of the latest, potentially preliminary findings of state-of-the-art research.

Following in the tradition of past EUMAS events (Oxford 2003, Barcelona 2004, Brussels 2005, Lisbon 2006, Hammamet 2007, Bath 2008, Agia Napa 2009, and Paris 2010), the aim of the 9th European Workshop on Multi-Agent Systems held in Maastricht (The Netherlands) during November 14–15, 2011, was to encourage and support activity in the research and development of multi-agent systems, in academic and industrial efforts.

In 2011, the EUMAS workshop had 45 papers accepted for oral presentation and the demo session hosted four contributions. The workshop was very well attended and the presentations gave the opportunity for several debates often continuing during the coffee breaks.

The two-day event also gave the opportunity to listen to three exciting invited talks given by Marie-Pierre Gleizes (Université Paul Sabatier, France), Peter McBurney (King's College London, UK), and Milind Tambe (University of Southern California, USA).

After the workshop, the best papers were selected taking into account the reviews they received during the pre-workshop review phase and the discussion generated by their presentations. The authors of these papers were asked to significantly improve their manuscripts and the resulting works passed through a new review cycle. These papers are the backbone of this book. They are perfectly completed by three papers written by the invited speakers, discussing key issues in multi-agent systems.

May 2012

Massimo Cossentino
Michael Kaisers
Karl Tuyls
Gerhard Weiss

# Organization

The 9th European Workshop on Multi-Agent Systems (EUMAS 2011) was held in Maastricht (The Netherlands) during November 14–15, 2011. It was hosted by the Department of Knowledge Engineering at Maastricht University, and co-organized by the Swarmlab at Maastricht University and the Istituto di Reti e Calcolo ad Alte Prestazioni, Consiglio Nazionale delle Ricerche, Palermo, Italy.

## Executive Committee

### Conference Chair

Karl Tuyls     Maastricht University, The Netherlands
Gerhard Weiss     Maastricht University, The Netherlands

### Program Chair

Massimo Cossentino     Consiglio Nazionale delle Ricerche, Italy

### Organizing Committee Chair

Michael Kaisers     Maastricht University, The Netherlands
Steven de Jong     Maastricht University, The Netherlands

## Local Organizing Committee

Sjriek Alers     Haitham Bou Ammar     Daniel Hennes
Daan Bloembergen     Joscha-David Fossel     Nyree Lemmens

## Reviewers

Leila Amgoud     Cristiano Castelfranchi     Bruce Edmonds
Matteo Baldoni     Vincent Chevrier     A. El-Fallah-Seghrouchni
Bernhard Bauer     Maria Chli     Edith Elkind
Michael Berger     Massimo Cossentino     Marc Esteva
Elizabeth Black     Paul Davidsson     Alessandro Farinelli
Olivier Boissier     Yves Demazeau     Nicoletta Fornara
Elise Bonzon     Marina Devos     Giancarlo Fortino
Rafael Bordini     Oguz Dikenelli     Martin Fredriksson
Vicent Botti     Yannis Dimopoulos     Rubén Fuentes-Fernández
Dídac Busquets     Juergen Dix     Chiara Ghidini
Javier Carbo     Kurt Driessens     Paolo Giorgini

Marie-Pierre Gleizes
Jorge Gomez-Sanz
J.C. González Moreno
Vladimir Gorodetsky
Nathan Griffiths
Vincent Hilaire
Koen Hindriks
Jomi Hubner
Wojciech Jamroga
Tomas Klos
Abderrafiaa Koukam
Daniel Kudenko
Joao Leite
Brian Logan
Nicolas Maudet
John-Jules Meyer
Simon Miles
Pavlos Moraitis
Marc Métivier

Pablo Noriega
Emma Norling
Ann Nowé
Eugénio Oliveira
Andrea Omicini
Santiago Ontañón
Nardine Osman
Mario Paolucci
Juan Pavón
Wojciech Penczek
Wolfgang Renz
Alessandro Ricci
J. Rodriguez-Aguilar
Jeff Rosenschein
Michael Rovatsos
Jordi Sabater-Mir
Luca Sabatucci
David Sarne
Michael Schumacher

Valeria Seidita
Murat Sensoy
Onn Shehory
Carles Sierra
Angelo Susi
Kuldar Taveter
Karl Tuyls
M. Birna Vanriemsdijk
László-Zsolt Varga
Wamberto Vasconcelos
Laurent Vercouter
Giuseppe Vizzari
Gerhard Weiss
Danny Weyns
Cees Witteveen
Michael Wooldridge
Pinar Yolum

## Subreviewers

Reyhan Aydogan
Cristina Baroglio
Volha Bryl
Henrique Cardoso
Pilar Dellunde
Oğuz Dikenelli
Henry Franks
Stéphane Galland
José M. Gascueña
   Noheda
Nicolas Gaud
A. Guerra-Hernández
Akin Gunay

Valeriia Haberland
Maaike Harbers
Majd Hawasly
Magdalena Kacprzak
Ozgur Kafali
Andrew Koster
Shahar Kosti
Jérôme Lacouture
Sylvain Lemouzy
Bin Lu
Msury Mahunnah
Elisa Marengo
Mirko Morandini

Ingrid Nunes
David Ramos-Valcarcel
Ana Paula Rocha
Igor Rochlin
Inna Shvartsman
Nadav Sofi
Nikolaos Spanoudakis
Jose M. Such
Maciej Szreter
Joana Urbano
Matthew Whitaker
Michael Winsper

## Editors of This Volume

Massimo Cossentino
Michael Kaisers
Karl Tuyls
Gerhard Weiss

# Sponsoring Institutions

# Table of Contents

## European Workshop on Multi-Agent Systems

# Reinforcement Learning Transfer Using a Sparse Coded Inter-task Mapping

Haitham Bou Ammar[1], Matthew E. Taylor[2], Karl Tuyls[1], and Gerhard Weiss[1]

[1] Department of Knowledge Engineering, Maastricht University
The Netherlands
[2] Department of Computer Science, Lafayette College
USA

**Abstract.** Reinforcement learning agents can successfully learn in a variety of difficult tasks. A fundamental problem is that they may learn slowly in complex environments, inspiring the development of speedup methods such as transfer learning. Transfer improves learning by reusing learned behaviors in similar tasks, usually via an inter-task mapping, which defines how a pair of tasks are related. This paper proposes a novel transfer learning technique to autonomously construct an inter-task mapping by using a novel combinations of sparse coding, sparse projection learning, and sparse pseudo-input gaussian processes. Experiments show successful transfer of information between two very different domains: the mountain car and the pole swing-up task. This paper empirically shows that the learned inter-task mapping can be used to successfully (1) improve the performance of a learned policy on a fixed number of samples, (2) reduce the learning times needed by the algorithms to converge to a policy on a fixed number of samples, and (3) converge faster to a near-optimal policy given a large amount of samples.

## 1 Introduction

Reinforcement Learning (RL)is a popular framework that allows agents to solve sequential-action selection tasks with minimal feedback. Unfortunately, RL agents may learn slowly in large or complex environments due to the amount of computational effort and/or experience needed to attain an acceptable performing policy. Transfer Learning [17] (TL) is one technique used to cope with this difficulty by providing a good starting prior for the RL agent attained in a related source task.

The source task can differ from the target task in many ways. If the tasks have different representations of state or action spaces, some type of mapping between the tasks is required. This inter-task mapping matches each state/action pair of the source task to its corresponding state/action pair in the target facilitating transfer. While there have been a number of successes in using such a mapping, the approaches are typically hand-coded and may require substantial human knowledge [17,19]. Our contributions in this paper are twofold. First, we propose a novel scheme to automatically learn an inter-task mapping between two tasks. Second, we introduce the new *Transfer Least Squares Policy Iteration* (TrLSPI) algorithm for transfer between tasks of continuous state spaces and discrete action spaces.

M. Cossentino et al. (Eds.): EUMAS 2011, LNAI 7541, pp. 1–16, 2012.
© Springer-Verlag Berlin Heidelberg 2012

To the best of our knowledge, this paper shows the first successful attempts to automatically transfer between RL benchmark tasks that are very different. Namely, we conduct experiments to automatically transfer from the Mountain Car to the Pole balancing problem. Our results show (1) improved performance on a fixed number of samples, (2) a reduction in the convergence times to attain a policy on a fixed number of samples, and (3) a reduction in the time needed to attain a near-optimal policy on a large amount of samples.

The rest of the paper proceeds as follows. Related work is discussed next in Section 2. Background information is presented in Section 3. Section 4 describes how an inter-task mapping can be learned between two tasks by leveraging sparse coding, sparse projection learning and sparse pseudo-input gaussian processes. In Section 5, we introduce our novel TrLSPI algorithm showing how the learned mapping can be used to transfer information between a source task and target task. Experiments of transfer between two very different tasks are presented in Section 6. Section 7 presents a discussion on the scope an applicability of our framework. Section 8 concludes and reflects upon interesting future work directions.

## 2   Related Work

In the past few years there has been a significant amount of work done in transfer learning for RL tasks. This section outlines the most related work and contrasts it with the work in this paper.

The majority of current transfer learning work in RL assumes that either 1) the two agents are very similar and no mapping is needed, or 2) the inter-task mapping is provided by a human. For instance, [19] transfers advice and [17] transfers Q-values — both methods assume that a mapping between the state and action variables in the two tasks has been provided. Another approach is to frame different tasks as having a shared *agent space* [5], so that no explicit mapping is needed. However, this requires that the agent acting in both tasks share the same actions and a human to map new sensors back into the agent space. The primary contrast between these methods and the current work is that we are interested in *learning* a mapping between states and actions in pairs of tasks, rather than assuming that it is provided or unnecessary.

Our previous work [1] required the presence of hand-coded features shared between two tasks in order to automatically learn the inter-task mapping. This work extends the previous approach to overcome the need for a *predefined common subspace* to determine the inter-task mapping.

There has also been recent work that approaches fully autonomous transfer. For example, semantic knowledge about state features between two tasks may be used [6,9], background knowledge about the range or type of state variables can be used [14,18], or transition models for each possible mapping could be generated and tested [15]. Transfer learning has also been successful across different domains, e.g., using a simple discrete, deterministic task to improve learning on a complex, continuous, noisy task [16]. However, there are currently no general methods to learn an inter-task mapping without requiring (1) background knowledge, which is not typically present in RL settings, or (2) an expensive analysis of an exponential number of inter-task mappings.

This paper overcomes these problems by automatically discovering high-level features and using them to conduct transfer within reasonable time requirements.

Unlike all other existing methods (to the best of our knowledge) and complementary to our previous work [1,15,16], we assume differences among all the variables of Markov Decision Processes describing the source and target tasks and focus on learning an *inter-state mapping*, rather than a state-variable mapping. Additionally, our framework can use state-dependent action mappings, allowing flexibility that other existing algorithms do not.

## 3  Background

This section provides the reader with a short overview of *sparse coding*, *reinforcement learning*, *gaussian processes*, *transfer learning* and other learning methods used in this paper.

### 3.1  Reinforcement Learning (RL)

In an RL problem, an agent must decide how to sequentially select actions to maximize its expected long term reward [3,13]. Such problems are typically formalized as Markov decision processes (MDPs). An MDP is defined by $\langle S, A, P, R, \gamma \rangle$, where S is the (potentially infinite) set of states, A is the set of all possible actions that the agent may execute, $P : S \times A \rightarrow S$ is a state transition probability function defining the transition dynamics, $R : S \times A \rightarrow \mathbb{R}$ is the reward function measuring the performance of the agent, and $\gamma \in [0, 1)$ is the discount factor. A policy $\pi : S \rightarrow A$ is defined as a probabilistic mapping from a state to an action, where $\pi(a|s)$, represents the probability of choosing an action $a$ in a state $s$. The goal of an RL agent is to improve its policy, potentially reaching the optimal policy $\pi^\star$ represented by taking greedy actions in the optimal Q-function:

$$Q^\star(s, a) = \max_\pi E[\sum_{t=0}^{\infty} \gamma^t R(s_t, a_t)|s = s_0, \pi] \tag{1}$$

In tasks with continuous state and/or action spaces, the $Q$ functions and policies cannot be represented in a table format, typically requiring sampling and function approximation techniques. This paper uses one such technique, *Least Squares Policy Iteration* (LSPI), which will be explained in Section 5.2.

### 3.2  Transfer Learning in RL Tasks

Typically, when using Transfer Learning (TL) in RL tasks, there is a source and a target task [17]. When the source and the target tasks are related, transferring a learned source behavior should improve learning in the target task by providing an informative prior. The prior will restrict the exploration in the target task by biasing the agent so that it chooses actions that are better than random exploration, reducing the target task learning times and improving the overall performance. In our formulation, each of these tasks is defined as an MDP which is a tuple of $\langle S^{(i)}, A^{(i)}, P^{(i)}(s,a), R^{(i)}, \gamma^{(i)} \rangle$ for $i \in \{1,2\}$ where $S^{(i)}$, $A^{(i)}$, $P^{(i)}(s,a)$, $R^{(i)}$ and $\gamma^{(i)}$ represent the state spaces, action spaces, state transition probabilities, reward functions and discount factors for each of the source $(i=1)$ and target $(i=2)$ tasks.

The source and the target task may differ in their state spaces and/or action spaces (as well as other components of the MDP). If transfer is to be useful when such differences exist, an inter-task mapping relating these state-action spaces differences [17] can be used. Traditionally, such a mapping was thought to be a one-to-one mapping between the state/action variables representing the tasks [17]. This paper instead considers a mapping that relates state-action successor state triplets from the source with the target task. Mathematically, $\chi : S_s \times A_s \times S_s \rightarrow S_t \times A_t \times S_t$, where $S$ and $A$ represent the state space and the action space of the source and the target task, respectively. This paper's inter-task mapping is more than just a one-to-one mapping between the state and/or action spaces of the MDPs. It also includes other terms that are automatically discovered by our global approximators, which ultimately enhance the transfer approach.

The main focus in this paper is the automatic discovery of an inter-task mapping to enable transfer. The upcoming sections will further clarify the need for such a mapping as well as describe our novel framework.

### 3.3  Sparse Coding

*Sparse coding* (SC) [8] is an unsupervised learning technique used to find a high-level representation for a given set of unlabeled input data. It does this by discovering a succinct over-complete basis for the provided data set. Given $m$ $k$-dimensional input vectors, $\zeta$, SC finds a set of $n$ basis vectors, $\mathbf{b}$, and activations, $a$, with $n > k$ such that $\zeta \approx \sum_{j=1}^{n} a_j^{(i)} \mathbf{b}_j$, where $i$ and $j$ represent the number of input data patterns and number of bases, respectively. SC begins by assuming a Gaussian and a sparse prior on the reconstruction error ($\zeta^{(i)} - \sum_{j=1}^{n} a_j^{(i)} \mathbf{b}_j$) and on the activations, leading to the following an optimization problem:

$$\min_{\{\mathbf{b}_j\},\{a_j^{(i)}\}} \sum_{i=1}^{m} \frac{1}{2\sigma^2} ||\zeta^{(i)} - \sum_{j=1}^{n} \mathbf{b}_j a_j^{(i)}||_2^2 \qquad (2)$$
$$+\beta \sum_{i=1}^{m} \sum_{j=1}^{n} ||a_j^{(i)}||_1$$
$$s.t. \ ||\mathbf{b}_j||_2^2 \le c, \forall j = \{1,2,\ldots,n\}$$

The problem presented in Equation 2 is considered to be a "hard" optimization problem as it is not jointly convex (i.e, in the activations and bases). However, fast and efficient optimization algorithms exist [8] and were used in our work.

### 3.4 Gaussian Processes

*Gaussian processes* (GPs) constitute a research field by themselves. It is beyond the scope of this paper to fully detail the mathematical framework. This section briefly explains GPs and refers the reader elsewhere [11] for a more in-depth treatment.

GPs are a form of supervised learning used to discover a relation between a given set of input vectors, $\mathbf{x}$, and set of output pairs, $\mathbf{y}$. As opposed to normal regression techniques that perform inference in the weight space, GPs perform inference directly in the functional space, making learning simpler. Following existing notation [11], if a function is sampled according to a GP we write:

$$f(\mathbf{x}) \sim \mathcal{GP}(m(\mathbf{x}), k(\mathbf{x}, \mathbf{x}')), \tag{3}$$

where $m(\mathbf{x})$ and $k(\mathbf{x}, \mathbf{x}')$, represent the mean and covariance function that fully specify a GP.

Learning in a GP setting involves maximizing the marginal likelihood:

$$\log p(\mathbf{y}|\mathbf{x}) = -\frac{1}{2}\mathbf{y}^T\mathbf{K}^{-1}\mathbf{y} - \frac{1}{2}log|\mathbf{K}| - \frac{n}{2}log2\pi. \tag{4}$$

Maximizing Equation 4 may be computationally complex as we must invert the covariance matrix $\mathbf{K}$, which is of order of $O(N^3)$, where $N$ is the number of input points. Therefore, we use a fast learning technique, *sparse pseudo-input gaussian processes* (SPGP), as proposed elsewhere [12].

SPGPs aim to reduce the complexity of learning and prediction in GPs by parametrizing the regression model with $M << N$ pseudo-input points, while still preserving the full Bayesian framework. The covariance of the GP model is parametrized by the location of the $M << N$ pseudo-inputs. Existing results [12] show a complexity reduction in the training cost (i.e., the cost of finding the parameters of the covariances) to $O(M^2N)$ and in the prediction cost (i.e., prediction on a new set of inputs) to $O(M^2)$.

## 4  Learning the Inter-task Mapping

In order to automatically construct an inter-task mapping, $\chi$, this paper proposes a novel framework using sparse coding, a $L_1$ projection scheme, and *sparse pseudo-input gaussian processes*. Each of these methods is necessary to solve a problem that is inherent to TL in RL tasks. We approach the problem of learning the inter-task mapping, $\chi$, as a supervised learning problem. As $\chi$ is a mapping relating state-action triplets from the source with the target task, related triplets should be provided as training data points. Unfortunately, this is itself a hard problem — it is not trivial for the user to describe what state triplets in the source task correspond to what in the target task. We therefore approach this problem by automatically transforming the problem spaces (i.e., the state-action spaces of the two tasks) into a higher representational space through SC, projecting the target task data onto those attained bases and then using a Euclidean distance measure to gauge similarity (Section 4.1). At this stage, the data set is provided to a regressor to construct the inter-task mapping. Many regression techniques could be applied to the approach but we chose to use a non-parametric approximation scheme because of its generalization advantages.

Our framework can conceptually be split into three essential parts. The first is the dimensional unification of both the source and target task state-action spaces of the MDPs. The second is the automatic discovery of a high dimensional informative space for the source task. This is achieved through SC, as described in Section 4.1, ensuring that transfer is conducted in a high representational space of the source task. In order to use a similarity measure among different patterns, the data should be present in the same space. That is why the target task samples still need to be projected to the attained high representational space of the source. This is done using sparse projection learning, described in Section 4.2. The third and final step is to approximate the inter-task mapping via a non-parametric regression technique, explained in Section 4.3.

### 4.1 Sparse Coding Transfer for RL

As described in Section 3.3, SC is an efficient way to discover higher level information in an unlabeled data set. We use SC to solve two inherent problems in transfer learning for RL tasks. The first is to unify the dimensions of the state action spaces of the two different MDPs. The second is to discover a higher level representation for the attained bases and activations of the source task state-action spaces. This step guarantees that our scheme works with the "best" available representation/information space of the source task.

**Unifying the Source and Target Dimensions.** Our problem commences by first unifying the dimensions of the state action spaces of the two MDPs, an essential step for discovering the inter-task mapping. After this step has finished, any existing TL in RL technique may be used. However, this paper goes further and proposes a new transfer framework based on the attained bases and activations, described in Section 5.

This "dimensional unification" process is described in Algorithm 1. In short, Algorithm 1 sparse codes random samples from the source task, constrained by learning the same number of bases ($d_t$) as the target task.

The algorithms proposed elsewhere [8] solve Equation 6 on line 3 of Algorithm 1. After this stage is done, new activations and bases describing the samples are attained.[1] Note that, these newly attained samples—described as a linear combinations of the bases and activations (**Ab**)—do not yet relate anything to the target task ones. The target task samples still need to be projected towards these bases. This is done as described in Section 4.2.

After Algorithm 1 is finished, new features in the source task state action spaces are discovered. This is reasonable as TL typically transfers between a low dimensional source task to a high dimensional target task. Here, SC is determining new bases that are of a higher number than the original state action dimensions in the source task. If successful, new patterns and representations are discovered in the source task state-action spaces. These new features describe new representations not anticipated by the original dimensions. Therefore, this new information can be used to help and guide the transfer learning scheme.

---

[1] Please note that while writing Algorithm 1 it was assumed that the dimensions of the source task $d_s$ are lower than those of the target task $d_t$. But it is worth noting that it works as well for the other cases with no restrictions.

---

**Algorithm 1.** Sparse Coding Transfer Reinforcement Learning

---

**Require:** Source MDP samples $\{\langle s_s, a_s, s_s' \rangle\}_{i=1}^m$, target MDP samples $\{\langle s_t, a_t, s_t' \rangle\}_{j=1}^f$

1: Calculate $d_s$ and $d_t$ which are the dimensions of each of the state action spaces of the MDPs
2: Sparse code the source by solving:
3:

$$\min_{\{b_j\},\{a_j^{(i)}\}} \sum_{i=1}^m \frac{1}{2\sigma^2} ||\langle s_s, a_s, s_s' \rangle^{(i)} - \sum_{j=1}^{d_t} b_j a_j^{(i)}||_2^2 \qquad (5)$$

$$+\beta \sum_{i=1}^m \sum_{j=1}^{d_t} ||a_j^{(i)}||_1$$

$$s.t. \ ||b_j||_2^2 \leq c, \forall j = \{1, 2, \ldots, d_t\}$$

4: Solve the problem of Equation 6 using the algorithm proposed in [8]
5: Return the activation matrix ($\mathbf{A} \in \mathbb{R}^{m \times d_t}$) and the bases ($\mathbf{b} \in \mathbb{R}^{d_t \times 1}$)

---

**High Information Representation.** After dimensional unification, as described in the previous section, SC is again used to discover a succinct higher informational/ representational bases of the activations than the unified dimensional spaces. This insures that our transfer approach operates in the "richest" space described through the samples. This is done in a similar framework to that in Section 4.1 and is described in Algorithm 2.

---

**Algorithm 2.** Succinct High Information Representation of MDPs

---

**Require:** Activations acquired through Algorithm 1, number of new high dimensional bases $d_n$

1: Represent the activations in the $d_n$ bases by solving the following problem using the algo- rithm in [8]:
2:

$$\min_{\{z_j\},\{c_j^{(i)}\}} \sum_{i=1}^m \frac{1}{2\sigma^2} ||\langle \mathbf{a}_{1:d_t} \rangle^{(i)} - \sum_{j=1}^{d_n} \mathbf{z}_j c_j^{(i)}||_2^2 \qquad (6)$$

$$+\beta \sum_{i=1}^m \sum_{j=1}^{d_n} ||c_j^{(i)}||_1$$

$$s.t. \ ||\mathbf{z}_j||_2^2 \leq o, \forall j = \{1, 2, \ldots, d_n\}$$

3: **return** activations $\mathbf{C} \in \mathbb{R}^{m \times d_n}$ and bases $\mathbf{z} \in \mathbb{R}^{d_n \times 1}$

---

The idea presented by Algorithm 2 is to sparse code the activations, representing the original samples of the MDPs, to a higher representational space, $d_n$.[2] This stage should guarantee that we project the samples of the source task MDP into a high informational

---

[2] In our experiments we have set $d_n$ to be 100, a relatively high number.

space where a similarity measure can be used to find a relation between the source and target task triplets. Noting that there are no restrictions on the number of bases to be determined: unneeded bases have an activation of zero once the SC problem has been solved.

At this stage, the source state action spaces are described in a rich informational space determined by the newly discovered bases and activations. The next step is to project the target task samples to that space described by $\mathbf{Z}$ so that triplets can be ordered and the inter-task mapping approximated.

### 4.2   $L_1$ Sparse Projection Learning

Once the above stages have finished, the source samples are described via the activations generated in Algorithm 2. However, target task samples still have no relationship to the learned activations. In other words, the bases and activations that have been attained successfully describe high informational patterns and representations in the source task state-action spaces but do not represent the target state-action spaces. Since we are seeking a similarity correspondence between the source and target task triplets, the target task samples should be represented in the same high informational space.

Therefore, the next step is to learn a sparse projection to project the target task samples onto the $\mathbf{Z}$ basis representing the source task MDP. In other words, the goal now is to learn a sparse projection that is capable of representing the random target task samples as a combination of some activations, automatically learned, and the $\mathbf{Z}$ bases generated by Algorithm 2. The overall scheme is described in Algorithm 3, where the activations are learned by solving the $L_1$ regularized least squares optimization problem of Equation 7. This optimization problem guarantees that the attained activations are as sparse as possible and is solved using the interior point methods [4].

At this stage all the samples from both the target and source task are projected to the same space described by the sparse coded vectors $\mathbf{Z}$. The next step will be to order the data points from both the source and the target task so to approximate the inter-task mapping.

---

**Algorithm 3.** Reflecting Target Task Samples

---

**Require:**  Sparse coded bases $\mathbf{Z}$ generated by Algorithm 2, target MDP samples $\{\langle s_t, a_t, s_t' \rangle\}_{i=1}^{f}$

1: **for** $i = 1 \to f$ **do**
2:     Represent the target data patterns in the sparse coded bases, $\mathbf{Z}$, by solving:
3:

$$\hat{\phi}^{(i)}(\langle s_t, a_t, s_t' \rangle) = \arg\min_{\phi^{(i)}} ||\langle s_t, a_t, s_t' \rangle - \sum_{j=1}^{d_n} \phi_j^{(i)} z_j||_2^2 \qquad (7)$$

$$+ \beta ||\phi^{(i)}||_1$$

4: **end for**
5: **return** activations $\Phi$

---

### 4.3   Similarity Measure and Inter-task Mapping Approximation

As mentioned previously, we tackle the problem of learning an inter-task mapping via supervised learning. Since $\chi$ maps triplets from the source task to their corresponding triplets in the target task, the problem at this stage is to attain the training patterns to approximate $\chi$.

After reaching the rich space representing the random samples of the 2 MDPs (i.e., $\mathbf{Z}$), a Euclidean distance measure is used to compare triplets, providing a data set to the regressor (i.e, SPGPs) to approximate the inter-task mapping $\chi$. This similarity measure is used to determine the correspondence of the source and target tasks triplets. Once applied, the similarity measure will seek the triplets of the source task closest to those of the target task and map them together as being inputs and outputs for the regression algorithm, respectively. This is shown on line 2 of Algorithm 4. Since the similarity measure is used in the sparse coded spaces, the distance is calculated using the attained activation ($\mathbf{C}$ and $\boldsymbol{\Phi}$) rather than the samples themselves. Therefore, the scheme has to trace the data back to the original dimensions of the state-action pairs of the MDPs.

There are few restrictions on the function approximation techniques that could be used. We use nonparametric regression with *sparse gaussian processes* technique [12]. We prefer *sparse gaussian processes* rather than normal *gaussian processes* regression technique as the latter may have problems dealing with large data sets. To clarify, consider the learning phase of a GP that involves maximizing Equation 4. It is clear that the inversion of the covariance matrix, $\mathbf{K}$, is required on each iteration with complexity $O(n^3)$, where $n$ is the number of samples. Additionally, the maximiztion algorithm (Conjugate Gradient Descent [10]) may get stuck in a local maximum of Equation 4, a common problem in function approximation schemes and maximization problems.

---

**Algorithm 4.** Similarity Measure & Inter-Task mapping approximation

---

**Require:** Sparse coded basis $\mathbf{Z}$, sparse coded activations of the source task $\mathbf{C} \in \mathbb{R}^{m \times d_n}$, projected target task activations $\phi \in \mathbb{R}^{m \times d_n}$

1: **for all** $\phi$ **do**
2:    Calculate the closest activation in $\mathbf{C}$ minimizing the Euclidean/similarity distance measure.
3: **end for**
4: Correspond the triplets with the minimum similarity measure as being inputs and outputs to create a data set $\mathcal{D}$
5: Approximate the inter-task mapping, $\chi$ using SPGPs
6: **return** The approximated inter-task mapping $\chi$

---

## 5   Transfer Scheme

Assuming there exists a "good enough" policy, $\pi_s^\star$ for the source task, we propose a novel transfer algorithm for pairs of tasks with continuous state spaces and discrete action spaces, titled Transfer Least Squares Policy Iteration.

This section describes the novel transfer scheme and reflects on the details and technicalities of the approach. It starts by describing a well-known reinforcement learning algorithm (LSPI), that our novel transfer algorithm builds on. Then clarifies all the technicalities involved in the proposed TrLSPI algorithm.

## 5.1 Least Squares Policy Iteration

LSPI [7] is an approximate RL algorithm that is considered an actor/critic method. LSPI is composed of two parts. The first is an evaluation step, *Least Squares Temporal Difference Q-learning* (LSTDQ) and the second is a policy improvement step. In LSTDQ the algorithm will update the weights representing the policy so that the new parameters minimize certain error criteria. For example, the LSTDQ could be set to minimize the Bellman residual error of the projected Bellman equations. Once this step has finished, LSPI uses the attained weights to improve the policy by taking greedy actions in the approximated $Q$-function.

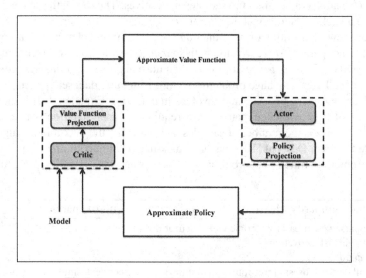

**Fig. 1.** Least Squares Policy Iteration schematic [7]

Figure 1 highlights the actor and critic organization of LSPI. Since LSPI uses function approximators to represent the $Q$-functions and/or policies, there also exist two projection phases for both the $Q$-function and the policy, as can been seen in the schematic. A more thorough treatment may be found elsewhere [7].

## 5.2 Transfer Least Squares Policy Iteration (TrLSPI)

TrLSPI, Algorithm 5, can be split into two sections. The first determines $\chi$ (Section 4), using source task samples[3] from $\pi_s^*$. The second provides those samples for the evaluation phase of the LSPI algorithm (LSTDQ), to learn a policy for the target task. The

---

[3] If using an approximate RL algorithm in the source task, the policy would instead by near-optimal.

---

**Algorithm 5.** TrLSPI

---

**Require:** Source MDP samples $\{\langle s_s, a_s, s_s' \rangle\}_{i=1}^m$, target MDP samples $\{\langle s_t, a_t, s_t' \}$, number for re-samples $n_s$, a (near-)optimal policy for the source system $\pi_s^\star$, state action basis functions for the target task $\psi_1, \ldots, \psi_k$

1: *Unify the dimensions* using Algorithm 1
2: Discover *high informational representation* using Algorithm 2
3: *Sparse project* the target task samples using Algorithm 3
4: Use a *similarity* measure to attain the data set and *approximate* $\chi$ using Algorithm 4
5: Randomly sample $n_s$ source task triplets $\langle s_s, a_s, s_s' \rangle_{i=1}^{n_s}$ greedily in the optimal policy $\pi_s^\star$, set of state-dependent basis function $\psi_1, \ldots, \psi_k : S_t \times A_t \to \mathbb{R}$
6: **for** $i = 1 \to n_s$ **do**
7:     Find the corresponding target task triplets as $\langle s_t^{(i)}, a_t^{(i)}, s_t^{(i)'} \rangle = \chi(\langle s_s^{(i)}, a_s^{(i)}, s_s^{(i)'} \rangle)$
8: **end for**
9: Find the closest triplet in the initial samples to the ones predicted by $\chi$
10: Use LSTDQ described by [7] to evaluate those samples
11: Learn and improve policy till convergence using LSPI [7]
12: **return** Learned policy $\pi_{target}^\star$

---

intuition here is that if the tasks are similar and if the inter-task mapping is "good enough," then those samples will bias the target task controller towards choosing good actions and restricting its area of exploration and reducing learning times and increasing performance.

Provided that the tasks are related, Algorithm 5 is capable of attaining a good starting behavior for the target task. The performance of this policy depends on the state space region where those samples were provided. In other words, it is not possible to achieve near-optimal performance with a small number of samples that are in regions far from the goal state.[4] Therefore, if the agent has to seek a near-optimal policy, then either a new sampling step using the current policy should be added to Algorithm 5, or a large amount of samples should be provided. It is worth noting that it is not necessary for the algorithm to be provided by a model for the system to perform that sampling. A black box generative model taking inputs being states and actions and producing outputs of successor states and rewards is sufficient.

## 6  Experiments and Results

Two very different tasks were chosen to evaluate the proposed framework, the RL benchmark tasks Mountain Car (MC) and Pole balancing (see Figure 2).

The control objective of MC, the source task, is to drive the car up the hill (Figure 2(a)). The difficulty is that gravity is stronger than the car's motor—even at maximum throttle the car can not directly reach the top of the hill. The solution is to first move away from the target to the opposite side of the hill and then accumulate enough energy to reach the top of the hill. The dynamics of the car are described via two continuous state variables $(x, \dot{x})$ representing the position and velocity of the center of gravity of the car, respectively.

---

[4] This is a problem that is inherentt to LSPI and is not due to the TrLSPI algorithm.

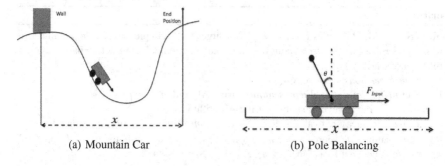

(a) Mountain Car                    (b) Pole Balancing

**Fig. 2.** Mountain Car to Pole Balancing Transfer

There are three actions: maximum throttle forward (+1), zero throttle (0), and maximum throttle reverse (-1). The car is rewarded by +1 once it reaches the top of the hill, −1 if it hits the wall, and zero elsewhere. At the end of each episode the start state is randomly initialized at the bottom of the hill.

The target task is the Pole Balancing problem described in Figure 2(b). The control goal of the pole balancing system is balancing the pole in an upright position (i.e., $\theta = \dot{\theta} = 0$). The allowed actions are (+1) for full throttle right and (-1) for full throttle left. The reward function of the system consists of two parts: (1) $cos(\theta)$, which yields its maximum value of +1 at the upright position of the pole, and (2) −1 if the cart hits the boundaries of the track. The angle was restricted to be within $|\theta| < \frac{\pi}{9}$ while the position was restricted to $|x| < 3$ and the start state was randomly chosen within that interval.

As is clear from the description, the two MDPs representing the tasks are significantly different. The source and target task have different state spaces, action spaces, transition probabilities, and reward functions. No previous work can learn to autonomously transfer between such different tasks.

Our framework requires an optimal policy in the MC source task, $\pi^{\star}_{MC}$. SARSA($\lambda$) [13] is used to learn $\pi^{\star}_{MC}$. The learned policy is then used to randomly sample different numbers of states, to be used by $\chi$. We started with 5000 and 2,000 randomly sampled states (using a random policy) for the MC and the Pole Balancing, respectively. These samples were used by the algorithm described in Section 4 to attain the inter-task mapping $\chi$. After $\chi$ has been learned, different amounts of samples were sampled from the source task using the optimal policy $\pi^{\star}_{MC}$. Specifically, we have sampled 500, 1, 000,... 20, 000 states as input to the TrLSPI algorithm to measure performance and convergence times.

Our results show 1) an increase in the performance on a fixed number of samples, 2) a decrease in the convergence time when using a predefined number of samples, and 3) a decrease in the time required to learn a near-optimal policy.

### 6.1  Performance on a Fixed Number of Samples

The first sets of experiments we conducted were to measure the performance in the target task, given a fixed number of source task transferred samples. Namely, we

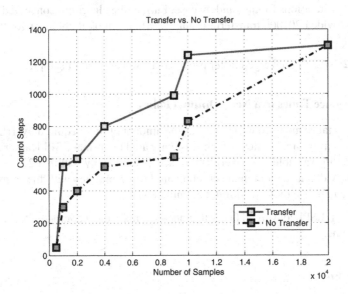

**Fig. 3.** Transfer Results on the Pole Balancing task

measured the number of successful control steps in the target task given a fixed number of $500, \ldots 20,000$ transferred MC samples. We compared the performance to a normal LSPI (i.e., random sampling) learner in the target task. The graph in Figure 3 summarizes the attained results and clearly shows an increase in the number of control steps in the case of the transferred samples compared to a random sampling scheme. For example it can be seen that at a small number of samples, e.g. $2,000$, our transfer scheme was able to attain an average of 600 control steps with about 400 for the random case. This performance increases with the number of samples to reach 800 steps at $4,000$ transferred samples. The random case needed to be provided by $9,000$ samples to attain an 800 steps performance. Finally, the transferred algorithm and the random selection scheme seem to converge, on a large amount of samples $20,000$ to the same number of control steps, about $1,300$. This leads to the following conclusion:

**Conclusion 1**: TrLSPI has provided a better distribution of samples compared to random policy in the target task. random what? a random policy in cart-pole?

## 6.2   Convergence Times on Fixed Number of Samples

The other improvement we report is the decrease in the convergence times, represented by the number of iterations in LSPI, provided a fixed amount of transferred sampled. This time was measured by comparing the convergence times of TrLSPI and LSPI on a fixed number of transferred and random samples, respectively. To clarify, LSPI was able to converge faster once provided the transferred samples compared to a random sample data set. For example, it took LSPI 7 iteration to converge provided $5,000$ transferred samples with 12 iterations for the random case. Further the algorithm converged within 14 iteration provided 20, 000 transferred samples while it took it about 21 for the random case.

**Conclusion 2**: TrLSPI converged faster provided a fixed amount of samples.

### 6.3   Convergence Times to a Near-Optimal Policy

The last performance measure we tested was the amount of time required by TrLSPI to converge to a near-optimal policy, which was compared to normal LSPI learners in the target tasks. LSPI was able to converge to an acceptable policy within a 22.5 minutes after being provided a random data set, compared to 17 minutes with the transferred data set[5]. Calculating $\chi$ took an addition 3.7 minutes.

**Conclusion 3**: TrLSPI converged faster to a near-optimal policy compared to a random selection scheme.

## 7   Discussion

The proposed TL framework is compatible with other sample-based model-free learning methods and can be used on a variety of RL tasks with continuous state spaces and discrete action spaces. The framework has the advantage of automatically finding the inter-task mapping using SC and any "good" regression technique. But there is one potential weakness, discussed next.

Our framework should work correctly when the two tasks at hand are *semantically* similar, as the rewards of the two systems were not taken into account in the explained scheme. For instance, consider the transfer example between the same robot but with opposite rewards.

Our mapping scheme from Section 4, once applied, will produce a one-to-one mapping from the source to the target task. In other words, since the two tasks have the same state and action spaces, the mapping that will be one-to-one, mapping the same state action successor state triplets of the two tasks together. Therefore, the transition of the robots to the rewardable/ un-rewardable states will map together. Since the optimal policies of the two robots are opposite, it is easy to see that in this case the target task has been provided with a "bad" biased starting policy which will decrease the agents performance rather than enhancing it. Such *negative transfer* is a well-known problem in TL for RL tasks. This paper's approach may be able to avoid this problem once rewards are added to the similarity measure, used to generate the training set to approximate the inter-task mapping $\chi$. However, this enhancement will be left to future work.

## 8   Conclusions and Future Work

This paper has presented a novel technique for transfer learning in reinforcement learning tasks. Our framework may be applied to pairs of reinforcement learning problems

---

[5] Our experiments were performed on a 2.8 Ghz Intel Core i7.

with continuous state spaces and discrete action spaces. The main contributions of this paper are (1) the novel method of automatically attaining the inter-task mapping, $\chi$ and (2) the new TrLSPI algorithm for tasks with continuous state spaces and discrete actions. We approached the problem by framing the approximation of the inter-task mapping as a supervised learning problem that was solved using *sparse pseudo input gaussian processes*. *sparse coding*, accompanied with a similarity measure, was used to determine the data set required by the regressor for approximating $\chi$. Our results demonstrate successful transfer between two very different tasks, the mountain car to the pole balancing task. Success was measured both in an increase in learning performance as well as a reduction in convergence time.

There are many exciting directions for future work. First, different distance metrics should be compared and their effects on the overall performance of the algorithm measured. Second, the distance measure will be improved by incorporating the rewards in the framework, helping to avoid the problem of negative transfer, as well as determine a criterion for TL in RL. Third, this approach should be applied to other RL method, such as our preliminary investigation described elsewhere [2].

# References

1. Ammar, H.B., Taylor, M.E.: Common subspace transfer for reinforcement learning tasks. In: Proceedings of the Adaptive and Learning Agents Workshop, at AAMAS 2011 (May 2011)
2. Ammar, H.B., Tuyls, K., Taylor, M.E., Driessens, K., Weiss, G.: Reinforcement learning transfer via sparse coding. In: Proceedings of the Eleventh International Joint Conference on Autonomous Agents and Multiagent Systems (AAMAS) (June 2012)
3. Buşoniu, L., Babuška, R., De Schutter, B., Ernst, D.: Reinforcement Learning and Dynamic Programming Using Function Approximators. CRC Press, Boca Raton (2010)
4. Jean Kim, S., Koh, K., Lustig, M., Boyd, S., Gorinevsky, D.: An interior-point method for large-scale l1-regularized logistic regression. Journal of Machine Learning Research (2007)
5. Konidaris, G.: A framework for transfer in reinforcement learning. In: Proceedings of the ICML 2006 Workshop on Structural Knowledge Transfer for Machine Learning (2006)
6. Kuhlmann, G., Stone, P.: Graph-Based Domain Mapping for Transfer Learning in General Games. In: Kok, J.N., Koronacki, J., Lopez de Mantaras, R., Matwin, S., Mladenič, D., Skowron, A. (eds.) ECML 2007. LNCS (LNAI), vol. 4701, pp. 188–200. Springer, Heidelberg (2007)
7. Lagoudakis, M.G., Parr, R.: Least-squares policy iteration. J. Mach. Learn. Res. 4, 1107–1149 (2003)
8. Lee, H., Battle, A., Raina, R., Ng, A.Y.: Efficient sparse coding algorithms. In: NIPS, pp. 801–808 (2007)
9. Liu, Y., Stone, P.: Value-function-based transfer for reinforcement learning using structure mapping. In: Proceedings of the Twenty-First National Conference on Artificial Intelligence, pp. 415–420 (July 2006)
10. Nocedal, J., Wright, S.J.: Numerical optimization. Springer (August 1999)
11. Rasmussen, C.E.: Gaussian processes for machine learning. MIT Press (2006)
12. Snelson, E., Ghahramani, Z.: Sparse gaussian processes using pseudo-inputs. In: Advance in Neural Information Processing Systems, pp. 1257–1264. MIT Press (2006)
13. Sutton, R.S., Barto, A.G.: Reinforcement learning: An introduction (1998)
14. Talvitie, E., Singh, S.: An experts algorithm for transfer learning. In: Proceedings of the Twentieth International Joint Conference on Artificial Intelligence (2007)

15. Taylor, M.E., Kuhlmann, G., Stone, P.: Autonomous transfer for reinforcement learning. In: Proceedings of the Seventh International Joint Conference on Autonomous Agents and Multiagent Systems (AAMAS), pp. 283–290 (May 2008)
16. Taylor, M.E., Stone, P.: Cross-domain transfer for reinforcement learning. In: Proceedings of the Twenty-Fourth International Conference on Machine Learning, ICML (June 2007)
17. Taylor, M.E., Stone, P.: Transfer learning for reinforcement learning domains: A survey. J. Mach. Learn. Res. 10, 1633–1685 (2009)
18. Taylor, M.E., Whiteson, S., Stone, P.: Transfer via inter-task mappings in policy search reinforcement learning. In: Proceedings of the Sixth International Joint Conference on Autonomous Agents and Multiagent Systems, AAMAS, pp. 156–163 (May 2007)
19. Torrey, L., Walker, T., Shavlik, J., Maclin, R.: Using Advice to Transfer Knowledge Acquired in One Reinforcement Learning Task to Another. In: Gama, J., Camacho, R., Brazdil, P.B., Jorge, A.M., Torgo, L. (eds.) ECML 2005. LNCS (LNAI), vol. 3720, pp. 412–424. Springer, Heidelberg (2005)

# Game Theory for Security: An Important Challenge for Multiagent Systems

Bo An and Milind Tambe

Computer Science Department
University of Southern California
Los Angeles, CA 90089, USA
{boa,tambe}@usc.edu

**Abstract.** The goal of this paper is to introduce a real-world challenge problem for researchers in multiagent systems and beyond, where our collective efforts may have a significant impact on activities in the real-world. The challenge is in applying game theory for security: Our goal is not only to introduce the problem, but also to provide exemplars of initial successes of deployed systems in this challenge problem arena, some key open research challenges and pointers to getting started in this research.

**Keywords:** Game Theory, Security, Multiagent Systems.

## 1 Introduction

Security is a critical concern around the world that arises in protecting our ports, airports, transportation or other critical national infrastructure from adversaries, in protecting our wildlife and forests from poachers and smugglers, and in curtailing the illegal flow of weapons, drugs and money; and it arises in problems ranging from physical to cyber-physical systems. In all of these problems, we have limited security resources which prevent full security coverage at all times; instead, limited security resources must be deployed intelligently taking into account differences in priorities of targets requiring security coverage, the responses of the adversaries to the security posture and potential uncertainty over the types, capabilities, knowledge and priorities of adversaries faced.

Game theory is well-suited to adversarial reasoning for security resource allocation and scheduling problems. Casting the problem as a Bayesian Stackelberg game, we have developed new algorithms for efficiently solving such games to provide randomized patrolling or inspection strategies. These algorithms have led to some initial successes in this challenge problem arena, leading to advances over previous approaches in security scheduling and allocation, e.g., by addressing key weaknesses of predictability of human schedulers. These algorithms are now deployed in multiple applications: ARMOR has been deployed at the Los Angeles International Airport (LAX) since 2007 to randomizes checkpoints on the roadways entering the airport and canine patrol routes within the airport terminals [1]; IRIS, is a game-theoretic scheduler for randomized deployment of the US Federal Air Marshals (FAMS) requiring significant scale-up in

M. Cossentino et al. (Eds.): EUMAS 2011, LNAI 7541, pp. 17–30, 2012.
© Springer-Verlag Berlin Heidelberg 2012

underlying algorithms has been in use since 2009 [2]; PROTECT, which uses a new set of algorithms based on quantal-response is deployed in the port of Boston for randomizing US coast guard patrolling [3, 4]; PROTECT has been deployed in the port of Boston since April 2011 and is now in use at the port of New York; GUARDS is under evaluation for national deployment by the US Transportation Security Administration (TSA) [5], and TRUSTS is being tested by the Los Angeles Sheriffs Department (LASD) in the LA Metro system to schedule randomized patrols for fare inspection [6]. These initial successes point the way to major future applications in a wide range of security arenas; with major research challenges in scaling up our game-theoretic algorithms, to addressing human adversaries' bounded rationality and uncertainties in action execution and observation, as well as in preference elicitation and multiagent learning.

This paper will provide pointers to our algorithms, key research challenges and how to get started in this research. While initial research has made a start, a lot remains to be done; yet these are large-scale interdisciplinary research challenges that call upon multiagent researchers to work with researchers in other disciplines, be "on the ground" with domain experts, and examine real-world constraints and challenges that cannot be abstracted away. Together as an international community of multiagent researchers, we can accomplish more!

## 2   Stackelberg Games Background

A generic Stackelberg game has two players, a *leader*, and a *follower*. These players need not represent individuals, but could also be groups that cooperate to execute a joint strategy, such as a police force or a terrorist organization. Each player has a set of possible *pure strategies*, or the actions that they can execute. A *mixed strategy* allows a player to play a probability distribution over pure strategies. Payoffs for each player are defined over all possible pure-strategy outcomes for both the players. The payoff functions are extended to mixed strategies by taking the expectation over pure-strategy outcomes. The follower can observe the leader's strategy, and then act in a way to optimize its own payoffs. Thus, the attacker's strategy in a Stackelberg game is a best response to the leader's strategy.

The most common solution concept in game theory is a *Nash equilibrium*, which is a profile of strategies for each player in which no player can gain by unilaterally changing to another strategy [7]. Strong Stackelberg equilibrium is a refinement of Nash equilibrium; it is a form of equilibrium where the leader commits to a strategy first, and the follower provides a best response while breaking ties in favor of the leader.[1] This Strong Stackelberg equilibrium is the solution concept adopted in security applications [7–10].

The Bayesian extension to the Stackelberg game allows for multiple types of players, with each type associated with its own payoff values [11, 12, 10]. For real-world security domains, we assume that there is only one leader type (e.g., only one police force), although there are multiple follower types (e.g. multiple groups of adversaries are trying to infiltrate security). Each follower type is represented by a different payoff matrix. The leader does not know the follower's type. The goal is to *find the optimal*

---

[1] The leader can always induce the follower to strictly break ties in favor of the leader by perturbing his strategy by an infinitesimal amount [8].

*mixed strategy* for the leader to commit to, given that each follower type will know the mixed strategy of the leader when choosing its own strategy.

## 3  Deployed and Emerging Security Applications

The last several years have witnessed the successful application of multi-agent systems in allocating limited resources to protect critical infrastructures [13–15, 5, 3]. The framework of game-theory (more precisely, Stackelberg games) is well suited to formulate the strategic interaction in security domains in which there are usually two players: the security force (defender) commits to a security policy first and the attacker (e.g., terrorist, poacher and smuggler) conducts surveillance to learn the policy and then takes his best attacking action.[2] Stackelberg games have been widely used for modeling/reasoning complex security problems and a variety of algorithms have been proposed to efficiently compute the equilibrium strategy, i.e., defender's best way of utilizing her limited security resources (there is actually a special class of Stackelberg games that often gets used in these security domains, and this class is referred to as security games). In the rest of this section, we describe the application of the Stackelberg game framework in multiple significant security domains.

### 3.1  ARMOR for Los Angeles International Airport

Los Angeles International Airport (LAX) is the largest destination airport in the United States and serves 60-70 million passengers per year. The LAX police use diverse measures to protect the airport, which include vehicular checkpoints, police units patrolling the roads to the terminals, patrolling inside the terminals (with canines), and security screening and bag checks for passengers. The application of game-theoretic approach is focused on two of these measures: (1) placing vehicle checkpoints on inbound roads that service the LAX terminals, including both location and timing (2) scheduling patrols for bomb-sniffing canine units at the different LAX terminals. The eight different terminals at LAX have very different characteristics, like physical size, passenger loads, foot traffic or international versus domestic flights. These factors contribute to the differing risk assessments of these eight terminals. Furthermore, the numbers of available vehicle checkpoints and canine units are limited by resource constraints. Thus it is challenging to optimally allocate these resources to improve their effectiveness while avoiding patterns in the scheduled deployments.

The ARMOR system (Assistant for Randomized Monitoring over Routes) focuses on two of the security measures at LAX (checkpoints and canine patrols) and optimizes security resource allocation using Bayesian Stackelberg games. Take the vehicle checkpoints model as an example. Assume that there are $n$ roads, the police's strategy is placing $m < n$ checkpoints on these roads where $m$ is the maximum number of checkpoints. The adversary may potentially choose to attack through one of these roads. ARMOR models different types of attackers with different payoff functions, representing different capabilities and preferences for the attacker. ARMOR uses DOBSS (Decomposed Optimal Bayesian Stackelberg Solver) to compute the defender's optimal strategy [10]. ARMOR has been successfully deployed since August 2007 at LAX.

---

[2] Or the attacker may be sufficiently deterred and dissuaded from attacking the protected target.

## 3.2    IRIS for US Federal Air Marshals Service

The US Federal Air Marshals Service (FAMS) allocates air marshals to flights orig-inating in and departing from the United States to dissuade potential aggressors and prevent an attack should one occur. Flights are of different importance based on a vari-ety of factors such as the numbers of passengers, the population of source/destination, international flights from different countries, and special events that can change the risks for particular flights at certain times. Security resource allocation in this domain is significantly more challenging than for ARMOR: a limited number of FAMS need to be scheduled to cover thousands of commercial flights each day. Furthermore, these FAMS must be scheduled on tours of flights that obey various constraints (e.g., the time required to board, fly, and disembark). Simply finding schedules for the marshals that meet all of these constraints is a computational challenge. Our task is made more dif-ficult by the need to find a randomized policy that meets these scheduling constraints, while also accounting for the different values of each flight.

Against this background, the IRIS system (Intelligent Randomization In Scheduling) has been developed and has been deployed by FAMS since October 2009 to randomize schedules of air marshals on international flights. In IRIS, the targets are the set of $n$ flights and the attacker could potentially choose to attack one of these flights. The FAMS can assign $m < n$ air marshals that may be assigned to protect these flights.

Since the number of possible schedules exponentially increases with the number of flights and resources, DOBSS is no longer applicable to the FAMS domain. Instead, IRIS uses the much faster ASPEN algorithm [16] to generate the schedule for thousands of commercial flights per day. IRIS also use an attribute-based preference elicitation system to determine reward values for the Stackelberg game model.

## 3.3    PROTECT for US Coast Guard

The US Coast Guard's (USCG) mission includes maritime security of the US coasts, ports, and inland waterways; a security domain that faces increased risks due to threats such as terrorism and drug trafficking. Given a particular port and the variety of critical infrastructure that an adversary may attack within the port, USCG conducts patrols to protect this infrastructure; however, while the adversary has the opportunity to observe patrol patterns, limited security resources imply that USCG patrols cannot be at every location 24/7. To assist the USCG in allocating its patrolling resources, the PROTECT (Port Resilience Operational / Tactical Enforcement to Combat Terrorism) model is be-ing designed to enhance maritime security and has been in use at the port of Boston since April 2011 and now is also in use at the port of New York (Figure 1). Similar to previous applications ARMOR and IRIS, PROTECT uses an attacker-defender Stack-elberg game framework, with USCG as the defender against terrorist adversaries that conduct surveillance before potentially launching an attack.

The goal of PROTECT is to use game theory to assist the USCG in maximizing its effectiveness in the Ports, Waterways, and Coastal Security (PWCS) Mission. PWCS patrols are focused on protecting critical infrastructure; without the resources to provide one hundred percent on scene presence at any, let alone all of the critical infrastructure, optimization of security resource is critical. Towards that end, unpredictability creates

(a) PROTECT is being used in Boston

(b) Extending PROTECT to NY

**Fig. 1.** USCG boats patrolling the ports of Boston and NY

situations of uncertainty for an enemy and can be enough to deem a target less appealing. The PROTECT system, focused on the PWCS patrols, addresses how the USCG should optimally patrol critical infrastructure in a port to maximize protection, knowing that the adversary may conduct surveillance and then launch an attack. While randomizing patrol patterns is key, PROTECT also addresses the fact that the targets are of unequal value, understanding that the adversary will adapt to whatever patrol patterns USCG conducts. The output of PROTECT is a schedule of patrols which includes when the patrols are to begin, what critical infrastructure to visit for each patrol, and what activities to perform at each critical infrastructure.

While PROTECT builds on previous work, it offers some key innovations. First, this system is a departure from the assumption of perfect adversary rationality noted in previous work, relying instead on a quantal response (QR) model [17] of the adversary's behavior. Second, to improve PROTECT's efficiency, a compact representation of the defender's strategy space is used by exploiting equivalence and dominance. Finally, the evaluation of PROTECT for the first time provides real-world data: (i) comparison of human-generated vs PROTECT security schedules, and (ii) results from an Adversarial Perspective Team's (human mock attackers) analysis. The PROTECT model is now being extended to the port of New York and it may potentially be extended to other ports in the US.

### 3.4 GUARDS for US Transportation Security Agency

The United States Transportation Security Administration (TSA) is tasked with protecting the nation's over 400 airports which services approximately 28,000 commercial flights and up to approximately 87,000 total flights per day. To protect this large transportation network, the TSA employs approximately 48,000 Transportation Security Officers, who are responsible for implementing security activities at each individual airport. While many people are aware of common security activities, such as individual passenger screening, this is just one of many security layers TSA personnel implement to help prevent potential threats [18, 19]. These layers can involve hundreds of heterogeneous security activities executed by limited TSA personnel leading to a complex resource allocation challenge. While activities like passenger screening are performed for every passenger, the TSA cannot possibly run every security activity all the time. Thus, while the resources required for passenger screening are always allocated by the TSA, it must also decide how to appropriately allocate its remaining security officers among the layers of security to protect against a number of potential threats, while facing challenges such as surveillance and an adaptive adversary as mentioned before.

To aid the TSA in scheduling resources to protect airports, a new application called GUARDS (Game-theoretic Unpredictable and Randomly Deployed Security) has been developed. While GUARDS also utilizes Stackelberg games as ARMOR and IRIS, GUARDS faces three key challenges [5]: 1) reasoning about hundreds of heterogeneous security activities; 2) reasoning over diverse potential threats; and 3) developing a system designed for hundreds of end-users. To address those challenges, GUARDS created a new game-theoretic framework that allows for heterogeneous defender activities and compact modeling of a large number of threats and developed an efficient solution technique based on general-purpose Stackelberg game solvers. GUARDS is currently under evaluation and testing for scheduling practices at an undisclosed airport. If successful, the TSA intends to incorporate the system into their unpredictable scheduling practices nationwide.

### 3.5   TRUSTS for Urban Security in Transit Systems

In some urban transit systems, including the Los Angeles Metro Rail system, passengers are legally required to purchase tickets before entering but are not physically forced to do so (Figure 2). Instead, security personnel are dynamically deployed throughout the transit system, randomly inspecting passenger tickets. This proof-of-payment fare collection method is typically chosen as a more cost-effective alternative to direct fare collection, i.e., when the revenue lost to fare evasion is believed to be less than what it would cost to directly preclude it.

Take the Los Angeles Metro as an example. With approximately 300,000 riders daily, this revenue loss can be significant; the annual cost has been estimated at $5.6 million [20]. The Los Angeles Sheriffs Department (LASD) deploys uniformed patrols on board trains and at stations for fare-checking (and for other purposes such as crime prevention), in order to discourage fare evasion. With limited resources to devote to patrols, it is impossible to cover all locations at all times. The LASD thus requires some mechanism for choosing times and locations for inspections. Any predictable patterns in such a patrol schedule are likely to be observed and exploited by potential fare-evaders. The LASD's current approach relies on humans for scheduling the patrols. However, human schedulers are poor at generating unpredictable schedules; furthermore such scheduling for LASD is a tremendous cognitive burden on the human schedulers who must take into account all of the scheduling complexities (e.g., train timings, switching time between trains, and schedule lengths).

(a) Los Angeles Metro          (b) Barrier-free entrance to transit system

**Fig. 2.** TRUSTS for transit systems

The TRUSTS system (Tactical Randomization for Urban Security in Transit Systems) models the patrolling problem as a leader-follower Stackelberg game [21]. The leader (LASD) precommits to a mixed patrol strategy (a probability distribution over all pure strategies), and riders observe this mixed strategy before deciding whether to buy the ticket or not. Both ticket sales and fines issued for fare evasion translate into revenue to the government. Therefore the optimization objective for the leader is to maximize total revenue (total ticket sales plus penalties). Urban transit systems, however, present unique computational challenges since there are exponentially many possible patrol strategies, each subject to both the spatial and temporal constraints of travel within the transit network under consideration. To overcome this challenge, TRUSTS uses a compact representation which captures the spatial as well as temporal structure of the domain. The LASD is currently testing TRUSTS in the LA Metro system by deploying patrols according to the generated schedules and measuring the revenue recovered.

## 3.6 Future Applications

Beyond the deployed and emerging applications above are a number of different application areas. One of those is protecting forests [22], where we must protect a continuous forest area from extractors by patrols through the forest that seek to deter such extraction activity. With limited resources for performing such patrols, a patrol strategy will seek to distribute the patrols throughout the forest, in space and time, in order to minimize the resulting amount of extraction that occurs or maximize the degree of forest protection. This problem can be formulated as a Stackelberg game and the focus is computing optimal allocations of patrol density [22].

Another potential application is police patrols for crime suppression which is a data-intensive domain [23]. Thus it would be promising to use data mining tools on a database of past reported crime and events to identify the locations to be patrolled, the times at which the game changes, and the types of adversaries faced. The idea is to exploit temporal and spatial patterns of crime on the area to be patrolled to determine the priorities on how to use the limited security resources. Even with all of these applications, we have barely scratched the surface of possibilities in terms of potential applications for multiagent researchers for applying game theory for security.

The Stackelberg game framework can also be applied to adversarial domains that exhibit 'contagious' actions for each player. For example, word-of-mouth advertising / viral marketing has been widely studied by marketers trying to understand why one product or video goes 'viral' while others go unnoticed [24]. Counterinsurgency is the contest for the support of the local leaders in an armed conflict and can include a variety of operations such as providing security and giving medical supplies. Just as in word-of-mouth advertising and peacekeeping operations, these efforts carry a social effect beyond the action taken that can cause advantageous ripples through the neighboring population. Moreover, multiple intelligent parties attempt to leverage the same social network to spread their message, necessitating an adversary-aware approach to strategy generation. Game-theoretic approaches can be used to generate resource allocations strategies for such large-scale, real world networks. The interaction can be modeled as a graph with one player attempting to spread influence while the other player attempts to stop the probabilistic propagation of that influence by spreading their own influence. This 'blocking' problem models situations faced by governments/peacekeepers combatting the spread of terrorist radicalism and armed conflict with daily/weekly/monthy visits with local leaders to provide support and discuss grievances [25].

Game-theoretic methods are also appropriate for modeling resource allocation in cybersecurity [26] such as packet selection and inspection for detecting potential threats in large computer networks [27]. The problem of attacks on computer systems and corporate computer networks gets more pressing each year as the sophistication of the attacks increases together with the cost of their prevention. A number of intrusion detection and monitoring systems is being developed, e.g., deep packet inspection method that periodically selects a subset of packets in a computer network for analysis. However, there is a cost associated with the deep packet inspection, as it leads to significant delays in the throughput of the network. Thus, the monitoring system works under a constraint of limited selection of a fraction of all packets which can be inspected. The attacking/pretecting problem can be formulated as a game between two players: the attacker (or the intruder), and the defender (the detection system) [27]. The intruder wants to gain control over (or to disable) a valuable computer in the network by scanning the network, hacking into a more vulnerable system, and/or gaining access to further devices on the computer network. The actions of the attacker can therefore be seen as sending malicious packets from a controlled computer (termed source) to a single or multiple vulnerable computers (termed targets). The objective of the defender is to prevent the intruder from succeeding by selecting the packets for inspection, identifying the attacker, and subsequently thwarting the attack. However, packet inspections cause unwanted latency and hence the defender has to decide where and how to inspect network traffic in order to maximize the probability of a successful malicious packet detection. The computational challenge is efficiently computing the optimal defending strategies [27].

# 4   Open Research Issues

While the deployed applications have advanced the state of the art, significant future research remains to be done. In the following, we highlight some key research challenges, including scalability, robustness, human adversary modeling and mixed-initiative optimization. The main point we want to make is that this research does not require access to classified information of any kind. Problems, solution approaches and datasets are well specified in the papers discussed below,

**Scalability:** The first research challenge is improving the scalability of our algorithms for solving Stackelberg (security) games. The strategy space of both the defender and the attacker in these games may exponentially increase with the number of security activities, attacks, and resources. As we scale up to larger domains, it is critical to develop newer algorithms that scale up significantly beyond the limits of the current state of the art of Bayesian Stackelberg solvers. Driven by the growing complexity of applications, a sequence of algorithms for solving security games have been developed including DOBSS [10], ERASER [15], ASPEN [16]. However, existing algorithms still cannot scale up to very large scale domains such as scheduling randomized checkpoints in cities. In such graph based security games, the strategy space of the defender grows exponentially with the number of available resources and the strategy space of the attacker grows exponentially with the size of the road network considered. The latest technique to schedule such checkpoints is based on a "double oracle approach" which does not require the enumeration of the entire strategy space for either of the players [28]. However, existing algorithms still cannot scale up to large scale domains such as scheduling randomized checkpoints in cities of the size of Mumbai (Figure 3).

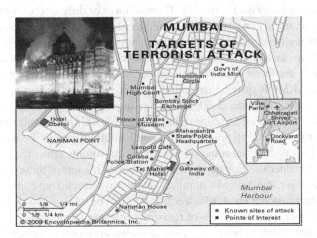

**Fig. 3.** The terrorist attacks of 2008 in Mumbai

**Robustness:** The second challenge is improving solutions' robustness. Classical game theory solution concepts often make assumptions on the knowledge, rationality, and capability (e.g., perfect recall) of players. Unfortunately, those assumptions could be wrong in real-world scenarios. Therefore, while computing the defender's optimal strategy, algorithms should take into account various uncertainties faced in the domain, including payoff noise [29], execution/observation error [30], uncertain capability [31]. While there are algorithms for dealing with different types of uncertainties, there is no general algorithm/framework that can deal with different types of uncertainty simultaneously. Furthermore, existing work assumes that the attacker knows (or with a small noise) the defender's strategy and there is no formal framework to model the attacker's belief update process and how it makes tradeoffs in consideration of surveillance cost, which remains an open issue for in future research.

One required research direction with respect to robustness is addressing bounded rationality of human adversaries, which is a fundamental problem that can affect the performance of our game theoretic solutions. Recently, there has been some research on applying ideas (e.g., prospect theory [32], and quantal response [17]) from social science or behavioral game theory within security game algorithms [33, 34]. Previous work usually applies existing frameworks and sets the parameters of these frameworks by experimental tuning or learning. However, in real-world security domains, we may have very limited data, or may only have some limited information on the biases displayed by adversaries. It is thus still a challenging problem to build high fidelity human adversary models that can address human bounded rationality. Furthermore, since real-world human adversaries are sometimes distributed coalitions of socially, culturally and cognitively-biased agents, acting behind a veil of uncertainty, we may need significant interdisciplinary research to build in social, cultural and coalitional biases into our adversary models.

**Mixed-Initiative Optimization:** Another challenging research problem in security games is mixed-initiative optimization in which human users and software assistants collaborate to make security decisions [35]. There often exist different types of constraints in security applications. For instance, the defender always has resource constraints, e.g., the numbers of available vehicle checkpoints, canine units, or air marshals. In addition, human users may place constraints on the defender's actions to affect the output of the game when they are faced with exceptional circumstances and extra knowledge. For instance, in the ARMOR system there could be forced checkpoints (e.g., when the Governor is flying) and forbidden checkpoints. Existing applications simply compute the optimal solution to meet all the constraints (if possible). Unfortunately, these user defined constraints may lead to poor (or infeasible) solutions due to the users' bounded rationality and insufficient information about how constraints affect the solution quality. Significantly better solution quality can be obtained if some of these constraints can be relaxed. However, there may be infinitely many ways of relaxing constraints and the software assistant may not know which constraints can be relaxed and by how much, as well as the real-world consequences of relaxing some constraints.

Thus, it is promising to adopt a mixed-initiative approach in which human users and software assistants collaborate to make security decisions. However, designing an efficient mixed-initiative optimization approach is not trivial and there are five major challenges. First, the scale of security games and constraints prevent us from using an exhaustive search algorithm to explore all constraint sets. Second, the user's incomplete information regarding the consequences of relaxing constraints requires preference elicitation support. Third, the decision making of shifting control between the user and the software assistant is challenging. Fourth, it is difficult to evaluate the performance of a mixed-initiative approach. Finally, it is a challenging problem to design good user interfaces for the software assistant to explain how constraints affect the solution quality. What remains to be done for the mixed-initiative approach includes sensitivity analysis for understanding how different constraints affect the solution quality, inference/learning for discovering directions of relaxing constraints, search for finding constraint sets to explore, preference elicitation for finding the human user's preference of different constraint sets, and interface design for explaining the game theoretic solver's performance.

**Multi-objective Optimization:** In existing applications such as ARMOR, IRIS and PROTECT, the defender is trying to maximize a single objective. However, there are domains where the defender has to consider multiple objectives simultaneously. For example, the Los Angeles Sheriff's Department (LASD) needs to protect the city's metro system from ticketless travelers, common criminals, and terrorists. From the perspective of LASD, each one of these attacker types provides a unique threat (lost revenue, property theft, and loss of life). Given this diverse set of threats, selecting a security strategy is a significant challenge as no single strategy can minimize the threat for all attacker types. Thus, tradeoffs must be made and protecting more against one threat may increase the vulnerability to another threat. However, it is not clear how LASD should weigh these threats when determining the security strategy to use. One could attempt to establish methods for converting the different threats into a single metric. However, this process can become convoluted when attempting to compare abstract notions such as safety and security with concrete concepts such as ticket revenue.

Multi-objective security games (MOSG) have been proposed to address the challenges of domains with multiple incomparable objectives [36]. In an MOSG, the threats posed by the attacker types are treated as different objective functions which are not aggregated, thus eliminating the need for a probability distribution over attacker types. Unlike Bayesian security games which have a single optimal solution, MOSGs have a set of Pareto optimal (non-dominated) solutions which is referred to as the Pareto frontier. By presenting the Pareto frontier to the end user, they are able to better understand the structure of their problem as well as the tradeoffs between different security strategies. As a result, end users are able to make a more informed decision on which strategy to enact. Existing approaches so far assume that each attacker type has a single objective and there is no uncertainty regarding each attacker type's payoffs. It is challenging to develop algorithms for solving multi-objective security games with multiple attacker objectives and uncertain attacker payoffs.

In addition to the above research challenges, there are other on-going challenges such as preference elicitation for acquiring necessary domain knowledge in order to build game models and evaluation of the game theoretic applications [37].

## 5    Resources for Starting This Research

Security is recognized as a world-wide grand challenge and game theory is an increasingly important paradigm for reasoning about complex security resource allocation.

While the deployed game theoretic applications have provided a promising start, very significant amount of research remains to be done. These are large-scale interdisciplinary research challenges that call upon multiagent researchers to work with researchers in other disciplines, be "on the ground" with domain experts, and examine real-world constraints and challenges that cannot be abstracted away.

There are a number of resources (mostly online) for starting this research. The research papers related to game theory for security have been extensively published at AAMAS conference[3] and the reader can also find some papers from AAAI[4] and IJ-CAI[5]. Additional resources:

- Key papers describing important algorithms and the deployed systems can also be found from a recently published book –*Security and Game Theory: Algorithms, Deployed Systems, Lessons Learned* [38].
- The details of those deployed systems as well as related publications can also be found at http://teamcore.usc.edu/projects/security/.
- From http://teamcore.usc.edu/projects/security/, the reader can also find a tutorial at UAI'2011 – Game Theory for Security: Lessons learned from deployed applications.

While we have focused on research conducted by our Teamcore group, there are a few other research groups that have started addressing challenges in security games [13, 14, 39–42].

**Acknowledgments.** This research is supported by MURI grant W911NF-11-1-0332 and ONR grant N00014-08-1-0733.

# References

1. Pita, J., Jain, M., Western, C., Portway, C., Tambe, M., Ordonez, F., Kraus, S., Parachuri, P.: Deployed ARMOR protection: The application of a game-theoretic model for security at the Los Angeles International Airport. In: Proc. of the 7th International Conference on Autonomous Agents and Multiagent Systems, AAMAS, pp. 125–132 (2008)
2. Tsai, J., Rathi, S., Kiekintveld, C., Ordonez, F., Tambe, M.: IRIS: a tool for strategic security allocation in transportation networks. In: Proc. of the 8th International Conference on Autonomous Agents and Multiagent Systems, AAMAS, pp. 37–44 (2009)
3. An, B., Pita, J., Shieh, E., Tambe, M., Kiekintveld, C., Marecki, J.: Guards and protect: Next generation applications of security games. SIGECOM 10, 31–34 (2011)
4. Shieh, E., An, B., Yang, R., Tambe, M., Baldwin, C., DiRenzo, J., Maule, B., Meyer, G.: PROTECT: A deployed game theoretic system to protect the ports of the united states. In: Proc. of the 11th International Conference on Autonomous Agents and Multiagent Systems, AAMAS (2012)
5. Pita, J., Tambe, M., Kiekintveld, C., Cullen, S., Steigerwald, E.: Guards - game theoretic security allocation on a national scale. In: Proc. of the 10th International Conference on Autonomous Agents and Multiagent Systems, AAMAS (2011)

---

[3] www.aamas-conference.org.

[4] www.aaai.org/.

[5] ijcai.org/.

6. Yin, Z., Jiang, A., Johnson, M., Tambe, M., Kiekintveld, C., Leyton-Brown, K., Sandholm, T., Sullivan, J.: Trusts: Scheduling randomized patrols for fare inspection in transit systems. In: Proc. of the 24th Conference on Innovative Applications of Artificial Intelligence, IAAI (2012)

7. Osbourne, M.J., Rubinstein, A.: A Course in Game Theory. MIT Press (1994)

8. von Stengel, B., Zamir, S.: Leadership with commitment to mixed strategies. Technical Report LSE-CDAM-2004-01, CDAM Research Report (2004)

9. Conitzer, V., Sandholm, T.: Computing the Optimal Strategy to Commit to. In: Proc. of the ACM Conference on Electronic Commerce, ACM-EC, pp. 82–90 (2006)

10. Paruchuri, P., Pearce, J.P., Marecki, J., Tambe, M., Ordonez, F., Kraus, S.: Playing games with security: An efficient exact algorithm for Bayesian Stackelberg games. In: Proc. of the 7th International Conference on Autonomous Agents and Multiagent Systems, AAMAS, pp. 895–902 (2008)

11. Harsanyi, J., Selten, R.: A Generalized Nash Solution for Two-Person Bargaining Games with Incomplete Information 18, 80–106 (1972)

12. Paruchuri, P., Pearce, J.P., Tambe, M., Ordonez, F., Kraus, S.: An efficient heuristic approach for security against multiple adversaries. In: Proc. of the 6th International Conference on Autonomous Agents and Multiagent Systems, AAMAS, pp. 311–318 (2007)

13. Basilico, N., Gatti, N., Amigoni, F.: Leader-follower strategies for robotic patrolling in environments with arbitrary topologies. In: Proc. of the 8th International Conference on Autonomous Agents and Multiagent Systems, AAMAS, pp. 500–503 (2009)

14. Korzhyk, D., Conitzer, V., Parr, R.: Complexity of computing optimal stackelberg strategies in security resource allocation games. In: Proc. of the 24th AAAI Conference on Artificial Intelligence, pp. 805–810 (2010)

15. Jain, M., Tsai, J., Pita, J., Kiekintveld, C., Rathi, S., Tambe, M., Ordonez, F.: Software assistants for randomized patrol planning for the lax airport police and the federal air marshal service. Interfaces 40, 267–290 (2010)

16. Jain, M., Kardes, E., Kiekintveld, C., Ordonez, F., Tambe, M.: Security games with arbitrary schedules: A branch and price approach. In: Proc. of the 24th AAAI Conference on Artificial Intelligence, pp. 792–797 (2010)

17. McKelvey, R.D., Palfrey, T.R.: Quantal response equilibria for normal form games. Games and Economic Behavior 10(1), 6–38 (1995)

18. TSA: Layers of Security: What We Do (2011)

19. TSA: Transportation Security Administration – U.S. Department of Homeland Security (2011)

20. Hamilton, B.A.: Faregating analysis. Report commissioned by the la metro (2007)

21. Jiang, A.X., Yin, Z., Kietkintveld, C., Leyton-Brown, K., Sandholm, T., Tambe, M.: Towards optimal patrol strategies for urban security in transit systems. In: Proc. of the AAAI Spring Symposium on Game Theory for Security, Sustainability and Health (2012)

22. Johnson, M., Fang, F., Yang, R., Tambe, M., Albers, H.: Patrolling to maximize pristine forest area. In: Proc. of the AAAI Spring Symposium on Game Theory for Security, Sustainability and Health (2012)

23. Ordonez, F., Tambe, M., Jara, J.F., Jain, M., Kiekintveld, C., Tsai, J.: Deployed security games for patrol planning. In: Handbook on Operations Research for Homeland Security (2008)

24. Trusov, M., Bucklin, R.E., Pauwels, K.: Effects of word-of-mouth versus traditional marketing: Findings from an internet social networking site. Journal of Marketing 73 (2009)

25. Howard, N.J.: Finding optimal strategies for influencing social networks in two player games. Master's thesis, MIT, Sloan School of Management (2011)

26. Alpcan, T.: Network Security: A Decision and Game-Theoretic Approach. Cambridge University Press (2010)

27. Vanek, O., Yin, Z., Jain, M., Bosansky, B., Tambe, M., Pechoucek, M.: Game-theoretic resource allocation for malicious packet detection in computer networks. In: Proc. of the 11th International Conference on Autonomous Agents and Multiagent Systems, AAMAS (2012)
28. Jain, M., Korzhyk, D., Vanek, O., Pechoucek, M., Conitzer, V., Tambe, M.: A double oracle algorithm for zero-sum security games on graphs. In: Proc. of the 10th International Conference on Autonomous Agents and Multiagent Systems, AAMAS (2011)
29. Kiekintveld, C., Marecki, J., Tambe, M.: Approximation methods for infinite bayesian stackelberg games: modeling distributional uncertainty. In: Proc. of the 10th International Conference on Autonomous Agents and Multiagent Systems, AAMAS (2011)
30. Yin, Z., Jain, M., Tambe, M., Ordonez, F.: Risk-averse strategies for security games with execution and observational uncertainty. In: Proc. of the 25th AAAI Conference on Artificial Intelligence, AAAI, pp. 758–763 (2011)
31. An, B., Tambe, M., Ordonez, F., Shieh, E., Kiekintveld, C.: Refinement of strong stackelberg equilibria in security games. In: Proc. of the 25th Conference on Artificial Intelligence, pp. 587–593 (2011)
32. Kahneman, D., Tvesky, A.: Prospect theory: An analysis of decision under risk. Econometrica 47(2), 263–291 (1979)
33. Yang, R., Kiekintveld, C., Ordonez, F., Tambe, M., John, R.: Improving resource allocation strategy against human adversaries in security games. In: IJCAI (2011)
34. Pita, J., Jain, M., Tambe, M., Ordóñez, F., Kraus, S.: Robust solutions to stackelberg games: Addressing bounded rationality and limited observations in human cognition. Artificial Intelligence 174(15), 1142–1171 (2010)
35. An, B., Jain, M., Tambe, M., Kiekintveld, C.: Mixed-initiative optimization in security games: A preliminary report. In: Proc. of the AAAI Spring Symposium on Help Me Help You: Bridging the Gaps in Human-Agent Collaboration, pp. 8–11 (2011)
36. Brown, M., An, B., Kiekintveld, C., Ordonez, F., Tambe, M.: Multi-objective optimization for security games. In: Proc. of the 11th International Conference on Autonomous Agents and Multiagent Systems, AAMAS (2012)
37. Taylor, M.E., Kiekintveld, C., Western, C., Tambe, M.: A framework for evaluating deployed security systems: Is there a chink in your armor? Informatica 34, 129–139 (2010)
38. Tambe, M.: Security and Game Theory: Algorithms, Deployed Systems, Lessons Learned. Cambridge University Press (2011)
39. Dickerson, J.P., Simari, G.I., Subrahmanian, V.S., Kraus, S.: A graph-theoretic approach to protect static and moving targets from adversaries. In: Proc. of the 9th International Conference on Autonomous Agents and Multiagent Systems, AAMAS, pp. 299–306 (2010)
40. Korzhyk, D., Conitzer, V., Parr, R.: Solving stackelberg games with uncertain observability. In: Proc. of the 10th International Conference on Autonomous Agents and Multiagent Systems, AAMAS (2011)
41. Korzhyk, D., Conitzer, V., Parr, R.: Security games with multiple attacker resources. In: Proc. of the International Joint Conference on Artificial Intelligence, IJCAI (2011)
42. Letchford, J., Vorobeychik, Y.: Computing randomized security strategies in networked domains. In: Proc. of the AAAI Workshop on Applied Adversarial Reasoning and Risk Modeling, AARM (2011)

# Local Coordination in Online Distributed Constraint Optimization Problems

Tim Brys, Yann-Michaël De Hauwere, Ann Nowé, and Peter Vrancx

Computational Modeling Lab - Vrije Universiteit Brussel,
Pleinlaan 2, B-1050 Brussels, Belgium
{timbrys,ydehauwe,anowe,pvrancx}@vub.ac.be
http://como.vub.ac.be

**Abstract.** In cooperative multi-agent systems, group performance often depends more on the interactions between team members, rather than on the performance of any individual agent. Hence, coordination among agents is essential to optimize the group strategy. One solution which is common in the literature is to let the agents learn in a joint action space. Joint Action Learning (JAL) enables agents to explicitly take into account the actions of other agents, but has the significant drawback that the action space in which the agents must learn scales exponentially in the number of agents. Local coordination is a way for a team to coordinate while keeping communication and computational complexity low. It allows the exploitation of a specific dependency structure underlying the problem, such as tight couplings between specific agents. In this paper we investigate a novel approach to local coordination, in which agents learn this dependency structure, resulting in coordination which is beneficial to the group performance. We evaluate our approach in the context of online distributed constraint optimization problems.

## 1 Introduction

A key issue in multi-agent learning is ensuring that agents coordinate their individual decisions in order to reach a jointly optimal payoff. A common approach is to let the agents learn in the joint action space. Joint Action Learning (JAL) enables agents to explicitly take into account the actions of other agents, but has the significant drawback that the action space in which the agents must learn scales exponentially in the number of agents [5], quickly becoming computationally unmanageable. In this paper, we investigate a novel approach in which agents adaptively determine when coordination is beneficial. We introduce *Local Joint Action Learners* (LJAL) which specifically learn to coordinate their action selection only when necessary, in order to improve the global payoff, and evaluate our approach in the context of distributed constraint optimization. We investigate teamwork among a group of agents attempting to optimize a set of constraints in an online fashion. Agents learn how to coordinate their actions using only a global reward signal resulting from the actions of the entire group of agents.

M. Cossentino et al. (Eds.): EUMAS 2011, LNAI 7541, pp. 31–47, 2012.
© Springer-Verlag Berlin Heidelberg 2012

The remainder of this paper is laid out as follows: in the next section we review some background material and related work on agent coordination. Section 3 introduces our local coordination method. Section 4 introduces the optimization problems we consider in this work. We demonstrate how optimization problems can have an inherent structure that can be exploited by LJALs. In Section 5, we propose and evaluate a method that allows LJALs to learn a coordination structure optimized for the specific problem task at hand. Finally, we offer some concluding remarks in Section 6.

## 2    Background and Related Work

The Local Joint Action Learner (LJAL) approach proposed below relies on the concept of a Coordination Graph (CG) [6], which describes action dependencies among agents. Coordination graphs formalize the way agents coordinate their actions. In a CG, vertices represent agents, and edges between two agents indicate a coordination dependency between these agents. Figure 1(a) is an example of a CG with 7 agents. In this graph, agent 1 coordinates with agents 2, 3 and 5; agent 4 does not coordinate and thus corresponds to an independent learner; and agent 6 coordinates with agents 5 and 7. Figure 1(a) represents an undirected CG where both agents connected by an edge explicitly coordinate. A CG can also be directed, as shown in Figure 1(b). In this graph, the same agents are connected as in Figure 1(a), but the edges are directed and the meaning of the graph thus differs. In Figure 1(b), agent 1 now coordinates with agents 2 and 5, but not with 3; agent 4 is still an independent learner; and agent 6 only coordinates with 5.

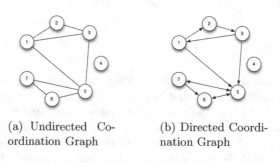

(a) Undirected Co-    (b) Directed Coordi-
ordination Graph         nation Graph

**Fig. 1.** Two coordination graphs with 7 agents

Guestrin [6] and Kok and Vlassis [8] propose algorithms where agents, using a message passing scheme based on a CG, calculate a global joint action by communicating their perceived local rewards. Below we describe a new approach which is an alternative to Independent Learning (IL) and Joint Action Learning (JAL) [5] based on CGs, where agents optimize their local joint actions without extensive communication, using global reward.

# 3  Local Joint Action Learners

We now introduce our Local Joint Action Learner (LJAL) framework. LJALs are a generalization of the Joint Action Learners proposed in [5]. The main idea is that agents keep estimates of expected rewards, not just for their own actions, but for combinations of actions of multiple agents. Contrary to the JALs, however, LJALs do not coordinate over the joint actions of all agents, but rather coordinate with a specific subset of all agents. An LJAL relies on a coordination graph to encode coordination, and will keep estimates only for the combinations of its own actions with those of its direct neighbors in the graph.

It can easily be seen that LJALs cover the entire range of possible coordination settings from Independent Learning (IL) agents, who only consider their own actions, to Joint Action Learners (JAL), who take into account the actions of all agents. As LJALs keep estimates for joint actions with their neighbours in the graph, ILs can be represented with a fully disconnected graph, whereas the coordination between JALs can be represented with a fully connected or complete graph.

Figure 2 illustrates the CGs for ILs and JALs, as well as showing another possible LJAL graph. Note that this representation is not directly related to the underlying structure of the problem being solved, but rather represents the solution method being used. In the experiments below, we will evaluate the effect of matching the CG to the problem structure on the performance, this in terms of learning speed and final performance.

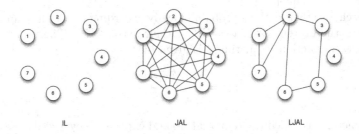

**Fig. 2.** Coordination graphs for independent learners and joint action learners and an example graph for local joint action learners

## 3.1  Action Selection

We view the learning problem as a distributed n-armed bandit problem, where every agent must individually decide which of n actions to execute and the reward depends on the combination of all chosen actions. In the case that the reward for each agent is generated by the same function, the game is said to be **cooperative**. It is with such cooperative or coordination games that we are concerned in this paper. Below, we describe the action estimation and action selection method used by LJALs.

Each agent estimates rewards for (possibly joint) action $a$ according to following incremental update formula [11]:

$$Q_{t+1}(a) = Q_t(a) + \alpha\,[r(t+1) - Q_t(a)] \tag{1}$$

where $\alpha$ is the step-size parameter, balancing the importance of recent and past rewards, and $r(t)$ is the reward received for action $a$ at time $t$. (L)JALs also keep a probabilistic model of the other agents' action selection, by using empirical distributions, i.e. counting the number of times $C$ each action has been chosen by each agent. Agent $i$ maintains the frequency $F_{a_j}^i$, that agent $j$ selects action $a_j$ from its action set $A_j$:

$$F_{a_j}^i = \frac{C_{a_j}^j}{\sum_{b_j \in A_j} C_{b_j}^j} \tag{2}$$

Using their estimates for joint actions and their probabilistic models of other agents' action selection, agents can evaluate the expected value for selecting a specific action from their individual action set:

$$EV(a_i) = \sum_{\mathbf{a} \in \mathbb{A}^i} Q(\mathbf{a} \cup \{a_i\}) \prod_j F_{\mathbf{a}[j]}^i, \tag{3}$$

where $\mathbb{A}^i = \times_{j \in N(i)} A_j$ and $N(i)$ represents the set of neighbors of agent $i$ in the CG. This means that the expected value for playing a specific action, is the average reward of the observed joint actions in which the action occurs, weighted by their relative frequencies.

Agents choose their actions probabilistically according to a Boltzmann distribution over the current estimates $EV$ of their actions [11]. The probability of agent $i$ selecting action $a_i$, at time $t$ is given by:

$$Pr(a_i) = \frac{e^{EV(a_i)/\tau}}{\sum_{b_i=1}^n e^{EV(b_i)/\tau}} \tag{4}$$

The parameter $\tau$ is called the temperature and expresses how greedy the actions are being selected. Low values for $\tau$ represent a more greedy action selection mechanism.

## 3.2   LJAL Performance

In this section, we briefly evaluate empirically how different types of LJALs relate to each other in terms of solution quality and computation speed. Specifically, we will evaluate the effect of increased graph density on performance; it results in more information, but also higher complexity for agents. Intuitively, we expect that ILs and JALs will lie at extreme ends of the performance spectrum that LJALs encompass. ILs possess little information and thus should yield the worst solutions, while JALs, who in theory have all possible information, should find the best solutions. On the other hand, JALs need to deal with the total complexity of the problem, resulting in long computation times, while ILs only reason about themselves and should logically compute fastest of all LJALs.

We compare respectively ILs, LJALs using randomly generated, directed CGs with an out-degree of 2 for each agent, random LJALs with out-degree 3, and JALs, see Figure 3. These types of learners were evaluated on randomly generated distributed bandit problems, i.e. for each possible joint action of the team, a fixed global reward is drawn from a normal distribution $\mathcal{N}(0, 50)$ ($50 = 10 \times \#$ agents). A single run of the experiment consists of 200 iterations, also referred to as plays, in which 5 agents choose between 4 actions, and receive a reward for the global joint action, as determined by the problem. Every run, LJAL-2 and LJAL-3 get a new random graph with the specified out-degree. All learners employ softmax action selection with temperature function $\tau = 1000 \times 0.94^{play}$. Figure 4 displays the results of this experiment averaged over 10000 runs and Table 1 shows the speed (running time needed to complete the experiment) and solution quality for the various learners, relative those of the JALs.

These results corroborate our hypothesis that ILs and JALs are both ends of the LJAL performance spectrum. Since any LJAL possesses no more information than JALs and no less than ILs, their solution quality lies in between these two extreme approaches. Moreover, because the complexity of LJAL joint actions lies in between ILs and JALs, we also observe that LJALs perform computationally

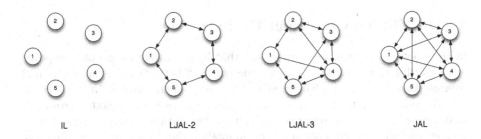

IL                    LJAL-2                    LJAL-3                    JAL

**Fig. 3.** Coordination graphs for independent learners and joint action learners, and examples of random coordination graphs for local joint action learners with out-degrees 2 and 3

**Table 1.** Comparison of speed and solution quality for independent learners, joint action learners and local joint action learners solving a typical distributed bandit problem. All differences are significant, $p < 0.05$.

| Learner | Avg # partners | Speed | Solution Quality |
|---------|----------------|-------|------------------|
| IL      | 0              | ×31.5 | 71.1%            |
| LJAL-2  | 2              | ×12.1 | 80.5%            |
| LJAL-3  | 3              | ×4.4  | 89.3%            |
| JAL     | 4              | ×1    | 100%             |

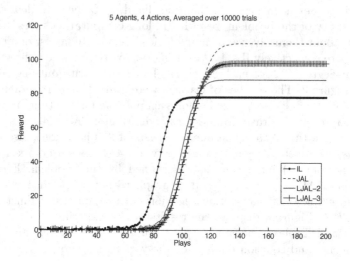

**Fig. 4.** Comparison of independent learners, joint action learners and local joint action learners on a typical distributed bandit problem

no faster than ILs and no slower than JALs. As expected, as the complexity of the CG used increases, so does the solution quality, but at the cost of a longer computation time.

## 4    Distributed Constraint Optimization

In the previous section, we have shown that it is possible to use our proposed local coordination method to balance the trade-off between solution quality and computation speed, a problem often encountered in real settings. In this section, we take this a step further, as we aim to show that we can exploit a problem's structure using local coordination, reducing computational complexity, but minimizing the corresponding loss in solution quality. Since the simple bandit problem of the previous section does not have such a structure, as the reward for every joint action is generated independently, we look at another type of problem, which is ideally suited to represent problems with an inherent structure, i.e. Distributed Constraint Optimization Problems.

A Constraint Optimization Problem (COP) describes the problem of assigning values to a set of variables, subject to a number of soft constraints. Each constraint takes the form of a function assigning rewards to variable assignments. A solution to a constraint optimization problem assigns a value to each variable and has an associated total reward, which is the sum of the rewards for every constraint. Solving a COP means maximizing this reward. A Distributed Constraint Optimization Problem (DCOP) describes the distributed equivalent of constraint optimization. A group of agents must solve a COP in a distributed way, each agent controlling a subset of the variables in the problem.

Formally, a DCOP is a tuple $(\mathcal{A}, \mathcal{X}, \mathcal{D}, \mathcal{C}, f)$, where:

- $\mathcal{A} = \{a_1, a_2, ..., a_\ell\}$, the set of agents.
- $\mathcal{X} = \{x_1, x_2, ..., x_n\}$, the set of variables.
- $\mathcal{D} = \{D_1, D_2, ..., D_n\}$, the set of domains. Variable $x_i$ can be assigned values from the finite domain $D_i$.
- $\mathcal{C} = \{c_1, c_2, ..., c_m\}$, the set of constraints. Constraint $c_i$ is a function $D_a \times D_b \times ... \times D_k \to \mathbb{R}$, with $\{a, b, ..., k\} \subseteq \{1, ..., n\}$, projecting the domains of a subset of variables onto a real number, being the reward.
- $f : \mathcal{X} \to \mathcal{A}$, a function mapping variables onto a single agent.

The total reward of a variable assignment $S$, assigning value $v(x_i) \in D_i$ to variable $x_i$, is:

$$C(S) = \sum_{i=1}^{m} c_i(v(x_a), \ldots, v(x_k)) \tag{5}$$

For simplicity, we assume only one variable per agent and only binary constraints. Unary constraints can easily be added and higher arity constraints can be constructed using unary and binary constraints.

Distributed Constraint Problems are used to model a variety of real problems, ranging from disaster response scenarios [2] and distributed sensor network management [7], to traffic management in congested networks [9].

## 4.1  Relation of LJAL to Other DCOP Algorithms

As noted in [12], a DCOP can be reformulated as a distributed n-armed bandit problem. Assign one variable to each agent and let it choose from the values in the domain corresponding to the variable as it would select an arm from an n-armed bandit. With such a formulation, we can apply our previously described learners to DCOPs. In this section, we briefly evaluate the relation of LJAL to other DCOP algorithms and in which context LJALs are best applied.

Comparing LJAL to the unifying DCOP algorithm framework proposed by Chapman et al. in [3], we see that it relates most to the "local iterative, approximate best response algorithms". Algorithms in this class are incomplete – they are not guaranteed to find the optimal solution –, but on the other hand, they only use local information, having neighbouring agents communicate only their state, and thus do not suffer from exponential complexity in the size of the problem. These algorithms typically converge to local optima, or Nash equilibria, and are often preferred in real-world settings, as these require a balance between solution quality and computational complexity, or timeliness, and communication overhead. In contrast, "distributed complete algorithms", such as ADOPT [1] are proven to find the optimal solution for a DCOP, although with an exponential communication or computational complexity[4,10].

We are not specifically interested in developing a state-of-the-art DCOP solver, but rather a multi-agent reinforcement learning technique which can trade-off solution quality and complexity, taking advantage of a problem's structure. Therefore, we explore solving DCOPs in an online reinforcement learning scenario.

This means that agents do not have any prior knowledge of the reward function and must sample actions in order to solve the problem. In conventional DCOP settings, local reward functions are assumed to be deterministic and available to the agent. As such the problem can be treated as a distributed planning problem. In our setting, the rewards associated with constraints can be stochastic and agents may have few opportunities to sample rewards. Moreover, the agents cannot directly observe the local rewards resulting from their actions, but only receive the global reward resulting from the joint action of all agents.

Finally, and most importantly, we do not assume knowledge of the constraint graph underlying the problem is always available, an assumption found all over the literature, and often not justifiable in real-world settings.

### 4.2  Experiments

Since each constraint in a DCOP has its own reward function and the total reward for a solution is simply the sum of all rewards, some constraints can have a larger impact on the solution quality than others, i.e. when there is a higher variance in their rewards. Therefore, coordination between specific agents can be more important than between others. In this section, we will investigate the performance of LJALs on DCOPs where some constraints are more important than others. We will generate random, fully connected DCOPs, drawing the rewards of every constraint function from different normal distributions. The variance in rewards is controlled by means of weights, formalizing the importance of specific constraints with respect to the whole problem. We attach a weight $w_i \in [0, 1]$ to each constraint $c_i$; the problem's variance $\sigma$ is multiplied with this weight when building the reward function for constraint $c_i$. A weight of 1 indicates the constraint is of the highest importance, while 0 makes the constraint of no importance. When building a DCOP, rewards for constraint $c_i$ are drawn from this distribution:

$$\mathcal{N}(0, \sigma w_i) \tag{6}$$

Figure 5 visualizes the structure of the problem we will compare different LJALs on in the first experiment. The colors of constraints or edges indicate the importance of that constraint. The darker the constraint, the higher the weight. The rewards for each constraint function are fixed before every run with $\sigma = 70$ ($10 \times \#$ agents). The black edges in the figure correspond to weights of 0.9, light-grey edges are weights of 0.1. What this graph formalizes, is that the constraints between agents 1, 2 and 3, and 5 and 6 are very important, while the contribution of all other constraints to the total reward is quite limited.

We state again that we are interested in using knowledge of the problem's underlying structure to minimize the loss in solution quality when reducing computational complexity. Therefore, in addition to independent learners (IL), joint action learners (JAL), and local joint action learners with a random 2-degree CG (LJAL-1), we compare LJALs with a CG matching the problem structure (LJAL-2), and the same graph, augmented with coordination between agents 1 and 5 (LJAL-3), see Figure 6.

**Fig. 5.** Distributed constraint satisfaction problem used in the experiments. Dark edges mean important constraints, light edges are unimportant constraints.

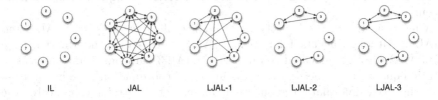

**Fig. 6.** Different local joint action learners, visualized by their coordination graphs. LJAL-1 is an example graph with outdegree 2.

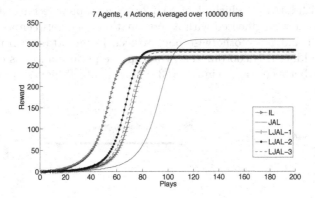

**Fig. 7.** Comparison of independent learners, joint action learners and local joint action learners on a distributed constraint optimization problem

**Table 2.** Comparison of speed and solution quality for independent learners, joint action learners and local joint action learners solving a distributed constraint optimization problem. All differences are significant $p < 0.05$.

| Learner | Avg # partners | Speed | Solution Quality |
|---------|----------------|-------|------------------|
| IL      | 0              | ×442  | 86.2%            |
| LJAL-1  | 2              | ×172  | 86.4%            |
| LJAL-2  | 1.14           | ×254  | 91.6%            |
| LJAL-3  | 1.43           | ×172  | 90.2%            |
| JAL     | 6              | ×1    | 100%             |

The results, averaged over 100000 runs, are shown in Figure 7 and Table 2. As seen in the previous section, ILs and JALs perform respectively best and worst in terms of solution quality. More importantly, as we compare LJAL-1 and LJAL-2, we see that LJAL-2 perform 6% better, while being at the same time 1.5× faster. The higher solution quality results from matching coordination with the problem structure, and lower computation times are due to the lower complexity (in LJAL-1, each agent coordinates with two partners, in LJAL-2, an agent coordinates with only 1.14 partners on average[1]). This shows that using a specific CG can help LJALs solve a problem better, using less computational resources.

A more surprising result is the performance difference between LJAL-2 and LJAL-3. Although agents 1 and 5 in LJAL-3 possess more information than in LJAL-2 through increased coordination, LJAL-3 performs worse in terms of solution quality (and speed, due to the increased coordination). We hypothesise that the extra information about an unimportant constraint complicates the coordination on important constraints.

We set up an experiment to evaluate the effect an extra coordination edge has on solution quality. It compares LJAL-2 and LJAL-3 from the previous experiment with LJAL-4, which like LJAL-2 uses a graph matching the problem structure, only now augmented with a coordination edge between agents 4 and 7. As agents 4 and 7 are otherwise not involved in important constraints, we predict that adding this coordination will improve performance, as opposed to the extra edge between 1 and 5 in LJAL-3. Figure 8 and Table 3 show the results this experiment.

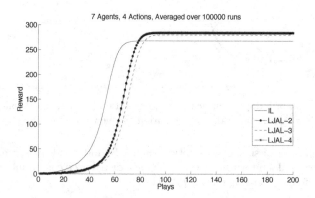

**Fig. 8.** Evaluating the effect of extra coordination edges on solution quality

Since agents 4 and 7 are not involved in important constraints as defined by the problem, the addition of this edge improves performance slightly; the agents will learn to optimize the marginally important constraint between them, without complicating the coordination necessary for important constraints. These

---

[1] Three agents with two partners, two with one and two without partners.

**Table 3.** Evaluating the effect of extra coordination edges on solution quality. Solution qualities are relative to that of independent learners. All differences are significant $p < 0.05$.

| Learner | Solution Quality |
|---------|------------------|
| IL      | 100%             |
| LJAL-2  | 105.9%           |
| LJAL-3  | 104.5%           |
| LJAL-4  | 106.2%           |

results show that the choice of the graph is very important and even small changes influence the agents' performance. In [12], Taylor et al. also conclude that increasing team work is not necessarily beneficial to solution quality.

# 5  Learning Coordination Graphs

In the previous sections, we have shown that matching the CG of local joint action learners to the inherent structure of a problem helps to improve solution quality without having to deal with the total complexity of the problem. The next problem we consider is learning this graph. In some problems, such as the graph colouring problem, this graph may be obvious. In others, the structure of the problem may not be known beforehand and thus the designer of the system has no way of knowing what graph to implement. In this section, we will investigate a way to allow the local joint action learners to optimize the CG themselves.

## 5.1  Method

We encode the problem of learning a CG as a distributed n-armed bandit problem. In the simplest case, each agent is allowed to pick one coordination partner and has as many actions as there are agents in the problem. For example, agent 2 choosing action 5 means a directed coordination edge in the CG from agent 2 to 5. Agent 3 choosing action 3 means agent 3 chooses not to coordinate, so no additional edge in the CG. The combined choices of the agents describe the coordination graph structure. In the experiments, we limit the learners to either one or two coordination partners, to evaluate how low complexity systems can perform on more complex problems. We map the two-partner selection to an n-armed bandit problem by making actions represent pairs of agents instead of single agents, e.g. action 10 means selecting agents 2 and 3. This is feasible in small domains, but with more agents and a higher complexity limit per agent, the problem of choosing multiple partners should be modelled as a Markov Decision Process, with partner selection spread out over multiple states, i.e. multi-stage.

After choosing coordination partners, the agents solve the learning problem using that coordination graph. The reward achieved after learning is then used as feedback for the choosing of coordination partners; agents estimate rewards for the partner choices. This constitutes one play at the meta-learning level. This process is repeated until the graph has converged due to decreasing temperature in the meta-bandit action selection. We choose to make the agents in the meta-bandit independent learners, although it would also be possible to allow them to coordinate. Only then the question of which CG to pick would arise again.

## 5.2    Learning in DCOPs with a Particular Structure

In our first experiment, we make agents learn a CG on the problem used in previous sections and illustrated in Figure 5. As such, we can compare the learned CGs with the (to us) known problem structure. One meta-bandit run consists of 1500 plays. In each play, the chosen CG is evaluated in 100 runs of 200 plays; 100 runs to account for the inherent stochasticity of the learning process so as to get relatively accurate estimates for the quality of the chosen graph. This evaluation is basically the same setup as the experiments in Section 4.2. The average of the reward achieved over these 100 runs is the estimated reward for the chosen CG.

In addition to ILs, JALs and LJALs with a CG matching the problem structure, LJAL-1, we compare two teams of LJALS who optimize their CG, with respective complexity limits of one, OptLJAL-1, and two, OptLJAL-2, coordination partners. Figure 9 and Table 4 show the results of this experiment, averaged over 1000 runs, each time a newly generated problem, although with the same inherent structure. Temperature $\tau$ in the meta-bandit is decreased as such: $\tau = 1000 \times 0.994^{play}$.

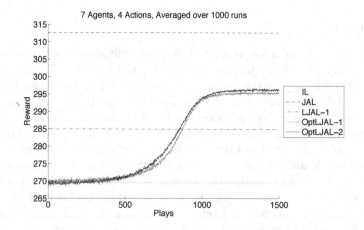

**Fig. 9.** Comparing the solution qualities of independent learners, joint action learners, local joint action learners with the supposedly optimal coordination graph and local joint action learners who optimize their coordination graph

**Table 4.** Comparing the computation speeds and solution qualities of independent learners, joint action learners, local joint action learners with the supposedly optimal coordination graph and local joint action learners who optimize their coordination graph, respectively limited to one and two coordination partners per agent. All differences are significant $p < 0.05$, except between OptLJAL-1 and OptLJAL-2.

| Learner | Avg # partners | Speed | Solution Quality |
|---|---|---|---|
| IL | 0 | ×374 | 86.2% |
| LJAL-1 | 1.14 | ×243 | 91.1% |
| OptLJAL-1 | 0.81 | ×290 | 94.5% |
| OptLJAL-2 | 1.28 | ×240 | 94.7% |
| JAL | 6 | ×1 | 100% |

The results show that not only can the agents adapt their coordination graph to the problem and thus improve performance over agents with random graphs, they also manage to outperform the LJALs that use the CG mimicking the problem structure. That graph is surprisingly not the optimal coordination structure, as the optimizing agents in general find better graphs, graphs with a lower complexity; a maximum complexity of one coordination partner in the case of OptLJAL-1, as opposed to two partners in the graph matching the problem. OptLJAL-2 has similar performance as OptLJAL-1, although with a slightly higher complexity and thus longer computation time. It is important to note that graphs optimized by OptLJAL-2 in general have a complexity of 1.28, which is very low considering the highest possible complexity is 2. More coordination again does not appear to be always beneficial. Compare for example the average complexities of the resulting graphs, 0.81 and 1.28 for limits 1 and 2 respectively, with that of the random graphs in the exploration stages: 0.86 and 1.59.

To get a better insight into how OptLJAL-1 and OptLJAL-2 can outperform LJAL-1, we look at some of the optimized graphs for this problem. Figure 10 shows the graphs learned by OptLJAL-1 and OptLJAL-2 respectively on five instances of the given problem. These graphs represent cases where optimizing agents significantly outperformed LJAL-1, who mimic the problem structure in their CG.

When viewing these optimized graphs, we would expect to find at least some of the problem structure reflected in them. This is clearly the case. In every single graph, we find that agents 5 and 6 learn to coordinate. There is also always some coordination in the agents 1-2-3 cluster. This is also reflected in Table 5, where the average number of edges between any two agents in a cluster is shown. Agents 1, 2 and 3, and agents 5 and 6 coordinate significantly more than they would in random graphs, while 4 and 7 coordinate less. Counting the incoming edges, we note that agents 1, 2, 3 have on average 1.0 agents adapting to them, 5 and 6 have 1.2 such agents, while 4 and 7 only 0.1.

This shows that the agents can determine which agents are more important to coordinate with. Still, this does not explain how the agents with an optimized

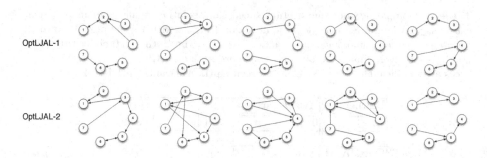

**Fig. 10.** Optimized coordination graphs. Graphs in the top row are limited to one coordination partner per agent, graphs in the bottom row are limited to two partners.

**Table 5.** The average number of directed edges between any two agents in a cluster. Agents in important problem substructures coordinate significantly more often in optimized graphs than in random graphs. The inverse is true for agents in unimportant substructures.

|           | 1-2-3 | 5-6  | 4-7  |
|-----------|-------|------|------|
| OptLJAL-1 | 0.68  | 1.53 | 0.13 |
| Random-1  | 0.28  | 0.28 | 0.28 |
| OptLJAL-2 | 0.85  | 1.54 | 0.33 |
| Random-2  | 0.53  | 0.53 | 0.53 |

graph can perform better with a lower coordination complexity than those who use the problem structure as a coordination graph. We believe the explanation is two-fold. First, in optimized graphs, agents often practice something we like to call "follow the leader". Basically, this comes down to one agent performing as leader, often an independent learner, while other agents coordinate unilaterally with that agent. This allows the other agents to choose actions in function of the same leader, while that leader can learn without knowing that other agents are coordinating, or rather adapting, to him, simplifying the problem for every agent by concentrating the exploration in certain parts of the search space. This is especially beneficial when only a limited amount of trials is allowed. Secondly, agents that do not coordinate directly are independent learners relative to each other. Independent learners have been shown to be able to find an optimum by climbing, i.e. each agent in turn changing an action [5]. The starting point for this climbing, in a two-dimensional game, is usually the row and column with the highest average reward. If the global optimum can be reached by climbing from this starting point, independent learning suffices to optimize the problem. When analysing the reward functions for these agents that choose to be independent learners, we see that they are involved in games where such climbing is possible. This is also the reason why a team of independent learners can perform reasonably well in this setting.

## 5.3   Learning in DCOPs with Random Structure

We have previously only focused on one specific problem, with only two very distinct categories of constraint importance, i.e. very important and very unimportant (respectively 0.9 and 0.1 as weight parameters). Such clear distinctions are not realistic and therefore we shall now investigate problems with constraints of varying importance. One issue with such problems is that, even if the structure of the problem is known, it is not easy to decide when coordination is important and when not. Is it necessary to coordinate over the constraint with weight 0.6, and not over the one with weight 0.59? Learning the graph should prove to be a better approach than guessing or fine-tuning by hand, as evidenced by the previous experiment where the preprogrammed graph was shown not to be optimal compared to other graphs of similar and even lower complexity.

The next experiment compares ILs, JALs, LJALs with a fixed CG, LJAL-1, and two teams of LJALs learning a CG, OptLJAL-1 and OptLJAL-2, on DCOPs with a randomly generated weights graph. The non-optimizing LJALs have a CG derived from the problem's weight graph; all constraints with weight 0.75 and higher are included in the graph. The results of this experiment are shown in Figure 11 and Table 6.

Although the LJALs with fixed CG coordinate over a quarter of all the constraints, and the most important ones at that, they do not manage to improve much over the solutions found by ILs. These LJALs have a CG with an average complexity of $\frac{7 \times 6 \times 0.25}{7} = 1.5$ coordination partners per agent. Compare that to the average complexity of 0.8 in OptLJAL-1. With less coordination and therefore less computation, they again manage to improve much on the solution quality.

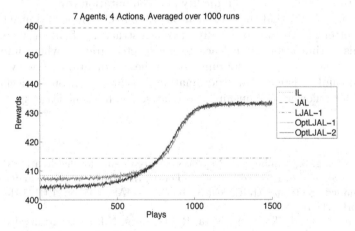

**Fig. 11.** Comparing the solution qualities of independent learners, joint action learners, local joint action learners with fixed coordination graph and local joint action learners who optimize their coordination graph on distributed constraint optimization problems with a random weights graph

**Table 6.** Comparing the computation speeds and solution qualities of independent learners, joint action learners, local joint action learners with the supposedly optimal coordination graph and local joint action learners who optimize their coordination graph, respectively limited to one and two coordination partners per agent. All differences are significant $p < 0.05$, except between OptLJAL-1 and OptLJAL-2.

| Learner | Avg # partners | Speed | Solution Quality |
|---|---|---|---|
| IL | 0 | ×315 | 88.9% |
| LJAL-1 | 1.5 | ×101 | 90.2% |
| OptLJAL-1 | 0.8 | ×254 | 94.2% |
| OptLJAL-2 | 1.28 | ×204 | 94.3% |
| JAL | 6 | ×1 | 100% |

# 6   Conclusion

In this paper, we investigated local coordination in a multi-agent reinforcement learning setting as a way to reduce complexity. *Local joint action learners* were developed as a trade-off between independent learners and joint action learners. Local joint action learners make use of a *coordination graph* that defines which agents need to coordinate when solving a problem. The density of the graph determines the computational complexity for each agent, and also influences the solution quality found by the group of agents.

Problems that have an inherent structure, making coordination between certain agents more important, can be solved by local joint action learners that have a coordination graph adapted to the structure of the problem. Learners using such a graph can perform better than those using a random graph of higher density, both in terms of solution quality and computation time.

We have also shown that the coordination graph itself can be optimized by the agents to better match the potentially unknown structure of the problem being solved. This optimization often leads to unexpected graphs, where important constraints in the problem are not mimicked in the coordination graph by a direct coordination link. Instead, this coordination is achieved through mechanisms such as leader-follower relationships and relative independent learning.

# References

1. Ali, S., Koenig, S., Tambe, M.: Preprocessing techniques for accelerating the dcop algorithm adopt. In: Proceedings of the Fourth International Joint Conference on Autonomous agents and Multiagent Systems, AAMAS 2005, pp. 1041–1048. ACM, New York (2005)
2. Chapman, A.C., Micillo, R.A., Kota, R., Jennings, N.R.: Decentralised dynamic task allocation: a practical game-theoretic approach. In: Proceedings of the 8th International Conference on Autonomous Agents and Multiagent Systems, AAMAS 2009, Richland, SC, vol. 2, pp. 915–922 (2009)
3. Chapman, A.C., Rogers, A., Jennings, N.R., Leslie, D.S.: A unifying framework for iterative approximate best-response algorithms for distributed constraint optimization problems. Knowledge Eng. Review 26(4), 411–444 (2011)

4. Chechetka, A., Sycara, K.: No-commitment branch and bound search for distributed constraint optimization. In: Proceedings of the Fifth International Joint Conference on Autonomous Agents and Multiagent Systems, pp. 1427–1429. ACM, New York (2006)

5. Claus, C., Boutilier, C.: The dynamics of reinforcement learning in cooperative multiagent systems. In: Proceedings of National Conference on Artificial Intelligence, AAAI 1998, pp. 746–752 (1998)

6. Guestrin, C., Lagoudakis, M., Parr, R.: Coordinated reinforcement learning. In: Proceedings of the ICML 2002 The Nineteenth International Conference on Machine Learning, pp. 227–234 (2002)

7. Kho, J., Rogers, A., Jennings, N.R.: Decentralized control of adaptive sampling in wireless sensor networks. ACM Trans. Sen. Netw. 5(3), 19:1–19:35 (2009)

8. Kok, J.R., Vlassis, N.: Using the Max-Plus Algorithm for Multiagent Decision Making in Coordination Graphs. In: Bredenfeld, A., Jacoff, A., Noda, I., Takahashi, Y. (eds.) RoboCup 2005. LNCS (LNAI), vol. 4020, pp. 1–12. Springer, Heidelberg (2006)

9. van Leeuwen, P., Hesselink, H., Rohling, J.: Scheduling aircraft using constraint satisfaction. Electronic Notes in Theoretical Computer Science 76, 252–268 (2002)

10. Modi, P.J., Shen, W.M., Tambe, M., Yokoo, M.: An asynchronous complete method for distributed constraint optimization. In: Autonomous Agents and Multiagent Systems, pp. 161–168 (2003)

11. Sutton, R.S., Barto, A.G.: Reinforcement Learning: An Introduction. The MIT Press (March 1998)

12. Taylor, M.E., Jain, M., Tandon, P., Yokoo, M., Tambe, M.: Distributed on-line multi-agent ooptimization under uncertainty: Balancing exploration and exploitation. Advances in Complex Systems (ACS) 14(03), 471–528 (2011)

# Improving Diagnosis Agents with Hybrid Hypotheses Confirmation Reasoning Techniques

Álvaro Carrera and Carlos A. Iglesias

Universidad Politécnica de Madrid,
Madrid, Spain
{a.carrera,cif}@dit.upm.es

**Abstract.** This article proposes a Multi-Agent Systems (MAS) architecture for network diagnosis under uncertainty. Network diagnosis is divided into two inference processes: hypotheses generation and hypotheses confirmation. The first process is distributed among several agents based on a Multiply Sectioned Bayesian Network (MSBN), while the second one is carried out by agents using semantic reasoning. A diagnosis ontology has been defined in order to combine both reasoning processes. To drive the deliberation process, the strength of influence obtained from Cumulative Distribution Function (CDF) method is used during diagnosis process. In order to achieve quick and reliable diagnoses, this influence is used to choose the best action to perform. This approach has been evaluated in a P2P video streaming scenario. Computational and time improvements are highlighted as conclusions.

**Keywords:** agent, Bayesian, ontology, diagnosis, network.

## 1 Introduction

The complexity of telecommunication networks has increased the demand for network and service management systems. Nowadays, network fault management requires high skilled engineers, which are not able to cope with the increasing heterogeneity and complexity of the network. The probability of occurrence of faults in large telecommunication networks grows as they become widespread, complex and heterogeneous [3]. Thus, the role of automatic diagnosis modules is getting more attention, in order to cover faults detection, isolation and recovery.

Furthermore, other important aspect to point out is the need for dealing with uncertainty during the diagnosis task, since many corroboration tasks cannot be carried out because of different reasons, such as the cost itself of the action or that the action requires to access the subscriber equipment and could cause him any trouble.

In recent past, several works have studied different approaches to deal with uncertainty using Bayesian networks for diagnosis [7,11]. The main focus of this work is to present a MAS architecture that combines two reasoning processes: semantic reasoning and Bayesian reasoning. This approach proposes to use Bayesian inference to handle uncertainty inherent in any diagnosis process and

M. Cossentino et al. (Eds.): EUMAS 2011, LNAI 7541, pp. 48–62, 2012.
© Springer-Verlag Berlin Heidelberg 2012

semantic inference to discriminate which action is the best one to perform depending on the available data.

The reminder of this article is structured as follows. Firstly, Sect. 2 shows the knowledge model used in this work. Sect. 3 proposes an agent architecture for reasoning during both phases of a diagnosis: hypotheses generation and hypotheses confirmation. Sect. 4 exposes the testbed scenario and exemplifies the diagnosis process. Sect. 5 shows the evaluation and presents the results of comparison with other approaches. Finally, Sect. 6 draws out the main conclusions about the application of this approach and, besides, a brief description of future possible improvements.

## 2 Knowledge-Level Model of the Diagnosis Task for Telecommunication Networks

Following the knowledge-level analysis of the diagnosis task by Benjamins [2], diagnosis can be decomposed into three subtasks: (i) *symptom detection*, finding out whether complaints are indeed symptoms, (ii) *hypotheses generation*, generating possible causes based on the symptoms, and (iii) *hypotheses discrimination*, discriminating between the hypotheses based on additional observations.

In this article, we focus on the last two tasks, hypotheses generation and discrimination, as well as in the repair task, as illustrated in Fig. 1.

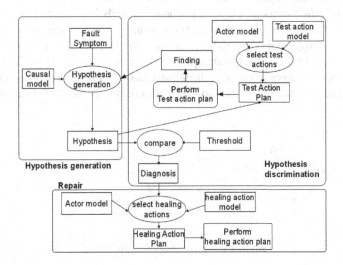

**Fig. 1.** Diagnosis inference structure. Legend: box (concept), oval (inference), rounded corner box (task).

The first process, *hypotheses generation*, consists of generating hypotheses from the notified fault based on a causal model. Since this process needs to handle uncertainty, a Bayesian network has been selected for expressing the causal model. Moreover, given that this Bayesian network could not scale well with the size and heterogeneity of telecommunication networks, our architecture proposes the usage of MSBN [13] technique, which allows to distribute this reasoning process across MASs.

The two other processes, *hypotheses discrimination* and *repairing*, follow a similar pattern. The first one obtains a test action plan to confirm the generated hypotheses. This process contains a list of ordered actions to be executed based on the expected benefits of the tests. The expected benefit of an action is defined as how relevant is for the current and is equal to the influence between variables inside causal model [8]. In this way, the system can perform more efficient hypotheses discrimination (as shown in Sect. 5).

Finally, the repair process obtains a healing action plan to repair the confirmed diagnosis. In order to reason under uncertainty, we propose to use an ontology based reasoning process, combining a diagnosis ontology expressed in Ontology Web Language (OWL) [14] with rules expressed in Semantic Web Rule Language (SWRL) [10].

Nevertheless, a technique to communicate both reasoning processes is needed, in order to be able to provide feedback and integrate learning mechanisms of the confidence of the generated hypotheses based on the results of the tests.

In order to carry out the exposed diagnosis process, an upper-ontology has been defined to facilitate the communication between the agents in the fault diagnosis task. This upper-ontology (Fig. 2) shows that *hypotheses* are generated according to *failure classes*. These hypotheses identify a suspected *component* as the *location* of the failure. In this way, the ontology represents what is happening and where is happening. Depending on the hypothesis class, different *actions* can be carried out for corroborating the hypothesis (*test actions*) or repairing the component (*healing actions*). All *actions* have *conditions*(preconditions and postconditions) that allow somebody to evaluate its eligibility for execution.

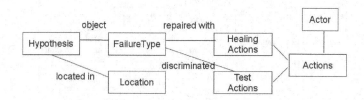

**Fig. 2.** Upper-ontology for diagnosis

Furthermore, the upper-ontology also includes the concept of *diagnosis*. A *diagnosis* has its set of hypotheses, its set of performed tests and its set of performed healing actions. This collection of data is useful for self-learning processes as reinforcement learning, for example which healing actions repaired a certain failure.

Another important assumption is that *actions* are executed by *actors*. *Actors* can be *humans* (manual actions) or *agents* (automatic actions). *Actions* can be

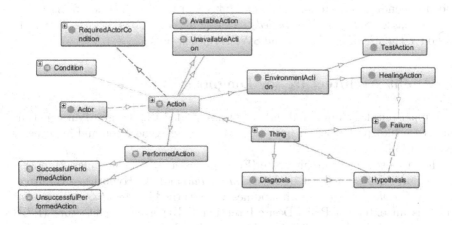

**Fig. 3.** Action upper-ontology

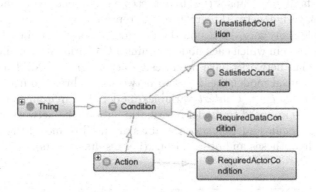

**Fig. 4.** Condition upper-ontology

classified according to the disjoint classes *Available / Unavailable*, when all preconditions are satisfied or not; and, if an *available action* has been performed, it
is classified according to the disjoint classes *Successful Performed / Unsuccess-
ful Performed*, when all postconditions are satisfied or not. This classification is
shown in Fig. 3.

   This model has been formalised as an OWL ontology for reasoning on diagnosis tasks. To adapt this generic diagnosis ontology for a specific diagnosis case,
the generic diagnosis ontology must be extended with specific concepts, i.e. possible faults, specific actors, specific conditions, etc. The conditions of *an action* are
modelled with the ontology class *Condition*. Fig. 4 shows two generic conditions:
*Required Data* that specifies a required parameter and *Required Actor* that specifies an actor to perform the action. The second one is condition for all actions,
because all actions need to be executed by someone. But these two conditions are
generic conditions; all conditions that particularise specific restrictions should be

added depending on the domain. *Conditions* can be classified according to the disjoint classes *Satisfied/Unsatisfied*. To check all conditions, we use SWRL. In section 4, the use of *conditions* and SWRL rules is shown.

## 3   Agent Architecture for Diagnosis

The upper-ontology presented in Sect. 2 has guided the design of an agent architecture that performs out both tasks: hypotheses generation and hypotheses confirmation.

The proposed agent architecture (Fig. 5) consists of four modules. Hypotheses generation is carried out by *Bayesian module* and the Hypotheses confirmation, by *Ontology module*. Both modules are governed by *Agent Control module* which is an extended Belief-Desire-Intention (BDI) agent architecture (B2DI Agent Model [4]) where beliefs are distributed and shared across the MAS. *Bayesian Module* is a reasoning inference engine that processes environment data to infer possible fault root causes (i.e. hypotheses with associated confidences). For this task, Bayesian networks are used to represent several concepts like symptom, possible root causes, etc. and the relations among them in a Directed Acyclic Graph (DAG) in which each node contains a Conditional Probability Table (CPT). Bayesian networks have been design accordign to BN3M model [9] which structures causal models in Bayesian networks to three groups of notes: *context*, *fault* and *evidence*. *Context* variables model the environment, in this case, these variables are used to model information about the network in which each agent resides. *Fault* and *Evidence* variables are used to model the possible failures through hypotheses and observations (i.e. results of tests).

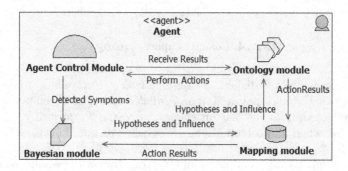

**Fig. 5.** Agent Architecture

Since a Bayesian network is a DAG with probability distributions, each node has a concrete influence on its neighbours [8]. The relevance of this influence in the diagnosis procedure varies depending on the available information about the environment. In other words, the influence represents how useful is the information that the agent would obtain if it would perform one action, for example, if it would execute a test. To obtain these data, CDF [9] distance is used. The outcomes of this method are used to sort all possible actions for an agent by relevance in order to reach a reliable and fast diagnosis.

The outcomes of hypotheses generation task is added to *Ontology-based Reasoning Module*. This module is responsible for deliberating which action should be performed out using the outcomes of the *Bayesian module*. This module filters the sorted action list based on preconditions of each action (see Sect. 2). After executing one action, its result is fedback to the *Bayesian module* to generate updated hypotheses.

It should pointed out that the mapping between *Bayesian module* and *Ontology module* is not trivial. So, *Mapping module* performs the mapping process to create ontology individuals and extract information from ontology concepts to probabilistic data that can be input to the Bayesian module. To perform this task, we use Probabilistic OWL (PR-OWL) [5] ontology that supports a way to add probabilistic information to others concepts defined using OWL.

SWRL rules are used before, during and after diagnosis process to choose which action is the best one to perform in each moment to diagnose a problem or to fix it, to check if the result of a performed action is the expected one or it was an error, to notify human operators, etc. Finally, the use of SWRL, OWL and Bayesian networks adds adaptability to the system since the behaviour of the agent can be deployed by a simple message with an OWL file as content that adds or modifies the current rules or Bayesian networks on the fly using PR-OWL.

Since presented modules can be split in different agents, some functionalities can be distributed across several agents in order to obtain more scalability, remote access to restricted data, less computational requirements, etc. Depending on which modules compound each agent, we can classify agents in three types:

- *Fully Autonomous Agent* which has all modules presented before. It is able to evaluate the environment, reason (in a distributed way) under uncertainty, perform actions, etc. It can work autonomously, but it has better performance working together with other agents.
- *Semi-Autonomous Agent* which has Agent Control Module and Ontology based Reasoning Module. It cannot deal with uncertainty, but it is able to interact with its environment. To reason with uncertainty, it has to interact with an *Fully Autonomous Agent*.
- *Dependent Agent* which has only the Agent Control Module. It is able only to perform prefixed request actions. For example, the execution of one test or one monitoring action.

Furthermore, the extensibility of the upper-ontology is possible using specific domain ontologies and Bayesian networks which represent diagnosis knowledge of a diagnosis domain.

Uncertainty handling and extensibility are highly recommended features for systems that work in complex environments like network management. Our proposal consists of defining a flexible agent architecture which integrates the previously identified modules. These functionalities can be distributed at design time or even run time by the agents themselves (creating agents on demand), depending on non functional requirements (time restrictions) or functional requirements (distribution requirements for complex actions on remote equipments).

# 4    Case Study

This section shows the case study used in this work. First of all, the scenario used to evaluate the model is presented in Sect. 4.1. Sect. 4.2 presents a example of the proposed agent architecture. In Sect. 4.3, the agents deployment is exposed in order to facilitate the explanation of a detailed diagnosis case, shown in Sect.4.4.

## 4.1    Scenario

To properly frame this study, a P2P streaming scenario (see Fig. 7) was chosen. In this scenario, there are a multimedia provider user and a multimedia consumer user. Multimedia contents are stored in a video server inside of the Multimedia Provider Home Area Network (HAN) and are remotely accessed from the Multimedia Consumer HAN. Multimedia contents are transmitted in real time using Real Time Streaming Protocol (RTSP) for session establishment and Real-time Transport Protocol (RTP) for content delivery. Many faults may occur both in connection and in services. The system is designed to provide, to an end-user or an operator, the result of the diagnosis made upon receipt of a failure symptom notification. The diagnosis result is expressed in percentages representing the certainty of the occurrence of a given hypothesis.

## 4.2    Agent Architecture Example

For exemplification purposes and facilitating the understanding of the deployment of agents in the scenario, an agent responsible to diagnose faults in Multimedia Provider HAN is presented.

*Agent Control Module* has a main goal that is to diagnose network faults. This module is responsible for acting as bridge between the other modules. *Bayesian module* contains a Bayesian network that models possible failures and possible tests in the Provider HAN region. A simplified version of this Bayesian network and one of its CPTs are shown in Fig. 6.

*Ontology based Reasoning module* works with a specific domain diagnosis ontology specialised for P2P streaming scenario. In other words, this ontology that extends the generic diagnosis ontology presented previously contains specific concepts like *Session* or *RTPMonitoringAction*, specific conditions like *RequiredRTPSessionCondition*, etc. *Mapping module* has been adapted to properly translate data between both domains: semantic and probabilistic domains.

## 4.3    Agents Deployment

In the scenario presented in Sect. 4.1, some agents have been deployed according to their geographic distribution for exemplification purposes. One *Fully Autonomous Agent* is executed inside each subnetwork. One agent has been deployed

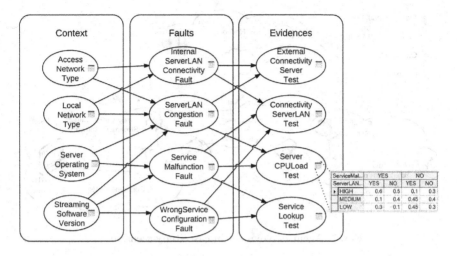

**Fig. 6.** Bayesian network for case study

in a internal server of ISP Network. The other two ones have been deployed in HAN gateways. Each one of these three agents is responsible to diagnose faults inside their domain. These agents have been deployed into devices with enough computational resources, but other three *Semi-Autonomous Agents* has been deployed taking care of minimising the consumed resources, since they are deployed in final user domain, such as multimedia consumer PC. One of them resides into the multimedia consumer PC. This agent has monitoring capabilities to detect and monitor quality of streaming sessions. The second one, into Multimedia Streaming Server with low resources. This agent has testing capabilities to know the server status. The other one is deployed in the network operator terminal to notify diagnosis results. These deployments are shown in Fig. 7.

Notice that these agents publish all actions they are able to perform in a directory facilitator like a service. Thus, any agent can request an action execution.

### 4.4    Streaming Diagnosis Case

In order to facilitate the understanding of the example, only three agents are involved in the exposed diagnosis case: "StreamingClientAgent" (Semi-Autonomous Agent), "DiagnosisClientAgent" and "DiagnosisServerAgent" (both Fully Autonomous Agents). Notice that all words with *italic* style in this section represent ontology classes, not ontology individuals.

The presented case study starts when a user requests a video streaming session. This streaming session is detected by the Semi-Autonomous Agent that resides inside multimedia client PC, named "StreamingClientAgent". This agent creates a new *RTPSession* individual in the ontology with properties that represents information about this session, like, which computer is the client and which computer is the streaming server. The creation of this individual triggers

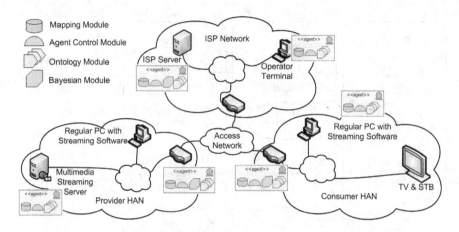

**Fig. 7.** Agent deployment in case study scenario

SWRL engine to evaluate if any possible action is now available, i.e. if all its preconditions are satisfied.

To simplify the explanation, we consider this agent is able to do only two types of actions: *RTPMonitoringAction* (to monitor Quality of Service (QoS) in RTP sessions) and *NotifySymptomAction* (to notify other agents about a new detected symptoms).

*RTPMonitoringAction* has two preconditions: *RequiredActorCondition* and *RequiredRTPSessionCondition*. To check if this conditions are satisfied, several SWRL rules are used. Rule 1 is used for *RequiredActorCondition* and Rule 2 for *RequiredRTPSessionCondition*.

**Rule 1.** Actor(?actor),
   RequiredActorCondition(?condition),
   hasPrecondition(?action, ?condition),
   canPerform(?actor, ?action)
   → satisfied(?condition, true)

Rule 1 searches all individuals of class *Actor* and class *RequiredActorCondition*. Then, it searches all actions which have one condition of this type. And finally, it searches if one agent can perform a determined action. If these subconditions are satisfied, the *RequiredActorCondition* individual changes its property "satisfied" to true.

**Rule 2.** RTPSession(?session),
   RequiredRTPSessionCondition(?condition),
   hasPrecondition(?action, ?condition),
   hasClient(?session, ?system),
   Actor(?agent),
   id(?agent, ClientAgent),
   isExecutingIn(?agent, ?system),
   → satisfied(?condition, true)

Rule 2 searches all individuals of class *RTPSession* and class *RequiredRTPSessionCondition*. Then, it searches all actions which have one condition of this type. It obtains the client system of the streaming session and gets the local system, i.e. the system in which the agent is executing currently. If both systems are the same, the condition is satisfied.

Once both conditions are satisfied, the *Action* individual changes its property "available" to true. Since "StreamingClientAgent" does not have more available actions, *RTPMonitoringAction* is selected to be executed. So, it performs a monitoring action to know the quality of the session. For this example, a quality degradation suddenly occurs and is detected. So, a new *Symptom* individual is generated in the ontology and SWRL engine is triggered again.

Now, *NotifySymptomAction* can be executed using rules similar to rules 1 and 2. "StreamingClientAgent" has not enough information to process this symptom, and it needs to cooperate with a Fully Autonomous Agent (in this case, the Fully Autonomous Agent that resides in the Multimedia Consumer Home Gateway, named "DiagnosisClientAgent"). "DiagnosisClientAgent" agent receives a message that notifies the new symptom. "StreamingClientAgent" receives an acknowledgement message and a new *SymptomACKMessage* individual is created and postcondition is evaluated (see Rule 3. When all postconditions are satisfied, "sucessfullyPerformed" property is set to true.

**Rule 3.** SymptomACKMessage(?msg),
  RequiredACKCondition(?condition),
  PerformedAction(?action),
  NotifySymptomAction(?action),
  hasPostcondition(?action, ?condition),
  hasSymptomContent(?msg,?symptom),
  hasSymptom(?action, ?symptom),
  → satisfied(?condition, true)

"DiagnosisClientAgent" is able to process symptoms performing Bayesian inference in a distributed way (using MSBN approach). In other words, this agent shares information with others Fully Autonomous Agents that are able to reason with high level data. So, the received *Symptom* individual is translated to Bayesian format through the Mapping module (see Sect. 3).

Once this information is inserted into Bayesian module (see Sect. 3), all *Fully Autonomous Agents* are working together and in parallel thanks to MSBN. Each one takes its own decisions using all available knowledge (shared knowledge and its own private knowledge).

When "DiagnosisClientAgent" has processed the new symptom and a set of hypotheses are obtained from Bayesian module, it has to decide which action is the best to be executed now. Depending on the state of the environment and the knowledge base of the agent, one action could change its influence in the diagnosis process. To deal with this issue, we use the CDF method (see Section 3). With this method, all possible actions are ordered by relevance to reach a reliable confidence in the diagnosis process. The first one whose preconditions are fulfilled is selected and executed. All Fully Autonomous Agents deployed in the scenario have to sort all possible actions to choose the best one.

For example, "DiagnosisServerAgent" has received shared knowledge when "DiagnosisClientAgent" has added the new symptom to the Bayesian module. So, "DiagnosisServerAgent" starts its own decision process to choose the best action that can be performed by itself. After it gets a set of *Hypothesis* individuals from Bayesian Module, then this agent chooses a *ConnectivityTestAction* to perform using CDF method (see Sect. 3). But it must check if all preconditions for this action are satisfied. In this case, two preconditions must be satisfied. One *RequiredActorCondition* (Rule 1) and one *RequiredDataCondition* (Rule 4).

**Rule 4.** RequiredDataCondition(?condition),
   Variable(?variable),
   requiredVariableType(?condition, ?typecond),
   variableType(?variable, ?typecond)
   → satisfied(?condition, true)

Rule 4 searches all individuals of class *Variable* and class *RequiredDataCondition*. Then, it searches type of the condition variables. If a variable has the wanted type, then the condition is satisfied. In the case of *ConnectivityTestAction* the required variable type is "Streaming Server LAN IP" and the variable value is "192.168.1.11".

Since both preconditions are satisfied, the agent executes the test and obtains more information about the environment. The postcondition of this action is a *RequiredDataCondition* which checks if a result is obtained later the test is executed. This result is added to Bayesian module as evidence. The output of Bayesian reasoning process is processed by Mapping module and inserted in Ontology module as a new set of *Hypothesis* individuals. Once all hypotheses are updated, CDF method is executed again to get which action is the most relevant to be executed in order to reach a fast and reliable diagnosis. Then, the most relevant available action is executed and the making decision process starts again, i.e., to sort possible actions by relevance, to check preconditions, to filter available actions, to choose the most relevant available action and to execute it.

This process is repeated until, at least, one hypothesis has enough confidence, i.e. the confidence is higher than a threshold. Diagnosis conclusions are shared using MSBN approach and, then, diagnosis finishes and a healing action is searched to fix the problem if it is possible, otherwise the system notifies a human operator.

To summarise the case study explanation, several agents have been deployed in different devices to perform distribute diagnosis and the proposed upper-ontology has been applied (see Fig. 7). Some agents have all modules proposed in section 3. These agents can work isolated without problems and offer more functionality to our diagnosis system. But, there are some devices such as *dedicated multimedia server* that have low performance computational resources and it is not possible to deploy Fully Autonomous Agents in these devices. On one hand, to solve this problem, we deploy only key modules in several agents to reduce required resources. But, on the other hand, an agent without Bayesian module cannot reach any diagnosis, because it only can perform actions (diagnosis tests), it does not perform inference. So, this *light-weight* agents have to share knowledge with Bayesian agents to reach diagnosis conclusions.

## 5   Evaluation

The benefits of the proposed upper-ontology have been evaluated comparing this approach with previous works [7,11]. In this paper, we compare the performance of the system using deliberation driven by "cost" or by "influence".

In previous works, test actions were ordered by estimated cost. This cost combined time cost and computational cost and it was estimated a priori by human experts. Then, all test actions are executed always in the same order. Even, sometimes, unneeded actions are executed.

In this work, test actions are sorted by relevance. Depending on the evidences about the environment, an action can modify its relevance for the current diagnosis (see Sect. 3).

The evaluation has been carried out based on a benchmark for a real diagnosis scenario of the R&D project Magneto [1]. With data stored in database with old diagnoses and the same Bayesian networks have been used in both cases. The volume of this data is around 500 diagnoses. We have clustered diagnoses in 13 diagnosis cases to simplify comparison and shown results.

As it is shown in Fig. 8, the number of performed tests has been reduced. Taking data from data base mentioned above, the average of performed test with deliberation driven by cost is 5.23 tests (with standard deviation 3.11). Using deliberation driven by influence, this number is reduced to 2.76 (with standard deviation 1.42); in other words, the number of performed tests has been reduced in 47.05%.

With deliberation driven by influence, there are two diagnosis cases that perform one test more than following the previous approach (driven by cost). The reason of this behaviour is that these are connectivity failures inside user HAN. These failures are very uncommon; for this reason, these hypotheses have, a priori, low confidence and other hypotheses have to be confirmed or refused first.

Table 1 shows the evaluation results in several columns. Mean Time to Diagnose (MTTD) [6] stands for the average time until the root cause of the failure is correctly diagnosed.

The column named "Result" represents if deliberation driven by influence improves driven by cost one or not in a specific diagnosis case.

The average of MTTD in previous approach is 25.47 seconds (with standard deviation 15.33), in proposed approach is 12.01 seconds (with standard deviation 7.12). Time improvement is 52.87%. These results show that the use of CDF method to extract the relevance of an action from Bayesian networks combained with semantic reasoning improves the performance of previous approaches driven by cost.

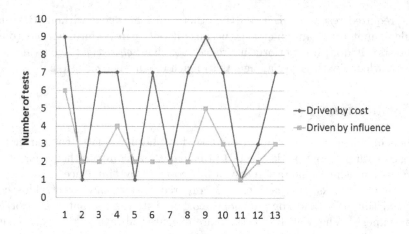

**Fig. 8.** Comparison: previous work vs proposed approach

**Table 1.** Evaluation of MTTD and number of tests using cost or influence metrics for ordering tests

| Diagnosis case | MTTD | | Number of tests | | Result |
|---|---|---|---|---|---|
| | Cost | Influence | Cost | Influence | |
| Case 1 | 41 | 29 | 9 | 6 | △ |
| Case 2 | 5 | 7 | 1 | 2 | ▽ |
| Case 3 | 36 | 8 | 7 | 2 | △ |
| Case 4 | 39 | 15 | 7 | 4 | △ |
| Case 5 | 4 | 8 | 1 | 2 | ▽ |
| Case 6 | 36 | 8 | 7 | 2 | △ |
| Case 7 | 9 | 9 | 2 | 2 | ~ |
| Case 8 | 34 | 8 | 7 | 2 | △ |
| Case 9 | 40 | 24 | 9 | 5 | △ |
| Case 10 | 33 | 13 | 7 | 3 | △ |
| Case 11 | 5 | 5 | 1 | 1 | ~ |
| Case 12 | 13 | 8 | 3 | 2 | △ |
| Case 13 | 36 | 14 | 7 | 3 | △ |

# 6    Conclusions and Future Work

We have presented a MAS that uses a diagnosis upper-ontology with Bayesian reasoning using OWL and SWRL to choose actions to perform. We focused on the deliberation process for hypotheses generation and discrimination. Our proposal of decision support improves previous approaches [7,11] both in time and in computational cost. Furthermore, the proposed modular architecture presents the capability to add or remove some modules of the architecture to reduce the resources required by agents, because there are important computational restrictions in devices like routers, TVs or STBs. Finally, one of the main advantages of use Bayesian Networks and semantic reasoning is the possibility of deploy new knowledge base or new reasoning rules on the fly, without restarting or deploying new agents.

As future work, we will study in depth the application of MSBNs [12,13] to distribute the Bayesian inference engine that offers support to self-organisation capabilities to add robustness and to maintain coherence and consistency in a distributed reasoning process. For depth comparisons, we plan to simulate more complex network environment and to test several agent architectures in order to measure the performance of each architecture.

**Acknowledgement.** This research has been partly funded by the Spanish Ministry of Science and Innovation through the projects Ingenio Consolider2010 AT Agreement Technologies (CSD2007-0022), Cenit THOFU (CEN-20101019) and CALISTA (TEC2012-32457) as well as the Spanish Ministry of Industry, Tourism and Trade through the project RESULTA (TSI-020301-2009-31).

The authors would also like to thank to J. García-Algarra, J. González-Ordás, P. Arozarena and R. Toribio for their support and collaboration in this research through the *Magneto R&D project* [1].

# References

1. Arozarena, P., Toribio, R., Kielthy, J., Quinn, K., Zach, M.: Probabilistic Fault Diagnosis in the MAGNETO Autonomic Control Loop. In: Stiller, B., De Turck, F. (eds.) AIMS 2010. LNCS, vol. 6155, pp. 102–105. Springer, Heidelberg (2010)
2. Benjamins, R.: Problem-solving methods for diagnosis and their role. International Journal of Expert Systems: Research and Applications 8(2), 93–120 (1995)
3. Berthet, G., Fischer, N.: A unified theory of fault diagnosis and distributed fault management in communication networks. In: Proceedings of IEEE AFRICON 1996, pp. 776–781. IEEE (1995)
4. Carrera, A., Iglesias, C.A.: B2DI - A Bayesian BDI Agent Model with Causal Belief Updating based on MSBN. In: Proceedings of the 4th International Conference on Agents and Artificial Intelligence, pp. 343–346 (2012)
5. Costa, P.C.G., Laskey, K.B.: PR-OWL: A framework for probabilistic ontologies. In: Proceedings of the 2006 Fourth International Conference on Formal Ontology in Information Systems, FOIS 2006, pp. 237–249. IOS Press (2006)
6. FitzGerald, J., Dennis, A.: Business Data Communications and Networking. John Wiley and Sons (2008)
7. García-Algarra, F.J., Arozarena-Llopis, P., García-Gómez, S., Carrera-Barroso, A.: A lightweight approach to distributed network diagnosis under uncertainty. In: INCOS 2009: Proceedings of the 2009 International Conference on Intelligent Networking and Collaborative Systems, pp. 74–80. IEEE Computer Society, Washington, DC (2009)
8. Kjaerulff, U.B., Madsen, A.L.: Bayesian Networks and Influence Diagrams. Information Science and Statistics. Springer, New York (2008)
9. Kraaijeveld, P., Druzdzel, M., Onisko, A., Wasyluk, H.: Genierate: An interactive generator of diagnostic bayesian network models. In: Proc. 16th Int. Workshop Principles Diagnosis, pp. 175–180. Citeseer (2005)

10. O'Connor, M., Knublauch, H., Tu, S., Grosof, B., Dean, M., Grosso, W., Musen, M.: Supporting Rule System Interoperability on the Semantic Web with SWRL. In: Gil, Y., Motta, E., Benjamins, V.R., Musen, M.A. (eds.) ISWC 2005. LNCS, vol. 3729, pp. 974–986. Springer, Heidelberg (2005)
11. Sedano-Frade, A., González-Ordás, J., Arozarena-Llopis, P., García-Gómez, S., Carrera-Barroso, A.: Distributed Bayesian Diagnosis for Telecommunication Networks. In: Demazeau, Y., Dignum, F., Corchado, J.M., Pérez, J.B. (eds.) Advances in PAAMS. AISC, vol. 70, pp. 231–240. Springer, Heidelberg (2010)
12. Xiang, Y.: Belief updating in multiply sectioned Bayesian networks without repeated local propagations. International Journal of Approximate Reasoning 23(1), 1–21 (2000)
13. Xiang, Y., Poole, D., Beddoes, M.P.: Multiply Sectioned Bayesian Networks and Junction Forests for Large Knowledge-based Systems. Computational Intelligence 9(2), 171–220 (1993)
14. Wang, X.H., Zhang, D.Q.: Ontology based context modeling and reasoning using OWL. IEEE (March 2004)

# Towards a Design Process for Modeling MAS Organizations

Massimo Cossentino[1], Carmelo Lodato[1], Salvatore Lopes[1], Patrizia Ribino[1], Valeria Seidita[2], and Antonio Chella[2]

[1] Istituto di Reti e Calcolo ad Alte Prestazioni,
Consiglio Nazionale delle Ricerche, Palermo, Italy
{cossentino,c.lodato,lopes,ribino}@pa.icar.cnr.it
[2] Dipartimento di Ingegneria Chimica Gestionale Informatica Meccanica
Università degli Studi di Palermo, Italy
{seidita,chella}@dinfo.unipa.it

**Abstract.** The design of MAS organizations is a complex activity where a proper methodological approach may offer a significant advantage in enabling the conception of the best solution. Moreover, the aid provided by a supporting tool significantly contributes to make the approach technically sound and it is a fundamental ingredient of a feasible strategy to the development of large MASs. In this paper, we introduce a portion of methodological approach devoted to design MAS organizations and a preliminary version of a specific case tool, named MoT (*Moise+ Tool*), for supporting activities from design production to automatic code generation. MoT provides four kinds of diagrams based on a definite graphical notation for representing organizational elements. Our process is applied to a classical write paper simulator example. Results include portion of the automatically generated code according to Moise+ specifications.

## 1 Introduction

Distributed and open systems are widely employed in the simulation and management of highly complex scenarios in dynamic environments. To this end, such systems should act in quasi-real time to changes occurring in the environment adopting the most suitable behavior for reacting to the new conditions. Agents can provide a good way for solving complex problems and they are very useful to both design and implementation levels [13][14].

The ability of simulating complex hierarchical organization provides further utility to the design of multi-agent systems (MAS from now on). In other words, organizations can be seen as a set of constraints [4] that rules the behavior of every single agent in a multi agent society.

The implementation of an organization in a MAS is normally decided at design time. The way in which a MAS may re-organize itself has then to be investigated from two different points of view, i.e. the design (methodological) and the implementation point of view. A robust approach to agent organizations comes from the work of Hubner et al. [10] where a definition of an organizational

M. Cossentino et al. (Eds.): EUMAS 2011, LNAI 7541, pp. 63–79, 2012.
© Springer-Verlag Berlin Heidelberg 2012

model (Moise+) is presented. MASs designed in accord with the Moise+ model are able to re-organize their processes and then react to what occurs in the environment.

Organizations are described in the Moise+ model by three main views: the structural, the functional and normative perspectives. In this model an organization is established a priori (created at design-time) and the agents ought to follow it. The structural and functional view are considered almost independent while the normative dimension is used for establishing a link between them. Furthermore, the Moise+ model is complemented with a development tool called J-Moise+[7], a Jason extension allowing developers to use Jason for programming agents and their organizations [1]. This is nevertheless a powerful tool, but it is not still adequately supported by a well defined methodological approach.

Some researchers have developed in the past other methodologies for MASs where some aspects of organization were modeled. In [16] the concepts of environment, roles, interactions and organizational rules are considered as organizational abstractions. Another example has been proposed in [3] where holarchy represents the organization structure of the MAS made of holons [5], hence the main element to be developed for building the MAS organization. Despite the number of methodologies only few of them cover the entire process lifecycle, from analysis to implementation, and above all very few is aided by tools.

In this paper we introduce a portion of methodological approach devoted to design MAS organizations and a preliminary version of a specific case tool, named MoT (*Moise+ Tool*), for supporting our approach from design production to automatic code generation.

In particular, MoT is based on a UML compliant graphical notation to represent the Moise+ specific elements and on a code generator in order to produce the final XML code containing the Moise+ organizational specification.

MoT has been realized by using a known tool, Metaedit+ by Metacase [12][6], that offers a valid environment for domain specific modeling. Metaedit+ provides means for creating an ad-hoc modeling language with concepts and rules from a well specific problem domain, and notation to be used for drawing diagrams.

The advantages of graphically representing organizations are evident: first of all, graphical notations are more readable and understandable at a glance than any coding language, secondly it is usually easier to explain a graphical notation to stakeholders involved in the design (that are not technical designers) than read the application code with them. The possibility of involving stakeholders like system users enables the adoption of agile or extreme development approaches and improves the flexibility of conventional ones.

The remainder of the paper is organized as follows. In section 2 the Moise+ organizational model and Metaedit+ are introduced. In section 3 we present our tool with the definite notation. Section 4 shows a portion of the design process for developing organizational MAS with the related work products. Such process is explained applying it to an example inspired by the Moise+ tutorial [8]. Moreover, in this section we address the issues concerning the Moise+ code generation. Finally some discussions and conclusions are drawn in section 5 together with a comparison with others MAS modeling proposals.

## 2    Background and Motivation

Since the beginning of computer science the need for adequately managing concepts related to the applications under development raised with the complexity of systems. A promising approach to this issue has been the definition of means for specifying what a system should do instead of how to do something. This approach led to formulation of the Model driven Engineering [11] (MDE) paradigm that deeply changed the way of thinking and then working of designers and programmers.

Designers and developers are no more involved in the specification of each single detail of the system using a programming language but they can model the needed functionalities and the architecture of the system. This fact presents many advantages like the increasing goodness of the softwares produced, the easiness and the rapidity of conveying information among team members and the possibility, through the use of model transformation techniques, of automatically generating code. However this latter issue is not still supported by adequately technology.

Our work focuses on the creation of a notation and a CASE tool, created as an instance of a meta-CASE tool (Metaedit+), for supporting the methodological activities involved in the development of organizational MASs. In so doing we exploited the Moise+ organizational model and the features of Metaedit+ for creating a graphical environment allowing the designer to implement concepts and rules of the Moise+ model in specific design diagrams and to automatically produce portions of code.

In the next subsections an overview of Moise+ and Metaedit+ is given.

### 2.1    Moise+

Moise+ [9][10] is an organizational model for MASs based on a few key elements to characterize an organization. It provides MASs with an explicit definition of their organizations. The organizational specification is useful both to the agents to clearly know their organizational structure and their particular purpose and to the organization framework, to ensure that the agents follow the specifications. More specifically, Moise+ looks at organization as a three dimensional element characterized by structural, functional and normative dimension.

Looking only at the structural dimension, an organization can be seen as a set of *Roles* linked by *Relations* and clustered into *Groups*. The functional dimension enriches the model showing the global objectives of the organization. It gives some information about the plans and the way for reaching the organizational global goals by means of *Social Schemes*. In these schemes the functionalities of the organization are represented as *Goals* grouped into *Missions*.

Finally, the normative dimension is fundamental into the Moise+ model because it shows the connecting elements, the *Norms*, between the functional and structural dimension of an organization. It defines the behavioral rules to be observed by *Roles* in order to reach the organizational global goal. Defining the norms basing on Moise+ means to create links between Roles and Missions. Actually, Moise+ supports two kinds of norms: the *Permission* and the *Obligation* norms.

Practically, designing an organization using the Moise+ model means to define an Organizational Specification (OS) which is the union of the structural, functional and normative specification corresponding to each dimension. An OS is an XML file with a precise structure that defines the features of the previously mentioned elements. In the following a portion of Moise+ XML code representing the skeleton of a classical Organizational Specification is reported. This code shows not only the main elements to be defined inside each specification but also the order in which the elements have to be defined.

```
< organisational − specification >
  < structural − specification >
    < role − definitions > ...
    < group − specification > ...
    < formation − constraints > ...
  < /structural − specification >

  < functional − specification >
    < scheme >
      < goal > ...
      < mission > ...
    < /scheme >
  < /functional − specification >

  < normative − specification >
    < normtype =?role =?mission =? > ...
  < /normative − specification >
< /organisational − specification >
```

**Fig. 1.** Moise+ XML code representing an organizational specification

In section 3 we present the proposed CASE tool developed in order to easily realize organization with Moise+.

## 2.2   Metaedit+

Recently designers manifested the need for changing CASE tools in order to customize them for their demands and to meet the features of different application domains. This customization is not possible with every CASE tool because tools constrain how the designer can do their work, how they can draw diagrams/models or manage tool concepts. Generally tools allow to use only fixed methods and notation.

What Metaedit+ proposes is a way for overcoming this limitation by adding the notion of meta-CASE tool to that of CASE tool. The meta-CASE tool is based on a three layered architecture in which the lowest level is the model level, hence the system design. The middle level contains a model of the bottom level, the model of a model is called metamodel. Metamodel contains concepts and rules for creating models. These two levels are already present in a CASE tool but the metamodel is imposed by the creators of the tool thus implying the previous said rigidity.

With the introduction of the third layer (the meta-metamodel one) Metaedit+ establishes concepts and rules for creating metamodels, indeed Metaedit+ offers the possibility of modifying the metamodel by following the rules established in the meta-metamodel, thus overcoming the constraints of CASE tools and having the possibility of specifying modeling languages that can then be used with the right tool. Metaedit+ is at the same time a CASE tool and a meta-CASE tool; by using the meta-CASE tool the designer may specify her/his own modeling language that (s)he can use by instantiating the meta-CASE tool in the CASE tool.

MetaEdit+ is based on a specific metamodeling language, GOPPRR that means Graph, Object, Property, Port, Relationship and Role. They are the metatypes used for defining modeling languages and each of them has its own semantic. Graph is the individual model, usually a diagram, the object is the main element of the graph, the relationships connect objects, the role connects relationships and objects, port gives the possibility to add semantics to the role and the property. The structure and the semantic of each modeling language can be described by a metamodel created by using these metatypes.

In addition to the previous features Metaedit+ offers an optimum support to the UML modeling language on which a lot of design methodologies are based. Finally Metaedit+ offers some preinstalled reports, or the possibility of creating new ones by using a specific language, the Metaedit Reporting Language (MERL). The report is a small program defined and working onto every diagram and, in addition to other facilities it offers, there is the document generation in html format or others and the generation of code skeleton in various programming languages (Java, C, C++, ... ). The more the description of each single element of the diagram is precise and detailed the more the produced code is complete.

This latter functionality has been highly exploited in order to create a report for each single newly introduced diagram of the proposed work and to generate the corresponding xml code.

## 3   An Organization Design Tool: MoT

The *Moise+ Tool* (MoT[1]) wants to be a tool supporting all the phases from the agent organization design to Moise+ code generation. MoT has been realized by using Metaedit+. It owns a graphical notation to represent the Moise+ specific elements and a code generator in order to produce the final XML code containing the Moise+ organizational specification. Fig. 2 shows a screenshot of MoT.

---

[1] MoT is available at http://www.pa.icar.cnr.it/aose/MoT.html

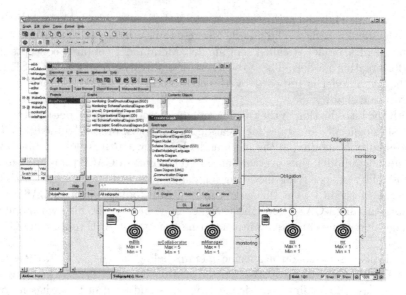

**Fig. 2.** A Screenshot of MoT

MoT is based on the metamodel shown in Fig. 3, it describes an organizational structure for MASs adapted from Moise+. The core element of the metamodel is the Organization that pursues some objectives (Goals), each of them reachable executing a particular Plan. A Group is usually responsible of at least a Scheme and a Scheme can be adopted to monitor the execution of another Scheme. A Scheme contains several Missions composed of a set of Goals. In addition, an Organization is composed of several Roles. When an agent adopts a Role it is committed to a Mission that is regulated by means of Norms. The Organizational Link and the Compatibility Link respectively define social exchanges and compatibility relations among agent roles.

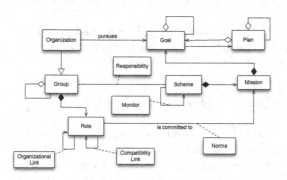

**Fig. 3.** Metamodel adopted in the MoT

In the following subsections we present the adopted notation.

**Fig. 4.** The Notation for MoT

## 3.1 Notation

MoT provides four kinds of diagrams: the *Organizational Diagram - OD*, the *Scheme Structural Diagram - SSD*, the *Goal Structural Diagram - GSD* and the *Goal Functional Diagram - GFD* that we will detail in the following.

These diagrams can be composed using the notation we present in this paper. Such notation allows to represent all the concepts involved in modeling and designing organizational MASs according to the metamodel shown in Fig. 3. This notation has been created as a UML profile. It allows to represent the following concepts (graphically shown in Fig. 4).

**Roles.** A Role is a UML class depicted as a sticky man. Its properties are represented in the form of class attributes. The main features of a MoiseRole are: a RoleName, a MaxAscribe and a MinAscribe representing the cardinality of the role in the organization. An abstract role, as usual, is identified using an italic font.

**Groups.** A Group is represented by means of a package with a sticky men icon. It may contain several structural elements (Roles) and other grouping elements (sub-groups). According to the Moise+ definition, the membership of an agent to a group constrains the agents that can cooperate with it.

**Goals.** In order to represent a goal in MoT we have used a UML class graphically depicted as circle with a check. Each goal element is characterized by a name and by a collection of attributes. Each attribute corresponds to a specific feature of the Moise+ concept of goal. As regard the attribute compartment, it basically contains the *GoalType* propriety that represents the two kinds of goal namely achievement and maintenance and the *ttf* attribute value prescribing the time requested for fulfilling the goal. The default type for every goal is achievement.

**Missions.** In the Moise+ model, a Mission is defined as a coherent set of authorized goals to achieve. In order to represent a mission in MoT we have used a UML class graphically depicted as a dartboard. Here the attributes' compartment contains values for the minimum and the maximum commitments to the mission.

**Social Schemes.** A Social Scheme or simply Scheme in Moise+ is composed of a functional goal decomposition tree (where the root is the objective of the

Scheme and the goals are decomposed within global plan) and a set of missions (where the responsibilities for the sub-goals are grouped to be distributed among Roles). In our tool, we prefer split its structural aspect (described in the SSD and represented by means of a UML package) from the functional one (described as a plan in the GFD). Thus, the schemes in the SSD are represented only as a set of associated missions while the GFD shows further features.

**Relationships.** The elements of the model can be logically related one another using several kinds of relationships. We omit to define the common UML relations that we use in MoT diagrams. In the following we describe those specially introduced for specifying Moise+ concepts.

▷ *Organizational Link* - It defines the way in which social exchanges between agent roles occur. Moise+ model defines three types of Organizational links: *communication* representing exchange of information; *authority* defining control power; *acquaintance* representing knowledge about other agents. In MoT these relations are graphically represented by the first relation shown in Fig. 4 and can be characterized by means of a label showing the type.

▷ *Compatibility Link* - It is always plotted between two roles and establishes the possibility for an agent to simultaneously play the two roles. It is graphically represented by the second relation shown in Fig. 4. When the link is oriented, it means that the agent playing the source role can play the target role but not the vice-versa.

▷ *Norm* - In the Moise+ model, a role is usually linked by means of Norms to one or more missions defined in a particular scheme. In our tool, we have defined a new link type named *MoiseNormLink* graphically represented by the third relation shown in Fig. 4. This link is characterized by the Norm-LinkType propriety and can take two values: *Obligation* and *Permission*. In MoT this link is a directed arc that starts always from a Role to a Mission. It expresses that an agent playing the role is obliged/allowed to fulfill the mission.

In the following section we introduce all phases of our methodological approach with the related work products (MoT diagrams). Our design process will be detailed with the aid of the the classical example ("Writing paper") reported in the Moise Tutorial [8].

## 4   Methodological Approach

We aim at defining a complete methodological approach ranging from requirements analysis to code production and system deployment. Such a methodology will include a goal oriented analysis (with some features inspired by the i* [15] and Tropos [2] approaches), the design of organizations that will be described below and the design of agents based on the Jason platform. The scope of this paper is limited to the organizational part of this work and therefore

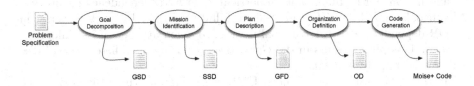

**Fig. 5.** Portion of the Design Process for Organizational Multi-Agent Systems

(also for space concerns) we skip the initial part of the methodology (requirements analysis) and the final one (the agent design and what follows it). In other words, this section introduces only the portion of our methodological approach devoted to instantiate the metamodel shown in Fig. 3. The diagrams we illustrated in the previous section are used for representing the outcome of this portion of design process, as it is sketched in Fig. 5. Let us assume that the problem specification document is already existing and it provides a list of system goals obtained for instance with a Tropos or i* like design process. The aim of our methodology is to model organizational multi-agent systems principally by means of goals, their decomposition, missions and roles; in the following table, we highlight the work product where each metamodel element of Fig. 3 is instantiated.

**Table 1.** Summary of instantiated element

| Work Product | Metamodel Element |
|---|---|
| Goal Structural Diagram | Goal |
| Scheme Structural Diagram | Scheme, Mission |
| Goal Functional Diagram | Plan |
| Organizational Diagram | Role, Group, Monitor, Norm, Organizational Link, Compatibility Link |

In the following subsections are detailed all phases of our approach shown in Fig. 5.

## 4.1 The Goal Decomposition Phase

The *Goal Decomposition* phase (see Fig.5) of the proposed design process involves activities for the decomposition of the identified goals and the identification of their dependencies. During this phase, goals are refined by means of an AND/OR decomposition. This allows to determine a hierarchical structure among goals and to individuate the dependencies between a high level goal and its subgoals. A dependency among goals implies that a given goal is constrained by another one for its fulfillment. In particular, an AND dependency means that all subgoals must be satisfied in order to fulfill the original goal. Vice versa, in an OR dependency the original goal is satisfied when any one of its children is fulfilled. This phase results in the *Goal Structural Diagram* where the *goal* (see metamodel Fig. 3) is instantiated.

In MoT, the GSD is an extended UML class diagram where the Goal is the only Moise+ element permitted.

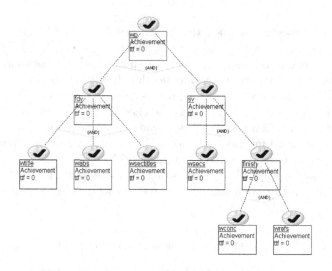

**Fig. 6.** Goal Structural Diagram for the Writing Paper example - GSD

In order to add a Goal in an GSD the *MoiseGoal* object from toolbar of the GSD must be selected. In this diagram, goals are related to other goals by means of an AND or OR dependency relation.

Fig. 6 shows the GSD for the "Writing paper" example. In this example, a set of agents wants to write a paper. In order to solve the problem, an organizational strategy is adopted. In this instance, we don't want to argue about the design choice. Vice versa, we accept the solution proposed in [8] because we want to show how it is represented in a GSD.

As we can see in Fig. 6, the global objective of the organization (to be created) is decomposed into two sub-goals *fdv* (first draft version) and *sv* (submit version). The *fdv* goal is, in turn, decomposed into three sub-goals: write a title (*wtitle*), an abstract (*wabs*), and the section titles (*wsectitles*). For the other hand, in order to fulfill the *sv*, it is necessary to write the sections (*wsecs*) and to finalize the paper (*finish*), that is to write the conclusion (*wconc*) and the bibliography (*wrefs*). The GSD for the "Writing paper" example highlights the root goal of the organization may be reachable only if all its subgoals have been satisfied. This is because all the relations linking goals with the related subgoals are AND relations.

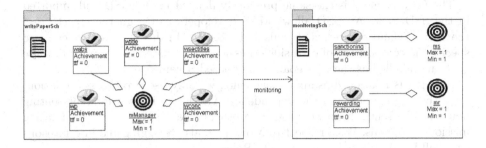

**Fig. 7.** The Writing Paper Example - SSD

## 4.2 Mission Identification Phase

The *Goal Structural Diagram* is the input of the *Mission Identification* phase where the main aim is to identify *Roles*, *Missions* and *Schemes*. This phase starts with the Roles Identification activity. Roles are identified by looking at *Positions* coming out from the previously report Tropos or i*-like analysis phase. We consider a *Position* characterized by its own competencies in order to fulfill its goals. Often Roles are identified in an iterative refinement process working in this way: some candidate Roles are identified, their consistency is verified against the Missions that is possible to assign them (see description of next activity). Roles are splitted or merged according to what emerges from the analysis of Mission assignments. Instantiating Missions is useful for the definition of organizations complying with the Moise specification. Thus it is necessary to establish how to group goals coming from the previous Goal Decomposition Phase. Practically, we group the leaf goals of the diagram into missions according to the previously identified candidate Roles, starting from the GSD. The Role involved in pursuing a Goal is sometimes the same Role who has a direct interest in its achievement, other times the goal is under the responsibility of other Roles. We assume that information about Roles responsibility are coming from the requirements analysis phase and guide this activity. The analysis of mission assignment to Roles may be useful for identifying Roles needing too many capacities or incoherent profiles. This may lead to split the candidate Role. Other times, missions analysis may indicate that similar Roles exist and their merging may be advisable. At the end of this iterative activity, missions are grouped into Schemes according to the high level goal to be satisfied. This series of iterations produces the *Scheme Structural Diagram*, where the *Mission* and *Scheme* metamodel elements (see Fig. 3) are instantiated.

In MoT, the SSD is an extended UML class diagram where main elements are Goal, Scheme and Mission. In the SSD, a Scheme is modeled by means of a package with a little sheet icon, where classes (i.e. missions) are grouped. The package's name corresponds to the social scheme id. In a SSD can be represented more than one Scheme, thus representing the existence of different schemes in the same organization with different objectives.

The Goal element is the same previously defined in the GSD and imported in the SSD view. An SSD allows MAS developers to design the structure of the Social Schemes in terms of goals and missions. In this diagram, we can also specify the composition of each single mission with related goals. Some of these goals are labelled as the root goal of the related Scheme.

As regards relationships among elements, we only use two kinds of relationship: the aggregation and the dependency. The latter is used for representing how two different schemes depend each others, the former is used for relating missions and goals. With respect to Moise+, goals are aggregated into missions that will be distributed/committed to Roles.

Fig. 7 shows a portion of the SSD for the "Writing paper" example. It is composed of two Social Schemes, *writePaperSch* and *monitoringSch*. The portion of *writePaperSch* scheme reported in Fig. 7 shows how the *mManager* mission is a composition of five goals: *wp, wtitle, concl, wabs, wsectitles*. This mission concerns the general management of the writing process. While the illustrated portion of *monitoringSch* scheme includes two missions: *ms* and *mr* mission formed by *sanctioning* and *rewarding* goal respectively. These missions concern the employment of sanctioning and rewarding policies in order to enforce rules. In the SSD, it is also possible to underline the dependences among different Social Schemes. As Fig. 7 shows, the Scheme *writePaperSch* is related to the *monitoringSch* Scheme through a "monitoring" dependency relationship. This is because the scheme *monitoringSch* is adopted in order to ensure the correct execution of the *writePaperSch*.

### 4.3   The Plan Description Phase

The *Plan Description* phase allows to establish the precedence relations among goals, that is the temporal sequence in which the goals are to be fulfilled. Establishing precedence relations among goals allows to consider different design choices. This phase is assisted by the *Goal Functional Diagram*. At this stage of the process, the functional aspect of goals (*Plan*) is determined.

The Goal Functional Diagram represents the functional view of the root goals of the schemes. In other words, it depicts how the task/activity related to each subgoal must be executed in order to fulfill the scheme root goal (that is the plans to reach the root goal). It is important to highlight that there are three different types of goal fulfillment: *sequential, parallel* and *choice*. If two goals are related with a sequential relationship then the target goal can be reached only after that the source goal is reached. If two goals are related with a parallel relationship then both goals can be simultaneously reached. Finally, a choice relationship indicates that it is possible to choose the goal to be achieved.

A GFD in MoT is realized by means of a UML activity diagram where the Goal is represented by an activity where the name is the goal's id. In a GFD the plans to reach the goals are also defined. There are three different kinds of plan operator: *sequence, parallelism* and *choice*, the first means that a goal $g_i$ (having

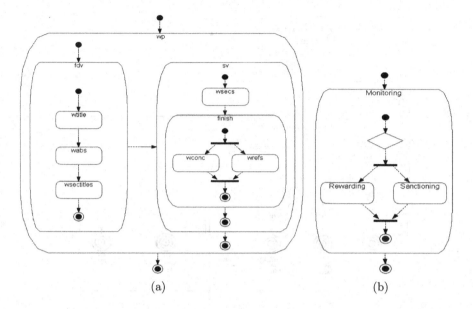

(a)                                              (b)

**Fig. 8.** Goal Functional Diagrams of the Writing Paper Example - GFD

two sub-goals $g_{i,i}$ and $g_{i,i+j}$) can be achieved only if the sequence of $g_{i,i}$ and $g_{i,i+j}$ is terminated. All of them can be easily represented by means of the UML activity diagram syntax, for instance the parallelism is represented through the fork and the choice through the decision diamond. Sequence is represented by a straight arrow line.

Fig. 8(a) and Fig. 8(b) show the Goal Functional Diagrams built for the *wp* and *monitoring* goals for the Writing Paper example which are the root goals of *writePaperSch* and *monitoringSch* (defined in the previous section) correspondingly. The GFD of the *writePaperSch* (see Fig. 8(a)) explains how to achieve the root goal of the scheme. In detail, the fulfillment of the *wp* goal depends on the achievement of the *fdv* and *sv* goal. The *sv* goal is reachable only after that the *fdv* is satisfied. In turn, *fdv* is achieved executing the atomic goals *wtitle*, *wabs* and *wsectitles* sequentially.

## 4.4   The Organizational Definition Phase

Finally, the *Organizational Definition* is the core phase of our methodology and it includes several steps. This phase uses the work products coming from the previous ones. Thus, it is almost natural finalizing the Roles of the Organization to be created, by means of the elements previously identified and instantiated. As a consequence, we can determine the kind of rule (*Norms*) that bind the Role to the mission and also the work teams (*Groups*) to Roles belong.

The set of all formed work groups compose the entire *Organization*. The last steps of this phase are to establish which Roles are compatibles (*Compatibility*

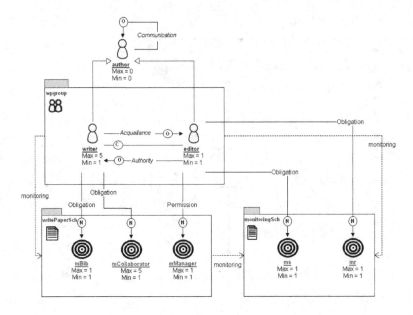

**Fig. 9.** The Writing Paper Example - OD

*Links*) with some others according to the policy adopted in the organization and which subordination relations exist among Roles (*Organizational links*). This phase is assisted by the *Organizational Diagram*.

In MoT, an Organizational Diagram is an extended UML class diagram for designing the structural and normative aspect of an organization. The OD focuses on Moise+ elements such as Roles, Groups, Missions, Schemes and different kinds of relationships.

Fig. 9 shows the Organizational Diagram for the Writing Paper example. A possible solution for this problem, can be provided defining an organization with one group (*wpgroup*) and two roles (*Writer* and *Editor*). These roles are an extension of the abstract role *Author*. As exemplified in Fig. 9, an agent playing the writer role can play the editor role at the same time and vice-versa because they are linked by a bidirectional *MoiseCompatibilityLink*. Moreover, in this diagram the organizational links existing between roles are also represented. For example, the MoiseOrganizationalLink between editor and writer role is of the type Authority. This means that an agent playing the role editor in the writing paper organization has some kind of control on agents playing the writer role.

Finally, the instantiated roles are linked by means of MoiseNormLinks to related missions. In the portion of diagram reported in Fig. 9, one of the *Writer*'s mission is *mbib* (i.e. getting references for the paper). The *norm* linking that mission to the role is an Obligation, that is the agent playing the Writer role must commit to this mission. The *Editor*, instead, may commit to the mission *mManager* because the link is a Permission norm.

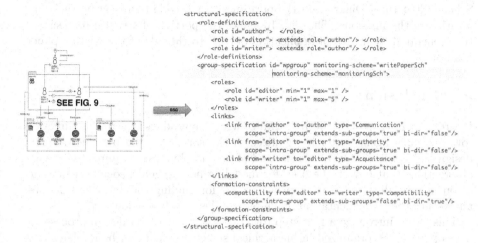

```
<structural-specification>
    <role-definitions>
        <role id="author">  </role>
        <role id="editor"> <extends role="author"/> </role>
        <role id="writer"> <extends role="author"/> </role>
    </role-definitions>
    <group-specification id="wpgroup" monitoring-scheme="writePaperSch"
                         monitoring-scheme="monitoringSch">
        <roles>
            <role id="editor" min="1" max="1" />
            <role id="writer" min="1" max="5" />
        </roles>
        <links>
            <link from="author" to="author" type="Communication"
                  scope="intra-group" extends-sub-groups="true" bi-dir="false"/>
            <link from="editor" to="writer" type="Authority"
                  scope="intra-group" extends-sub-groups="true" bi-dir="false"/>
            <link from="writer" to="editor" type="Acquaintance"
                  scope="intra-group" extends-sub-groups="true" bi-dir="false"/>
        </links>
        <formation-constraints>
            <compatibility from="editor" to="writer" type="compatibility"
                  scope="intra-group" extends-sub-groups="false" bi-dir="true"/>
        </formation-constraints>
    </group-specification>
</structural-specification>
```

**Fig. 10.** Moise+ Structural Specification generated code from OD

## 4.5   Code Generation Phase

The last phase of our process is the Code Generation. This phase is devoted to produce the Moise+ organizational specifications of the MAS to be developed. MoT supports this phase generating Moise+ code automatically.

In the previous sections we have defined the domain-specific modeling language in order to design agent organizations to be implemented in Moise+. The resulting metamodel containing the domain concepts with their relations and notation is shown in Fig.3. In this subsection, instead, we want to specify the mapping from model to code by defining a domain-specific code generator using MetaEdit+. In MetaEdit+, code generators are defined in the Generator Editor using the MERL scripting language. MERL enables navigating through the elements of the user designed diagrams accessing the data according to the defined metamodel. Moreover, MERL allows translating the design data into the formats required by the generation target language.

For our purposes, we have defined the main generators associated with the diagram types defined in the section 3.1. Each generator is responsible of producing a Moise+ specification portion.

Specifically, the *Structural Specification Generator* (SSG) and the *Normative Specification Generator* (NSG) produces the XML portion of code concerning the Moise+ Structural and Normative Specification by respectively analyzing the elements designed in the Organizational Diagram.

The Functional Specification Generator (FSG) generates the Moise+ Functional Specification. This (as hinted in the section 2) shows how the organizational goals can be reached and how to compose the missions to be assigned to a specific role. For these reasons, the FSG is obtained merging two sub-generators: the former maps of the Goal Functional Diagram in the XML code concerning the Moise+ goal decomposition tree; the latter traduces the design data of the

Scheme Structural Diagram in the portion of XML code representing the composition of the missions. The Fig. 10 shows the portion of structural specification generated by means of application of SSG to the OD of the writing paper example.

## 5    Conclusion

In order to fully exploit the powerful of agents nowadays research is directing towards multi agent systems organized in the same way the humans do. The design and implementation of this kind of system obviously requires to manage abstractions that have to be used for modeling norms, goals, social schemes ad so on. Above all it requires supporting tools for guiding the designer from the analysis to the implementation in simple and less costly fashion.

This paper introduce a first step towards the creation of a design process for developing MASs organized in hierarchical structures that can be implemented with Moise+ and supported by a CASE tool using a specific notation for representing organizations. In particular, we illustrated a portion of our methodological approach devoted to instantiate the main elements necessary to create an agent organization with Moise+.

Moreover, we developed a CASE tool by using Metaedit+ that allows to generate specific code for each kind of diagrams, in so doing we are able to support the designer in producing organizational multi agent systems models and then implementing them in a semi automatic way. The Moise+ metamodel is the basis for our tool that, thanks to automatic generation of code from diagrams, lets the designer free from the heavy work related to the manual production of organization XML code.

Finally it is worth noting that the use of Metaedit+ constitutes a first experiment that produced very good results in terms of CASE tool for supporting design activities. The approach we adopted for the creation of the UML profile for representing organizations is general enough for being applied with every kind of tools since it is grounded on the creation of a metamodel that complement the one of Moise+ with that of UML.

For the future we are planning to develop a CASE tool as an extension of Eclipse that might let us overcome the age-old limit of Metaedit+ in managing images and easily positioning elements in the diagrams.

**Acknowledgment.** This work was realized within IMPULSO and partially supported by the EU project FP7-Humanobs and by the FRASI project.

## References

1. Bordini, R.H., Hübner, J.F., Wooldridge, M.J.: Programming multi-agent systems in AgentSpeak using Jason. Wiley-Interscience (2007)
2. Bresciani, P., Giorgini, P., Giunchiglia, F., Mylopoulos, J., Perini, A.: Tropos: An agent-oriented software development methodology. Autonomous Agent and Multi-Agent Systems 3(8), 203–236 (2004)

3. Cossentino, M., Gaud, N., Hilaire, V., Galland, S., Koukam, A.: ASPECS: an agent-oriented software process for engineering complex systems. Autonomous Agents and Multi-Agent Systems 20(2), 260–304 (2010)
4. Dignum, V., Dignum, F.: Modelling Agent Societies: Co-ordination Frameworks and Institutions. In: Brazdil, P.B., Jorge, A.M. (eds.) EPIA 2001. LNCS (LNAI), vol. 2258, pp. 191–204. Springer, Heidelberg (2001)
5. Fischer, K., Schillo, M., Siekmann, J.: Holonic Multiagent Systems: A Foundation for the Organisation of Multiagent Systems. In: Mařík, V., McFarlane, D.C., Valckenaers, P. (eds.) HoloMAS 2003. LNCS (LNAI), vol. 2744, pp. 71–80. Springer, Heidelberg (2003)
6. Isazadeh, H., Lamb, D.A.: Case environments and metacase tools (1997)
7. Hübner, J.F.: J-moise+ programming organizational agents with moise+ and jason (2007)
8. Hübner, J.F., Sichman, J.S., Boissier, O.: Moise tutorial (for moise 0.7)
9. Hübner, J.F., Sichman, J.S., Boissier, O.: Moise+: towards a structural, functional, and deontic model for mas organization. In: Proceedings of the First International Joint Conference on Autonomous Agents and Multiagent Systems: Part 1, p. 502. ACM (2002)
10. Hübner, J.F., Sichman, J.S., Boissier, O.: Developing organised multiagent systems using the MOISE+ model: programming issues at the system and agent levels. International Journal of Agent-Oriented Software Engineering 1(3), 370–395 (2007)
11. Schmidt, D.C.: Model-driven engineering. Computer 39(2), 25–31 (2006)
12. Tolvanen, J.-P., Rossi, M.: Metaedit+: defining and using domain-specific modeling languages and code generators. In: OOPSLA 2003: Companion of the 18th Annual ACM SIGPLAN Conference on Object-Oriented Programming, Systems, Languages, and Applications, pp. 92–93. ACM Press, New York (2003)
13. Wooldridge, M., Jennings, N.R.: Intelligent Agents: Theory and Practice. The Knowledge Engineering Review 10(2), 115–152 (1995)
14. Woolridge, M., Wooldridge, M.J.: Introduction to Multiagent Systems. John Wiley & Sons, Inc., New York (2001)
15. Yu, E.: Modeling organizations for information systems requirements engineering. In: Proceedings of IEEE International Symposium on Requirements Engineering, pp. 34–41 (1993)
16. Zambonelli, F., Jennings, N.R., Wooldridge, M.: Developing multiagent systems: The Gaia methodology. ACM Transactions on Software Engineering and Methodology (TOSEM) 12(3), 317–370 (2003)

# Argumentation Strategies for Task Delegation

Chukwuemeka David Emele[1], Timothy J. Norman[1],
and Simon Parsons[2]

[1] University of Aberdeen, Aberdeen, AB24 3UE, UK
[2] Brooklyn College, City University of New York, 11210 NY, USA
{c.emele,t.j.norman}@abdn.ac.uk,
parsons@sci.brooklyn.cuny.edu

**Abstract.** What argument(s) do I put forward in order to persuade another agent to do something for me? This is an important question for an autonomous agent collaborating with others to solve a problem. How effective were similar arguments in convincing similar agents in similar circumstances? What are the risks associated with putting certain arguments forward? Can agents exploit evidence derived from past dialogues to improve the outcome of delegation decisions? In this paper, we present an agent decision-making mechanism where models of other agents are refined through evidence derived from dialogues, and where these models are used to guide future argumentation strategy. We combine argumentation, machine learning and decision theory in a novel way that enables agents to reason about constraints (e.g., policies) that others are operating within, and make informed decisions about whom to delegate a task to. We demonstrate the utility of this novel approach through empirical evaluation in a plan resourcing domain. Our evaluation shows that a combination of decision-theoretic and machine learning techniques can significantly help to improve dialogical outcomes.

## 1 Introduction

It is typical in collaborative settings for agents (human or artificial) to work together, act on each others' behalf, share resources, etc [4,8]. This presupposes that there exist some kind of relationship or agreement between collaborators. Regardless of whether such relationships are transient or permanent, collaborators often engage in dialogue regarding task delegation, or resources sharing. Agents in such settings may, however, be subject to policy restrictions. Such policies might regulate what resources may be released to an agent from some other organisation, under what conditions they may be used, and what information regarding their use is necessary to make a decision.

Given that agents are operating under policies, and some policies may prohibit an agent from performing an action under certain circumstances, how can we utilise models of others' policies that have been learned to devise a strategy for selecting an appropriate agent from a pool of potential providers? To do this, we propose an approach based on decision theory, which utilises a model of the policies and resource availabilities of others to aid in deciding who to talk to and what information needs to be revealed. We explore, in this paper, strategies for task delegation where agents operate under policies, and we intend to validate the following hypothesis: *agents that build more accurate models of others and use this to drive argumentation strategy will perform better*

M. Cossentino et al. (Eds.): EUMAS 2011, LNAI 7541, pp. 80–96, 2012.
© Springer-Verlag Berlin Heidelberg 2012

*than those that do not. More specifically, exploiting appropriate decision-theoretic and machine learning techniques will mean that agents can: (1) significantly improve the cumulative utility of dialogical outcomes; (2) reduce communication overhead; and (3) strike a balance between maximising utility and minimising communication overhead.*

The remainder of this paper is organised as follows: Section 2 presents our framework and describes how policies are learned through evidence, and Section 3 discusses our decision-theoretic model. Section 4 presents a number of strategies for selecting arguments. Section 5 reports the results of our evaluation, and Section 6 discusses related work and future direction. Section 7 concludes.

## 2    Our Framework

One of the core goals of this research is to learn models of the policies of others. In this section, we describe how policies are captured and learned. We begin by formulating a mechanism to capture agents' policies.

### 2.1    Agents' Policies

Agents' policies regulate how tasks are delegated or resources deployed to others. Here, we develop an abstract model of policies, which provides the basis for designing a framework that allows agents to reason about others' policies as they collaborate, communicate and coordinate their activities. In this model, we assume that agent policies can be described in terms of features that characterise the prevailing circumstances. Our approach of using features to model systems has been used in data mining and machine learning problems [2,10], where features capture the attributes and characteristics of objects. We model policies as conditional entities that are relevant to an agent under specific circumstances only. These circumstances are characterised by a set of features such as the type of resource required, the location of an operation, and so on.

We define a feature as a characteristic of the prevailing circumstance within which an agent operates. Let $\mathcal{F}$ be the set of all features such that $f_1, f_2, \ldots \in \mathcal{F}$. Our concept of policy maps a set of features into an appropriate policy decision. In our framework, an agent can make one of two policy decisions at a time, namely (i) *grant*, which means that the policy allows the agent to provide the resource when requested, and (ii) *decline*, which means that the policy prohibits the agent from providing the resource.

**Definition 1.** *(Policies) A policy is a function $\Pi : 2^{\mathcal{F}} \to \{grant, decline\}$, which maps feature vectors of agents to appropriate policy decisions.*

We illustrate, by examples, the way policies may be captured in this model.

$\mathbb{P}_1$: You are **prohibited** from releasing a *helicopter* to any agent if the weather report says there are volcanic clouds (vc) in the location the agent intends to deploy the *helicopter*.

$\mathbb{P}_2$: You are **permitted** to release a *helicopter* ($h$), to any agent if the *helicopter* is required for transporting relief materials ($trm$) and the weather is good.

$\mathbb{P}_3$: You are **permitted** to release a *jeep* ($j$) to any agent for any purpose, irrespective of the day and the weather report.

In the above example, if a *helicopter* is intended to be deployed in an area with volcanic clouds then the provider is prohibited from providing the resource but might offer a ground vehicle (e.g., *jeep*) to the consumer if the resource is available. Policies are important factors that regulate agents' behaviour in a society. Given that policies are often private, and agents are required to work together as they collaborate to solve a problem then *how can agents identify what policies others are working within?* Our claim is that there is useful evidence that one can extract from interactions with other agents. Such additional evidence can help to build more accurate models of others' policies. In the next section, we discuss how argumentation-based dialogue allows us to gather such useful evidence.

## 2.2   Argumentation-Derived Evidence (ADE)

We explore the evidence that argumentation-based dialogue provides in revealing underlying policy constraints, and thereafter we present the interaction protocol employed in this research. Three important types of evidence are considered in this paper, namely: (i) seeking information about the issue under negotiation; (ii) providing explanations or justifications; and (iii) suggesting alternatives. This is not intended as an exhaustive list, but do represent three of the most common sources of evidence in argument-based dialogue in general [14].

**Seeking Further Information.** When an agent receives a request to provide a resource, it checks whether or not it is permitted to honour the request. To do this, it must compare the details provided by the consumer with the policies it must operate within to make a decision. If the details of the task context provided by the consumer is insufficient for the provider to make a decision, it will need to seek further information. The consumer could use that information as input to try to model what policies the provider agent may be operating with. Such a request for further information could mean that there are specific values of certain features that may lead to different policy-governed decisions.

**Suggesting Alternatives.** When an agent is unable to grant a request because there is either a policy restriction or a resource availability constraint, it may wish to suggest alternatives. For example, a consumer may request the use of a *helicopter* to transport relief materials in bad weather conditions. If the provider is prohibited from providing a *helicopter* in such conditions but permitted to provide a *jeep* then it may offer a *jeep* as an alternative for transporting those materials. If we assume that an agent will only suggest an alternative if that alternative is available and there is no policy that forbids its provision, then the suggestion provides evidence regarding the policies of the provider with respect to the suggested resource. While the issue of deception remains an open problem, some techniques for addressing this assumption have been investigated [12].

**Justifications.** Following a request for a resource, ultimately the provider agent will either agree to provide it or decline the request (though further information may be sought in the interim and suggestions made). In the case where the provider agent agrees to grant the request, the consumer agent obtains a positive example of a task context that

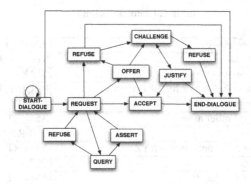

**Fig. 1.** The interaction protocol

the provider agent's policies permit the provision of the resource. On the other hand, if the request is refused then the consumer may seek further explanation for the refusal. The justification provided in response to the challenge may offer further evidence that may help to identify the underlying constraints.

**Interaction Protocol.** Here, we present the protocol employed in this framework which guides the interaction between agents (see Figure 1). Our approach is similar to [1,5] in negotiating for resources required to enact a plan. To illustrate the sorts of interaction between agents, consider the example dialogue in Table 1. Let $x$ and $y$ be consumer and provider agents respectively. Suppose we have an argumentation framework that allows agents to ask for and receive explanations (as in Table 1, *lines* 11 *to* 14), offer alternatives (*line* 10 in Table 1), or ask and receive more information about the attributes of requests (*lines* 4 *to* 9 in Table 1), then $x$ can gather additional information regarding the policy rules guiding $y$ concerning the provision of resources.

Negotiation for resources takes place in a turn-taking fashion. The dialogue starts, and then agent $x$ sends a request to agent $y$ (e.g., *line* 3, Table 1). The provider, $y$, may respond by conceding to the request (accept), refusing, offering an alternative resource, or asking for more information (query) such as in *line* 4 in Table 1. If the provider agrees to provide the resource then the negotiation ends. If, however, the provider declines the request then the consumer may challenge that decision, and so on. If the provider suggests an alternative (*line* 10 in Table 1) then the consumer evaluates it to see whether it is acceptable or not. Furthermore, if the provider needs more information from the consumer in order to decide, the provider would ask questions that will reveal the features it requires to make a decision (query, assert/refuse in Figure 1). There is a cost attached to the revelation of private information to another agent. An agent might refuse to reveal a piece of information if doing so is expensive [9].

## 2.3 Policy Modelling through Argumentation-Derived Evidence (ADE)

When an agent has a collection of experiences with other agents described by feature vectors (see Section 2.1), we can make use of existing machine learning techniques for

**Table 1.** Dialogue example

| # | Dialogue Sequence | Locution Type |
|---|---|---|
| 1 | $x$: Start dialogue. | START-DIALOGUE |
| 2 | $y$: Start dialogue. | START-DIALOGUE |
| 3 | $x$: Can I have a *helicopter* for $0.1M reward? | REQUEST |
| 4 | $y$: What do you need it for? | QUERY |
| 5 | $x$: To transport relief materials. | ASSERT |
| 6 | $y$: To where? | QUERY |
| 7 | $x$: A refugee camp near region XYZ. | ASSERT |
| 8 | $y$: Which date? | QUERY |
| 9 | $x$: On Friday 16/4/2010. | ASSERT |
| 10 | $y$: I can provide you with a *jeep* for $5,000. | OFFER |
| 11 | $x$: But I prefer a *helicopter*, why offer me a *jeep*? | CHALLENGE |
| 12 | $y$: I am not allowed to release a *helicopter* in volcanic eruption. | JUSTIFY |
| 13 | $x$: There is no volcanic eruption near region XYZ. | CHALLENGE |
| 14 | $y$: I agree, but the ash cloud is spreading, and weather report advises that it is not safe to fly on that day. | JUSTIFY |
| 15 | $x$: Ok then, I accept your offer of a *jeep*. | ACCEPT |
| 16 | $y$: That's alright. Good-bye. | END-DIALOGUE |

learning associations between sets of features and policy decisions. For each interaction, which involves resourcing a task $t$ using provider $y$, we add the example $(\vec{F}_y, grant)$ or $(\vec{F}_y, decline)$ to the training set, depending on the evidence obtained from the interaction where $\vec{F}_y \in 2^{\mathcal{F}}$. Specifically, we investigate three classes of machine learning algorithms [6,15], namely: decision tree learning (using C4.5), instance-based learning (using k-nearest neighbours), and rule-based learning (using sequential covering).

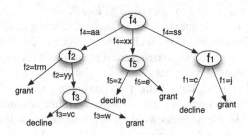

**Fig. 2.** Example decision tree

Figure 2 shows an example tree representing an agent's policy model learned from interactions. Nodes of the decision tree capture features of an agent's policy, edges denote feature values, while the leaves are policy decisions.

# 3   Decision-Theoretic Model

We have described how the policies of other agents can be learned with the help of evidence derived from argumentation. In this section, we demonstrate the use of such structures in developing argumentation strategies for deciding which agent(s) to negotiate with and what arguments to put forward. Our model takes into account communication cost and utility to be derived from fulfilling a task. Agents attempt to complete tasks by approaching the most promising provider. Here, we formalise the decision model developed for this aim; a model that we empirically evaluate in Section 5.

Let $\mathcal{A}$ be a society of agents. Agents play one of two roles: consumer and provider. Let $\mathcal{R}$ be the set of resources such that $r_1, r_2, \ldots \in \mathcal{R}$ and $\mathcal{T}$ be the set of tasks such that $t_1, t_2, \ldots \in \mathcal{T}$, and, as noted above, $\mathcal{F}$ is the set of features of possible task contexts such that $f_1, f_2, \ldots \in \mathcal{F}$. Each consumer agent $x \in \mathcal{A}$ maintains a list of tasks $t_1, t_2, \ldots t_n \in \mathcal{T}$ and the rewards $\Omega_x^{t_1}, \Omega_x^{t_2}, \ldots \Omega_x^{t_n}$ to be received for fulfilling each corresponding task. We assume here that tasks are independent; in other words, $x$ will receive $\Omega_x^{t_1}$ if $t_1$ is fulfilled irrespective of the fulfilment of any other task. Further, we assume that tasks require single resources that can each be provided by a single agent; i.e. we do not address problems related to the logical or temporal relationships among tasks or resources. Providers operate according to a set of policies that regulate its actions, and (normally) agents operate according to their policies.

Each consumer agent $x \in \mathcal{A}$ has a function $\mu_x^r$ with signature $\mathcal{A} \times \mathcal{R} \times \mathcal{T} \times 2^{\mathcal{F}} \to \mathbb{R}$ that computes the utility gained if $x \in \mathcal{A}$ acquires resource $r \in \mathcal{R}$ from provider $y \in \mathcal{A}$ in order to fulfil task $t \in \mathcal{T}$, assuming that the information revealed to $y$ regarding the use of $r$ is $F \subseteq \mathcal{F}$. This $F$ will typically consist of the information features revealed to persuade $y$ to provide $r$ within a specific task context. (Although we focus here on resource provision, the model is equally applicable to task delegation, where we may define a function $\mu_x^t : \mathcal{A} \times \mathcal{T} \times 2^{\mathcal{F}} \to \mathbb{R}$ that computes the utility gained if $y$ agrees to complete task $t$ for $x$, assuming that the information revealed to $y$ to persuade it to do $t$ is $F \subseteq \mathcal{F}$.)

Generally, agents receive some utility for resourcing a task and incur costs in providing information, as well as paying for the resource. In some domains, there may be other benefits to the consumer and/or provider in terms of some kind of non-monetary transfers between them, but we do not attempt to capture such issues here. Hence, in our case, the utility of the consumer is simply the reward obtained for resourcing a task minus the cost of the resource and the cost of revealing information.

**Definition 2.** *(Resource Acquisition Utility) The utility gained by $x$ in acquiring resource $r$ from $y$ through the revelation of information $F$ is:*

$$\mu_x(y, r, t, F) = \Omega_x^t - (\Phi_y^r + Cost_x(F, y)) \tag{1}$$

*where $\Omega_x^t$ is the reward received by $x$ for resourcing task $t$, $\Phi_y^r$ is the cost of acquiring $r$ from $y$ (which we assume to be published by $y$ and independent of the user of the resource), and $Cost_x(F, y)$ is the cost of revealing the information features contained in $F$ to $y$ (which we define below).*

The cost of revealing information to some agent captures the idea that there is some risk in informing others of, for example, details of private plans[1]. Even in a cooperative setting, there is a chance that information revealed to others can be exploited. We agree, however, that there might be situations where revealing more information could lead to better outcomes for both agents. Notwithstanding, this does not rule out the fact that revealing too much information in a current dialogue might damage an agent's chance of winning a future argument. This line of argument has seen use in many practical applications. For example, during job interviews, applicants often plan to reveal information that they think is likely to project them as the right candidate for the job. In that regard, they usually plan not to present any information that could reveal otherwise. In another practical example, [11] speculates that certain government spying organisations are easily able to break most forms of encryption. However, when required to present evidence in a court of law, these organisations try to pose arguments that avoid revealing such information. This is because they consider revealing such information to be expensive.

**Definition 3.** *(Information Cost) We model the cost of agent $x$ revealing a single item of information, $f \in \mathcal{F}$, to a specific agent, $y \in \mathcal{A}$, through a function: $cost_x : \mathcal{F} \times \mathcal{A} \to \mathbb{R}$. On the basis of this function, we define the cost of revealing a set of information $F \in \mathcal{F}$ to agent $y$, as the sum of the cost of each $f \in F$.*

$$Cost_x(F, y) = \sum_{f \in F} cost_x(f, y) \qquad (2)$$

Cost, therefore, depends on $y$, but not on the task/resource. This definition captures a further assumption of the model; i.e. that information costs are additive. In general, we may define a cost function $Cost'_x : 2^{\mathcal{F}} \times \mathcal{A} \to \mathbb{R}$. Such a cost function, however, will have some impact upon the strategies employed (e.g. if the cost of revealing $f_j$ is significantly higher if $f_k$ has already been revealed), but the fundamental ideas presented in this paper do not depend on this additive information cost assumption.

Predictions regarding the information that an agent, $x$, will need to reveal to $y$ for a resource $r$ to persuade it to make that resource available is captured in the model that $x$ has developed of the policies of $y$. For example, if, through prior experience, it is predicted that a car rental company will not rent a car for a trip outside the country, revealing the fact that the destination of the trip is within the country will be necessary. The actual destination may not be necessary, but would also be sufficient. The costs incurred in each case may differ, however. Let $Pr(Permitted|y, r, F)$ be the probability that, according to the policies of $y$ (as learned by $x$), $y$ is permitted to provide resource $r$ to $x$ given the information revealed about the context of the use of this resource is $F$.

Predictions about the availability of resources also form part of the model of other agents. Let $Pr(Avail|y, r)$ be the probability of the resource being available given we ask agent $y$ for resource $r$. These probabilities are captured in the models learned about other agents from previous encounters.

---

[1] It is worth noting that the utility derived by the agent to whom the information was revealed is beyond the scope of this paper, and so is not discussed here.

**Definition 4.** *(Resource Acquisition Probability) A prediction of the likelihood of a resource being acquired from an agent y can be computed on the basis of predictions of the policy constraints of y and the availability of r from y:*

$$Pr(Yes|y, r, F) = Pr(Permitted|y, r, F) \times Pr(Avail|y, r) \qquad (3)$$

With these definitions in place, we may now model the utility that an agent may expect to acquire in approaching some other agent to resource a task.

**Definition 5.** *(Expected Utility) The utility that an agent, x, can expect by revealing F to agent y to persuade y to provide resource r for a task t is computed as follows:*

$$E(x, y, r, t, F) = \mu_x(y, r, t, F) \times Pr(Yes|y, r, F) \qquad (4)$$

At this stage we again utilise the model of resource providers that have been learned from experience. The models learned also provide the minimal set of information that needs to be revealed to some agent $y$ about the task context in which some resource $r$ is to be used that maximises the likelihood of there being no policy constraint that restricts the provision of the resource in that context. This set of information depends upon the potential provider, $y$, the resource being requested, $r$, and the task context, $t$. (If, according to our model, there is no way to convince $y$ to provide the $r$ in context $t$, then this is the empty set.)

**Definition 6.** *(Information Function) The information required for y to make available resource r in task context t according to x's model of the policies of y is a function* $\lambda_x : \mathcal{A} \times \mathcal{R} \times \mathcal{T} \to 2^{\mathcal{F}}$

Now, we can characterise the optimal agent to approach for resource $r$, given an information function $\lambda_x$ as the agent that maximises the expected utility of the encounter:

$$y_{opt} = \arg \max_{y \in \mathcal{A}} E(x, y, r, t, F) \text{ s.t. } F = \lambda(y, r, t) \qquad (5)$$

Our aim here is to support decisions regarding which agent to approach regarding task resourcing (or equivalently task performance); an aim that is met through the identification of $y_{opt}$. The question remains, however, how the agent seeking a resource presents arguments to the potential provider, and what arguments to put forward. To this end, we present strategies for selecting arguments in the next section.

## 4   Strategies for Selecting Arguments

We focus on minimising communication overhead (i.e. reducing the number of messages between agents) and minimising the information communicated (i.e. reducing the cost incurred in revealing information). To illustrate these strategies, consider a situation in which, according to the evaluation made by $x$ (the consumer) of $y_{opt}$'s (the provider's) policies, $\lambda_x(y_{opt}, r, t) = \{f_1, f_2, f_3, f_4\}$ for resource $r$ used for task $t$. The costs for revealing each feature is, as described above, $cost_x(f_1, y_{opt})$, etc. Using this situation, in the following sections we discuss 3 strategies: message minimisation; profit maximisation; and combined.

## 4.1  Profit Maximisation

The rationale for this strategy is to attempt to maximise the profit acquired in resourcing a task by attempting to reduce the information revelation costs in acquiring a resource. To effectively specify this heuristic, we define a function *power*, which returns the strength or persuasive power of a feature in leading to a positive response from the provider as follows.

**Definition 7.** *(Persuasive Power) The persuasive power of a single item of information* $f \in \mathcal{F}$ *with respect to a specific agent,* $y \in \mathcal{A}$ *regarding a specific resource* $r \in \mathcal{R}$, *denoted as* $power_x(y, r, f)$, *is defined as the confidence that agent* $x$, *has in the fact that revealing* $f$ *to another agent,* $y$, *will contribute positively towards persuading* $y$ *along the desired (or positive) direction regarding the provision of* $r$.

$$power_x : \mathcal{A} \times \mathcal{R} \times \mathcal{F} \rightarrow \mathbb{R} \qquad (6)$$

Computationally, this can be done by generating confidence values (or probabilities over the information features) with respect to how features have contributed to positive responses in past dialogues. We leave the choice of which approach to use in generating the persuasive power or strength of arguments (that is, information feature) to system designers who can decide based on their objectives and the peculiarities of the domain of interest.

Using this strategy, the agent uses the models of other agents developed from past encounters to compute confidence values (or persuasive power) for each diagnostic information feature. Suppose that the persuasive power of the features from $\lambda_x(y, r, t)$ are $f_3 > f_1$, $f_3 > f_2$, $f_1 > f_4$ and $f_2 > f_4$. Using this information, the agent will inform the potential provider of these features of the task context in successive messages according to this order when asked for justification of its request until agreement is reached (or the request fails). In the above example, if the most persuasive justification (feature of the task context) succeeds, it will achieve an outcome of $\Omega_x^t - (\Phi_y^r + Cost_x(f_3, y))$, if further justification is required either $f_1$ or $f_2$ is used, and so on.

Other strategies are, of course, possible. An immediate possibility is to order the features to be released on the basis of cost, or a combination of persuasive power and cost. Rather than discussing these relatively simple alternatives, in the following we discuss how such simple strategies could be combined.

## 4.2  Message Minimisation

The rationale for the use of this first strategy is for the consumer agent, $x$, to resource task, $t$, as soon as possible. To this aim, $x$ seeks to minimise the number of messages exchanged with potential providers required to release the required resource, $r$. The consumer, therefore, reveals all the information that, according to $\lambda_x$, the provider will require to release the resource in a single proposal. Since cost is incurred when information is revealed, however, this strategy will, at best, get the *baseline* utility; i.e. the utility expected if the provider indeed requires all information predicted to release the resource. In the example introduced above, the consumer, $x$, will send

$\lambda_x(y, r, t) = \{f_1, f_2, f_3, f_4\}$ to the provider in one message, and, if the request is successful, the utility gained will be:

$$\mu_x(y, r, t, \lambda_x(y, r, t)) = \Omega_x^t - (\Phi_y^r + Cost_x(\lambda_x(y, r, t), y))$$

This strategy ensures minimal messaging overhead if the consumer has an accurate model of the policy and resource availability models of providers. A number of variations can be formulated for this strategy. An immediate possibility is for agents to anticipate the next question of the other party and provide a response in advance. To demonstrate this variation, we refer to the dialogue captured earlier in Table 1. In *line 4* of the dialogue, $y$ asks *"What do you need it for?"*. Agent $x$, rather than just respond with *"To transport relief materials".*, may prefer to respond with *"To transport relief materials to refugee camp near region XYZ"*. In our evaluation, we implement the variation of message minimisation strategy that reveals all the information (in one response) that, according to $\lambda_x$, will be required to release $r$.

## 4.3 Combined Strategies

The rationale for these combined strategies is to capture the trade-off between presenting all the features of the task context in a single message, thereby, reducing the communication, and attempting to extract as much utility as possible from the encounter (in this case by utilising information regarding relative persuasive power). One way of doing this, is to set a message threshold (a limit to the number of messages sent to a potential provider), $\sigma_m$. In other words, an agent can try to maximise utility (using the *profit maximising strategy*) in $\sigma_m - 1$ steps (or messages) and if the information revealed is insufficiently persuasive then the agent reveal all remaining task context features in the final message. It is easy to see that when $\sigma_m$ is set to 1 then the agent adopts the *message minimisation* strategy, and if $\sigma_m$ is set to $|\lambda_x(y, r, t)|$ this is equivalent to the *profit maximising* strategy.

Another way, is to identify the diagnostic features of the provider's decision (from the model), and compute the confidence values (persuasive power) for each feature. If the confidence value of a given feature exceeds some threshold, $\sigma_c$, then that feature is included in the set of information that will be revealed first (under the assumption that this set of features is most likely to persuade the provider to release the resource). If this does not succeed, the remaining features are revealed according to the profit maximisation strategy. For example, if $f_3$, $f_2$ and $f_1$ all exceed $\sigma_c$, these are sent in the first message, providing an outcome of $\Omega_x^t - (\Phi_y^r + Cost_x(\{f_1, f_2, f_3\}, y))$ if successful, and, if not, $f_4$ is used in a follow-up message.

Again, other strategies are possible such as computing a limited number of clusters of features on the basis of their persuasive power, or clustering by topic (if such background information is available). Our aim here is not to exhaustively list possible strategies, but to empirically evaluate the impact of utilising information from the models of others learned from past encounters to guide decisions regarding whom to engage in dialogue and what arguments to put forward to secure the provision of a resource (or, equivalently, a commitment to act). We turn to the evaluation of our model in the following section.

# 5  Evaluation

In evaluating our approach, we employed a simulated agent society where a set of consumer agents interact with a set of provider agents with regard to resourcing tasks assigned to them, and we test the following hypothesis:

- *Hypothesis 1:* Incremental revelation of information ordered by *persuasive power* significantly improves the cumulative utility of dialogical outcomes.
- *Hypothesis 2:* Anticipation of information needs of others leads to significant reduction in the number of messages exchanged (i.e. communication overhead).

## 5.1  Experimental Setup

The scenario involves a team of five software agents (one consumer and four provider agents) collaborating to complete a joint activity over a period of three simulated days. There are five resource types, five locations, and five purposes that provide the possible task context of the use of a resource (375 possible task configurations). A task involves the consumer agent identifying resource needs for a plan and collaborating with provider agents to see how that plan can be resourced. Experiments were conducted with consumer agents initialised with random models of the policies of provider agents. In the control condition, the consumer simply memorises outcomes from past interactions (see SM configuration below). Since there is no generalisation in the control condition, the *confidence* (or prediction accuracy) is 1.0 if there is an exact match in memory, otherwise we assume there is a 50:50 chance of the prediction being accurate. Typically, if there is no exact match the control condition does not look for the best match (because this will involve some generalisation, which is not allowed in this configuration). In other configurations involving machine learning (e.g., SC, see below), the confidence can be generalised from past interactions.

In our experimental setup, the consumer's policies allow it to delegate the provision of resources to any of the four providers in the system. However, the cost of revealing information to various providers differ. This could be used to model such things as trust (or distrust). Each provider is assigned a set of resources, and resources are associated with some charge, $\Phi_r$. Providers also operate under a set of policy constraints that determine under what circumstances they are permitted to provide a resource to a consumer. We conducted 800 experiments, and in each experiment 100 tasks were randomly generated (from the 375 possible task configurations) and assigned to a consumer, and the consumer attempts to delegate to others the provision of resources required to fulfil each task. Based on previous experience (that is, the policy model built so far), an agent tries to predict whether or not a provider is permitted to release a given resource. The prediction is logged and after the experiment the predictions are checked against the agent's policies. The more accurate the policy model built, the more accurate the predictions.

For example, suppose a consumer is assigned to deliver relief materials to victims of a natural disaster in a certain location. The consumer then probes the environment for provider agents that can provide required resources. After identifying potential providers, it employs our decision model to select the most promising candidate. Thereafter, it engages in argumentation-based negotiation with the agent in an attempt to acquire such resources. The procedure for the negotiation follows the interaction protocol (presented in Section 2). For example, in the argumentation-based dialogue captured in Table 1, the consumer $x$, initiated the dialogue. The provider had a policy that forbid it from releasing a *helicopter* but was allowed to release a *jeep* and so it offered the consumer a *jeep*.

**Table 2.** Experimental Conditions

| Condition | Description |
|---|---|
| SM | Simple memorisation of outcomes |
| SMMMS | SM + message minimising strategy |
| SMPMS | SM + profit maximising strategy |
| SC | Sequential covering rule learning algorithm |
| SCMMS | SC + message minimising strategy |
| SCPMS | SC + profit maximising strategy |

In this evaluation, we aim to demonstrate that a careful combination of machine learning and decision theory can be used to aid agents in choosing who to partner with, and what information needs to be revealed in order to persuade the partner to release the resource. We consider six experimental conditions in total (i.e. SM, SMMMS, SMPMS, SC, SCMMS, SCPMS). In an earlier research [3], Emele *et al.* explored the performance of different classes of machine learning techniques in building accurate models of the policies of others through argumentation-derived evidence. Out of all the algorithms investigated in that research, SC was one of the best performers, and so we use it as the learning algorithm for the remaining parts of this evaluation. The SC algorithm also has the benefit of representing models of others' policies as rules, and hence are amenable to presentation to human decision makers.

Table 2 outlines the configurations tested in our experiments while Table 3 captures the cost that the consumer associates with revealing the various features of a task to different providers ($y_1, y_2, y_3$ and $y_4$). We assume that these costs are constant throughout the experiment. This simplification is to enable us concentrate on such things as identifying the most promising candidate and what information features are more persuasive in a given context. In addition, the reward offered for fulfilling tasks were randomly generated and range between $18 and $25. The price of resources were also randomly generated and lies between $7 and $12. Once the price of resources are generated at the beginning of the experiment, it remains the same throughout the experiment. Again, the reason for this is both to simplify the experiment and to allow us investigate the effect of our decision model without bias.

**Table 3.** Cost associated with revealing various features to various providers

| Feature | $Cost_x(F, y_1)$ | $Cost_x(F, y_2)$ | $Cost_x(F, y_3)$ | $Cost_x(F, y_4)$ |
|---|---|---|---|---|
| *Resource* | $2 | $2 | $2 | $2 |
| *Day* | $1 | $1 | $1 | $2.50 |
| *Location* | $4 | $1.50 | $1 | $3 |
| *Purpose* | $6 | $4 | $7 | $2 |

## 5.2   Results

We aim to confirm whether or not agents that utilise a combination of machine learning and decision theory to guide their argumentation strategies can perform better than those that do not.

**Hypothesis 1**

In a set of experiments, we evaluate the performance of incremental revelation of information features, ordered by *persuasive power* of arguments, on the cumulative utility gained from dialogical encounters.

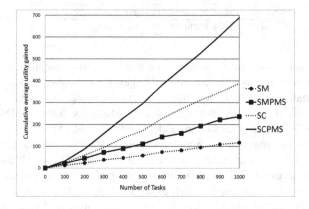

**Fig. 3.** SC vs. SM, cumulative average utility

Figure 3 t agents perform better (that is, gain higher cumulative average utility) when they reveal information in incremental fashion given that such information is ordered by its *persuasive power*. Regardless of how simple or sophisticated an agents learning approach is, results show that if agents can (somehow) order the information according to its *persuasive power* and incrementally reveal them during negotiation the agent is more likely to perform better and thereby gain higher cumulative average utility. More specifically, the SMPMS consistently gained higher utility than the SM configuration. Likewise, the SCPMS recorded greater improvement in the cumulative utility gained than its counterpart (i.e. SC). For example, after 800 tasks, the cumulative average utility gained by agents using the incremental revelation approach had risen above $190 and $520 (in SMPMS and SCPMS configurations respectively) while the configuration that reveals information without considering the *persuasive power* approaches $96 and $312 (in SM and SC configurations respectively). Clearly, the configurations in which incremental revelation of information takes into account the persuasive power significantly and consistently outperforms those without such consideration. These results show that incremental revelation of information ordered by *persuasive power* significantly improves the cumulative utility of dialogical outcomes, which confirms our hypothesis.

In order to test the statistical significance of the results of our evaluation, we carried out a paired t-test to determine whether or not the null hypothesis $H_0$ should be rejected in favour of the alternative hypothesis $H_1$.

- $H_0$ = There is NO significant difference in the performance of agents that revealed information incrementally (based on the *persuasive power*) and those that revealed information without paying attention to the *persuasive power* of arguments being put forward.
- $H_1$ = There is a significant difference between the performance of agents that revealed information incrementally (based on the *persuasive power*) and those that revealed information without paying attention to the *persuasive power* of arguments being put forward.

**Table 4.** Statistical analysis of utility gained across different configurations

| Configuration | t-statistic | p-value | 95% Conf. interval | | Significant |
|---|---|---|---|---|---|
| | | | From | To | |
| SM vs SMPMS | 1.71 | 0.033 | 0.56 | 2.86 | Yes |
| SC vs SCPMS | 24.34 | $\ll 0.001$ | 23.19 | 25.49 | Yes |

In Table 4, we summarise the results of the statistical analysis performed on the experimental data in various configurations of the agent. From the statistical analysis, the results show that there is a significant difference in the performance of agents in the SM vs SMPMS and SC vs SCPMS configurations. With each pairwise comparison recording $p < 0.05$, we reject the null hypothesis, and conclude that agents that reveal information incrementally (based on the persuasive power) perform better than those that reveal information without considering the persuasive power of arguments being put forward. This further confirms our hypothesis.

## Hypothesis 2

In a series of experiments, we evaluate the effectiveness of anticipating the information needs of others, and how it affects the number of messages exchanged (i.e. communication overhead) during dialogical encounters. We considered the following configurations — SM, SMMMS, SC, and SCMMS.

For all the configurations considered, the number of messages exchanged during dialogical encounters was considerably reduced in configurations where agents anticipate the information needs of others (and therefore provide it ahead of time) than those without such capability. Figures 4 shows the effectiveness of anticipation of information needs of others using simple memorisation, and rule learning respectively. In each case, results clearly show that communication overhead is reduced when agents anticipate others' information needs. Irrespective of the complexity or simplicity of the learning approach employed, results show that if agents can accurately predict the information requirement of other partners in collaborative problem solving activities then they can significantly reduce the communication overhead. For example, after 600 tasks, the number of messages exchanged per 100 tasks by agents that anticipate the information needs of others had fallen below 595 and 240 messages (averaging about 6, 3 messages per task) in SMMMS and SCMMS configurations respectively, while configurations in which agents do not anticipate others' information needs is above 845 and 510 messages

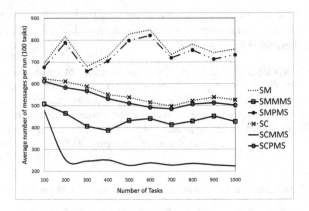

**Fig. 4.** SC vs. SM, number of messages exchanged

per 100 tasks (that is, more than 8 and 5 messages per task) in SM, and SC configurations respectively. Clearly, these results show that anticipation of information needs of others consistently and significantly reduces the number of messages exchanged (i.e. communication overhead) during dialogical encounters. This confirms our hypothesis.

We carried out a paired t-test analysis to test the statistical significance of the results of our evaluation. The null hypothesis $H_0$ and the alternative hypothesis $H_1$ are as follows:

- $H_0$ = The number of messages exchanged by agents that anticipate the information needs of others is equal to those exchanged by agents that do not anticipate the information needs of others.
- $H_1$ = There is a significant difference between the number of messages exchanged by agents that anticipate the information needs of others and those that do not anticipate others' information needs.

**Table 5.** Statistical analysis of messages exchanged across configurations

| Configuration | $t$-statistic | p-value | 95% Conf. interval | | Significant |
|---|---|---|---|---|---|
| | | | From | To | |
| SM vs SMMMS | 1.90 | 0.030 | 0.75 | 3.05 | Yes |
| SC vs SCMMS | 14.32 | $\ll 0.001$ | 13.17 | 15.47 | Yes |

In Table 5, we summarise the results of the statistical analysis performed on the experimental data in various configurations of the agent. From the statistical analysis, the results show that there is a significant difference in the number of messages exchanged by agents in the SM vs SMMMS and SC vs SCMMS configurations. With each pairwise comparison recording $p < 0.05$, we reject the null hypothesis, and conclude that agents that anticipate the information needs of others perform better (lead to significant reduction in communication overhead) than those that do not consider such anticipation in their interactions. This further confirms our hypothesis.

# 6  Discussion

The results we have presented show that a decision-making mechanism based on a combination of decision-theoretic and machine learning techniques can clearly help agents to improve their performance both in terms of utility and communication overhead. Our approach represents the first model for combining argumentation, machine learning and decision theory to learn underlying social characteristics (e.g. policies/norms) of others and exploit the models learned to reduce communication overhead and improve strategic outcomes. There is, however, some prior research in combining machine learning and argumentation, and in using argument structures for machine learning. In that research, Možina et al. [7] propose an induction-based machine learning mechanism using argumentation. However, the framework developed in that research will struggle to learn and build an accurate model of policies from argumentation-derived evidence, which is the main issue we are addressing in our work. Also, the authors assume that the agent knows and has access to the arguments required to improve the prediction accuracy, but we argue that it is not always the case. As a result, we use dialogue to tease out evidence that could be used to improve performance.

In recent research, Sycara et al. [13] investigate agent support for human teams in which software agents aid the decision making of team members during collaborative planning. One area of support that was identified as important in this context is guidance in making policy-compliant decisions. This prior research focuses on giving guidance to humans regarding their own policies. An important and open question, however, is how can agents support humans in developing models of others' policies and using these in decision making? We use a novel combination of techniques to build accurate models of others' policies, and use these to aid decision making. We believe that our research contributes both to the understanding of argumentation strategy for dialogue among autonomous agents, and to applications of these techniques in agent support for human decision-making.

In the evaluation presented in this paper, we assume that the consumer makes a single decision per task about which provider to choose, irrespective of whether it fails or succeeds. In our future work, we plan to make the decision process more iterative such that if the most promising candidate fails to provide the resource, the next most promising is approached and the sunk cost incurred while interacting with the previous provider is taken into account in computing the total cost of resourcing the task, etc. We are hoping that some of these ideas will provide helpful feedback to future research on developing strategies for delegation in which there might be a cost for failing to resource a task.

# 7  Conclusions

In this paper, we have presented an agent decision-making mechanism where models of other agents are refined through evidence from past dialogues, and are used to guide future argumentation strategy. Furthermore, we have empirically evaluated our approach and the results of our investigations show that decision-theoretic and machine learning techniques can individually and in combination significantly improve the cumulative utility of dialogical outcomes, and help to reduce communication overhead. The results also demonstrate that this combination of techniques can help in developing more robust and adaptive strategies for advising human decision makers on how a plan may be resourced (or a task delegated), who to talk to, and what arguments are most persuasive.

# References

1. Amgoud, L., Parsons, S., Maudet, N.: Argument, dialogues and negotiation. In: Horn, W. (ed.) Proceedings of European Conference on Artificial Intelligence 2000, pp. 338–342. IOS Press, Amsterdam (2000)
2. Blum, A.L., Langley, P.: Selection of relevant features and examples in machine learning. Artificial Intelligence 97(1-2), 245–271 (1997)
3. Emele, C.D., Norman, T.J., Guerin, F., Parsons, S.: On the Benefits of Argumentation-Derived Evidence in Learning Policies. In: McBurney, P., Rahwan, I., Parsons, S. (eds.) ArgMAS 2010. LNCS, vol. 6614, pp. 86–104. Springer, Heidelberg (2011)
4. Grosz, B., Kraus, S.: Collaborative plans for group activities. In: Proceedings of the 13th International Joint Conference on Artificial Intelligence, pp. 367–373 (1993)
5. McBurney, P., Parsons, S.: Games that agents play: A formal framework for dialogues between autonomous agents. Journal of Logic, Language and Information 12(2), 315–334 (2002)
6. Mitchell, T.M.: Machine Learning. McGraw Hill (1997)
7. Možina, M., Žabkar, J., Bratko, I.: Argument based machine learning. Art. Intel. 171(10-15), 922–937 (2007)
8. Norman, T.J., Reed, C.: A logic of delegation. Art. Intel. 174(1), 51–71 (2010)
9. Oren, N., Norman, T.J., Preece, A.: Loose lips sink ships: A heuristic for argumentation. In: Proc. of the 3rd Int'l Workshop on ArgMAS, pp. 121–134 (2006)
10. Ren, L., Shakhnarovich, G., Hodgins, J.K., Pfister, H., Viola, P.: Learning silhouette features for control of human motion. ACM Trans. Graph. 24(4), 1303–1331 (2005)
11. Schneier, B.: Applied Cryptography: Protocols, Algorithms, and Source Code in C. John Wiley & Sons, Inc., New York (1993)
12. Sensoy, M., Zhang, J., Yolum, P., Cohen, R.: Context-aware service selection under deception. Computational Intelligence 25(4), 335–364 (2009)
13. Sycara, K., Norman, T.J., Giampapa, J.A., Kollingbaum, M.J., Burnett, C., Masato, D., McCallum, M., Strub, M.H.: Agent support for policy-driven collaborative mission planning. The Computer Journal 53(5), 528–540 (2010)
14. Walton, D.N., Krabbe, E.C.W.: Commitment in Dialogue: Basic Concepts of Interpersonal Reasoning. SUNY Press, USA (1995)
15. Witten, I.H., Frank, E.: Data Mining: Practical machine learning tools and techniques, 2nd edn. Morgan Kaufmann (2005)

# Using OWL 2 DL for Expressing ACL Content and Semantics

Nicoletta Fornara[1,*], Daniel Okouya[1,**], and Marco Colombetti[2,***]

[1] Università della Svizzera Italiana,
via G. Buffi 13, 6900 Lugano, Switzerland
{nicoletta.fornara,daniel.okouya}@usi.ch
[2] Politecnico di Milano, Piazza Leonardo Da Vinci 32, Milano, Italy
marco.colombetti@polimi.it

**Abstract.** The design and implementation of open interaction systems is widely recognized to be a crucial issue in the development of innovative applications on the Internet. In this paper we pursue the goal of enhancing interoperability and openness in open interaction systems by systematic use of web standards. We propose a way of using the semantic web language OWL 2 DL to represent both the content of an ACL message, whose structure is compatible with FIPA-ACL, and the meaning of the whole message, adopting a commitment-based semantics, in such a way that OWL reasoning on message meaning is made possible. To this purpose we specify a number of ACL conventions regarding the domain independent components of the content language and the semantics of messages; we describe a set of supporting OWL ontologies, and exemplify our proposal with the analysis of a commissive message: a promise to perform a certain action within a given deadline if certain conditions hold. We then describe a demonstrative prototype of a system where those conventions are concretely implemented that is based on Web Service technologies (WSDL, SOAP, and HTTP for message transport).

## 1 Introduction

The design and implementation of *open interaction systems* (OISs) is widely recognized to be a critical issue in the development of innovative applications on the Internet, like e-commerce systems, e-marketplaces, and applications for the management of virtual enterprises. Basically, we can conceive an OIS as a distributed system which different computer programs (regarded as autonomous agents) may freely enter or leave, with the purpose of achieving their individual goals by interacting with other agents according to shared rules. In an OIS,

---

* Supported by the Hasler Foundation project Nr. 11115-KG and by the SER project Nr. C08.0114 within the COST Action IC0801 Agreement Technologies.
** Supported by the Swiss National Science Foundation project Nr. 200020_134790.
*** This research has been carried out as part of the activities of the author at Università della Svizzera italiana, Switzerland.

M. Cossentino et al. (Eds.): EUMAS 2011, LNAI 7541, pp. 97–113, 2012.
© Springer-Verlag Berlin Heidelberg 2012

rules cover several aspects of the interaction, and in particular the *communication conventions* regulating the exchange of messages and their semantics, and the *artificial institutions* [7,5,3] specifying the roles, powers, and norms that constitute the social environment within which the interactions are carried out.

It has long been recognized that the set of conventions regulating the exchange of messages is particularly important. Since the 1990s this fact has led to a flourishing of studies on Agent Communication Languages (ACLs), and there are signs that this area of research may take front stage once again [1]. Indeed, in an OIS the *communication conventions* have to cover several layers, all of which are crucial to the successful exchange of messages between agents; moving bottom-up, such layers concern:

1. *connectivity*: the ability of agents to exchange messages as binary data with other agents, typically running on different and possibly heterogeneous platforms;
2. *data format*: the concrete serialization of the binary data that represent messages;
3. *message structure*: the application-independent component of messages (i.e., the abstract syntax);
4. *terminology*: the application-independent and the application-dependent terms contained in a message;
5. *semantics*: the contribution of the message structure and of the application-independent and application-dependent terminology to the meaning of the message;
6. *conversation management*: the rules concerning how a conversation should be initiated, carried out, and terminated.

In Section 2 and 3 we mainly focus on the message structure, terminology, and semantics, whereas in Section 4 we propose an approach for the connectivity and data format based on web services technologies. As far as possible, we follow the spirit of FIPA-ACL specifications[1]. In particular, we take from such specifications that:

1. a message is articulated in a set of sections, each of which is introduced by a specific *parameter* (like sender, receiver, etc.);
2. every message realizes a *communicative act*, whose type (like inform, request, etc.) is explicitly represented in the message;
3. the content of the message is expressed in a suitable Content Language (CL).

The main goal of this paper is to propose an approach to agent communication that maximizes *interoperability*, at both the syntactic and the semantic level, as a means to achieve true openness. For this reason we conform, as far as possible, to the suitable W3C recommendations, and in particular to those concerning the Semantic Web and the Service Oriented Architecture (SOA). More precisely, we show how agent communication can be based on OWL ontologies, used to specify the semantics of the application-independent component of the content language,

[1] http://www.fipa.org/repository/aclspecs.html

the application-dependent terminology, and the semantics of the whole message (inclusive of the illocutionary force of the message).

In particular in Section 2 we define a minimal set of *conventions* concerning the message structure, the content language, and the semantics of performatives, that would guarantee agent interoperability if adopted as interaction standards. In Section 3 we present the semantics of commissive communicative acts. In Section 4 we describe a demonstrative prototype which implements the various layers of communication conventions for an OIS. Finally, in Section 5 we discuss the contribution of this paper with respect to other relevant proposals available in the literature and draw some conclusions.

## 2   Message Structure and Content Language

An OIS is a system where agents can interact to achieve their individual goals by coordinating and negotiating their activities. Contrary to more traditional distributed systems, the distinctive feature of an OIS is that it allows external agents to enter the system, participate in the activities, and then leave the system at will. This brings to the foreground the problem of *interoperability*, because for the interaction to be successful all agents have to comply with a set of *shared conventions*, which will have to be taken as *standards* by the designers of the agents. In this section we introduce a set of possible conventions, covering the structure of the messages (i.e. their *abstract syntax*), the syntax and semantics of the application-independent part of the *content language*, and the syntax and semantics of the application-dependent *terminology* used in the content expression.

Regarding the structure of messages and the content language, when possible we will try to roughly follow FIPA-ACL specifications[2]. Regarding the semantics of the message, as discussed in [12,4], we depart significantly from the semantics of FIPA-ACL; this because, among other problems, FIPA-ACL is unable to account for the normative consequences of message exchanges, which are essential to a satisfactory treatment of agent interactions. More specifically, we adopt commitment-based semantics for communicative acts and institutional semantics for declarations. In the past we have expressed the semantics of communicative acts using the Event Calculus [5]; however, given the current importance of exploiting industry-level technology, in this paper we consider the application of Semantic Web technologies [9]. For the moment, in the next section we propose a semantics of commissive communicative acts, using an extension of the OWL ontology of obligations presented in [3]. We plan to further extend this ontology in the future, to express the semantics of *directive* and *assertive* communicative acts and of *declarations*.

### 2.1   Message Structure

In this section we propose the message structure of our ACL. Like in FIPA-ACL, a message contains an acl-envelope, used to correctly route the message

---

[2] http://www.fipa.org/repository/aclspecs.html

to the final destination and comprised of a number of attributes, including to, from, length, encoding, and others. The message also contains an acl-payload, characterized by the following components:

- performative: a symbol denoting the type of the communicative act, that in our ACL may be: promise, inform, request, agree, refuse, cancel, query-ref, query-if, declare; further types may be added and specified according to need;
- sender: the identifier of the agent that sends the message;
- receiver: the identifier of the recipients of the message;
- content: a complex expression that can represent: a state of affair if the performative is assertive (like inform); an action with a deadline if the performative is commissive (like promise) or directive (like request); and an institutional action if the performative is declare;
- reply-by: the time within which it is possible to answer to a request;
- msg-id: the unique identifier of the message, generated by the sender of the message by using its name as namespace followed by a progressive number, for example John:001.

The following parameters are used to describe the content of the message:

- language: denotes the name of the formal language in which the value of the content parameter is expressed;
- ontology: denotes the name of the ontology that specifies the concepts used in the content expression.

FIPA-ACL defines other parameters (like reply-to, protocol, conversation-id, reply-with, in-reply-to) that can be used for conversation management but that are nor relevant for the goals of this paper.

## 2.2   Content Language

Content expressions are sentences belonging to a *content language* (CL). This consists of: (i) *application-independent* terms, like for example those used to describe the logical structure of *actions* and *events*; and (ii) *application-dependent* terms used in relation to specific domains, for example to describe actions of payment, delivery, bidding, and so on. All such terms must merge to form a unique formal language.

As we have already remarked, in the attempt to maximize interoperability we conform as far as possible to widely adopted standards, like those recommended by W3C. A similar attempt has been made by FIPA, which proposes FIPA-RDF[3], an application-independent content language whose application-independent classes and properties are defined using RDF Schema. However RDF-based solutions, while very flexible and expressive, are limited in the complexity of the inferences they can support. This is due to the limited expressive power of RDF Schema, which for example does not allow one to specify the

---

[3] http://www.fipa.org/specs/fipa00011/

disjointness of classes, cardinality restrictions of properties, and formal characteristics of properties like transitivity.

We thus opted for OWL (more precisely, OWL 2 DL[4] that is briefly described in Appendix A) as the formal language for the specification of both the
application-independent and the application-dependent terms of our content language. The reasons of our choice are that: (i) OWL, recommended by W3C, is by
now a fairly well-known standard; (ii) OWL is a very expressive, but still decidable, logical language, which licenses powerful reasoning procedures; (iii) many
open source tools are already available for editing OWL ontologies, carrying out
reasoning, and realizing applications like Development Environments and APIs[5];
(iv) there are many available OWL ontologies, which can be easily integrated in
our proposal thanks to the fact that two ontologies can be usually merged by
simply taking the union of their axioms; (v) as discussed in Section 3, OWL 2
DL can be used to specify both the semantics of the content of messages and
the semantics of the whole messages (inclusive for example, of its performative).

In this section we describe the application-independent concepts that can be
used in the content of ACL messages: the specification of these concepts makes
up what we call the *CL Ontology* (i.e., the Content Language Ontology). In
turn, this ontology imports the OWL *Time Ontology*[6] that defines classes like
Instant $\sqsubseteq$ TemporalEntity, Interval $\sqsubseteq$ TemporalEntity, ProperInterval $\sqsubseteq$ Interval,
Discla(ProperInterval,Instant), and properties like hasBeginning: TemporalEntity
$\rightarrow$ Instant, hasEnd: TemporalEntity $\rightarrow$ Instant (for connecting a temporal entity
to its start and end instant of time) and before: TemporalEntity $\rightarrow$ TemporalEnty
(for expressing that a temporal entity is before another temporal entity).

**The Content of Assertive Messages.** The content of assertive messages,
like for example an *inform* message, is the description of a state of affairs, that
is, a *proposition*. For the moment, in our content language we consider only
a restricted type of propositions, namely those that can be expressed as a set
of positive or negative OWL assertions (i.e., the elements of an OWL ABox).
Such assertions in the set are implicitly in logical conjunction. For example, the
proposition "John owns a red car" must first be analysed as the conjunction
of four atomic propositions, and then represented as the following set of OWL
assertions:

Agent(john-001), Car(car-001), owns(john-001,car-001), Red(car-001),

where: the Agent class is defined in the *CL Ontology*; the Car and Red classes,
and the property owns: Agent $\rightarrow$ Car, are defined in what we call the *Domain
Ontology*. As we shall see, similar OWL assertions appear also as parts of the
content of non-assertive messages.

**The Content of Directive and Commissive Messages.** The content of
a *directive* or *commissive* message (like a request and a promise, respectively)
includes the description of an *action*, which ought to be carried out in the future.

---

[4] http://www.w3.org/2007/OWL/wiki/OWL_Working_Group
[5] http://www.w3.org/2007/OWL/wiki/Implementations
[6] http://www.w3.org/TR/owl-time/

The semantics behind the exchange of a promise (as we shall see in Section 3) is that the sender is in charge of performing, within a given deadline, an instance of the action described in the message.

In the *CL Ontology* we define the Action class for representing the description of actions. The Action class is the domain of the following properties that can be used to characterize the action that has to be performed:

- The property hasActor, used to represent the agent responsible for the execution of the action; the range of this property is the application-independent class Agent.
- The property hasDeadline, that represents the instant of time within which the action has to be performed. It is empty if the deadline for the performance of the action is not known when the message is sent. In this case the deadline depends on the time when some other event happens; for example, in the promise to pay a given book within one week from delivery, the deadline depends on the date of delivery. The range of this property is the Instant class.
- The property hasDuration, which can be used to specify the interval of time within which the action has to be performed, starting from the instant of time when the event described in the condition component of the message will happen. Its range is the DurationDescription class.
- Other properties that can be defined in the *Domain Ontology* for describing specific types of actions. For instance, in an application where agents talk about payment and delivery, a *Commercial Ontology* will define the class Pay $\sqsubseteq$ Action and Deliver $\sqsubseteq$ Action (for representing the action of paying and delivering), with properties hasAmount and hasRecipient, hasObject, and the class Item for representing the items exchanged in the commercial transaction.

In many commissive and directive messages, the action is specified as a *conditional action*, that is, as an action that has to be executed if certain conditions obtain. The ConditionalAction class is used for representing an *action* that ought to be executed, on condition that a given *condition event* occurs; this is very frequent in both *request* and *promise* communicative acts. The content and the condition part are inserted in the message by introducing the property hasContentPart, whose range is the Action class, and the property hasConditionPart, whose range is the Event class.

To this purpose we introduce in the *CL Ontology* the application-independent Event class that generalizes the class Action $\sqsubseteq$ Event (in fact an action is regarded as an event with an actor). The Event class has some subclasses, and in particular: the class TimedEvent $\sqsubseteq$ Event, used to represent those events that are connected through the property atTime: TimedEvent $\rightarrow$ Instant to exactly one instant of time, as specified by the following axiom: TimedEvent $\sqsubseteq$ =1atTime.Instant; and the class TimeEvent $\sqsubseteq$ TimedEvent, used to specify as condition event the elapsing of a given instant of time.

Finally, we require that the content of directive or commissive messages are a set of OWL assertions specifying *exactly one* individual belonging to the ConditionalAction class.

**Example: The Promise Communicative Act.** To exemplify the proposed message structure and content language we formalize a type of commissive act, the *promise*. We use as an example the following promise that can be useful in an electronic commerce application: "agent John promises to agent Mary that John will pay 5 euro to Mary within 2 days from the delivery of book1". The message with the content expressed in the *Commercial Ontology* which imports the *CL Ontology*, which in turn imports the *Time Ontology* is:

```
(promise
  :sender John          :receiver Mary
  :language OWL-2-DL    :ontology Commercial Ontology
  :msg-id John:001
  :content
     ConditionalAction(condAct),
       hasActionPart(condAct, promisedAction),
         Pay(promisedAction), hasActor(promisedAction, John),
         hasAmount(promisedAction, 5), hasDuration(promisedAction, 2),
       hasConditionPart(condAct, cond),
         Deliver(cond), hasActor(cond, Mary),
         hasRecipient(cond, John), hasObject(cond, book1)
)
```

## 3   Message Semantics

Basically, the meaning of a message derives from a combination of the message's performative and content expression. Different performatives combine with the content expression in different ways; this approach is compatible with the idea, which is fundamental in Speech Act Theory, that the meaning of a message depends on its illocutionary force (denoted by the performative) and propositional content (represented by the content expression) [11].

One of our assumptions is that the content expression of a message is a set of OWL axioms, which represent the *propositional content* of the speech act performed by sending the message. More precisely, such propositional content coincides with the meaning that the set of OWL axioms have under standard OWL 2 DL semantics [9] in the context of the *Domain Ontology* referred with the ontology parameter of the message. Such a propositional content is suitably transformed to obtain the *meaning of the whole message*, in a way that depends on the message *performative*. What remains to be decided is how the performative transforms the propositional content to produce a representation of the meaning of the whole message and how to represent this meaning.

The semantics of the whole message that we adopt in this paper is inspired by the commitment-based semantics that we firstly presented in [4], enriched with the semantics of declarations expressed via institutional concepts as presented in [5]. In this work we only formalize the semantics of the promise communicative act; we plan to cover other types of communicative acts, extending the approach proposed in this section, in our future works.

There is, we believe, no single solution to the problem of choosing a representation for the message meaning: the choice depends on what the representation is going to be used for. For the same reasons expounded in the previous section, we chose to base our representation of message meaning on OWL. That is, we propose to express the semantics of the whole message as a set of OWL axioms, which extend a pre-existing ontology representing the meanings of the previous messages belonging to the same conversation (this aspect is not treated in the current paper).

In the case of a promise (and, more generally, of commissive messages), an important point is the ability to represent, and reason on, the obligations brought about by making the promise. The matter here is more complex than with the representation of propositional content (i.e., of the meaning of the content expression). The reason is that a representation of obligations is already problematic in full First Order Logic (FOL), and even more so in the fragment of First Order Logic covered by OWL 2 DL. A suitable representation can be developed, however, if there is a clear specification of the reasoning tasks that the representation is intended to support. At the present stage of our research, we intend to use the representation of message meanings for *monitoring* the temporal evolution of commitments, obligations, etc., that are incurred by the agents as an effect of communication (either in a real OIS or in simulations). Therefore, to deal with the meaning of promises we designed an OWL representation of obligations that allows us to exploit standard OWL reasoning to monitor the temporal evolution of an obligation, as part of the *state of the interaction* of certain agents at any time instant.

We represent the state of an interaction (which includes the relevant events and actions that happen in the system) in a specific OWL ontology, the *State Ontology*. This ontology imports the *Domain Ontology* (introduced in the previous section) and the *Obligation Ontology*, which specifies the concepts needed to represents obligations of the interacting agents. The overall picture of the ontologies used and their dependencies is depicted in Figure 1.

Many classes and properties of the *Obligation Ontology* were formalized in [3], and some of them have been customized to the need of representing the semantics of communicative acts. More precisely the *Obligation Ontology* defines the classes and properties for the management of the obligations derived from the exchange of certain messages (like promises) and for the monitoring of their *state* (from activated to fulfilled or violated). It imports the *CL Ontology*, because this specifies some classes (like Agent, Action, Event) that are used as domain or range of properties related to obligations. The *Obligation Ontology* defines the

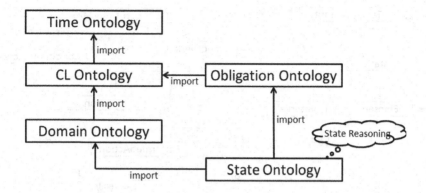

**Fig. 1.** Overall picture of the OWL ontologies used and their dependencies

class Obligation, which is the domain of a set of properties used to represent the *debtor* and the *creditor* of the obligation (their range being the Agent class). The *start event* of an obligation is a subclass of the Event class: when an event that belongs to the start event class of an obligation takes place, the obligation becomes activated. The *content* of the obligation is a subclass of the Action class: when an action that belongs to the content class of an obligation is executed within a given deadline the obligation becomes fulfilled.

The *State Ontology* is used to represent and monitor the temporal evolution of the interaction, therefore it defines the class Elapsed $\sqsubseteq$ Instant, used to model that an instant of time is elapsed. As this ontology is used to represent the events and the actions that happen during an interaction, we introduce the class OccurredEvent $\sqsubseteq$ TimedEvent defined by the following axiom: OccurredEvent $\equiv \forall$ atTime.Elapsed; this class contains the events that happened up to an elapsed instant of time. Finally we introduce the class PerformedAction defined by the following axiom: PerformedAction $\equiv$ Action $\sqcap$ OccurredEvent; it is necessary for distinguishing between the description of an action used in the content of messages, and an action that has been executed, and is actually related to its elapsed instant of execution by means of the atTime property. The main classes and properties of the *State Ontology* (some of them are imported from the other ontologies) are represented in Figure 2.

As we already said, the *State Ontology* is used to represent at run-time the state of the interaction among agents; this is the ontology on which we run a reasoner for deducing relevant facts. As already proposed in [3], a program is in charge of representing the elapsing of time and the functionalities necessary to perform closed-world reasoning on certain classes, with the goal of monitoring the state of obligations and reacting to their fulfillment or violation. This program is also in charge of inserting into the *State Ontology* the new assertions and axioms used for representing the semantics of the messages.

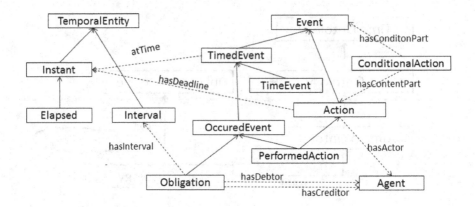

**Fig. 2.** Graphical representation of the main classes and properties of the *State Ontology* (some of them imported). Properties are represented with dotted lines, solid lines are used for subclasses.

### 3.1   Semantics of the Promise Communicative Act

A communicative act performed by exchanging a message is characterized by: a set of *preconditions* that need to be evaluated for the successful performance of the communicative act, and a set of *effects* that affect the state of the interaction if the communicative act is successfully performed and represent its meaning.

For a *promise* to be a valid communicative act it is necessary that: (i) the content belongs to the ConditionalAction class, with its action part belonging to the Action class and its condition part, if specified, belonging to the Event class; (ii) the action has to be performed in the future (i.e., if a deadline is specified it has to be in the future of the message exchange); and (iii) the sender of the message has to coincide with the actor of the promised action.

Following the commitment-based semantics for ACL proposed in [5], the performance of communicative acts has the effect of creating or changing *social commitments* [4]. The semantics of a promise communicative act is represented by a commitment of the message sender to perform the communicated action; this commitment can be viewed as a special case of social commitment, and coincides with the obligation to perform the action. Therefore in our proposal the effects of a promise are represented by creating in the state of the interaction an obligation of the message sender, directed to the receiver, to perform the action described in the content of the message within the specified deadline, if a certain communicated condition holds. Those effects are represent in the *State Ontology* by a program that is in charge of extending its *ABox* and *TBox* with a set of OWL axioms used to define the new obligation generated by the message and to monitor its state.

We now exemplify the axioms that need to be defined by using the promise message presented in the previous section; this procedure can be easily generalized and automatically applied to every promise message received by an agent. First of all we insert in the *ABox* of the *State Ontology* the following assertions:

Obligation(obl-1),     Instant(instant1),     atTime(obl-1,instant1)
hasDebtor(obl-1,John),     hasCreditor(obl-1,Mary),
ProperInterval(interval1), hasInterval(obl-1,interval1),
Instant(instant2),     hasEnd(interval1, instant2),
days(duration1, 2),     hasDurationDescription(interval1,duration1),

The intuitive meaning of these assertions is as follows. A new individual obl-1 belonging to the class Obligation is created at the time instant instant1, equal to the instant of time when the message is received. The debtor of the obligation is the sender of the message and its creditor is the receiver of the message. The obligation is related to an interval of time that starts at the time instant when the obligation is activated and ends in the time instant communicated in the message as the deadline (if any). The instant of time at which this interval starts is computed as soon as an individual starts to belong to the Start-Event-1 class (defined below). If the message communicates a duration for the interval (in this case for example the duration is 2), the end instant of time is computed summing the duration to the start instant of time as soon as it becomes known.

The *TBox* of the *State Ontology* has also to be updated with the axioms necessary for representing the start event and the content of the newly created obligation. A crucial aspect of our model is that the start event and the content of an obligation are represented as OWL classes. Any instance belonging to such classes will satisfy the corresponding representations. The fact that a concrete action belongs to the start event class or to the content class can be established through an OWL 2 DL reasoner; therefore, an agent may exploit reasoning to choose which action to perform in order to fulfill a given obligation. We define the StartEvent-1 class of obligation obl-1 as a class of possible events. This class is defined as the intersection of a set of classes, defined using the properties communicated in the condition event part of the message content, and some other classes that are necessary to express the fact that the start event has to occur after the creation of the obligation:

StartEvent-1 ≡ Deliver ⊓ hasActor∋Mary ⊓ hasRecipient∋John ⊓
    hasObject∋book1 ⊓ OccurredEvent ⊓ (∃evBefore⁻∋obl-1).

The content of the obligation, the Content-1 class, is defined as the intersection of a set of classes that are defined using the properties communicated in the content of the message, the class of the content, and the PerformedAction class:

Content-1 ≡ Pay ⊓ hasActor∋John ⊓ hasRecipient∋Mary ⊓ hasAmount∋5 ⊓
    PerfomedAction.

The Deadline-1 class of the obligation obl-1 contains only the time event that happens at the instant of time which terminates the interval of the obligation (which may be known or unknown when the obligation is created), and it is defined by the following axiom:

Deadline-1 ≡ ∃ atTime.(∃ hasEnd⁻.(hasInterval⁻ ∋ obl-1))

For those obligations whose deadline event is a fixed time event, it is important to check that the start event happens before the end event. By introducing the following axiom, if the deadline time event is before or equal to the start time event, then the ontology becomes contradictory:

Deadline-1 $\sqcap$ (evBefore.StartEvent-1 $\sqcup$ evSameTime.StartEvent-1) $\sqsubseteq$ $\bot$

The EndEvent-1 class for this obligation is equivalent to the empty set: EndEvent-1 $\equiv$ $\bot$ because in this example the message does not specify an event that will terminate the obligation.

When a new obligation is created, we introduce in the *TBox* of the *Sate Ontology* also the following four axioms, necessary to deduce the state of a given obligation, that is, to deduce if the obligation belongs to the Activated, Cancelled, Fulfilled, or Violated classes. As we have already shown in [6], we need to perform some form of closed-world reasoning on the Cancelled and Fulfilled classes; this is done by a program, which computes the class KCancelled $\sqsubseteq$ Cancelled as the class that contains all obligations that are known to be in the Cancelled class, and the class KFulfilled $\sqsubseteq$ Fulfilled as the class that contains all obligations that are known to be in the Fulfilled class.

{obl-1} $\sqcap$ $\neg$ KCancelled $\sqcap$ ($\exists$evBefore.(StartEvent-1 $\sqcap$ $\exists$atTime.Elapsed) $\sqcup$ $\exists$evSameTime.(StartEvent-1 $\sqcap$ $\exists$atTime.Elapsed) ) $\sqsubseteq$ Activated

{obl-1} $\sqcap$ $\exists$evBefore.(EndEvent-1 $\sqcap$ $\exists$atTime.Elapsed) $\sqsubseteq$ Cancelled

{obl-1} $\sqcap$ Activated $\sqcap$ ($\exists$evBefore.(Content-1 $\sqcap$ $\exists$atTime.Elapsed) $\sqcup$ $\exists$evSameTime.(Content-1 $\sqcap$ $\exists$atTime.Elapsed)) $\sqcap$ $\exists$evBefore.(Content-1 $\sqcap$ $\exists$evBefore.Deadline-1) $\sqsubseteq$ Fulfilled

{obl-1} $\sqcap$ Activated $\sqcap$ $\neg$KFulfilled $\sqcap$ $\exists$evBefore.(Deadline-1 $\sqcap$ $\exists$ atTime.Elapsed) $\sqsubseteq$ Violated

## 4   Demonstrative Prototype

In this section we describe the demonstrative prototype that we have implemented for testing the various layers of communication conventions for OIS proposed in this paper. Due to the openness of the proposed framework we based our approach to message structure and terminology on Semantic Web Technologies that are W3C recommendations. Similarly we based our approach to connectivity and data format on principles and standards of Service Oriented Architecture (SOA); this because they address crucial low-level aspects of openness and interoperability [2], are sufficiently mature and relatively stable, and are already accepted and used by a large industrial community.

For realizing the *connectivity* layer we adopted current SOA standards: the *transport protocol* is HTTP, and the *message structure protocol* is SOAP[7](Simple Object Access Protocol). In the most popular implementation of the Service Oriented Architecture two distinct software applications play the role of *Service Requestor* and the role of *Service Provider*. This architecture can be adapted to our need of peer to peer (P2P) interactions by merging the two roles into one software application that plays both roles simultaneously.

---

[7] http://www.w3.org/TR/2007/REC-soap12-part0-20070427/

All the components of our open system possess a *listening point* to receive messages and a *talking point* to send messages. The listening point is represented as a *web-service service*[8]. As such it is exposed on the Internet via a contract defined in a WSDL (Web Service Definition Language) file. The talking point is a *web-service client*, which communicates in conformance with the previously mentioned contract. More precisely the contract defines an operation called send-message, which expects as input a message with the parameters described in Section 2, and the listening point that provides the service of delivering the message. The corresponding service contract contains a reference to the abstract syntax of the messages proposed in this paper, specified using an XML schema. Both the envelope and the payload of the messages are serialized as an XML document and they constitute the body of a SOAP message. The content part of the message is serialized in XML using the RDF/XML syntax of OWL. A crucial advantage of this approach is the provision of a human-readable communication contract that can be easily handled with the support of runtime frameworks coming along with web-service technology, such as for example Apache CXF. Hence anyone can easily generate the infrastructure to handle the transmission of a message abiding to the exposed messaging protocol and adapt it to his needs, in order to participate in the OIS. Effort will only be required for the handling of ACL communication content.

Our approach assumes that each agent has a well-defined identity, which is kept constant across different interactions. This justifies the assumption that every agent has a unique *agent identifier*. The fact that it is unique implies the existence of a service for the registration of unique names. We do not assume that such an identifier is initially known to all possible partners: this implies the need of *agent directories*. Those services plus the description of the services provided by the participants in SOA are provided by the UDDI (Universal Description Discovery and Integration) component. In our open interaction system those services (plus other services in support of the communication layer) are provided by an *intermediary* that should not be understood as an agent (in that it has no autonomy in the choice of goals or strategies), but rather as a component of the OIS whose function is to enable and support openness. The intermediary interacts with all participating agents through the communication interface and may provide the following functions in support of the communication among agents: (i) checking messages for compliance at the levels of syntax, terminology, and preconditions; (ii) forwarding messages to receivers, provided that they are correct at all these levels (otherwise an error message will be sent to the sender); (iii) keeping track of the semantics of messages and monitoring the evolution of the state of the system (for example by checking if obligations are fulfilled and applying sanctions if they are violated).

---

[8] This name is due to the fact that we consider "web-service" as the name of a technology, that we differentiate from the formal concept of service and client as understood in SOC/SOA; in principle this can be provided on the web using web-service technology or something else.

To run the experiment, we have implemented the intermediary in Java and two dummy participant agents in JADE (Java Agent DEvelopment Framework), but in principle a participant agent can be any software able to comply with the communication conventions and with the web-service contract. The Java components of the implemented framework use the JENA[9] API for accessing and modifying the ontologies and the Pellet OWL 2 DL reasoner[10] for reasoning on the ontologies.

## 5   Discussion and Conclusions

The contribution of this paper regards mainly the formalization and implementation of a proposal for using OWL 2 DL as content language of an ACL and for expressing the commitment-based semantics [4] of the whole message.

The advantages of using Semantic Web languages, like OWL 2 DL, with respect to other formal languages proposed in other approaches, like FIPA SL or FIPA KIF[11], or formalisms like the Event Calculus [5], [13] are mainly due to the fact that: (i) Semantic Web languages are international standards, and therefore it is possible to realize systems able to reuse existing ontologies (like for example the FOAF ontology), and to use numerous existing tools for programming, editing, validating, and reasoning on ontologies; (ii) OWL 2 DL is a decidable fragment of FOL, for which several reasoners are available; (iii) ontologies from different sources can be merged by taking the union of their axioms (or using ontology alignment mechanisms when the different ontologies are not immediately compatible), making it possible for an agent to participate to different interactions using one knowledge base; (iv) the same ontologies can be adopted for defining the concepts to be used in the content language and in the *State Ontology*.

The idea of using Semantic Web languages for the specification of the content of communicative acts has been proposed for the first time by FIPA in 2001. The main differences between the FIPA's proposal and the one presented in this paper are that: (i) FIPA proposed to use RDF and RDF Schema for expressing the content of messages instead of using OWL 2 DL with the limitations discussed in Section 2.2; (ii) in FIPA's application-independent content language, fipa-rdf0, there is no definition of the concept of event, which is useful to specify conditions for the performance of actions, there is no formal definition of the notion of time, and actions are not related to their deadlines; (iii) FIPA's ACL semantics is only based on agents' beliefs and intentions and, differently from what we propose in this paper, it does not take into account the deontic consequences of the exchange of messages.

In [10] a proposal for using OWL DL as content language of FIPA-ACL is presented and the limits of FIPA SL and FIPA KIF as content languages are widely discussed. This work and our proposal have in common the use OWL DL

---

[9] http://incubator.apache.org/jena/
[10] http://clarkparsia.com/pellet/
[11] http://www.fipa.org/repository/cls.php3

for expressing the content of messages but in [10] the focus is on the semantics of the content part of messages, that is, the semantics of the OWL language. This approach is exemplified by the formalization of a query-ref message whose content is a referential expression formulated as an OWL DL class expression followed by an inform message whose content is a set of assertions in OWL DL. Differently in the ACL proposed in this paper we distinguish the semantics of the propositional content from the meaning of the whole message, which depends also from the message performative. We exemplified this approach with the formalization of a distinctive communicative act, the promise. In this type of acts the content of the message describes the action that has to be performed within a given deadline, and the meaning of the whole message is to commit the sender of the message to the actual performance of the action within the given deadline.

In [14] a proposal of using the Darpa Agent Markup Language (DAML) language for expressing the content of message is presented. The main concepts formalized in the content language are similar to the one presented in this paper, except for the use of a question part and a result part for queries. The main problem of the proposal of using DAML as content language is that it is not a current standard for representing knowledge in the Semantic Web.

Regarding our proposal of using Web Service technologies like WSDL, SOAP, and HTTP for message transport, our approach is similar to the one proposed in [8], where messages are sent between JADE platforms using SOAP over HTTP; in our proposal, however, the content of SOAP messages is described with an XML Schema instead of using JADE custom binary data format, a solution that better supports openness.

In this work we formalized the semantics of the whole message only for the promise communicative act; we plan to formalize the semantics of other types of communicative acts, like request, query-ref, inform, and declare by extending the approach proposed in this paper, in our future works.

# References

1. Chopra, A.K., Artikis, A., Bentahar, J., Colombetti, M., Dignum, F., Fornara, N., Jones, A.J.I., Singh, M.P., Yolum, P.: Research directions in agent communication. ACM Transactions on Intelligent Systems and Technology (in press)
2. Erl, T.: Service-Oriented Architecture: Concepts, Technology, and Design. Prentice Hall PTR, Upper Saddle River (2005)
3. Fornara, N.: Specifying and Monitoring Obligations in Open Multiagent Systems Using Semantic Web Technology. In: Elçi, A., Koné, M.T., Orgun, M.A. (eds.) Semantic Agent Systems. SCI, vol. 344, pp. 25–45. Springer, Heidelberg (2011)
4. Fornara, N., Colombetti, M.: Operational specification of a commitment-based agent communication language. In: Proceedings of the First International Joint Conference on Autonomous Agents & Multiagent Systems, AAMAS 2002, Bologna, Italy, July 15-19, pp. 536–542. ACM (2002)
5. Fornara, N., Colombetti, M.: Specifying Artificial Institutions in the Event Calculus. In: Dignum, V. (ed.) Handbook of Research on Multi-Agent Systems: Semantics and Dynamics of Organizational Models. Information Science Reference, ch. XIV, pp. 335–366. IGI Global (2009)

6. Fornara, N., Colombetti, M.: Representation and monitoring of commitments and norms using OWL. AI Commun. 23(4), 341–356 (2010)
7. Fornara, N., Viganò, F., Verdicchio, M., Colombetti, M.: Artificial institutions: A model of institutional reality for open multiagent systems. Artificial Intelligence and Law 16(1), 89–105 (2008)
8. Greenwood, D., Lyell, M., Mallya, A., Suguri, H.: SOAP based Message Transport for the Jade Multiagent Platform. In: Industry Track Proceedings of the 8th International Joint Conference on Autonomous Agents and Multiagent Systems, AAMAS 2009, pp. 101–104. ACM (2009)
9. Hitzler, P., Krötzsch, M., Rudolph, S.: Foundations of Semantic Web Technologies. Chapman & Hall/CRC (2009)
10. Schiemann, B., Schreiber, U.: OWL-DL as a FIPA-ACL content language. In: Proceedings of the Workshop on Formal Ontology for Communicating Agents, Malaga, Spain (2006)
11. Searle, J.R.: Speech Acts: An Essay in the Philosophy of Language. Cambridge University Press, Cambridge (1969)
12. Singh, M.P.: A Social Semantics for Agent Communication Languages. In: Dignum, F.P.M., Greaves, M. (eds.) Agent Communication. LNCS, vol. 1916, pp. 31–45. Springer, Heidelberg (2000)
13. Yolum, P., Singh, M.: Reasoning about commitment in the event calculus: An approach for specifying and executing protocols. Annals of Mathematics and Artificial Intelligence 42, 227–253 (2004)
14. Zou, Y., Finin, T., Peng, Y., Joshi, A., Cost, S.: Agent Communication in Daml World. In: Truszkowski, W., Hinchey, M., Rouff, C. (eds.) WRAC 2002. LNCS, vol. 2564, pp. 347–354. Springer, Heidelberg (2003)

# Appendix A: OWL 2 DL

OWL 2 DL is a practical realization of a Description Logic known as $\mathcal{SROIQ(D)}$. It allows one to define *classes*, *properties*, and *individuals*. An OWL ontology consists of: a set of class axioms that specify logical relationships between classes, which constitutes the *Terminological Box* (*TBox*); a set of property axioms to specify logical relationships between properties, which constitutes a *Role Box* (*RBox*); and a collection of assertions that describe individuals, which constitutes an *Assertion Box* (*ABox*).

Classes are formal descriptions of sets of objects (taken from a nonempty universe), and individuals can be regarded as names of objects of the universe. A class is either a *basic class* (i.e., an atomic class name) or a *complex class* build through a number of available *constructors*. Properties can be either *object properties*, which represent binary relations between objects of the universe, or *data properties*, which represent binary relationships between objects and data values (taken from XML Schema datatypes).

Through *class axioms* one may specify that subclass ($\sqsubseteq$) or equivalence ($\equiv$) relationships hold between certain classes, and that certain classes are disjoint. In particular, class axioms allow one to specify the domain and range of a property $p$ ($p: A \rightarrow B$ where class A is the domain and class B is the range), and that a property is functional or inverse functional. *Property axioms* allow one to specify that a given property (or chain of subproperties) is a subproperty of another property, that two properties are equivalent, or that a property is reflexive, irreflexive, symmetric, asymmetric, or transitive. Finally, *assertions* allow one to specify that an individual a belongs to a class C, C(a), that an individual a is or is not related to another individual b through an object property R, R(a,b) or ¬R(a,b), that an individual is or is not related to a data value through a data property, or that two individuals are equal or different.

*Complex classes* can be specified by using Boolean operations on classes: C ⊔ D is the union of classes, C ⊓ D is the intersection of classes, and ¬ C is the complement of class C. Classes can be specified also through *property restrictions*: (i) ∃ R.C denotes the set of all objects that are related through property R to some objects belonging to class C, at least one; if we want to specify to how many objects an object is related we should write: $\leq$nR, $\geq$nR, =nR where n is any natural number; (ii) ∀ R.C denotes the set of all objects that are related through R only to objects belonging to class C; (iii) R∋a denotes the set of all objects that are related to a through R.

We use capital initials for classes, and lower case initials for properties and individuals. We assume that all individuals introduced in the *ABox* are asserted to be different individuals.

# Self-adaptive Complex Systems

IRIT (Institut de Recherche en Informatique de Toulouse), Toulouse University, 118
Route de Narbonne, F-31062 Toulouse Cedex 9, France
gleizes@irit.fr

**Abstract.** Nowadays and in the near future, the complexity of computer applications is exponentially increasing. This complexity comes from the inherent properties of such applications: the great number of their involved components, the distribution of their control and skills, the nonlinearity of their process and their increasing openness. This is also caused by the unpredictable coupling with their environment due to high dynamicity. To fulfill these requirements, systems have to adapt themselves in order to be robust and efficient. This paper will deal with self-adaptation in software systems, particularly from a multi-agent viewpoint and will focus on the Adaptive Multi-Agent Systems theory.

## 1 Introduction

Nowadays and in the near future, the complexity of computer applications is exponentially increasing. This complexity comes from the inherent properties of such applications: the great number of their involved components, the distribution of their control and skills, the nonlinearity of their process and their increasing openness. This is also caused by the unpredictable coupling with their environment due to high dynamicity. Complexity was previously studied in a formal way, mainly by Kurt Gödel who stated that some inherent limitations exist about completeness and consistency for formal theories including arithmetic. This means that their own validity can only be proved outside of them. Demonstration of Gödel 's incompleteness theorem introduced the computable function, formalized later in computer science (such as pi-calculus, Turing machines, recursive functions, Post's machine). These lead to main several limitations in complex artificial systems: we cannot prove in a general way that they cannot be free of bugs, and these bugs can only be detected at runtime. From this very basic result, it is possible to define some directions to design complex systems:

- A complex system must be able to self-adapt during its execution because of the dynamics but also because residual bugs are potentially included despite the design and verification phases. For the same reasons, classical learning methods cannot be sufficiently general in order to suppress these residual bugs and we must discover new approaches able to self-adapt at the micro-level without any knowledge of the global goal to achieve at the macro-level.

M. Cossentino et al. (Eds.): EUMAS 2011, LNAI 7541, pp. 114–128, 2012.
© Springer-Verlag Berlin Heidelberg 2012

- Each component of the system has only to be coupled with a small number of the total amount composing the global system. This constraint comes from the previously quoted inapplicability of the global function at the micro-level, but implies the definition of micro-theories able to converge towards the desired emergent global functions.
- Designing systems in a top-down manner presupposes that the assembling of the specified components provide the desired global behaviour. Unfortunately, it is well-known that non-linearities and the multiplicity of dynamics lead to emergent phenomena at the macro-level. Consequently top-down design is fundamentally inappropriate for complex systems design.

These reasons lead us to change the perspective in order to design complex adaptive systems from satisfaction of system requirements by global and top-down activity to satisfaction of system requirements by local and bottom-up activity. Self-organisation is a way to achieve this change by allowing the design of system with emergent funtionality. To contribute to this approach, the Adaptive Multi-Agent Systems (AMAS) theory provides a guide to design self-organising systems. This theory is based on the observation that the cooperation enables to guide the agent behaviour at the micro-level, helping the agents to self-organise and to obtain adaptation at the macro-level. The modification of the interactions between the agents of the system modifies also the global function and makes the system able to adapt to changes in its environment. The interactions between agents depend on the local view these agents have and on their ability to "cooperate" with each other.

In section 2, the motivations leading to design self-adaptive complex systems are expounded. Then, section 3 presents the concepts of self-organisation and emergence. Section 4 details the AMAS theory which is studied in the SMAC[1] research group in Toulouse and has lead to Research led to a Spin off, UPETEC[2]. Then, section 5 concludes and proposes some perspectives.

# 2   Motivations

Nowadays, applications to design and problems to solve become more and more complex such as energy management [1], aircraft design [2], crisis management [3], maritime surveillance systems [4], ambient systems [5]... This complexity is due to a combination of aspects such as the great number of components involved in the applications, the fact that knowledge and control have to be distributed, the presence of non linear processes in the system, the fact that the system is more and more often open, its environment dynamic and the interactions unpredictable [6]. So, these properties motivate designer to realize software systems taking into account scalability, difficulty to solve problems, dynamics and under-specifications. In order to tackle the design of such complex

---

[1] SMAC Systèmes Multi-Agents Coopératifs www.irit.fr/SMAC
[2] www.upetec.fr

systems, self-adaptive multi-agent systems represent a promising approach providing the needed robustness and adaptation in the light of the aforementioned difficulties.

## 2.1   Scalability

The scalability of MAS [7] means that the system well behaves with a small numbers of agents but also with a great number of agents. A scalable system is a system which reaches scalable solutions that is to say with "reasonable" performances regardless of problem size.

The need of large-scale systems is an obvious fact in numerous domains as traffic control systems, maritime surveillance systems, simulation of biochemical reactions [8]. These domains provide strong constraints for the designer. The first one concerns the **control** which must be decentralized. Decentralization is required because it is too much difficult to get all informations about all entities in a single point without leading to a bottleneck. Decentralization enables to improve the system performances. The second point is about the **solving** which also must be distributed. It is a quite obvious consequence of the first point and this is also inevitable in systems composed of different physical agents such as cars or aircrafts in a traffic control system. The last point refers to the **accessibility of a global knowledge** about the system. Usually, because the system is too large, an agent inside the system has only a partial knowledge about the system,which is acquired from its environment. Depending on the size of the system, a global knowledge is available or not.

## 2.2   Problems Difficult to Solve

Several reasons can explain the difficulty for humans to solve some types of problems. The problem can present some non-linearity, some interdependencies between its parameters. The most representative classes of these problems are the multi-disciplinary, multi-objective, multi-level optimisation problems [2] and the distributed constraint-satisfaction problems [9]. The recognition of the whole problem is not possible because of its complexity. This has led to design self-organising systems presenting emergent functionalities [10], [11]. Those systems are necessarily composed of several autonomous interacting agents, plunged into an environment. In general, the global behaviour of the system emerges from the local interactions between agents. The potential of this approach is important because it simplifies the design and diminishes the design delays. But this is not so easy to do, as Van Parunak & Zambonelli [12] have claimed: "Such behaviour can also surface in undesirable ways". So, systems can reach undesirable states because the main difficulty lies in controlling the global behaviour while designing at micro-level.

## 2.3   Dynamics

Challenges of current systems are to take into account the dynamics. This dynamics is the result of changes that may be endogenous or exogenous to the system. Endogenous changes are generated by the system and derive, for example, from hardware failures or errors of the software behavior. Exogenous disturbances come from the system environment. To enable the system to continue to fulfill the function for which it was designed, it is necessary that it can adapt in real time. The system must also be open which means that an entity of the system (agent) may be added or removed at runtime. Disturbances from the environment of the system cause it to adapt.

## 2.4   High Level Expression of Requirement or under-Specified Problems

The way we usually design computational systems requires for the designer, to have some important initial knowledge. The first information a designer has to know is the exact purpose of the system. But sometimes, the main goal of the system is described at a very high level such as, for example: the system must satisfy the end-user. It is difficult to freeze this goal at the design time. Or the solution to be reached can be modified during the execution and in order to do this, the end-users have to be able to interact with the system. The system and the user have to co-construct the solution. It is the case, for example, for complex constraints problem solving in which the user can relax some constraints. The second kind of knowledge that the engineer has to know, concerns every interaction to which the system may be confronted in the future. The environment of the system can evolve and by consequences, the designer is not able to know all these situations at design time. The evolution of computer science forces us to consider that it is more and more difficult - if not impossible - not only to control accurately the activity of software with increasing complexity but also to describe completely how they work [17]. Making systems more autonomous and more adaptive is a way to simplify the task of the designer. That means that systems are able to modify their behaviour in order to achieve what they have to do at a given time.

# 3   Self-adaptation

As we have seen in section 2, the system to be designed must tackle complexity by using self-adaptation.

## 3.1   Self-adaptive Systems

In [13], according to the DARPA definition, it is said "self-adaptive software evaluates its own behavior and changes behavior when the evaluation indicates that it is not accomplishing what the software is intended to do, or when better functionality or performance is possible". This definition must be completed by the fact that the system realizes the adaptation in an autonomous way, without the designer intervention and at runtime. So, we do not have to stop the system in order to adapt it, it is able to adapt its behaviour, by itself, without stopping its execcution. This explains the prefix "self".

Designing these self-adaptive systems requires a radical change of perspective. Classicaly, designers satisfy the requirements by a global and top-down activity. They usually know the purpose of the system (main objective) and the interactions corpus in the future between the system and its environment. Designers must switch to the requirements satisfaction by a local and bottom-up activity. Furthermore, they do not know the purpose of the system and the body of interactions occuring in the future between the system and its environment. One of the most well-known mechanism used to enable adaptation of a system is inspired from natural systems and social animals like ants, termites... and is called self-organisation.

## 3.2   Self-organisation and Emergence

The works of the Agentlink Technical Forum on Self-Organisation in Multi-Agent Systems[14] have established two definitions of self-organising systems:

- **Strong self-organising systems** are systems that change their organisation without any explicit, internal or external, central control;
- **Weak self-organising systems** are systems where reorganisation occurs as a result of an internal central control or planning.

Furthermore, self-organisation implies organisation, which in turn implies some ordered structure and component behaviour. In this respect, the process of self-organisation changes the respective structure and behaviour and a new distinct organisation is self-produced [14]. Finding a solution with this kind of systems is equivalent to find the right organisation [15]. For designers, the benefits of self-organising systems are mainly due to the fact that the resolution process as a whole is not to be designed. To develop a complex system, it is sufficient to design its agents, to provide them with means to self-organise and to enable them to interact with the environment. Then, the solving process is self-constructed: it emerges from the interactions between agents [6].

The concept of self-organisation is often coupled with the concept of emergence. Emergence is the result of a collective activity and self-organisation is the means to obtain an emergent phenomenon. And it seems that emergence is a suitable context to design complex systems that cannot be controlled by a human in a centralised way. We commonly agree with the fact that an emergent phenomenon must be observable. From an observer point of view, we assume that if one can observe the content of the entities of a system and if one can observe at the system level a behaviour that cannot be reduced to the behaviour of the entities, the global behaviour can be qualified as emergent. In other words, we can say that a human cannot determine the global behaviour of the system only by looking at the agent behaviour. We can also qualify a phenomenon as emergent if we need different terms, vocabularies to explain the micro and the macro levels. This leads to give the following operational definition of emer-

gence in artificial systems, based on three points: what we want to be emergent
(subject), at what condition it is emergent and how we can use it (method) [16].

1. **Subject.** The goal of a computational system is to realise an adequate function, judged by a relevant user. This "function" can be for instance a behaviour, a pattern, a property (which may evolve during time) that has to
   emerge.
2. **Condition.** This function is emergent if the coding of the system does not
   depend on the knowledge of this function. This coding has to contain the
   mechanisms facilitating the adaptation of the system during its coupling with
   the environment, so as to tend toward a coherent and relevant function.
3. **Method.** The mechanisms which allow the changes are specified by self-
   organisation rules, providing autonomous guidance to the components' behaviour without any explicit knowledge about the collective function nor
   how to reach it.

### 3.3   Self-organisation / Re-organization

Two well-known communities focus on the design of adaptive and robust systems: SASO(Self-Adaptive and Self-Organising systems) and COIN (Coordination, Organisation, Institutions and Norms in agent systems). The SASO
community studies self-adaptation and self-organisation. In a self-organising
multi-agent systems context, the designer of such systems first focuses on agent
local behaviours and peer-to-peer interactions. The organisation is the result
of the collective emergent behaviour due to how agents act their individual
behaviours and interact in a common shared and dynamic environment. The
designer does not put any global knowledge about the organisation inside the
agents.

In the COIN community, the designer provides on one hand, the entire organisation and coordination patterns, and on the other hand, the agents local
behaviours . At runtime, the agents may consider the constraints imposed by the
defined organisation as compulsory or possible guidelines for the coordination of
their local behaviours. The organisation exists at design time. The designer puts
this knowledge inside the system and allows the agent access to this information.

Both communities are interested in adaptation and self-adaptation and use
the organisation concept but the hypothesis for designing systems are different.
Organisation is a first-abstract class in the design of COIN systems, required
at design time. In self-organising systems, the organisation is the result of the
collective behaviour.

### 3.4   Self-organisation Mechanisms

Currently, a lot of mechanisms of self-organisation are implemented in artificial systems [11] and cannot be all detailed here. The older are nature-inspired
mechanism and copy the activity of social animals such as: foraging, nest building, sorting, web weaving... The most well-known technique is the **stigmergy**

mechanism. It has been widely used and was first observed in societies of social insects by Grassé and can be summarised as "*the work excites the workers*" [17]. Agents leave information in the environment which can be perceived by the others. This information, usually evaporates after a given time. This mechanism allows task coordination and regulation within a group, using only indirect interactions and without any central control. There is no method to develop this technique and the primary difficulty is to adjust the different parameters such as the speed of evaporation or the amount of information dropped. Because the solution must be represented in the environment, the final goal of the system guides the design phase. Some mechanisms are inspired from physics such as the gradient fields. They are based on attraction and repulsion behaviours and show self-organised behaviour [18]. We can also find mechanisms imitating human behaviour such as gossip. It enables to spread information and to create evolving organisations [19].

In all these works, researchers have applied a mechanism observed or not in the nature, a theory to an application. Sometimes the phenomenon observed by simulating the system is interesting such as web weaving. But it is difficult to find a real application which can be realized by the system. Concerning web weaving, researchers have applied it to regions detection but they do not propose another application. What we try to do in my research group is to constantly go from applications to theory but also from the theory to applications. We realize specific applications by highlighting generic behaviours and then, we reuse these behaviours by improving them to design other applications. Applications enrich theory and theory enables to develop new applications. This theory: the Adaptive Multi-Agent Systems theory [20],[21],[16], [6] is presented in the following sections.

## 4    AMAS Theory

The first aim of the AMAS theory is to design MAS having a coherent collective activity that achieves the right task. We name this property "functional adequacy" and we proved the following theorem: "For any functionally adequate system, there is at least a cooperative interior medium system which fulfills an equivalent function in the same environment". Therefore, we focused on the design of cooperative interior medium systems in which agents are in cooperative interactions. The specificity of the theory resides in the fact that we do not code the global function of the system within the agents. Agents have only a partial knowledge. The global function of this system emerges from the collective behavior of the different agents composing it. Each agent possesses the ability of self-organisation i.e. the capacity to locally rearrange its interactions with others depending on the individual task it has to solve. Changing the interactions between agents can indeed lead to a change at the global level. This induces the modification of the global function. This capacity of self-organisation enables to change the global function without coding this modification at the upper level of the system. An intuitive example is the realisation of an elementary mathematical function. Let five agents be *, +, 2, 100, 5, if the organisation is the following: 2+(5*100) the result is 502 but if the organisation was (2+5)*100, the result would be 700. With this simple example, we can see that a change inside an organisation, changes the results provided by it. Self-organization in AMAS is based on the capacity an agent possesses to be locally "cooperative".

These agents, called **cooperative agents** are composed of five parts contributing to their behavior: skills (what the agent is able to do), representations of the world (the knowledge it has about itself, about the others or about its environment), an interaction language (to communicate with others or with its environment), aptitudes (the capacities it possesses to reason on its knowledge) and a social attitude led by what we call cooperation.

## 4.1  Definition of Cooperation

The basic definition of the cooperation between two agents is that an agent helps the other to execute a task. For example, two agents are needed to carry a very heavy object and they must help each other to do it. In Artificial Intelligence [22] cooperation means that, if two agents have two different goals then the fact that an agent can reach its goal, does not prevent the other to reach its own one. In the AMAS theory, cooperation defines more an attitude, a behaviour that an agent has to follow.

In the AMAS theory, an agent is benevolent, sincere, willing, fair and implements reciprocity. Benevolence is different from altruistism and means that for a limited duration, an agent can leave its individual goal to help another agent or to adopt the goal of another one. An agent is sincere if it never lies to other agents. A willing agent is an agent which tries to satisfy a request if it is coherent with its own skills and the current state of the world, and if no damage results from the action, either to the acting agent or to another. If there is a resulting damage, refer to property four. A fair agent always tries to satisfy, when it is possible, agents with the highest level of difficulty for reaching their goals. Reciprocity is the fact that each agent of the same society knows that itself and the others verify these four main properties.

## 4.2  Cooperative Agent Behaviour

A cooperative agent aims at always being in a cooperative state that is in cooperative interactions with its environement. However, because of the dynamic nature of the environment of the system, as well as the dynamics of the interactions between agents, an agent can be in a non cooperative state or can be at the origin of cooperation failures. We call these states: "Non Cooperative Situations" (NCS). More precisely an agent can detect NCS at three different steps during its lifecyle:

- when a signal perceived from its environment is not understood and not read without ambiguity;
- when the information perceived is not useful for the agent's reasoning;
- when concluding results lead to act in a useless way in the environment.

The general algorithm followed by a cooperative agent (see 1) consists in executing what the agent has been created for (called its Nominal behaviour), if it does not detect NCS. But if a cooperation problem occurs, it can realize one or more of the three following behaviours: tuning, reorganisation and evolution. For tuning, an agent changes the value of some of its internal parameters. For reorganising, an agent modifies the way it interacts with its neighbours by: adding or removing a neighbour, modifying the trust it has in a neighbour. Concerning the evolution, the agent self-removes or creates another agent (a replication of it for example). Note that these behaviours lead to self-organisation.

**Begin while** *The agent is alive* **do**
    **if** *The agent does not detect any Non Cooperative Situation* **then**
       | Execute the Nominal Behaviour;
    **else**
       | The agent tries to:
       Adjust its internal parameters: **Tuning**;
       and/or Change its interactions: **Reorganization**;
       and/or Add or remove an agent: **Evolution**;
    **end**
**end**

**Algorithm 1.** Cooperative agent's behaviour

In the algorithm, we can note that the detection of NCS infuences the agent behaviour. As a consequence, a central point in the AMAS theory has been the definition of NCS. At this step of our work, we have registered seven NCS [23]:

- **Incomprehension** is related to the interpretation of the messages and informs that the agent is not able to extract any understandable information from the received message.
- **Ambiguity** informs the agent that different interpretations are possible, and therefore, an accurate representation update is not possible. That can be due for instance to missing information.
- **Incompetence** is detected when the agent does not have the competence to process the received information such as answering an agent request.
- **Unproductivity** is detected when the agent has accurately interpreted the received information but cannot use it to produce any useful information for itself because it already has this information, it is of no interest for it or the received information is incomplete.
- **Conflict** is detected either when considering the list of possible future actions or when detecting a conflict in the environment. In the first case, among the list of possible actions some are conflicting and such actions cannot be performed by the agent at the same time (i.e. lack of resources). In the second case, the conflict can either be due to a previous action performed by the agent or another agent, or a change in the environment not related to the agent activity. This situation is also detected when the agent considers

that modifying the environment can prevent other agents from reaching their goals.
- **Concurrence** concerns the interactions between the agent and its environment. It is detected when among the list of possible actions, some can put the agent in concurrence or competition with other agents.
- **Uselessness** is detected when the agent considers itself not useful for the system or its environment. This can be due to a lack of information or unused knowledge.

Depending on the application, only some of these NCS are relevant. For example, in an ant simulation, the notion of incomprehension is not necessary because an ant can always understand what it perceives (food, pheromone, ant, obstacle).

## 4.3   Mechanisms for Implementing Cooperation

Cooperation is considered as an attitude which guides the agent behaviour in using only a partial knowledge: the agent's knowledge and its local perceptions. The cooperation is implemented inside an agent with the four following mechanisms:

- spontaneously communicate,
- anticipate cooperation failures,
- repair cooperation failures,
- act for helping its worst neighbours.

Notice that depending on the application, not all these mechanisms must be implemented by the designer inside the agent.

**Spontaneous Communication.** Spontaneous communication consists in communicating to an agent an information not requested by it. An agent sends a piece of information if it thinks that this information can be useful to another agent. An example of this action has been implemented in the simulation of foraging ants [24]. In this simulation, the environment is composed of the nest, some obstacles, pheromone, pieces of food and ants. The pheromone self-evaporates during time and can be accumulated when several ants drop pheromone at the same place. The foraging ants are the cooperative agents of the multi-agent system. Their behaviour is copied from natural ants and consists first in exploring the environment. When it encounters an obstacle, it avoids it. When it encounters food, it can harvest it. When it is loaded, it goes back to nest in dropping a given quantity of pheromone on the ground. By consequence, tracks of pheromone appear in the environment. During its exploration, an ant is attracted by pheromone and leads to follow pheromone track. This behaviour implies a reinforcement of the existing tracks. In the following situation called "come back to the nest": when an ant is loaded and comes back to the nest, it puts pheromone on the ground to mark the location. The spontaneous communication is implemented as follows: in the "come back to the nest" situation

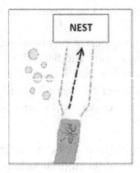

**Fig. 1.** Spontaneous communication of an ant

if in addition the ant perceives new pieces of food, it drops a higher quantity of pheromone on the ground (see figure 1). This is done to provide a better information about the environment to other ants.

**Anticipation of Non Cooperative Situations.** If it is possible, an agent can try to anticipate NCS. The designer has to implement the detection of possible NCS due to the future action of the agent. If an agent can know in advance that its action will lead to a NCS, it has to avoid it. For example, an agent can anticipate an **Unproductivity** NCS by informing other agents about the update of its profile such as the agents main interest or the information produced by the agent and judged helpful for others. The NCS anticipation can be illustrated in

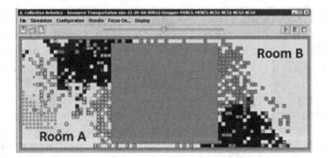

**Fig. 2.** Carrier robots

the carrier robots application [25]. In this application, see figure 2, there are two rooms A and B, separated by two narrow corridors (where two robots cannot cross). The robots have to take a box in the room A and to drop it in the room B. They have only local perceptions (only adjacent cases). For each robot, we store the ten last locations where the robot has encountered problems (most of the time a location where it cannot move because something is in front of it). These locations are in blue in the figure 2. There are a lot because all locations marked by all robots are visualised on this figure. Of course for one robot there are no more than ten blue locations. Therefore thanks to this memory a robot can anticipate that there is a robot coming in the opposite diretion in front of it, and choose another direction to avoid the conflict.

**Treatment of Non Cooperative Situations.** If an agent detects NCS, it must act to repair them. By consequence, the designer has to provide for each NCS an handler which will be executed by the agent to come back in a cooperative state. This handler is application-dependent. For example, if an **Incomprehension** NCS is detected, to solve this NCS, the agent can for instance ask the sender to modify its message, or ask other agents that may understand it for a translation/decryption.

The NCS treatment can be illustrated in the carrier robots application see figure 2. A conflict occurs when inside the corridor, one robot is in front of another robot moving in the opposite direction. In this case, if it is possible, the agent must move to its sides (left or right). If it cannot move laterally, two other solutions are opened. If the other robot has an antagonist goal, the robot which is the most far from its goal will move backward to free the way for the robot which is the closest to its goal. Robots can evaluate which is the most distant since they know their goals and the associated zones.

**Action to Help Its Worst Neighbour.** Each agent can measure the degree of difficulty it has to reach its individual goal. This measure is called criticality. When an agent receives a request from its neighbours, the request can be provided with the criticality of the sender agent. So a cooperative attitude is to try to help its neighbours which have the most difficulties to reach their goals. In fact, in doing this the satisfaction of all the agents in the system tends to be balanced. No agent is very satisfied and no agent is not satisfied at all.

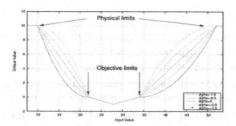

**Fig. 3.** Criticality in the MASCODE system

The criticality notion can be showed in the MASCODE system [2]. MAS-CODE is an aircraft design system which realizes multi-disicplinary and multi-objective optimisation. When designing a new aircraft, a designer defines his objective parameters, the main constraints on the design and the main expected performances. Each of these parameters are agentified. The criticality of an agent provides information on the fact that the value of the parameter (it represents) found by the agent is inside or outside the validity interval (see figure 3). With the curve of figure provided to the agent, this latter is able to compute its criticality. Within the objective limits, the agent is completely satisfied and it is not critical. Outside its physical limits, it is not at all satisfied and its criticality is equal to the maximum value.

### 4.4   Designing Self-adaptive MAS

To facilitate the design of systems based on the AMAS theory, we have proposed a methodology called ADELFE [26] and a framework called MAY[3]. These two tools will not be described here, only the main steps the designer has to follow are summarized. First of all the designer has to determine the agents and their nominal behaviour. He has also to verify which mechanism is needed and relevant i.e. he has to decide if spontaneous communication is needed. Then, he has to find for every type of agents, which NCS among the seven NCS (described in section 4.2) an agent can encounter. For every possible NCS, he has to provide a handler to treat this NCS and for every anticipated NCS, to provide a handler to avoid it. At the end, he has to explore the utility of using or not criticality notion.

All these steps are more or less simple, the expertise acquired in building AMAS systems is of course very useful to design a new system. But the main difficulty is to think "local". Because the designer knows what the collective has to do, he tends to put this knowledge inside the agents. This is the wrong way to design adaptive complex systems. Because of the difficulty to realize the global task or at the deployment phase with a great number of agents, this global knowledge is no more accessible.

## 5   Conclusion

Self-adaptive complex systems are relevant systems to cope with scalability, dynamics, difficulty to solve a problem, and under-specification. The AMAS theory, presented in this paper, is our contribution to design a class of self-adaptive systems: the self-adaptive multi-agent systems. This theory was and is also currently applied in numerous research projects but also in industrial ones: maritime surveillance, aircraft electric harness optimisation, energy management,... Future systems will be composed of systems and will be system of systems which will not be designed by the same designer. In this context, interoperability and openess will be the main future research challenges. The large scale of systems will require to find new means to evaluate and validate them. The context in which

---

[3] www.irit.fr/MAY

the system will be deployed will not be known in advance. The designer will have to tackle unanticipated adaptation. This means that he will not precisely know this context at design time. Self-adaptive complex systems should be improved to answer to these fascinating and open challenges.

**Acknowledgements.** I want to thank all members of the SMAC team: permanent researchers, students supervised in the past and ongoing PhD who contributed to the work presented in this paper.

# References

1. Lagorse, J., Paire, D., Miraou, A.: A multi-agent system for energy management of distributed power sources. Renewable Energy 35(1), 174–182 (2010)
2. Welcomme, J.B., Gleizes, M.P., Redon, R.: Adaptive multi-agent systems for multi-disciplinary design optimisation. In: 16th International Conference on Engineering Design (ICED 2007), Paris, The Design Society (2007)
3. Lacouture, J., Gascueña, J.M., Gleizes, M.-P., Glize, P., Garijo, F.J., Fernández-Caballero, A.: ROSACE: Agent-Based Systems for Dynamic Task Allocation in Crisis Management. In: Demazeau, Y., Müller, J.P., Rodríguez, J.M.C., Pérez, J.B. (eds.) Advances on PAAMS. AISC, vol. 155, pp. 255–260. Springer, Heidelberg (2012), http://www.springerlink.com
4. Mano, J.-P., Georgé, J.-P., Gleizes, M.-P.: Adaptive Multi-agent System for Multi-sensor Maritime Surveillance. In: Demazeau, Y., Dignum, F., Corchado, J.M., Pérez, J.B. (eds.) Advances in PAAMS. AISC, vol. 70, pp. 285–290. Springer, Heidelberg (2010)
5. Georgé, J.P., Camps, V., Gleizes, M.P., Glize, P.: Ambient Intelligence as a Never-Ending Self-Organizing Process: Analysis and Experiments. In: ASAMi 2007 (2007)
6. Gleizes, M.-P., Camps, V., Georgé, J.-P., Capera, D.: Engineering Systems Which Generate Emergent Functionalities. In: Weyns, D., Brueckner, S.A., Demazeau, Y. (eds.) EEMMAS 2007. LNCS (LNAI), vol. 5049, pp. 58–75. Springer, Heidelberg (2008)
7. Turner, P.J., Jennings, N.R.: Improving the Scalability of Multi-agent Systems. In: Wagner, T.A., Rana, O.F. (eds.) Infrastructure for Agents 2000. LNCS (LNAI), vol. 1887, pp. 246–262. Springer, Heidelberg (2001)
8. Videau, S., Bernon, C., Glize, P.: Towards Controlling Bioprocesses: A Self-adaptive Multi-agent Approach. Journal of Biological Physics and Chemistry 10(1), 24–32 (2010)
9. Liu, J., Jing, H., Tang, Y.Y.: Multi-agent Oriented Constraint Satisfaction. Artificial Intelligence 136(1), 101–144 (2002)
10. Di Marzo Serugendo, G., Gleizes, M.P., Karageorgos, A.: Self-Organization in Multi-Agent Systems. The Knowledge Engineering Review 20(2), 165–189 (2005)
11. Di Marzo Serugendo, G., Gleizes, M.P., Karageorgos, A. (eds.): Self-organising Software - From Natural to Artificial Adaptation. Natural Computing Series. Springer (Octobre 2011), http://www.springerlink.com
12. Zambonelli, F., Van Dyke Parunak, H.: Signs of a Revolution in Computer Science and Software Engineering. In: Petta, P., Tolksdorf, R., Zambonelli, F. (eds.) ESAW 2002. LNCS (LNAI), vol. 2577, pp. 13–28. Springer, Heidelberg (2003)

13. Robertson, P., Laddaga, R., Shrobe, H.: Introduction: The First International Workshop on Self-Adaptive Software. In: Robertson, P., Shrobe, H.E., Laddaga, R. (eds.) IWSAS 2000. LNCS, vol. 1936, pp. 1–10. Springer, Heidelberg (2001)
14. Di Marzo-Serugendo, G., Gleizes, M.P., Karageorgos, A.: Self-Organisation and Emergence in MAS: An Overview. Informatica 30(1), 45–54 (2005)
15. Georgé, J.P., Picard, G., Gleizes, M.P., Glize, P.: Living Design for Open Computational Systems. In: International Workshop on Theory and Practice of Open Computational Systems (TAPOCS) at IEEE 12th International Workshop on Enabling Technologies: Infrastructure for Collaborative Enterprises (WETICE 2003), Linz, Austria, Juin 09-Juin 11, pp. 389–394. IEEE Computer Society (2003), http://www.computer.org
16. Capera, D., Georgé, J.P., Gleizes, M.P., Glize, P.: Emergence of Organisations, Emergence of Functions. In: AISB 2003 Symposium on Adaptive Agents and Multi-Agent Systems, pp. 103–108. University of Wales, Aberystwyth, Society for the Study of Artificial Intelligence and the Simulation of Behaviour (2003)
17. Grassé, P.: La reconstruction du nid et les interactions inter-individuelles chez les bellicositermes natalenis et cubitermes sp. La théorie de la stigmergie: essai d'interprétation des termites constructeurs. Insectes Sociaux 6, 41–83 (1959)
18. Mamei, M., Zambonelli, F.: Field-based Coordination for Pervasive Multiagent Systems. Springer Series on Agent Technology (2006)
19. Jelasity, M., Voulgaris, S., Guerraoui, R., Kermarrec, A., van Steen, M.: Gossip-based peer sampling. ACM Transactions on Computer Systems 25(3) (2007)
20. Camps, V., Gleizes, M.P., Glize, P.: A self-organization process based on cooperation theory for adaptive artificial systems. In: 1st International Conference on Philosophy and Computer Science "Processes of evolution in real and Virtual Systems", Krakow, Poland (1998)
21. Gleizes, M.P., Camps, V., Glize, P.: A Theory of Emergent Computation Based on Cooperative Self-Oganization for Adaptive Artificial Systems. In: 4th European Congress of Systems Science (1999)
22. Ferber, J.: Multi-Agent Systems: An Introduction to Distributed Artificial Intelligence. Addison Wesley (1999)
23. Kaddoum, E.: Optimisation sous contraintes de problèmes distribués par auto-organisation coopérative. Thèse de doctorat, Université de Toulouse, Toulouse, France (Novembre 2011)
24. Topin, X., Fourcassié, V., Gleizes, M.P., Theraulaz, G., Régis, C.: Theories and experiments on emergent behaviour: From natural to artificial systems and back. In: European Conference on Cognitive Science, Siena (Octobre 1999)
25. Picard, G., Gleizes, M.P.: Cooperative Self-Organization to Design Robust and Adaptive Collectives. In: 2nd International Conference on Informatics in Control, Automation and Robotics (ICINCO 2005), Barcelona, Spain, September 14-17, vol. I, pp. 236–241. INSTICC Press (2005)
26. Rougemaille, S., Migeon, F., Maurel, C., Gleizes, M.P.: Model Driven Engineering for Designing Adaptive Multi-Agent Systems. In: European Workshop on Multi-Agent Systems (EUMAS), Hammamet, Décembre 13-Décembre 14. Ecole Nationale des Sciences de l'Informatique, ENSI, Tunisie (2007) (electronic medium)

# Argumentation Semantics for Agents

Cristian Gratie and Adina Magda Florea

Computer Science Department,
University "Politehnica", Bucharest, Romania

**Abstract.** The paper introduces an argumentation semantics that can
deal with several challenges that arise when using abstract argumentation within multi-agent systems. The extensions are computed with
respect to initial constraints that specify the desired justification state
of some arguments. The constraints can come from the agent's goals, its
confidence in information from other agents or they may describe a decision context, where the agent must choose between several alternatives.
The core idea behind the approach is the fact that, in order to find an
extension that satisfies the constraints, an agent needs to find a suitable
set of arguments to defeat.

We provide a full scenario where an auction for two items is modeled
as a game where the participating agents take turns at updating an argumentation framework describing the possible states of the environment
as well as the agents' intentions. The agents' goals and the consistency of
the environment's state are described with constraints. Our argumentation semantics is shown to provide a very natural strategy for the agents
playing this game. It can also be used at the end of the game for deciding
its outcome, namely the final state of the environment and the actions
of the agents.

**Keywords:** argumentation, semantics, multi-agent systems.

## 1   Introduction

Abstract argumentation was introduced by Dung [8] in 1995 and has been a
hot research topic since. Several approaches were defined in the literature for
using argumentation in artificial intelligence and several works deal with abstract
argumentation itself.

The most common approach for using argumentation with multi-agent systems relies on extending the model with some additional features that make it
more expressive for use with agents, such as preferences or values.

This paper aims to provide a different approach, by defining an argumentation
semantics that can deal with the challenges of using argumentation frameworks
in multi-agent systems. More precisely, our approach does not change the formal
model proposed by Dung, it only defines a new semantics that has properties
relevant for use in multi-agent systems.

Section 2 provides some argumentation background, together with a discussion of related work. Our approach is presented in Section 3. The details of an

M. Cossentino et al. (Eds.): EUMAS 2011, LNAI 7541, pp. 129–144, 2012.
© Springer-Verlag Berlin Heidelberg 2012

argumentation-based multi-agent system corresponding to an auction scenario is discussed in Section 4. The paper ends in Section 5 with conclusions and ideas for future research.

## 2    Argumentation Basics and Related Work

This section is focused on argumentation research that is relevant to this paper, but is also aimed at providing the reader with basic argumentation background. We start with the definition of argumentation frameworks, as introduced by Dung in [8], and the basic terminology used when talking about arguments.

**Definition 1.** *An **argumentation framework** is a pair $F = (\mathcal{A}, \mathcal{R})$, where $\mathcal{A}$ is a set of arguments and $\mathcal{R} \subseteq \mathcal{A} \times \mathcal{A}$ is a binary attack relation on $\mathcal{A}$. We say that an argument $a$ **attacks** another argument $b$ and we write this as $a \to b$ iff $(a, b) \in \mathcal{R}$. Otherwise, $a$ does not attack $b$ and we write $a \not\to b$. Also, we say that a set of arguments $S$ attacks an argument $a$ iff $S$ contains an attacker of $a$. A set of arguments $S$ **defends** an argument $a$ iff $S$ attacks all the attackers of $a$. The **characteristic function** $\mathcal{F}_F$ returns, for every set of arguments $S$, the set of arguments defended by $S$ in $F$.*

We have split the presentation of argumentation research related to our work into several subsections with respect to different facets of our approach.

### 2.1    Extension-Based Semantics

Given a set of arguments and the attack relation between them, one must be able to identify the arguments that are acceptable. Several semantics were defined in the literature for finding the extensions of an argumentation framework, namely the sets of arguments that satisfy certain properties. Definition 2 lists the semantics introduced by Dung himself in [8].

**Definition 2.** *Let $F = (\mathcal{A}, \mathcal{R})$ be an argumentation framework and let $S$ be a set of arguments.*

- *$S$ is **conflict-free** (CF) iff $S$ does not attack any of its arguments.*
- *$S$ is **admissible** (AS) iff $S$ is conflict-free and $S$ defends all its arguments.*
- *$S$ is a **complete extension** (CO) iff $S$ is admissible and it contains all the arguments it defends.*
- *$S$ is a **stable extension** (ST) iff $S$ is conflict-free and it attacks all the arguments it does not contain.*
- *$S$ is a **preferred extension** (PR) iff $S$ is a maximal (with respect to set inclusion) admissible set.*
- *$S$ is the **grounded extension** (GR) of $F$ iff $S$ is the least fixed point of the characteristic function.*

*For an argumentation semantics Sem we will use $\mathcal{E}_{Sem}$ to denote the set of all extensions prescribed by it, for example $\mathcal{E}_{CO}(F)$ stands for all the complete extensions of $F$.*

Of the six types of sets introduced in Definition 2, only the last four correspond to actual argumentation semantics, whereas the first two describe properties satisfied by almost all semantics defined in the literature. The four semantics are not independent: stable extensions are also preferred, preferred extensions are also complete and the grounded extension is the minimal (with respect to set inclusion) complete extension [8].

Several additional semantics were defined in the literature, such as: semi-stable [3], ideal [9], eager [4], prudent [6], $CF2$ [2], resolution-based grounded [1], enhanced preferred [11]. We will provide more details about the last two, as this work combines ideas from both of them.

For the resolution-based grounded semantics we introduce the corresponding terminology in Definition 3.

**Definition 3.** *Two arguments a and b are **conflicting** iff $a \to b$ or $b \to a$. For an argumentation framework F, the set of all conflicting pairs of arguments is denoted by $\mathcal{CONF}(F)$. Given two argumentation frameworks $F_1 = (\mathcal{A}_1, \mathcal{R}_1)$ and $F_2 = (\mathcal{A}_2, \mathcal{R}_2)$, we say that $F_1$ is **more skeptical** than $F_2$ and we write $F_1 \preceq F_2$ iff $\mathcal{CONF}(F_1) = \mathcal{CONF}(F_2)$ and $\mathcal{R}_2 \subseteq \mathcal{R}_1$. Two frameworks $F_1$ and $F_2$ are **comparable** (with respect to skepticism) iff $F_1 \preceq F_2$ or $F_2 \preceq F_1$. The set of maximal (with respect to $\preceq$) frameworks comparable with a given framework F is denoted with $\mathcal{RES}(F)$. The **resolution-based version** of a given argumentation semantics $\mathcal{S}em$ is defined as $\mathcal{E}_{\mathcal{S}em^*}(F) = \mathcal{MIN}(\bigcup_{F' \in \mathcal{RES}(F)} \mathcal{E}_{\mathcal{S}em}(F'))$, where $\mathcal{MIN}(X)$ denotes the minimal (with respect to set inclusion) elements of X.*

In other words, it is easy to see that an argumentation framework $F_1$ is less skeptical than a framework $F_2$ iff some of $F_2$'s mutual attacks are replaced with unidirectional attacks in $F_1$. With the terminology in [10], $F_1$ is a partial resolution of $F_2$. In a complete resolution, all mutual attacks are replaced with unidirectional ones. Thus, computing the resolution-based version of some argumentation semantics $\mathcal{S}em$ consists of taking all the complete resolutions of the argumentation framework, applying $\mathcal{S}em$ to each of them, then choosing the minimal (with respect to set inclusion) of all the resulting extensions.

In the partial resolution of an argumentation framework, some of the mutual attacks are converted to unidirectional ones, which is the same as discarding some attacks. In our approach we apply the same idea, but to arguments instead of attacks.

We now turn to the work of Zhang and Lin on enhanced preferred extensions [11]. We summarize their work in Definition 4, but using defense instead of acceptability with respect to a set.

**Definition 4.** *A pair of sets of arguments (S, H) defends an argument a iff $a \notin H$, $H \cap S = \varnothing$ and S defends a against all attacks that do not come from H. Given a framework $F = (\mathcal{A}, \mathcal{R})$ a conflict-free set of arguments S and a set of arguments H, we say that (S, H) is an **admissible pair** iff (1) $S \neq \varnothing$ or $H = \mathcal{A}$, and (2) (S, H) defends all arguments in S. A pair (S, H) is a **minimal admissible pair** if it is an admissible pair and its second element H is minimal (with respect to cardinality) among all admissible pairs. A pair (S, H) is an* *enhanced preferred extension* iff its first element $S$ is maximal (with respect to set inclusion) among all minimal admissible pairs. The first element of an enhanced preferred extension is called **proper enhanced preferred extension.**

In other words, for computing the enhanced preferred extension, admissible extensions are computed with respect to subframeworks of $F$, then the maximal extensions are picked among those of all subframeworks of maximal cardinality.

As we have already mentioned while discussing resolution-based semantics, our approach relies on ignoring arguments as well and computing a given semantics on subframeworks. However, the sets of ignored arguments are minimized with respect to set inclusion instead of cardinality, additional constraints are imposed on the pair of sets and the extensions are not maximized, nor is the second element dropped. Instead we work with several sets (we actually use labelings).

## 2.2   Argument Labelings

In this section we will focus on argument labelings, as proposed in [3]. We do this because our proposal is most intuitively expressed in terms of labelings. At the same time, using labels allows us to compare our approach with existing semantics.

**Definition 5.** *Let $F = (\mathcal{A}, \mathcal{R})$ be an argumentation framework. A **labeling** is a total function $\mathcal{L} : \mathcal{A} \to \{\text{in}, \text{out}, \text{undec}\}$. A labeling $\mathcal{L}$ is complete iff (1) an argument is labeled* in *iff all its attackers are labeled* out, *and (2) an argument is labeled* out *iff it has an attacker that is labeled* in.

Alternatively, a labeling $\mathcal{L}$ can be seen as a partition of the set of arguments into three sets $(\text{in}(\mathcal{L}), \text{out}(\mathcal{L}), \text{undec}(\mathcal{L}))$. It is shown in [3] that any complete labeling $\mathcal{L}$ is uniquely defined by either $\text{in}(\mathcal{L})$ or $\text{out}(\mathcal{L})$. For the grounded labeling, $\text{in}(\mathcal{L})$ and $\text{out}(\mathcal{L})$ are minimal, whereas $\text{undec}(\mathcal{L})$ is maximal. Preferred labelings have maximal $\text{in}(\mathcal{L})$ and $\text{out}(\mathcal{L})$, whereas the semi-stable extensions correspond to labelings that have a minimal $\text{undec}(\mathcal{L})$.

We will provide a labeling-based definition for our approach and then compare it with complete labelings in Section 3.

## 2.3   Constrained Argumentation Frameworks

Our proposal is also related to constrained argumentation frameworks [7], but we prefer to relate the constraints to the labelings rather than to the framework itself, thus obtaining parameterized semantics.

The basic idea, roughly speaking, for constrained argumentation frameworks is that the extensions are computed for regular semantics, then only the extensions satisfying the constraints are kept. We do something similar, but with labelings and we apply constraints on a general enough set of labelings so as to be able to satisfy any reasonable constraint.

# 3   Constrained Strict Semantics

In this section we introduce the constrained strict semantics, describing it in terms of labelings. In order to do this, we first enrich the usual set of labels $\{\text{in}, \text{out}, \text{undec}\}$ with an additional label, ign, which stands for arguments that are ignored.

The idea behind ignoring arguments is that a rational agent may choose to doubt some of the information it has in order to be able to take a decision or enforce one of its goals in the extensions of the corresponding argumentation framework.

**Definition 6.** *Let $F = (\mathcal{A}, \mathcal{R})$ be an argumentation framework. An **open labeling** is a mapping $\mathcal{L} : \mathcal{A} \to \{\text{in}, \text{out}, \text{undec}, \text{ign}\}$ such that:*

- *an argument is labeled* in *iff all its attackers are labeled either* out *or* ign
- *an argument is labeled* out *iff it has an attacker labeled* in

As one can see from Definition 6, the open labelings can be seen as complete labelings for subframeworks that ignore some arguments from the original framework. Note that arguments are only provisionally ignored, while computing extensions and searching for those satisfying certain constraints (as we shall see further on). In the end, however, the ignored arguments must be defeated (with new arguments, for example) so that the corresponding open labeling becomes a complete labeling of the framework. More about this aspect in Section 4.

We regard the ability to ignore arguments as a tool for being more decided about the status of the arguments that are not ignored. This leads to the definition of decided open labelings.

**Definition 7.** *An open labeling is said to be **decided** iff it has no* undec-*labeled argument.*

Let us first see that such labelings exist for any argumentation framework. Just as in [5], we will use $\text{in}(\mathcal{L})$ to stand for the set of in-labeled arguments for an open labeling $\mathcal{L}$ and so on for the other labels. A complete labeling $\mathcal{L}_c$ can thus be viewed as a partition of the set of arguments into three sets $(\text{in}(\mathcal{L}_c), \text{out}(\mathcal{L}_c), \text{undec}(\mathcal{L}_c))$, whereas an open labeling $\mathcal{L}$ corresponds to a partition into four sets $(\text{in}(\mathcal{L}), \text{out}(\mathcal{L}), \text{undec}(\mathcal{L}), \text{ign}(\mathcal{L}))$.

**Proposition 1.** *For any argumentation framework $F = (\mathcal{A}, \mathcal{R})$, the following open labelings are decided:*

*(i) $\mathcal{L} = (S, \varnothing, \varnothing, \mathcal{A} \setminus S)$, where $S$ is any conflict-free set of $F$.*
*(ii) $\mathcal{L} = (\text{in}(\mathcal{L}_c), \text{out}(\mathcal{L}_c), \varnothing, \text{undec}(\mathcal{L}_c))$, where $\mathcal{L}_c$ is any complete labeling of $F$.*

Note that applying the condition from Definition 7 to complete labelings leads to stable labelings, which may not exist for certain argumentation frameworks. So ignoring some arguments does indeed enable us to enforce stronger restrictions on the arguments that are not ignored.

Since a decided open labeling only uses three labels (in , out and ign), similarly to the complete labelings, it is natural to ask ourselves whether our approach does indeed bring something new. It may seem that decided open labelings are only able to ignore parts of a complete labeling, thus only reducing the in and out parts. We show that this is not the case.

*Example 1.* Consider the argumentation framework $F = (\mathcal{A}, \mathcal{R})$, with $\mathcal{A} = \{a, b, c\}$ and $\mathcal{R} = \{(a, b), (b, c), (c, a)\}$. Its only complete labeling is $\mathcal{L}_c = (\varnothing, \varnothing, \{a, b, c\})$. On the other hand, the framework has 7 decided labelings: $\mathcal{L}_1 = (\{a\}, \{b\}, \varnothing, \{c\})$, $\mathcal{L}_2 = (\{b\}, \{c\}, \varnothing, \{a\})$, $\mathcal{L}_3 = (\{c\}, \{a\}, \varnothing, \{b\})$, $\mathcal{L}_4 = (\{a\}, \varnothing, \varnothing, \{b, c\})$, $\mathcal{L}_5 = (\{b\}, \varnothing, \varnothing, \{a, c\})$, $\mathcal{L}_6 = (\{c\}, \varnothing, \varnothing, \{a, b\})$, $\mathcal{L}_7 = (\varnothing, \varnothing, \varnothing, \{a, b, c\})$. All labelings except the trivial $\mathcal{L}_7$ are able to accept one argument, whereas the complete labeling was undecided.

It is known that complete labelings are uniquely identified by either their in or out parts. For open labelings this is generally not the case, as for each ign part there are several complete labelings for the resulting subframework. This means that the open labelings are uniquely identified by two of their sets, either ign and in or ign and out. These observations hold even if we focus on decided labelings only. Indeed, consider the following example:

*Example 2.* Let $F = (\mathcal{A}, \mathcal{R})$, with $\mathcal{A} = \{a, b, c, d\}$ and $\mathcal{R} = \{(a, b), (b, c), (c, d), (d, a)\}$. We consider the following decided labelings: $\mathcal{L}_1 = (\{a, c\}, \{b, d\}, \varnothing, \varnothing)$, $\mathcal{L}_2 = (\{a, c\}, \{b\}, \varnothing, \{d\})$, $\mathcal{L}_3 = (\{a\}, \{b\}, \varnothing, \{c, d\})$ and $\mathcal{L}_4 = (\{b, d\}, \{a, c\}, \varnothing, \varnothing)$. Note that we have $\text{in}(\mathcal{L}_1) = \text{in}(\mathcal{L}_2)$, $\text{out}(\mathcal{L}_2) = \text{out}(\mathcal{L}_3)$ and $\text{ign}(\mathcal{L}_1) = \text{ign}(\mathcal{L}_4)$. Thus, none of the labels can uniquely identify decided labelings on its own (the undec label is not part of this discussion, as $\text{undec}(\mathcal{L}) = \varnothing$ for any decided labeling $\mathcal{L}$). On the other hand, let us see that $\mathcal{L}_2$ and $\mathcal{L}_3$ are uniquely determined by their ign parts. We consider this property useful because, given a set of such labelings, choosing the desired one only depends on choosing the arguments to ignore (and later defeat).

**Definition 8.** *An open labeling of an argumentation framework F is **unique** if no other open labeling of F has the same set of ign-labeled arguments.*

Such labelings exist for all argumentation frameworks, as the labelings from Proposition 1 (i) are also unique. In the general case, however, not all unique labelings are also decided. Indeed, consider the framework from Example 1 and notice that $\mathcal{L} = (\varnothing, \varnothing, \{a, b, c\}, \varnothing)$ is a unique but not decided open labeling of $F$.

In fact, the decided labelings correspond to stable labelings of subframeworks, whereas the unique labelings correspond to grounded labelings of subframeworks that have a single complete labeling.

**Definition 9.** *An open labeling is said to be **strict** iff it is both decided and unique.*

Again, we rely on Proposition 1 (i) to see that strict labelings exist for any argumentation framework.

We are now ready to add constraints to our labelings. The approach is similar to that used for constrained argumentation frameworks in [7] We will use $PL_S$ to denote the propositional language defined in the usual inductive way from the set of propositional symbols $S$ and the logical connectives $\top, \bot, \neg, \wedge, \vee$.

**Definition 10.** *Let $F = (\mathcal{A}, \mathcal{R})$ be an argumentation framework, $\mathcal{L}$ one of its open labelings and $\varphi \in PL_{\mathcal{A}}$. We say that $\mathcal{L}$* **satisfies** *$\varphi$ and write $\mathcal{L} \vDash \varphi$, where satisfiability is recursively defined for each formula as follows:*

- $\mathcal{L} \vDash \top$
- $\mathcal{L} \nvDash \bot$
- $\mathcal{L} \vDash a$ *iff $a \in \mathsf{in}(\mathcal{L})$, for all $a \in \mathcal{A}$*
- $\mathcal{L} \vDash \neg a$ *iff $a \in \mathsf{out}(\mathcal{L})$ or $a \in \mathsf{ign}(\mathcal{L})$, for all $a \in \mathcal{A}$*
- $\mathcal{L} \vDash \phi \wedge \psi$ *iff $\mathcal{L} \vDash \phi$ and $\mathcal{L} \vDash \psi$, for all $\phi \in PL_{\mathcal{A}}$ and $\psi \in PL_{\mathcal{A}}$*
- $\mathcal{L} \vDash \phi \vee \psi$ *iff $\mathcal{L} \vDash \phi$ or $\mathcal{L} \vDash \psi$, for all $\phi \in PL_{\mathcal{A}}$ and $\psi \in PL_{\mathcal{A}}$*

Note that in Definition 10 there is no rule for arbitrary negations, but only for negated propositional symbols. This is because the negation of a propositional symbol does not only mean that the corresponding argument is not **in**, but also that it is not **undec**. We have chosen this approach because we consider that it makes little sense to actually want an argument to be undecided. Whenever writing constraints, we will make sure that all negations are applied to propositional symbols.

The interesting question is whether, given a formula $\varphi$, there is an open labeling that satisfies it. Clearly this is not possible for inconsistent formulas. Furthermore, consistency of a formula should also be related in some way to the attack relation, as it is clearly not possible to have both an argument and its attacker marked as **in**, for example.

**Definition 11.** *Let $F = (\mathcal{A}, \mathcal{R})$ be an argumentation framework and $\varphi \in PL_{\mathcal{A}}$ a satisfiable formula. We say that $\varphi$ is* **consistent with** *$F$ iff the set of formulas $\{\varphi\} \cup \{\neg a \vee \neg b \mid (a, b) \in \mathcal{R}\}$ is satisfiable.*

Satisfiability in Definition 11 refers to the usual satisfiability in propositional logic and is not connected to labelings. Whenever we talk about satisfiability with respect to labelings, we will explicitly say that the formula is satisfied by a labeling, to avoid any confusion.

**Proposition 2.** *A satisfiable formula $\varphi$ is consistent with an argumentation framework $F$ iff its disjunctive normal form contains at least one conjunction whose positive literals correspond to the elements of a conflict-free set of $F$.*

*Proof.* For the "$\Leftarrow$" part, suppose that the disjunctive normal form of $\varphi$ contains the conjunction $\psi = a_1 \wedge \ldots \wedge a_n \wedge \neg b_1 \wedge \ldots \wedge \neg b_k$ such that the set $S = \{a_1, \ldots, a_n\}$ is a conflict-free set of $F$. We assign $a_i = \top$ for all $i$'s and we assign $\bot$ to all the other arguments. This assignment is correct because the $a$'s and the $b$'s are distinct, as a result of the fact that $\varphi$ is satisfiable. Suppose that there is a formula $\neg a \vee \neg b$ that corresponds to an attack in $\mathcal{R}$ and is not satisfied. That would mean that both $a$ and $b$ are true and, thus, are elements of the conflict-free set $S$. But then they cannot attack one another, which contradicts our assumption. We can conclude that $\varphi$ is consistent with $F$.

For the "$\Rightarrow$" part, consider a truth assignment that satisfies $\varphi$. Then the disjunctive normal form of $\varphi$ contains at least one conjunction that is satisfied. The positive literals of that conjunction correspond to a conflict-free set, because otherwise there would be an attack whose corresponding formula is not satisfied, which would in turn violate the fact that $\varphi$ is consistent with $F$. This completes our proof.                                                                                    □

Note that, as a term in some conjunction of the disjunctive normal form of a formula, $\top$ corresponds to the empty set, which is a conflict-free set of every framework. This is in accordance with the expected fact that $\top$ is consistent with every framework.

We are now ready for the main theoretical result of this paper, namely the existence of strict labelings satisfying any reasonable constraint.

**Proposition 3.** *Any formula $\varphi$ that is consistent with an argumentation framework $F$ is satisfied by at least one strict labeling of $F$.*

*Proof.* From Proposition 2 we have that the disjunctive normal form of $\varphi$ contains a conjunction $\psi = a_1 \wedge \ldots \wedge a_n \wedge \neg b_1 \wedge \ldots \wedge \neg b_k$ such that the set $S = \{a_1, \ldots, a_n\}$ is a conflict-free set of $F$. We denote $B = \{b_1, \ldots, b_k\}$. Let $T = \{b \mid \exists a(a \in S \wedge (b, a) \in \mathcal{R})\}$, the set of arguments that attack elements of $S$. Let $\mathcal{L}_{gr}$ denote the grounded labeling of the restricted argumentation framework $F \downarrow_{A \setminus (B \cup T)}$, where $F \downarrow_X = (X, \mathcal{R} \cap (X \times X))$. We consider the open labeling $\mathcal{L} = (\text{in}(\mathcal{L}_{gr}), \text{out}(\mathcal{L}_{gr}), \varnothing, \text{undec}(\mathcal{L}_{gr}) \cup B \cup T)$.

First, let us see that $S \subseteq \text{in}(\mathcal{L}_{gr})$. Indeed, since all attackers of arguments from $S$ were ignored, all elements of $S$ are unattacked in the restricted framework so they must be part of the grounded extension. Coupled with the fact that all arguments in $B$ are ignored, this leads to the fact that $\mathcal{L}$ satisfies $\psi$ and hence it satisfies $\varphi$ as well.

What is left to show is that $\mathcal{L}$ is indeed a strict labeling. Since the **in** and **out** parts come from $\mathcal{L}_{gr}$, the labeling satisfies the conditions for an open labeling. Also, the **in** and **out** arguments of the grounded labeling form a subframework that allows no other complete labeling, so $\mathcal{L}$ is unique. Since $\text{undec}(\mathcal{L}) = \varnothing$, $\mathcal{L}$ is also decided and thus strict.                                                                                    □

The result of Proposition 3 is quite strong as it shows that, given any reasonable constraints, one can find strict labelings that satisfy them. This is the most important feature that distinguishes our work from the constrained argumentation frameworks in [7].

Since there may still be several labelings to choose from, we can refine the approach even more and finally define the constrained strict labelings.

**Definition 12.** *A **constrained strict labeling** of an argumentation framework $F$ with respect to a formula $\varphi$ that is consistent with $F$ is a strict open labeling*

$\mathcal{L}$ that satisfies $\varphi$ and has $\mathrm{ign}(\mathcal{L})$ minimal (with respect to set inclusion) among all strict open labelings that satisfy $\varphi$.

The intuition behind Definition 12 is that one should decide the status of as many arguments as possible, while not violating the constraint $\varphi$ or the restrictions of strict labelings.

# 4   Constrained Argumentation Game

In this section we show that the constrained strict semantics is relevant for the multi-agent systems community by introducing an argumentation-based game featuring agents. We instantiate the approach by modeling a special auction scenario and we show how desired features of the scenario can be mapped into game elements.. At the end of the section we discuss the critical role that the constrained strict semantics plays for this game.

## 4.1   Auction Scenario

The example scenario that we will translate into a constrained argumentation game consists in a special kind of multiple items auction. To keep things simple, we will use an unspecified currency (just a positive integer). We will consider just three persons in our scenario: Anthony, Brian and Carol.

Anthony has two old pieces of furniture, a chair and a table, that he would like to sell. Since he has been a collector for quite some time now, he is rather good at appraising antiques so he knows that the chair values 200, while the table values 300. Anthony is determined to get at least these prices or keep the items. Anthony is familiar with most types of auctions, but he would like a bit more control over the outcome, so he organizes a special kind of auction.

The auction starts with Anthony announcing the rules, the items for sale and the minimum prices. To avoid any suspicions, the bidding process is public, spoken out loud. In a round-robin order, each participant can place, update or retract bids for any of the items that are put up for sale. Anthony can benefit from auctioning both items at the same time, as he is part of the auction himself and, on his turn, he reserves the right to impose additional restrictions or, on the contrary, relax some constraints. Each participant may also choose to pass, if satisfied with the current outcome (unless other restrictions are applicable, the highest bidder for each item wins that item). The auction ends when all participants pass.

We assume, for simplicity, that only two potential buyers show up for the auction: Brian and Carol. Brian is rather rich and knows very little about antiques, so he is willing to pay even twice their value: 400 for the chair and 600 for the table. However, he is determined to either get both items or none of them. That is why he likes Anthony's idea of an auction: he does not risk buying the first item only to find himself unable to acquire the second as well. Carol, on the other hand, has more limited resources so she cannot afford both items. However, she would really like acquiring one of them. She is willing to pay 300 for the chair and 500 for the table.

In the following subsections we will translate this auction scenario step by step into a turn-based game featuring agents that work with an abstract argumentation framework and constraints.

## 4.2   Arguments for the Environment

We start by discussing the environment of the multi-agent system and its representation using arguments. We will use a first order language containing predicates for various aspects of possible states of the environment and constants for the relevant objects. For our particular scenario, we have two items (*chair* and *table*) and three agents (*Anthony*, *Brian* and *Carol*).

The only relevant outcome of our auction is the final owner of each item. First, we consider the (rather naive) approach of assigning a first-order formula for each possible state: $s_1 = has(Anthony, chair) \wedge has(Anthony, table)$, $s_2 = has(Anthony, chair) \wedge has(Brian, table)$, and so on, for a total of $3^2 = 9$ states. We can read these states as arguments, deduce that no two of them can hold at the same time and decide to add attacks between all pairs of arguments. In order to ensure that any extension of the framework does select a state, we can add the constraint $\phi_{\mathcal{E}} = s_1 \vee \ldots \vee s_9$ and use strict constrained labelings. Since $\phi_{\mathcal{E}}$ can be satisfied, the corresponding strict constrained labelings ignore no argument so they are in effect complete labelings. Each of the 9 possible states forms a singleton complete extension. This representation, although semantically reasonable, is exponential in the number of items.

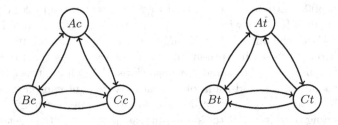

**Fig. 1.** State arguments for the auction example

We can come up, on the other hand, with an approach that is linear in the number of items. Indeed, it is rather easy to see that our states depend on two distinguishable parameters, the owners of each item. Thus, we can use just the following arguments: $Ac = has(Anthony, chair)$, $At = has(Anthony, table)$, $Bc = has(Brian, chair)$, $Bt = has(Brian, table)$, $Cc = has(Carol, chair)$ and $Ct = has(Carol, table)$. A suitable and intuitive framework for this case is the one in Figure 1, in conjunction with the following constraint: $\phi_{\mathcal{E}} = (Ac \vee Bc \vee Cc) \wedge (At \vee Bt \vee Ct)$. The constraint ensures that each item will have at least one owner, whereas the attacks between the states enforce at most one owner, thus leading to the desirable outcome that each item has exactly one owner. Let us note that the number of possible states is again given by the number of complete labelings, but this time each extension has exactly two elements.

## 4.3    Action and Reaction

We will use first order predicates to talk about actions as well. In fact, since our auction is more like a negotiation game, what we talk about are intentions of taking some action. We will see them as action arguments, to distinguish them from those describing the environment, which we shall call state arguments.

In our scenario, the only possible action consists in placing a bid for an item, for example $bids(table, 350)$. Such actions will be annotated with the name of the agent performing them, as in $Carol : bids(table, 350)$. The implicit attacks between such arguments come from the fact that a higher bid on the same item is preferred to a lower one.

Furthermore, actions may have an impact on the state of the environment. For example, the bid $Carol : bids(table, 350)$, if highest, should imply that Carol becomes the owner of the table. For this, we should have the following attacks: $Carol : bids(table, 350) \rightarrow At$ and $Carol : bids(table, 350) \rightarrow Bt$. We assume that such implicit attacks are common knowledge for all the participants at the auction.

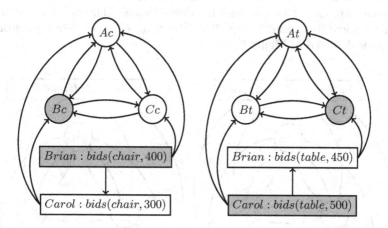

**Fig. 2.** Simple bid scenario on top of the initial environment representation. Grayed arguments form the only complete extension of the framework.

The framework in Figure 2 describes a possible moment from our auction. The grayed arguments form the only complete extension of the framework which, in addition, satisfies the environment constraint formula from the previous subsection. We will say that the extension is a valid outcome of the framework. Should this be the final state of the framework, it would mean that Brian is bound to pay 400 for the chair and Carol should pay 500 for the table. The resulting state after these actions would be the one also described by the extension, where the winning bidders actually get the items they pay for. But more about commitment and the outcome of a game later on.

## 4.4   Beliefs, Desires, Intentions

In this subsection we explore the role that beliefs, desires and intentions play
in our model. While there is no one-to-one correspondence, we have several
mechanisms that can help. First of all, let us see that the action arguments can
be seen as intentions, or even plans, of the agents. They turn into actions only
once an extension is chosen as the outcome of the framework.

Another mechanism consists in restricting the action arguments that are available to each agent. This can help us express the desires of the agent (the agent
only considers the actions it would do) but it may also describe the abilities
of the agent (some agents may have a smaller set of abilities with respect to
others). In our case, we have that Brian's actions range from $bids(chair, 1)$
to $bids(chair, 400)$ and from $bids(table, 1)$ to $bids(table, 600)$, while Carol's actions range from $bids(chair, 1)$ to $bids(chair, 300)$ and from $bids(table, 1)$ to
$bids(table, 500)$.

We also know that Carol can only afford one item. In order to say this, we
will add attacks between Carol's bid for the chair and her bid for the table. Furthermore, Anthony wants some minimum price for each item. We can simulate
this by having him bid as well, with the desired values. Thus, if he is the highest
bidder for some item, that item will not be sold. The complete framework for
this case is depicted in Figure 3.

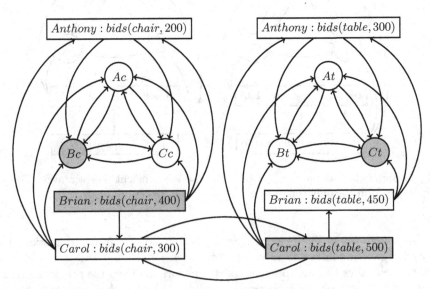

**Fig. 3.** Complete bid scenario extended from Figure 2. Grayed arguments form the
only complete extension of the framework.

The goals of the agents can be expressed by means of constraints. Brian's
desire to buy either both items or none can be expressed by $\phi_{Brian} = Bc \wedge$
$Bt \vee \neg Bc \wedge \neg Bt$. Carol's wish to buy one of the items can be expressed by

$\phi_{Carol} = Cc \lor Ct$. Anthony's wish to sell both items can be written as $\phi_{Anthony} = \neg Ac \land \neg At$. We can see in Figure 3 that the only complete extension does satisfy the environment constraint, but does not satisfy Brian's.

Beliefs may also be encoded by means of additional state arguments that are not common knowledge, but are private to one or several agents. The agent may choose to disclose such information or not. For example, Carol may wish to debate the authenticity of the table. For this, she may provide the state arguments $auth(table)$ and $\neg auth(table)$, each attacking the other, then also add an action argument defeating the former: $Carol : newPaint(table) \to auth(table)$. It may also be implied that Anthony is no longer able to sell the table or that he must settle for a lower price. We will not detail this spin-off here, as it is not part of the initial scenario.

## 4.5    The Outcome of Changing the World

What we have seen so far is that the instantaneous state of the game can be described using an argumentation framework plus constraints. But we have said nothing about moving from one state to the other or about how the framework actually changes.

The auction will run as a turn-based game. During its turn, each agent can change the current argumentation framework so that it satisfies its goals (described with the corresponding constraint formula). However, not everything can be changed, as we shall see.

First of all, an agent is free to retract any of its own action arguments (intentions) or to add new ones to the framework Furthermore, each agent may have some influence on some of the state arguments. To maintain a unified approach, we shall assume that for each agent we can define the set of arguments it can control and that the set always includes its own actions. Now, given an argument it can control, an agent may add or remove attacks against it in order to express certain states of affairs. Let us explain this on our auction example.

All state arguments in our scenario are controlled by Anthony, since he is the one organizing the auction. This means that, if he so chooses, Anthony may change the rules of the game, for example by adding or removing attacks between state arguments. If Anthony prefers Carol to Brian, he may choose to favor her by removing the attacks $Bc \to Cc$ and $Bt \to Ct$. Thus, whenever both Carol and Brian might win, Carol will be preferred.

The bidding agents, each during its own turn, may change their bid on some of the items. They will generally do so by looking at the outcome of the current framework. From a strategical perspective, constrained strict labelings are fit for this task, because the agents may use their goals as constraints and find minimal sets of arguments that are to be attacked. From the arguments they have available, they may then choose which of them to put forward or in what way to change the framework.

The outcome of an instantaneous configuration, as well as the outcome of the game's final configuration, consists in the choice of a constrained extension of the framework, using an algorithm that is known to all participants of the game in advance, for example the constrained strict semantics. If all agents strive to maintain the environment constraint satisfiable at all times by a complete labeling, then at the end of the game this will also hold so none of the arguments will need to be ignored.

Let us consider the example in Figure 3 again and see how that configuration looks for each of the participants and what might be their next move, were it to be their turn. The only complete labeling is the one depicted in the figure and it also satisfies the environment constraint. Anthony gets to sell both items, so his goal is fulfilled. Thus, Anthony will pass. So will Carol, whose goal is to obtain one of the objects. However, this configuration is not good for Brian, who wishes either both objects or none.

What Brian must do in this case is recompute the open labelings using both the environment constraint and his own goal. In this case he will end up with sets of arguments to ignore. All such sets that contain arguments that Brian himself cannot control are to be discarded. He may then choose between remaining alternatives, if any.

In the particular case of Figure 3, Brian may notice that a simple solution to his problem consists in ignoring Carol's bid. Since actually ignoring it is not an option, Brian must defeat it. For this, it is enough to put forward a higher bid for the table.

### 4.6   End of the Game and Commitment

We have seen that the game proceeds in turn-based fashion, each agent changing the current configuration to better fulfill its goals. Whenever an agent is satisfied with the current configuration, or has no available action arguments to put forward for producing a favorable change, the agent will pass. The game ends after every agent has passed in a full round.

Once the game has reached its final configuration, all agents are committed to fulfill their intentions executing the corresponding actions. In doing so, the environment will also enter the state described by the chosen extension of the argumentation framework for the configuration.

An additional challenge for such a game is to arrange the initial configuration in such a way as to describe the actual initial state. In our auction scenario, instead of letting all states be acceptable, one might add Anthony's arguments so that the ownership of the items can only be his in acceptable extensions of the initial framework.

### 4.7   Discussion

We will end this section with a discussion of the relevance of constrained strict labelings for the presented argumentation-based multi-agent system. These extensions may play a part at the end of the game, where a suitable outcome is to be chosen. Since the environment constraint must be satisfied, in more liberal games, where it is not enforced at all points, it may be needed to ignore some of the arguments at the end of the game.

On the other hand, for the outcome algorithm it might be better to consider frameworks where there is a single extension satisfying the environment constraint. Of course, it may be declared in the beginning of such a game that some semantics that provides multiple extensions will be used and that the result will be undecided if several extensions are available. Thus, this may work as an incentive for participants that would not be satisfied with an undecided negotiation to work towards reaching a final state that has a single extension.

The most important part where our semantics can undoubtedly be put to good use is the agent's strategy for executing its move. At that point, the agent may use the same semantics as the one used for the game outcome, but update the constraint to include its own goals thus identifying arguments that are to be attacked or ignored. It is important that all the arguments found in the chosen ignored set can actually be controlled or attacked by the agent.

## 5   Conclusions

We have introduced a new argumentation semantics, based on labelings, which allows us to impose constraints on the labelings. We have proved that for any reasonable constraint we get at least one constrained strict labeling and we have shown how to use these labelings in an agent setting.

We have provided a detailed scenario that can be modeled as a multi-agent system based on argumentation where our semantics can play a significant part in determining the next move for each agent. The proposal is a significant contribution in itself, as it provides an alternative approach for using argumentation in multi-agent systems. Future work will compare our turn-based game with other approaches in the literature.

It would be interesting to analyze the proposed semantics with respect to its computational complexity, this being an important goal of future research, as the applicability of our approach in real multi-agent systems strongly depends on this.

**Acknowledgement.** This work has been funded by the Sectoral Operational Programme Human Resources Development 2007-2013 of the Romanian Ministry of Labour, Family and Social Protection through the Financial Agreement POSDRU/88/1.5/S/61178 and by project ERRIC (Empowering Romanian Research on Intelligent Information Technologies), number 264207/FP7-REGPOT-2010-1. We would like to thank the reviewers for their useful comments that have helped us improve this paper.

## References

1. Baroni, P., Giacomin, M.: Resolution-based argumentation semantics. In: Proceedings of the 2nd Conference on Computational Models of Argument (COMMA 2008), Tolouse, France, pp. 25–36 (2008)
2. Baroni, P., Giacomin, M., Guida, G.: SCC-recursiveness: a general schema for argumentation semantics. Artificial Intelligence 168(1-2), 162–210 (2005)

3. Caminada, M.: Semi-stable semantics. In: Dunne, P.E., Bench-Capon, T.J.M. (eds.) Computational Models of Argument: Proceedings of COMMA 2006, September 11-12. Frontiers in Artificial Intelligence and Applications, vol. 144, pp. 121–130. IOS Press (2006)
4. Caminada, M.: Comparing two unique extension semantics for formal argumentation: Ideal and eager. In: Proceedings of the 19th Benelux Conference on Artificial Intelligence (BNAIC 2007), pp. 81–87 (2007)
5. Caminada, M., Gabbay, D.: A logical account of formal argumentation. Studia Logica 93(2), 109–145 (2009)
6. Coste-Marquis, S., Devred, C., Marquis, P.: Prudent semantics for argumentation frameworks. In: Proceedings of the 17th IEEE International Conference on Tools with Artificial Intelligence (ICTAI 2005), Hong-Kong, China, pp. 568–572 (2005)
7. Coste-Marquis, S., Devred, C., Marquis, P.: Constrained argumentation frameworks. In: Proceedings of the 10th International Conference on Practices in Knowledge Representation and Reasoning, pp. 112–122 (2006)
8. Dung, P.M.: On the acceptability of arguments and its fundamental role in non-monotonic reasoning, logic programming and n-person games. Artificial Intelligence 77(2), 321–357 (1995)
9. Dung, P.M., Mancarella, P., Toni, F.: Computing ideal sceptical argumentation. Artificial Intelligence 171(10-15), 642–674 (2007)
10. Modgil, S.: Hierarchical Argumentation. In: Fisher, M., van der Hoek, W., Konev, B., Lisitsa, A. (eds.) JELIA 2006. LNCS (LNAI), vol. 4160, pp. 319–332. Springer, Heidelberg (2006)
11. Zhang, Z., Lin, Z.: Enhancing Dung's Preferred Semantics. In: Link, S., Prade, H. (eds.) FoIKS 2010. LNCS, vol. 5956, pp. 58–75. Springer, Heidelberg (2010)

# Multi-agent Learning
# and the Reinforcement Gradient

Michael Kaisers, Daan Bloembergen, and Karl Tuyls

Department of Knowledge Engineering, Maastricht University

**Abstract.** This article shows that seemingly diverse implementations of multi-agent reinforcement learning share the same basic building block in their learning dynamics: a mathematical term that is closely related to the gradient of the expected reward. Gradient Ascent on the expected reward has been used to derive strong convergence results in two-player two-action games, at the expense of strong assumptions such as full information on the game that is being played. Variations of Gradient Ascent, such as *Infinitesimal Gradient Ascent* (IGA), *Win-or-Learn-Fast* IGA, and *Weighted Policy Learning* (WPL), assume a known value function for which the reinforcement gradient can be computed directly. In contrast, independent multi-agent reinforcement learning algorithms that assume less information on the game being played such as *Cross learning*, variations of *Q-learning* and *Regret minimization* base their learning on feedback from discrete interactions with the environment, requiring neither an explicit representation of the value function nor its gradient. Despite this much stricter limitation on information available to these algorithms, they yield dynamics which are very similar to Gradient Ascent and exhibit equivalent convergence behavior. In addition to the formal derivation, directional field plots of the learning dynamics in representative classes of two-player two-action games illustrate the similarities and strengthen the theoretical findings.

## 1  Introduction

Recent multi-agent learning survey papers and publications at agents and machine learning conferences make clear that the number of newly proposed multi-agent learning algorithms is constantly growing. Many domain-specific problems are tackled by modifying or refining the learning algorithms in question for the task at hand. An overview of well-established multi-agent learning algorithms with their various purposes is given in [5]; it demonstrates the need for a comprehensive understanding of their similarities and differences. The diversity of learning algorithms makes it imperative to specify the assumptions (*learning bias*) which precede any discussion [6]. Within the scope of this article, agents can only observe their own actions and payoffs (i.e., learning with *Minimal Information*).

Q-learning has been linked to a dynamical system which allows decomposing the learning dynamics into exploitation and exploration terms [20]. This reveals that the exploitation terms, which move the behavior toward higher payoff, are

M. Cossentino et al. (Eds.): EUMAS 2011, LNAI 7541, pp. 145–159, 2012.
© Springer-Verlag Berlin Heidelberg 2012

equivalent to Cross Learning as described in [3]. The remaining terms allow for inferior strategies to be explored. This article extends this decomposition, and further relates Cross Learning to the most fundamental concept of learning to increase payoff – learning along the reinforcement gradient.

Specifically, two independent branches of multi-agent learning research can be distinguished based on their respective assumptions and premises. The first branch assumes that the value function of the game is known to all players, which is then used to update the learning policy based on *Gradient Ascent*. Notable algorithms in this branch include Infinitesimal Gradient Ascent (IGA) [17], the variation Win or Learn Fast IGA (WoLF) [4] and the Weighted Policy Learner [1]. The second branch of multi-agent learning is concerned with learning in unknown environments, using interaction-based *Reinforcement Learning*, and contains those algorithms which have been shown to be formally connected to the replicator equations of *Evolutionary Game Theory*. In this case, the learning agent updates its policy based on a sequence of ⟨*action, reward*⟩ pairs that indicate the quality of the actions taken. Notable algorithms include Cross Learning [7], Regret Minimization [13], and variations of Q-learning [11,21]. This article demonstrates inherent similarities between these diverse families of algorithms by comparing their underlying learning dynamics, derived as the continuous time limit of their policy updates. These dynamics have already been investigated for algorithms from each family separately [1,3,4,11,13,17], however, they have not yet been discussed in context of the relation to each other, and the origin of their similarity has not been discussed satisfactorily.

The remainder of this article is structured as follows: Section 2 formally introduces Gradient Ascent, Reinforcement Learning, and the concepts of Evolutionary Game Theory that are used in the analysis. This analysis is presented in Section 3 and starts with a comparison of the evolutionary dynamics of reinforcement learning. Representative two-player two-action games serve as an illustrative example for the comparison of these dynamics to gradient ascent. This comparison is then generalized to two-player normal form games. Section 4 emphasizes the practical differences between reinforcement learning and gradient ascent, and sketches the merits of evolutionary game theory. Finally, Section 5 concludes the article.

## 2  Background

This section provides an overview of the basic concepts of Gradient Ascent, Reinforcement Learning, and Evolutionary Game Theory, that are necessary to understand the remainder of this paper. This overview is not meant to be complete; references are provided for those readers that want to delve deeper into these diverse fields.

### 2.1  Gradient Ascent

The idea of gradient ascent (or decent) is a well known optimization technique in the field of Machine Learning. If an appropriate objective function can be defined, the learning process can be directed in the direction of its gradient in order to find an optimum. This concept can be adapted for multi-agent learning by having the learning agents' policies follow the gradient of their expected payoff. Naturally, this approach assumes that the expected payoff function is known to the learners, which is not generally feasible in practice.

One algorithm that implements gradient ascent is **Infinitesimal Gradient Ascent** (IGA) [17], in which a learner updates its policy by taking infinitesimal steps in the direction of the gradient of its expected payoff. It has been proven that in two-player two-action games IGA either converges to a Nash equilibrium or the asymptotic expected payoff of the two players converges to the expected payoff of a Nash equilibrium. A discrete time algorithms using a finite decreasing step size is shown to share these properties as well.

A learner's policy $\pi(t) = \{\pi_1, \pi_2, \ldots, \pi_n\}$ denotes a probability distribution over its $n$ possible actions at time $t$, where $\pi_i$ is the probability of selecting action $i$, i.e., $\forall i : 0 \leq \pi_i \leq 1$, and $\sum_i \pi_i = 1$. Take $V(\pi) : \mathbb{R}^n \to \mathbb{R}$ to be the value function that maps a policy to its expected payoff. The policy update rule for IGA can now be defined as

$$\Delta\pi_i(t) \leftarrow \alpha \frac{\partial V(\pi(t))}{\partial \pi_i(t)}$$

$$\pi_i(t+1) \leftarrow projection(\pi_i(t) + \Delta\pi_i(t)) \tag{1}$$

where $\alpha$ denotes the learning step size. The intended change $\Delta\pi(t)$ may take $\pi$ outside of the valid policy space, in which case it is projected back to the nearest valid policy by the *projection* function.

**Win or Learn Fast.** (WoLF) [4] is a variation on IGA which uses a variable learning rate. The intuition behind this scheme is that an agent should adapt quickly if it is performing worse than expected, whereas it should be more cautious when it is winning. The modified learning rule of IGA-WoLF is

$$\Delta\pi_i(t) \leftarrow \frac{\partial V(\pi(t))}{\partial \pi_i(t)} \begin{cases} \alpha_{min} & \text{if } V(\pi(t)) > V(\pi^*) \\ \alpha_{max} & \text{otherwise} \end{cases}$$

$$\pi_i(t+1) \leftarrow projection(\pi_i(t) + \Delta\pi_i(t)) \tag{2}$$

where $\pi^*$ is an arbitrary Nash equilibrium policy. This means that, next to the assumption that the value function is known to all agents, WoLF also assumes that the agents have knowledge of at least one strategy which is part of a Nash equilibrium of the learning problem.

The **Weighted Policy Learner** (WPL) [1] is a second variation of IGA that also modulates the learning rate, but in contrast to WoLF-IGA does not require knowledge of Nash equilibria. The update rule of WPL is defined as

$$\Delta\pi_i(t) \leftarrow \alpha \frac{\partial V(\pi(t))}{\partial \pi_i(t)} \begin{cases} \pi_i(t) & \text{if } \frac{\partial V(\pi(t))}{\partial \pi_i(t)} < 0 \\ 1 - \pi_i(t) & \text{otherwise} \end{cases}$$

$$\pi_i(t+1) \leftarrow projection(\pi_i(t) + \Delta\pi_i(t)) \tag{3}$$

where the update is weighted either by $\pi_i$ or by $1 - \pi_i$ depending on the sign of the gradient. This means that $\pi$ is driven away from the boundaries of the policy space. The *projection* function is slightly different from IGA, in that the policy is projected to the closest valid policy that lies at distance $\epsilon$ within the boundary of the policy space. Note that while WPL does not require the Nash equilibria to be known, it still requires that the gradient of the value function is known.

## 2.2   Reinforcement Learning

Reinforcement Learning starts from a different premise than gradient ascent. Instead of assuming full knowledge of the value function, a reinforcement learning agent learns from scratch by repeatedly interacting with its environment. After taking an action, the agent perceives the resulting state of the environment and receives a reward that captures the desirability of that state and the cost of the action. While the single-agent reinforcement learning problem is well defined as a Markov decision process, the multi-agent case is more complex. As state transitions and rewards are influenced by the joint action of all agents, the Markov property is no longer satisfied from a single agents' point of view. In essence, each agent is chasing its optimal policy, which depends on what the other agents do – and since they change as well, all agents chase a moving target. Nevertheless, single-agent reinforcement learning algorithms have been shown to produce good results in the multi-agent case [5]. Three independent reinforcement algorithms are selected for this article: the policy iterator Cross Learning; and the value iterators Regret Minimization and Q-learning.

This article considers the special case of stateless reinforcement learning, which facilitates the analysis of the algorithms and enables natural comparison to the similarly stateless gradient ascent algorithms. One of the most basic reinforcement learning algorithms is **Cross Learning** [3,7], which updates its policy $\pi$ based on the reward $r$ received after taking action $j$:

$$\pi_i(t+1) \leftarrow \begin{cases} r(t) + [1 - r(t)]\,\pi_i(t) & \text{if } i = j \\ [1 - r(t)]\,\pi_i(t) & \text{otherwise} \end{cases} \qquad (4)$$

In this case, no projection function is needed as a valid policy is ensured by the update rule as long as the rewards are normalized, i.e., $0 \leq r \leq 1$. Cross Learning is closely related to Finite Action-set Learning Automata (FALA) [15,19]. In particular, it is equivalent to a learning automaton with a linear reward-inaction ($L_{R-I}$) scheme and a learning step size of 1.

The notion of **Regret Minimization** (RM) forms the basis for a different type of reinforcement learning algorithms. In the Polynomial Weights algorithm [2], the learner calculates the loss $l_i$ of taking action $i$ rather than the best action in hindsight as $l_i = r^* - r$ where $r$ is the reward received, and $r^*$ is the optimal reward. The learner maintains a set of weights $w$ for its actions, updates these weights according to the perceived loss, and derives a new policy by normalization:

$$\begin{pmatrix} A_{11}, B_{11} & A_{12}, B_{12} \\ A_{21}, B_{21} & A_{22}, B_{22} \end{pmatrix}$$

**Fig. 1.** General payoff bi-matrix (A, B) for two-player two-action games

$$w_i(t+1) \leftarrow w_i(t)\left[1 - \alpha l_i(t)\right]$$
$$\pi_i = \frac{w_i}{\sum_j w_j} \tag{5}$$

Like Cross Learning, this algorithm ensures a valid policy as long as the rewards are normalized. There is however a difference in information requirements: Regret Minimization requires to know the optimal reward in hindsight.

Arguably the best-known reinforcement learning algorithm is **Q-learning**. Q-learning estimates the expected discounted future reward achievable for every action from the learner's current state [21]. In the stateless learning problem, learning the expected discounted future reward is equivalent to learning the expected instantaneous reward. The action-value function $Q$ is updated at each step according to

$$Q_i(t+1) \leftarrow Q_i(t) + \alpha\left[r(t) - Q_i(t)\right] \tag{6}$$

after which a new policy can be derived. Various schemes exist to derive the policy, which mainly differ in the way they balance exploration and exploitation. The Boltzmann scheme [18] allows controlling this balance using a temperature parameter $\tau$:

$$\pi_i = \frac{e^{Q_i \cdot \tau^{-1}}}{\sum_j e^{Q_j \cdot \tau^{-1}}} \tag{7}$$

A high temperature promotes exploration, whereas a low temperature favors exploitation and generates a close-to-greedy policy. Q-learning using the Boltzmann scheme ensures a valid policy independent of the reward range, and does not require the reward function to be known.

## 2.3   Evolutionary Game Theory

Game theory models strategic interactions in the form of games. Each player has a set of actions, and a preference over the joint action space which is captured in the numerical payoff signal. For two-player games, the payoffs can be represented by a bi-matrix $(A, B)$, that gives the payoff for the row player in $A$, and the column player in $B$ (see Figure 1). In this example, the row player chooses one of the two rows, the column player chooses on of the columns, and the outcome of this joint action determines the payoff to both. The goal for each player is to come up with a strategy (a probability distribution over its actions) that maximizes its expected payoff in the game.

It is assumed that the players are hyper-rational, in the sense that each player purely tries to maximize its own payoff, and assumes the others are doing likewise. Under this assumption, the Nash equilibrium prescribes what players will reasonably choose to do. A set of strategies forms a Nash equilibrium if no single player can do better by unilaterally switching to a different strategy [8]. In other words, each strategy in a Nash equilibrium is a best response against all other strategies in that Nash equilibrium.

Classical game theory requires that full information about the game is available to each player, which together with the assumption of hyper-rationality does not reflect the dynamical nature of most real world environments [9]. Evolutionary Game Theory (EGT) replaces the assumption of rationality by concepts like natural selection and mutation from evolutionary biology [14]. Since EGT relies on relaxed assumptions, it provides a solid basis to study the decision making process of bounded rational players in an uncertain environment.

Central to evolutionary game theory are the replicator dynamics, that describe how a population of candidate strategies evolves over time. Suppose that each player is represented by a population consisting of pure strategies. The fact that a player plays action $i$ with probability $\pi_i$ can then be translated as a fraction $\pi_i$ of the population playing pure strategy $i$. In this evolutionary setting, the fitness of each candidate strategy is defined by its expected payoff against a randomly selected individual from the opponent's population. The reproduction rate of each strategy depends on the difference between its individual fitness and the average fitness of the whole population: if a strategy does better than average, its population share will increase; if it does worse, it will decrease.

In a two-player game with payoff bi-matrix $(A, B)$, where the two players use the strategies $\pi$ and $\sigma$ respectively, the fitness of row player's $i^{th}$ candidate strategy can be calculated as $\sum_j A_{ij}\sigma_j$. Similarly, the average fitness of the population is defined as $\sum_i \pi_i \sum_j A_{ij}\sigma_j$. In matrix form, this leads to the following dynamical system describing the change over time in the frequency distribution of the candidate strategies:

$$\begin{aligned}
\dot{\pi}_i &= \pi_i \left[ e_i A\sigma^T - \pi A\sigma^T \right] \\
\dot{\sigma}_i &= \sigma_i \left[ \pi B e_i^T - \pi B\sigma^T \right]
\end{aligned} \tag{8}$$

where $e_i$ is the $i^{th}$ unit vector. These differential equations are the replicator dynamics that encode the evolutionary concept of selection based on fitness.

## 2.4   Linking Reinforcement Learning to Evolutionary Game Theory

Multi-Agent Learning and Evolutionary Game Theory share a substantial part of their foundation, in that they both deal with the decision making process of bounded rational agents, or players, in uncertain environments. The link between these two field is not only an intuitive one, but was made formal with the proof that the continuous time limit of Cross Learning converges to the replicator dynamics [3].

Recall the update rule of Cross Learning given in Equation 4. This update rule can be rewritten to take the form $\pi_i(t+1) = \pi_i(t) + \Delta\pi_i(t)$ as

$$\pi_i(t+1) \leftarrow \pi_i(t) + \begin{cases} r(t) - r(t)\pi_i(t) & \text{if } i = j \\ -r(t)\pi_i(t) & \text{otherwise} \end{cases}$$

Note that the probability $\pi_i$ of action $i$ is affected both if $i$ is selected and if another action $j$ is selected, and let $r_i$ or $r_j$ be the reward received for taking action $i$ or $j$ respectively. The expected change $E\left[\Delta\pi_i(t)\right]$ can now be calculated as

$$E\left[\Delta\pi_i(t)\right] = \pi_i(t)\left[r_i(t) - r_i(t)\pi_i(t)\right] + \sum_{j \neq i} \pi_j\left[-r_j(t)\pi_i(t)\right]$$

$$= \pi_i(t)\left[r_i(t) - \sum_j \pi_j(t)r_j(t)\right]$$

If the discrete updates are considered learning steps of time 1, then the continuous limit of this process can be taken as $\pi_i(t + \delta) = \pi_i(t) + \delta\Delta\pi_i(t)$, with $\lim \delta \to 0$. This yields a continuous system which can be expressed with a partial differential equation as

$$\dot{\pi}_i = \pi_i\left[f_i - \sum_j x_j f_j\right] \quad \text{where } f_i = E\left[r_i\right]$$

which is the single-population replicator dynamic. In a two-agent scenario with rewards defined by the payoff bi-matrix $(A, B)$ and agents following policies $\pi$ and $\sigma$, the multi-population replicator dynamics of Equation 8 turn up again. This can be seen by replacing the expected reward $f_i = e_i A\sigma$ for the first agent.

# 3   Analysis

This section presents an overview of the dynamics of the different algorithms, and highlights their similarities. The discussion is limited to the domain of two-player normal form games for the sake of clarity. First, the evolutionary game theoretic models that have been derived for Cross Learning, Frequency Adjusted Q-learning and Regret Minimization are described and compared. Next, the similarities between these evolutionary dynamics and the gradient ascent algorithms are derived for two-player two-action games. In addition, the various dynamics are visualized in directional field plots. Finally, these findings are generalized to two-player normal-form games.

## 3.1   Evolutionary Dynamics of Reinforcement Learning

**Cross Learning** (CL) was the first algorithm to be linked to a dynamical system from evolutionary game theory [3]. As described in Section 2.4, the learning dynamics of CL in the limit of an infinitesimal update step approach the replicator dynamics of Equation 8, which is reiterated here for one player:

$$\dot{\pi}_i = \pi_i\left[e_i A\sigma^T - \pi A\sigma^T\right]$$

The link between a policy learner like CL and a dynamical system in the policy space may be rather straight forward. However, the link has been extended to value based learners as well. A model of Q-learning with the Boltzman update scheme has been proposed in [20], given the additional assumption of updating all actions simultaneously. The variation **Frequency-Adjusted Q-learning** (FAQ-learning) [11] implements this model by modulating the update rule inversely proportional to $\pi_i$, thereby approximating simultaneous action updates.

$$Q_i(t+1) \leftarrow Q_i(t) + \frac{1}{\pi_i}\alpha\left[r_i(t) - Q_i(t)\right]$$

This update rule corresponds to a dynamical system that can be decomposed into the replicator dynamics and terms for randomization, where the temperature parameter $\tau$ tunes the balance between the two. The replicator dynamics enforce the selection of knowingly better actions (exploitation), while randomization corresponds to mutations (exploration). In brief, the FAQ-learning dynamics are a weighted average between CL and exploration.

$$\dot{\pi}_i = \frac{\alpha\pi_i}{\tau}\underbrace{\left[e_iA\sigma^T - \pi A\sigma^T\right]}_{\text{selection}} - \alpha\pi_i\underbrace{\left[\log\pi_i - \sum_k \pi_k\log\pi_k\right]}_{\text{mutation}}$$

Recently, the evolutionary framework has also been extended to the Polynomial Weights algorithm, which implements **Regret Minimization** [2,13]. Despite the great difference in update rule and policy generation (see Eq. 5), the infinitesimal limit has been linked to a dynamical system with CL dynamics in the nominator.

$$\dot{\pi}_i = \frac{\alpha\pi_i\left[e_iA\sigma^T - \pi A\sigma^T\right]}{1 - \alpha\left[\max_k e_kA\sigma^T - \pi A\sigma^T\right]}$$

The denominator can be interpreted as a learning rate modulation dependent on the best action's relative fitness.

### 3.2 Similarities in Two-Player Two-Action Games

For two-agent two-action games, the dynamics can be simplified. Let $h = (1, -1)$, $\pi = (x, 1-x)$ and $\sigma = (y, 1-y)$. The dynamics are completely described by the pair $(\dot{x}, \dot{y})$, which denote the probability changes of the first actions. For CL in self-play, this leads to the following simplified form:

$$\dot{x} = x(1-x)\left[yhAh^T + A_{12} - A_{22}\right]$$
$$\dot{y} = y(1-y)\left[xhBh^T + B_{21} - B_{22}\right]$$

Here, the payoff matrices $A$ and $B$ are again taken from the bi-matrix given in Figure 1. The second player's update $\dot{y}$ is completely analogous to $\dot{x}$, and will be omitted in the subsequent discussion. Similarly, for FAQ-learning the simplified dynamics read

$$\dot{x} = \alpha x(1-x)\left(\tau^{-1}\left[yhAh^T + A_{12} - A_{22}\right] - \log\frac{x}{1-x}\right)$$

The dynamics of RM are slightly more complex. To simplify the notation for two-action games, let $\eth = e_1 A \sigma^T - e_2 A \sigma^T = yhAh^T + A_{12} - A_{22}$. The numerator is equal to Cross Learning with an additional step size parameter $\alpha$, and the denominator depends on which action gives the highest reward. This can be derived from the gradient: the first action will be maximal iff $\eth > 0$. If the first action is maximal, the denominator can be worked out to read $1 - \alpha(1-x)\eth$. Similarly, when the second action is maximal the denominator reads $1 + \alpha\eth$. The dynamics of RM in two action games can then be written as follows:

$$\dot{x} = \alpha x(1-x)\eth \cdot \begin{cases} (1 + \alpha x \eth)^{-1} & \text{if } \eth < 0 \\ (1 - \alpha(1-x)\eth)^{-1} & \text{otherwise} \end{cases}$$

For **Gradient Ascent**, the update rule can be worked out in a similar fashion. The main term in this update rule is the gradient of the expected reward, which in two player two-action games can be written as

$$\begin{aligned} \frac{\partial V(x,y)}{\partial x} &= \frac{\partial}{\partial x}(x, 1-x) A \begin{pmatrix} y \\ 1-y \end{pmatrix} \\ &= y(A_{11} - A_{12} - A_{21} + A_{22}) + A_{12} - A_{22} \\ &= yhAh^T + A_{12} - A_{22} \\ &= \eth \end{aligned}$$

This reduces the dynamics of the update rule for IGA in two-player two-action games to

$$\dot{x} = \alpha\eth$$

The extension of the dynamics of IGA to IGA-WoLF and WPL are straightforward. Table 1 lists the dynamics of the six discussed algorithms: IGA, WoLF, WPL, CL, FAQ and RM. It is immediately clear from this table that *all algorithms have the same basic term in their dynamics*: the gradient $\eth$. Depending on the algorithm, the gradient is scaled with a learning speed modulation. FAQ-learning yields the only dynamics that additionally add exploration terms to the process.

In order to illustrate the similarities between the algorithms, their dynamics are visualized in representative classes of two-player two-action games. Three distinct classes can be identified [9]. The first class consists of games with one pure Nash equilibrium, such as the Prisoner's Dilemma. The second class of games has two pure and one mixed Nash equilibrium, such as the Battle of the Sexes. Finally, the third class of games has only one mixed Nash equilibrium; an example is the Matching Pennies game. The payoff bi-matrices of these games are presented in Figure 2.

Since the dynamics in two-player two-action games are completely described by the pair $(\dot{x}, \dot{y})$ as described above, it is possible to plot the dynamics in the unit square that makes up the joint policy space. The dynamics can be visualized using a directional field plot, where each arrow indicates the direction of change at that point $(x, y)$ in the policy space.

**Table 1.** This table shows an overview of the learning dynamics, rewritten for the specific case of two-agent two-action games. For simplicity, the common gradient is abbreviated $\eth = \left[ yhAh^T + A_{12} - A_{22} \right]$.

| Algorithm | $\dot{x}$ |
|---|---|
| IGA | $\alpha\eth$ |
| WoLF | $\eth \cdot \begin{cases} \alpha_{min} & \text{if } V(x,y) > V(x^e,y) \\ \alpha_{max} & \text{otherwise} \end{cases}$ |
| WPL | $\alpha\eth \cdot \begin{cases} x & \text{if } \eth \; \mathrm{¡} \; 0 \\ (1-x) & \text{otherwise} \end{cases}$ |
| CL | $\alpha x(1-x)\,\eth$ |
| FAQ | $\alpha x(1-x)\left[\eth \cdot \tau^{-1} - \log \frac{x}{1-x}\right]$ |
| RM | $\alpha x(1-x)\,\eth \cdot \begin{cases} (1+\alpha x\eth)^{-1} & \text{if } \eth < 0 \\ (1-\alpha(1-x)\eth)^{-1} & \text{otherwise} \end{cases}$ |

$$
\begin{array}{cc}
 & \begin{array}{cc} C & D \end{array} \\
\begin{array}{c} C \\ D \end{array} & \left( \begin{array}{cc} \frac{3}{5},\frac{3}{5} & 0,1 \\ 1,0 & \frac{1}{5},\frac{1}{5} \end{array} \right)
\end{array}
\qquad
\begin{array}{cc}
 & \begin{array}{cc} O & F \end{array} \\
\begin{array}{c} O \\ F \end{array} & \left( \begin{array}{cc} 1,\frac{1}{2} & 0,0 \\ 0,0 & \frac{1}{2},1 \end{array} \right)
\end{array}
\qquad
\begin{array}{cc}
 & \begin{array}{cc} H & T \end{array} \\
\begin{array}{c} H \\ T \end{array} & \left( \begin{array}{cc} 1,0 & 0,1 \\ 0,1 & 1,0 \end{array} \right)
\end{array}
$$

Prisoner's Dilemma        Battle of the Sexes        Matching Pennies

**Fig. 2.** Normalized payoff matrices for three representative two-player two-action games

Figure 3 shows the learning dynamics of the different algorithms in the Prisoner's Dilemma, Battle of the Sexes, and Matching Pennies game. The dynamics of RM are not shown, as they are visually indistinguishable from CL. Figure 3 illustrates the high similarity between all algorithms in the first two games. They all share the same convergence properties, and follow similar trajectories. The dynamics of IGA and WoLF in the Prisoners' Dilemma show the need for the *projection* function to prevent the update from taking the policies $\pi$ and $\sigma$ out of the valid policy space.

In the Matching Pennies, IGA and CL both cycle around the Nash equilibrium. The other three algorithms all spiral inwards and eventually converge, but do so in a different manner. The dynamics of WoLF clearly show the effect of the *win or learn fast* scheme, switching between the two discrete learning step values at $x = 0.5$ and $y = 0.5$.

### 3.3   Generalization to Two-Player Normal Form Games

The previous section has show the gradient $\eth$ to be a basic building block of several learning algorithms in two-action games, where the policy can be written as $\pi = \{x, 1-x\}$. This section extends the definition to the more general case of two-player normal form games, where each player has a finite discrete set of actions, and $\pi = \{\pi_1, \pi_2, \ldots, \pi_n\}$ such that $\sum_i \pi_i = 1$ and $\forall \pi_i : 0 \leq \pi_i \leq 1$. To ensure satisfying the first constraint the gradient needs to be normalized such that $\sum_i \eth_i = 0$, where $\eth_i$ is the $i^{th}$ component of the gradient, i.e., $\eth_i$ is the

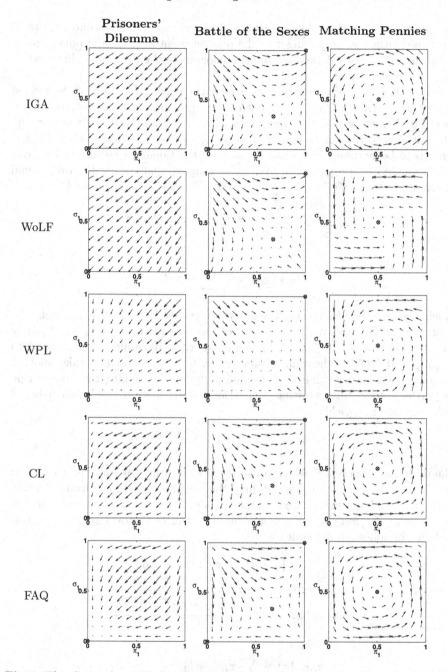

**Fig. 3.** This figure shows the learning dynamics of the various algorithms in the Prisoners' Dilemma, Battle of the Sexes, and Matching Pennies. The Nash Equilibria are indicated with ⊗.

partial derivative of the value function with respect to $\pi_i$. The second constraint is satisfied either by projecting $\pi$ to the (closest point in the) valid policy space, or by making $\dot{\pi}_i$ itself dependent on $\pi$, analogous to the different policy update rules of the algorithms.

Recall that the value function in two-player normal form games is defined as $V(\pi, \sigma) = \pi A \sigma^T$. The $i^{th}$ element of the gradient can be calculated as the partial derivative of $V$ with respect to $\pi_i$. Let $e_i$ denote the $i^{th}$ unit vector, the differential with respect to $\pi_i$ can then be defined as $\delta e_i$. However, recall that $\dot{\pi}$ needs to be normalized in order to stay on the tangent space of $\pi$. This can be guaranteed by projecting $\delta e_i$ onto the tangent space using the orthogonal projection function $\Phi(\zeta) = \zeta - \frac{1}{n} \sum_j \zeta_j$ [16]. This gradient can now be written as

$$\frac{\partial V(\pi, \sigma)}{\partial \pi_i} = \lim_{\delta \to 0} \frac{[\pi + \Phi(\delta e_i)] A \sigma^T - \pi A \sigma^T}{\delta}$$

$$= \Phi(e_i) A \sigma^T$$

$$= e_i A \sigma^T - \frac{1}{n} \sum_j e_j A \sigma^T$$

which closely resembles the replicator dynamics (see Equation 8). As explained in Section 2, IGA and WoLF use a projection function to ensure a valid policy (i.e., to satisfy $\forall \pi_i : 0 \le \pi_i \le 1$). Similarly, their dynamical models need to be projected back to the valid policy space. CL, FAQ and RM take another approach, and ensure validity of the policy update by making the update rule proportional to $\pi$. Incorporating proportional updating into the gradient-based policy update rule yields

$$\pi_i(t+1) \leftarrow \pi_i(t) + \pi_i \frac{\partial V(\pi, \sigma)}{\partial \pi_i}$$

The projection function $\Phi$ which projects $\delta e_i$ to the tangent space of $\pi$ needs to change as well in order to properly map the weighted gradient. Intuitively, this can be achieved by using a weighted mean instead of a standard mean, such that $\hat{\Phi}(\zeta, w) = \zeta - \sum_j w_j \zeta_j$ where $w$ is a normalized weight vector. Using $w = \pi$, this leads to the following dynamics:

$$\dot{\pi}_i = \pi_i \lim_{\delta \to 0} \frac{\left[\pi + \hat{\Phi}(\delta e_i, \pi)\right] A \sigma^T - \pi A \sigma^T}{\delta}$$

$$= \pi_i \lim_{\delta \to 0} \frac{\pi A \sigma^T + \hat{\Phi}(\delta e_i, \pi) A \sigma^T - \pi A \sigma^T}{\delta}$$

$$= \pi_i \hat{\Phi}(e_i, \pi) A \sigma^T$$

$$= \pi_i [e_i A \sigma^T - \sum_j \pi_j e_j A \sigma^T]$$

$$= \pi_i [e_i A \sigma^T - \pi A \sigma^T]$$

These resulting dynamics are exactly the replicator dynamics of Equation 8, which shows that Cross Learning is equal to Gradient Ascent with proportional updates. This provides a strong link between the two families of algorithms, gradient ascent on the one hand and independent multi-agent reinforcement learning on the other.

All of the algorithms described in this section reveal dynamics that follow the reinforcement gradient. The terms of the gradient appear to be the foundation of multi-agent reinforcement learning, with learning rate modulations and some deviations for the sake of exploration and coordination.

## 4   Discussion

Gradient Ascent on the expected reinforcement assumes that the gradient is known or can be computed by the agent. This is typically not the case in reinforcement learning problems. The merits of Gradient Ascent are more theoretical – it allows to provide convergence guarantees at the cost of stronger assumptions. Recently, similar guarantees have also been derived for evolutionary models of independent multi-agent reinforcement learning. These guarantees either draw on well established models from evolutionary biology, or study newly derived variations. For example, the cyclic behavior of the replicator dynamics is a well studied phenomenon [10], while the dynamics of FAQ-learning have been thoroughly analyzed in two-agent two-action games showing convergence to Nash equilibria [12]. In addition, the findings presented in this article highlight the commonalities of gradient ascent and reinforcement learning. Future research can build on this basis and further unite the two parallel streams of literature.

## 5   Conclusions

This article relates two seemingly diverse families of algorithms within the field multi-agent learning: gradient ascent and independent reinforcement learning. The main contributions can be summarized as follows: First, it is shown that the replicator dynamics are a prime building block of various types of independent reinforcement learning algorithms, such as Cross Learning, Regret Minimization, and Q-learning. Second, the replicator dynamics are shown to relate to the gradient of the expected reward, which forms the basis of Gradient Ascent. Both the replicator dynamics and gradient ascent base their update on the difference between the expected reward of an action and the average expected reward over all actions. The difference lies in the weight given to each action's update: gradient ascent assumes uniform weights as given by the gradient, whereas the replicator dynamics use the action-selection probabilities as weights. The theoretical comparison is complimented by a visualization of the different learning dynamics in representative two-agent two-action games – a class in which their similarity is particularly compelling.

In sum, this article structures a highly diversified field such as multi-agent learning. The number of proposed learning algorithms is continuously increasing, and we deem recognizing persistent principles such as learning along the reinforcement gradient crucial to the integrity of the field. This approach provides the basis for an analysis of the inherent capabilities but also limitations of what is learnable with independent reinforcement learning in multi-agent games. Eventually, we are seeking to establish lower bounds on the performance in multi-agent games similar to Probably Approximately Correct Learning guarantees in single-agent learning.

# References

1. Abdallah, S., Lesser, V.: A multiagent reinforcement learning algorithm with nonlinear dynamics. Journal of Artificial Intelligence Research 33(1), 521–549 (2008)
2. Blum, A., Mansour, Y.: Learning, regret minimization and equilibria. Cambridge University Press (2007)
3. Börgers, T., Sarin, R.: Learning through reinforcement and replicator dynamics. Journal of Economic Theory 77(1) (November 1997)
4. Bowling, M., Veloso, M.: Multiagent learning using a variable learning rate. Artificial Intelligence 136, 215–250 (2002)
5. Busoniu, L., Babuska, R., De Schutter, B.: A comprehensive survey of multiagent reinforcement learning. IEEE Transactions on Systems, Man, and Cybernetics, Part C: Applications and Reviews 38(2), 156–172 (2008)
6. Crandall, J.W., Ahmed, A., Goodrich, M.A.: Learning in repeated games with minimal information: The effects of learning bias. In: Twenty-Fifth AAAI Conference on Artificial Intelligence (2011)
7. Cross, J.G.: A stochastic learning model of economic behavior. The Quarterly Journal of Economics 87(2), 239 (1973)
8. Gibbons, R.: A Primer in Game Theory. Pearson Education (1992)
9. Gintis, H.: Game Theory Evolving, 2nd edn. University Press, Princeton (2009)
10. Hofbauer, J., Sigmund, K.: Evolutionary Games and Population Dynamics. Cambridge University Press (2002)
11. Kaisers, M., Tuyls, K.: Frequency adjusted multi-agent Q-learning. In: Proc. of 9th Intl. Conf. on Autonomous Agents and Multiagent Systems (AAMAS 2010), May 10-14, pp. 309–315 (2010)
12. Kaisers, M., Tuyls, K.: Faq-learning in matrix games: Demonstrating convergence near nash equilibria, and bifurcation of attractors in the battle of sexes. In: Proceedings of the Workshop on Interactive Decision Theory and Game Theory (2011)
13. Klos, T., van Ahee, G.J., Tuyls, K.: Evolutionary Dynamics of Regret Minimization. In: Balcázar, J.L., Bonchi, F., Gionis, A., Sebag, M. (eds.) ECML PKDD 2010, Part II. LNCS, vol. 6322, pp. 82–96. Springer, Heidelberg (2010)
14. Maynard Smith, J., Price, G.R.: The logic of animal conflict. Nature 246(2), 15–18 (1973)
15. Narendra, K.S., Thathachar, M.A.L.: Learning automata - a survey. IEEE Transactions on Systems, Man, and Cybernetics 4(4), 323–334 (1974)
16. Sandholm, W.H.: Population Games and Evolutionary Dynamics. The MIT Press, Cambridge (2010)
17. Singh, S., Kearns, M., Mansour, Y.: Nash convergence of gradient dynamics in general-sum games. In: Proc. of the 16th Conference on Uncertainty in Artificial Intelligence, pp. 541–548 (2000)

18. Sutton, R., Barto, A.: Reinforcement Learning: An introduction. MIT Press, Cambridge (1998)
19. Thathachar, M.A.L., Sastry, P.S.: Varieties of learning automata: An overview. IEEE Transactions on Systems, Man, and Cybernetics - Part B: Cybernetics 32(6), 711–722 (2002)
20. Tuyls, K., Jan't Hoen, P., Vanschoenwinkel, B.: An evolutionary dynamical analysis of multi-agent learning in iterated games. Autonomous Agents and Multi-Agent Systems 12, 115–153 (2006)
21. Watkins, C.J.C.H., Dayan, P.: Q-learning. Machine Learning 8(3), 279–292 (1992)

# A Methodology for the Generation of Multi-agent Argumentation Dialogue Scenarios

Eric M. Kok, John-Jules Ch. Meyer, Herre van Oostendorp,
Henry Prakken, and Gerard A. W. Vreeswijk

Department of Information and Computing Sciences,
Utrecht University,
The Netherlands

**Abstract.** Increasingly research into the uses of argumentation in multi-agent dialogues takes an experimental approach. Such studies explore how agents can successfully employ argumentation besides the best and worst case situations of formal analysis. While a vital part in these experiments is influenced by the scenarios from which dialogues are generated, there is very little research on how these can be generated in a meaningful way, respecting the characteristics of the underlying dialogue problem. This paper proposes, by means of an example system for deliberation dialogues, a methodology for the construction and evaluation of a scenario generation process. It is shown how scenarios can accommodate argumentation with structured arguments and how it is tested whether the generated scenarios are interesting for experimentation.

## 1 Introduction

One of the key components of multi-agent systems is communication and in recent years systems have been developed to model agent communication using argumentation-enabled dialogue systems. Such systems promise to be more efficient in bringing agents to a decision and yield better agreements. [10]

While formal studies have indeed provided insights into theoretical reachability of ideal and intuitive conclusions, more and more research is looking to empirically investigate benefits to overcome the often strong limitations that are introduced in formal studies and to find results besides best and worst case situations. Through a software experiment unique situations, called scenarios, are generated. Agents are run to construct a dialogue from the scenario, after which the efficiency and effectiveness of the dialogue is measured. Inherently this specific scenario directly influences the results and it is therefore crucial that it is generated in a meaningful fashion. However, very little research has focussed on how scenarios can be generated while respecting the characteristics of the underlying dialogue problem.

This paper, being part of a project taking the experimental approach to finding the use of argumentation for agents, will provide a methodology to generate scenarios in a structured way. An example dialogue system with BDI-based

M. Cossentino et al. (Eds.): EUMAS 2011, LNAI 7541, pp. 160–174, 2012.
© Springer-Verlag Berlin Heidelberg 2012

agents is introduced for which scenarios are generated. Several desirable metrics are introduced by which it is shown how the most influential input parameters of the system can be found.

## 2    Background on Experimentation in Argumentation-Enabled Dialogues

Computational argumentation is roughly divided in the areas of argumentation logics and dialogical argumentation. The former pertains to the evaluation of an argumentation system as to identify the justified arguments while the latter usually makes use of such logics but studies the effects of arguments in agent dialogues instead. Agents engage in various types of dialogues where argumentation is useful; notably, as classified by Walton and Krabbe [12], negotiation, persuasion and deliberation.

### 2.1    Existing Work

Several works explored the practical benefits of argumentation in dialogues. In both Karunatillake et al. [3] and Paquier et al. [8] argumentation-based negotiation is studied. While the focus of the systems is different (social agent societies and exploring the negotiation space respectively) the argumentative parts of agents are modelled alike. Within a dialogue agents may ask for and supply a motivation behind proposals. However, the language does not allow agents to build structured arguments, which severely limit the expressivity of agents.

Black and Bentley [1] empirically investigated the use of argumentation in two-party deliberation dialogues. Agents are initialized with a set of abstract value-based arguments which are used in the dialogue to decide on some action. The argumentative strategy is shown to outperform a simple consensus forming strategy in randomly generated dialogues with a wide variety in number of arguments, values and actions.

Ontañón and Plaza [6] experiment with two-agent inductive learning dialogues using structured arguments. Evaluation is performed using examples from an existing repository, in contrast to generating new scenarios for the agents.

### 2.2    Characteristics of Deliberation Dialogues

While the existing work already points towards useful applications, there has not yet been a project that uses argumentation with structured arguments, formed from an agents beliefs and goals. This paper shows a methodology to generate scenarios that accommodate for argumentation with structured arguments while strongly reflecting the characteristics of deliberation dialogue type as identified from the existing literature on argumentation-based dialogues [1,4,5]:

- Mutual deliberation goal
- Unequal roles between agents
- Not all options (possible actions) are known by all agents
- Both compatible and conflicting goals between agents
- Incomplete information and from different sources

The scenario generation process that is now introduced is grounded in and supports these characteristics. A similar analysis of the characteristics of the underlying problem structure should be performed for any dialogue type that is under experimentation.

### 2.3   Generating Interesting Scenarios for Experimentation

Scenarios generated using the methodology proposed in this paper will reflect the unique features of the deliberation dialogue as just identified. However, we also need to evaluate whether the generated scenarios will be interesting enough to use in argumentation dialogue experiments. That is, the scenarios need to provide incentive to the deliberation process. When testing argumentation in deliberation dialogues it is desired that agents can indeed make proposals for some action, forward (counter-)arguments and question statements. Scenarios can be interesting in two ways: to which degree it allows for the justification of doing some action and to which degree proposals for these actions can be attacked. How to test scenarios on these qualities will be discussed in section 5.

## 3   Deliberation Model

To facilitate scenarios with the complexity of the deliberation dialogues a model is now introduced that combines a structured argumentation logic with a multi-agent deliberation dialogue system. This forms the example system for which a scenario generation process is modelled and evaluated.

### 3.1   Argumentation Logic

Arguments in the deliberation dialogues are formed using a simple instantiation of the abstract ASPIC framework for argumentation with structured arguments [9], which is an instance of the Dung [2] abstract argumentation model. It allows agents to create structured arguments, modelled as inference trees of applied strict and defeasible rules.

An argument can be attacked by rebutting a conclusion of a defeasible inference, by undermining one of its premises or by undercutting one of its defeasible inferences. From the resulting attack relation and a preference relation on the arguments the status of an argument can be evaluated.

In this paper a simple instantiation of the ASPIC framework is assumed, with a simple logical language consisting of propositional literals, only defeasible rules and no preference ordering on arguments (such an instantiation is called an *ASPIC argumentation system*). Rules are written as $p \Rightarrow_\varrho q$, where the rule name $\varrho$ is omitted for clarity when appropriate and where the premise $p$ and conclusion $q$ are literals in the topic language. Arguments are written as $A \mathrel{\vdash\!\sim} p$ where $A$ is the set of used premises and inferences and $p$ is the conclusion. Extended versions of this simple instantiation will be studied in later work.

## 3.2  Dialogue Context

The deliberation dialogues consist of a series of moves that, except for proposals, always reply to a previous move. In these moves the agents make proposals, question statements, provide arguments or surrender to a previous statement. Although the full dynamics of an argumentation-based deliberation dialogue model are not needed for this paper, it is still good to briefly cover the interplay between agents, arguments and the proposals. The multi-agent deliberation model here is a simplification from that of Kok et al. [4].

First of all the dialogue takes place in a deliberation dialogue context.

**Definition 1.** A deliberation dialogue context consists of:

- An ASPIC *argumentation system* $\mathcal{L}$
- A *topic language* $L_t$ consisting of
  - options $L_o \subseteq L_t$
  - goals $L_g \subseteq L_t$
  - beliefs $L_b \subseteq L_t$
- A mutual deliberation goal $g_d \in L_g$

Agents engage in a dialogue and make proposals for action respecting a mutual goal describing their shared interest, like making profit. Reasons for submitting proposals can in turn be requested to which arguments can be forwarded showing how some goal is achieved by performing the proposed action. From there the agents question or surrender to premises and provide arguments.

Agents take turns and every turn they may submit multiple moves to the dialogue. Except the *propose* move every move has a specific target that it attacks or to which it surrenders. In this way multiple distinct proposal trees can be constructed by the agents. When no agent makes any more moves the dialogue ends and the winning proposal can be determined according to some heuristic. Figure 1 show an example in which a proposed option $o$ is supported by two arguments with a goal as conclusion, one of which is has a counter-argument causing agent $b$ to retract his earlier claim.

## 3.3  Agent Model

Every participating agent has a certain role in the system, such as a topic expert or nancial agent. This role describes the duties and desires of an agent as being a part of its context.

**Definition 2.** A set of roles $\mathcal{R}$ is defined where every role $r \in \mathcal{R}$ in a deliberation context with mutual goal $g_d$ and set sizes $n_{O_r}$ and $n_{G_r}$ is assigned:

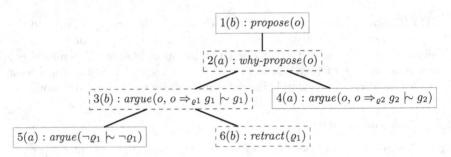

**Fig. 1.** Example of a proposal tree with two arguments from option $o$

- A set of options $O_r \subseteq L_o$ defined by $O_r = \{o_1, \ldots, o_i\}$ such that $|O_r| = n_{O_r}$
- A set of goals $G_r \subseteq L_g$ defined by $G_r = \{g_1, \ldots, g_j\}$ such that $|G_r| = n_{G_r}$

The idea is that the role accounts for the basic set of options that the agent knows about and the goals the agent has. The variables $n_{O_r}$ and $n_{G_r}$ are used to vary the number of options and goals associated with a role.

Internally the agents are modelled using the influential BDI architecture [11], which is also a natural way of designing argumentation-enabled agents. [7] An agent maintains a set of goals that it wants to bring about and a set of beliefs consisting of facts and rules. For deliberation systems this is extended with a set of options, which are the actions that an agent knows it can propose to solve the deliberation problem at hand.

**Definition 3.** A set of agents $\mathcal{A}$ is defined where every agent $a \in \mathcal{A}$ has:

- A role $r \in \mathcal{R}$
- A set of *options* $O_a \subseteq L_o$
- A set of *goals* $G_a \subseteq L_g$
- A set of *beliefs* $B_a \subseteq L_b$

## 4    Scenario Generation

As established above, generated scenarios will need to support full structured argumentation using the agents' beliefs and goals. Options in a deliberation problem typically exist because, through some line of reasoning, they promote the achievement of a goal, as supported by an argument for the option. This property forms the idea behind the five-step process for the generations of scenarios.

To illustrate the generation process a running example is used. Three agents will participate in a deliberation dialogue with mutual goal $g_d$. These agents are split into two different roles, both of which are assigned two options and two goals, as visualized in Table 1.

### 4.1    Rule Chaining

The first step in generating scenarios is to create a body of knowledge that, as is typical in deliberation problems, forms lines of reasoning between options and

Table 1. Example dialogue with three agents

| $n_{\mathcal{A}} = 3$ | $\mathcal{A} = \{a_1, a_2, a_3\}$ | |
|---|---|---|
| $n_{\mathcal{R}} = 2$ | $\mathcal{R} = \{r_1, r_2\}$ | |
| $n_{O_r} = 2$ | $O_{r_1} = \{o_1, o_2\}$ | $O_{r_2} = \{o_2, o_3\}$ |
| $n_{G_r} = 2$ | $G_{r_1} = \{g_1, g_d\}$ | $G_{r_2} = \{g_3, g_4\}$ |
| $n_S = 10$ | $S = \{p_1, p_2, p_3, p_4, p_5, p_6, p_7, p_8, p_9, p_{10}\}$ | |

the goals that they promote. These are called rule chains and will connect a role's option to one of the role's goals. Rules in these chains are built from a limited set of atoms called the chaining seed set.

**Definition 4.** A *chaining seed set* of atoms $S \subseteq L_b$ is defined as $S = \{p_1, \ldots, p_i\}$ such that $|S| = n_S$

The variable $n_S$, the running example uses $n_S = 10$, is used to control the number of atoms that are used to generate rules for a chain. A chain starts with a rule with an option as premise and ends with a rule with a goal as conclusion. The consequence to all other rules is an atom from the chaining seed set and in turn is the antecedent for the follow-up rule. Although chains of rules with only one positive antecedent may seem restricted, it will already support a sufficiently complex scenario as will be shown in Section 5.

**Definition 5.** Given a goal $g$, an option $o$ and a chain length $l$ a *rule chain* is a set of rules $C_{g,o}$ such that

- if $l = 1$ then $C_{g,o} = \{o \Rightarrow g\}$
- if $l > 1$ then $C_{g,o} = \{o \Rightarrow p_1, \ldots, p_i \Rightarrow p_j, \ldots, p_n \Rightarrow g\}$ where $n = l - 1$ and $\{p_1, \ldots, p_n\} \subseteq S$

Intermediate atoms used to create rules are chosen arbitrarily from the chaining seed set. Note that only one chain is possible with chain length 1, but multiple paths with larger chain lengths, using different intermediate atoms. Also, the option $o$ is the only required premise to generate a full argument in $\mathcal{L}$ for the goal $g$ and every $p_i$ is a sub-conclusion in such an argument.

When generating a chain for the running example, we may for instance chain role $r_1$'s goal $g_d$ to its option $o_1$. With $l = 3$ and the seed set $S$ a chain $C_{g_2,o_1} = \{o_1 \Rightarrow_{\varrho 1} p_5, p_5 \Rightarrow_{\varrho 2} p_2, p_2 \Rightarrow_{\varrho 3} g_2\}$ is constructed. Agents that know about all rules in this chain as well as the option $o_1$ will be able to construct a single argument for $g_2$.

## 4.2  Conflict Generation

Scenarios do not only contain reasons why an option will lead to some goal being achieved. An important part of deliberation problems is that there are conflicts between what is known and what the rule chains proclaim. Therefore, the second generation step is to extend the scenario with conflicting knowledge. This is modelled using negated facts which are created based on a rule chain. A negated fact is generated for every way that a rule in some chain can be attacked in $\mathcal{L}$, that is by undercutting, undermining or rebutting. These negated facts represent the contrary views in the deliberation problem over the truth status of relevant facts.

**Definition 6.** A rule chain $C_{g,o}$ with length $l$ linking some goal $g$ and option $o$ has a set of *possible conflicts* $\bar{C}_{g,o}$ containing for every rule $p \Rightarrow_\varrho q \in C_{g,o}$:

- a fact $\neg\varrho$ (an undercutter)
- a fact $\neg p$ (an underminer)
- a fact $\neg q$ (a rebuttal)

A set of possible conflicts $\bar{C}_{g,o}$ thus contains facts that can be used to generate counter-arguments to arguments formed using $C_{g,o}$. Note that no rule weights are used in both chains and conflict set. Therefore the attack between two arguments as formed from these rules is always be symmetric, i.e. they are equally acceptable. Although this is a simplification of the complex knowledge of real world deliberation problems it does already allow for structured arguments and counter arguments and, as demonstrated later, can be sufficiently complex to generate interesting dialogues.

Consider the example chain $C_{g2,o1} = \{o_1 \Rightarrow_{\varrho 1} p_5, p_5 \Rightarrow_{\varrho 2} p_2, p_2 \Rightarrow_{\varrho 3} g_2\}$ then there is a set of possible conflicts $\bar{C}_{g2,o1} = \{\neg\varrho_1, \neg o_1, \neg p_5, \neg\varrho_2, \neg p_2, \neg\varrho_3\}$.

## 4.3   Completing the Knowledge Pool

As a third step the pool of knowledge is completed before being allocated to the agents. The options and goals in the pool are aggregated from the roles in the system.

**Definition 7.** A knowledge pool $K$ is assigned:

- a set of pool options $O_K = \bigcup_{r \in \mathcal{R}} O_r$
- a set of pool goals $G_K = \bigcup_{r \in \mathcal{R}} G_r$

Beliefs are derived from roles as well, by, for every option in the pool, generating either a chain or a set of conflicts, depending on whether the role was assigned the specific option.

**Definition 8.** For every option $o \in O_K$, given some role $r \in \mathcal{R}$ and a set size $n_{B_r^o}$ a set of *role-option beliefs* $B_r^o$ is any set such that:

- if $o \in O_r$ then $B_r^o = C_{g_d,o} \cup C_{g,o}$ for some goal $g \in G_r$
- if $o \notin O_r$ then $B_r^o \subseteq \bar{C}_{g,o}$ for an arbitrary goal $g \in G_r$ such that $|B_r^o| = n_{B_r^o}$

The knowledge pool now contains both full paths from some option to some goal as well as negated facts to form counter arguments. The variable $n_{B_r^o}$ can be used to tweak the number of generated negated beliefs for options not assigned to a role. Table 2 shows the rule chains that are generated for the roles in the running example as well as the selected negated beliefs for every chain.

**Table 2.** Belief assignment in the example's knowledge pool

| $l = 3$ | (chains with length 3) |
|---|---|
| $n_{B_{\bar{r}}^o} = 2$ | (full chain or 2 negated beliefs) |

$r_1$

$B_{r_1}^{o1}$  $o_1 \Rightarrow_{\varrho 1} p_5,\ p_5 \Rightarrow_{\varrho 2} p_2,\ p_2 \Rightarrow_{\varrho 3} g_2,$
   $o_1 \Rightarrow_{\varrho 4} p_6,\ p_6 \Rightarrow_{\varrho 5} p_4,\ p_4 \Rightarrow_{\varrho 6} g_d$

$B_{r_1}^{o2}$  $o_2 \Rightarrow_{\varrho 7} p_5,\ p_5 \Rightarrow_{\varrho 2} p_2,\ p_2 \Rightarrow_{\varrho 8} g_1,$
   $o_2 \Rightarrow_{\varrho 9} p_9,\ p_9 \Rightarrow_{\varrho 10} p_1,\ p_1 \Rightarrow_{\varrho 11} g_d$

$B_{r_1}^{o3}$  $\neg \varrho 17, \neg p_3$

$r_2$

$B_{r_2}^{o1}$  $\neg p_2, \neg \varrho 3$
$B_{r_2}^{o2}$  $o_2 \Rightarrow_{\varrho 9} p_9,\ p_9 \Rightarrow_{\varrho 12} p_8,\ p_8 \Rightarrow_{\varrho 13} g_4,$
   $o_2 \Rightarrow_{\varrho 14} p_1,\ p_1 \Rightarrow_{\varrho 15} p_9,\ p_9 \Rightarrow_{\varrho 16} g_d$

$B_{r_2}^{o3}$  $o_3 \Rightarrow_{\varrho 17} p_7,\ p_7 \Rightarrow_{\varrho 18} p_3,\ p_3 \Rightarrow_{\varrho 19} g_4,$
   $o_3 \Rightarrow_{\varrho 17} p_7,\ p_7 \Rightarrow_{\varrho 21} p_8,\ p_8 \Rightarrow_{\varrho 22} g_d$

## 4.4  Option and Goal Allocation

Following the characteristics of deliberation problems, agents inherit options and goals associated with their roles. Additionally, agents have personal goals that they do not necessarily share with other agents. Examples of such goals are those originating from personal values or goals transcending an agent's current role.

**Definition 9.** An agent $a \in \mathcal{A}$ with role $r$ and a set size $n_{G_{\bar{r}}}$ has:

- A set of *options* $O_a = O_r$
- A set of *non-role originating goals* $G_a^{\bar{r}}$ where for every $g \in G_a^{\bar{r}}$ it holds that $g \in G_K \setminus G_r$ and such that $|G_a^{\bar{r}}| = n_{G_a^{\bar{r}}}$
- The combined set of *goals* $G_a = G_r \cup G_a^{\bar{r}} \cup \{g_d\}$

Non-role originating goals are only goals that already exist in the knowledge pool. This is not for simplicity but ensures partial overlap between the goals of agents with different roles, as is typical for deliberation situations. The variable $n_{G_a^{\bar{r}}}$ will be used to set the number of non-role goals allocated to an agent.

## 4.5  Role and Non-role Belief Allocation

The final step is to allocate the beliefs that an agent will have in the deliberation scenario. We will again use an agent's role to allocate knowledge from the pool to an agent. Since we have seen that agents usually have incomplete knowledge we will not assign all of a role's rule chains or negated facts.

**Definition 10.** An agent $a \in \mathcal{A}$ with some role $r$ is assigned a set of $n_{B_a^r}$ *role-originating beliefs*

$$B_a^r \subseteq \bigcup_{o \in O_K} B_r^o \text{ such that } |B_a^r| = n_{B_a^r}$$

**Table 3.** Information allocation to the agents for the example

| $n_{G_a^{\bar{r}}} = 1$ | (Agents $a_1$ and $a_2$ have role $r_1$; agent $a_3$ has role $r_2$) |
|---|---|
| | (Agents inherit goals, $g_d$ and get one non-role goal) |
| | $O_{a_1}$   $o_1, o_2$   $G_{a_1}$   $g_d, g_1, g_2, g_4$ |
| | $O_{a_2}$   $o_1, o_2$   $G_{a_2}$   $g_d, g_1, g_2, g_3$ |
| | $O_{a_3}$   $o_2, o_3$   $G_{a_3}$   $g_d, g_3, g_4, g_2$ |
| $n_{B_a^r} = 13$ | (Agents inherit 13 of their 14 role beliefs) |
| $n_{B_a^{\bar{r}}} = 2$ | (And get 2 non-role beliefs) |
| | $B_{a_1}$   $o_1 \Rightarrow_{\varrho 1} p_5,\ p_5 \Rightarrow_{\varrho 2} p_2,\ p_2 \Rightarrow_{\varrho 3} g_2,$ |
| | $o_1 \Rightarrow_{\varrho 4} p_6,\ p_4 \Rightarrow_{\varrho 6} g_d,$ |
| | $o_2 \Rightarrow_{\varrho 7} p_5,\ p_5 \Rightarrow_{\varrho 2} p_2,\ p_2 \Rightarrow_{\varrho 8} g_1,$ |
| | $o_2 \Rightarrow_{\varrho 9} p_9,\ p_9 \Rightarrow_{\varrho 10} p_1,\ p_1 \Rightarrow_{\varrho 11} g_d,$ |
| | $\neg \varrho 17, \neg p_3,$ |
| | $o_1 \Rightarrow_{\varrho 23} p_2,\ p_3 \Rightarrow_{\varrho 19} g_4$ |
| | $B_{a_2}$   $p_5 \Rightarrow_{\varrho 2} p_2,\ p_2 \Rightarrow_{\varrho 3} g_2,$ |
| | $o_1 \Rightarrow_{\varrho 4} p_6,\ p_6 \Rightarrow_{\varrho 5} p_4,\ p_4 \Rightarrow_{\varrho 6} g_d,$ |
| | $o_2 \Rightarrow_{\varrho 7} p_5,\ p_5 \Rightarrow_{\varrho 2} p_2,\ p_2 \Rightarrow_{\varrho 8} g_1,$ |
| | $o_2 \Rightarrow_{\varrho 9} p_9,\ p_9 \Rightarrow_{\varrho 10} p_1,\ p_1 \Rightarrow_{\varrho 11} g_d,$ |
| | $\neg \varrho 17, \neg p_7,$ |
| | $o_2 \Rightarrow_{\varrho 25} p_2,\ o_1 \Rightarrow_{\varrho 25} p_5$ |
| | $B_{a_3}$   $\neg \varrho 4,$ |
| | $o_2 \Rightarrow_{\varrho 9} p_9,\ p_9 \Rightarrow_{\varrho 12} p_8,\ p_8 \Rightarrow_{\varrho 13} g_4,$ |
| | $o_2 \Rightarrow_{\varrho 14} p_1,\ p_1 \Rightarrow_{\varrho 15} p_9,\ p_9 \Rightarrow_{\varrho 16} g_d,$ |
| | $o_3 \Rightarrow_{\varrho 17} p_7,\ p_7 \Rightarrow_{\varrho 18} p_3,\ p_3 \Rightarrow_{\varrho 19} g_4,$ |
| | $o_3 \Rightarrow_{\varrho 17} p_7,\ p_7 \Rightarrow_{\varrho 21} p_8,\ p_8 \Rightarrow_{\varrho 22} g_d,$ |
| | $p_8 \Rightarrow_{\varrho 26} p_7,\ p_2 \Rightarrow_{\varrho 3} g_2$ |

The variable $n_{B_a^r}$ is used to set the number of role-option beliefs, which for simplicity is equal for all agents. Since no agent will be assigned full knowledge, it is likely to miss some rule needed to construct a full argument for a chain, or that it cannot construct a counter-argument.

Agents also have beliefs that not necessarily originate from the role they have in the system. Such beliefs can come from various sources, such as an agent's expertise or prior encounters. It will be modelled as a set of rules taken from newly generated chains for some of the agent's options and goals, not different than how chains are generated for roles.

**Definition 11.** An agent $a \in \mathcal{A}$ is assigned a set of $n_{B_a^{\bar{r}}}$ *non-role originating beliefs*

$$B_a^{\bar{r}} \subseteq \bigcup_{o \in O_a} C_{g,o} \text{ for an arbitrary goal } g \in G_a \text{ such that } |B_a^r| = n_{B_a^{\bar{r}}}$$

The variable $n_{B_a^{\bar{r}}}$ is used to set the number of non-role originating beliefs known to the agent. The additional chains, if fully assigned to the agent, can be used to create supplementary arguments from some option to an agent's goal. In addition, the individual rules in the chain can solve the problem of missing rules in the chains it was assigned from its role. For instance if, in our running example, agent $a_2$ was not assigned the rule $\varrho_4$ it no longer knows all rules in the chain and cannot construct an argument for $g_1$ any more. However, its non-role originating beliefs set may include a supplementary chain $\{o_2 \Rightarrow p_1, p_1 \Rightarrow p_2, p_2 \Rightarrow g_d\}$ which again allows him to construct an argument for $g_1$ from $o_2$.

The total set of beliefs is the union of role and non-role originating beliefs.

**Definition 12.** An agent $a \in \mathcal{A}$ is assigned a set of *beliefs* $B_a = B_a^r \cup B_a^{\bar{r}}$

The running example's allocated options, goals and beliefs are listed in Table 3. Agents $a_1$ and $a_2$ share a role $r_1$ in the system, while agent $a_3$ has role $r_2$. Every agent inherits the options, goals and an arbitrary part of the beliefs from their role (as specified in Table 2), but also is assigned a supplementary non-role originating goal and a small arbitrary set of non-role originating beliefs.

## 5  Evaluation of Generated Scenarios

A method to structurally generate deliberation scenarios has been presented that models the dynamics of deliberation problems using goals, rule chains and (non-)role based belief allocation. Recall from 2.3 that generated scenarios should be tested on to what extent they have the potential to produce interesting dialogues, which is defined by to what degree an agent has an argument for its options and to what degree counter-arguments to those exist.

It is now shown how an experimental approach, similar to experimentation with a full dialogue system, can be used to evaluate the scenario generation process. Importantly, the generation process uses 10 input parameters, as collected in Table 4 for the system in this paper, which directly influence how a scenario looks like and therefore to what degree the scenario is interesting.

### 5.1  Metrics for Interesting Scenarios

For an agent to propose one of its options in a deliberation dialogue it needs to be able to generate an argument from the option to one of its goals. Consequently, the first metric for interesting scenarios is to test if agents can form such arguments, in which case the option is called justified.

**Definition 13.** An agent $a$'s option $o \in O_a$ is a *justified option* if, on the basis of the beliefs $B_a \cup \{o\}$, an argument $A \mathrel{|\!\sim} g$ can be constructed for some goal $g \in G_a$ such that $o \in A$.

Note that depending on the exact deliberation dialogue system used the argument may be required to be a credulously or sceptically acceptable argument or even have the mutual deliberation goal as conclusion. For the system in this paper we will require an argument that is defensible under preferred semantics, matching the credulous nature of practical reasoning in deliberation dialogues.

**Table 4.** Input parameters used in the scenario generation process

|  |  | min | example | max |
|---|---|---|---|---|
| $n_\mathcal{A}$ | The number of agents | 1 | 3 | 6 |
| $n_\mathcal{R}$ | The number of roles | 1 | 2 | 6 |
| $n_{O_r}$ | A role $r$'s options set size | 2 | 2 | 5 |
| $n_{G_r}$ | A role $r$'s goals set size | 2 | 2 | 5 |
| $n_S$ | The chaining seedset size | 10 | 10 | 100 |
| $l$ | The length of rule chains | 3 | 3 | 9 |
| $n_{B_a^{\bar{o}}}$ | An agent $a$'s negated role-option beliefs set size | 0 | 3 | 15 |
| $n_{G_a^{\bar{r}}}$ | An agent $a$'s non-role originating goals set size | 0 | 1 | 2 |
| $n_{B_a^r}$ | An agent $a$'s role-originating beliefs set size | 1 | 7 | 15 |
| $n_{B_a^{\bar{r}}}$ | An agent $a$'s non-role originating beliefs set size | 0 | 2 | 20 |

It is now possible to define a metric that indicates to what extent a scenario is interesting, that is, which of the options of the agents are justified.

**Definition 14.** A generated scenario with a set of agents $\mathcal{A}$ has an *option justification percentage*

$$j_\mathcal{A} = \frac{|\bigcup_{a \in \mathcal{A}}\{o|o \in O_a \text{ where } o \text{ is a justified option}\}|}{n_\mathcal{A} \times n_{O_r}} \times 100$$

Consider again the generated example scenario. For each of the three agents their two options are tested. Table 5 shows the arguments that the agents can form. Agents $a_1$ and $a_2$ have arguments from both their options, while agent $a_3$ was able to construct an argument for $o_2$ but not for $o_3$ since it misses the rule $p_8 \Rightarrow_{\varrho16} g_3$. Hence, the option justification percentage $j_\mathcal{A} = \frac{5}{6} \times 100 = 83\%$.

To see if scenarios also spur counter-arguments to the arguments used for justified options a second metric is defined. The idea is that for every justified option of an agent the other agents' knowledge is used to construct a counter-argument as so to allow attacks on proposals as made in a deliberation dialogue.

**Definition 15.** An agent $a$'s justified option $o$, as supported by argument $A \mathrel{|\!\sim} g$, is also a *countered justified option* if some agent $a' \in \mathcal{A}$, where $a \neq a'$, can, on the basis of beliefs $B_{a'} \cup \{o\}$, construct a counter-argument $B \mathrel{|\!\sim} p$ that defeats $A \mathrel{|\!\sim} g$.

Analogous to the degree of option justification we define a metric for the degree of justified options that are also countered by some argument.

**Definition 16.** A generated scenario with a set of agents $\mathcal{A}$ has an *option countered justification percentage*

$$\bar{j}_\mathcal{A} = \frac{|\bigcup_{a \in \mathcal{A}}\{o|o \in O_a \text{ where } o \text{ is a countered justified option}\}|}{|\bigcup_{a \in \mathcal{A}}\{o|o \in O_a \text{ where } o \text{ is a justified option}\}|} \times 100$$

The example's countered option justification percentage $\bar{j}_\mathcal{A} = \frac{3}{5} \times 100 = 60\%$ since agent $a_3$ can construct a counter-argument for three of the justified options: to both agent $a_1$'s and $a_2$'s argument for $o_1$ and to agent $a_2$'s argument for $o_2$.

**Table 5.** Arguments for option justification in the example scenario

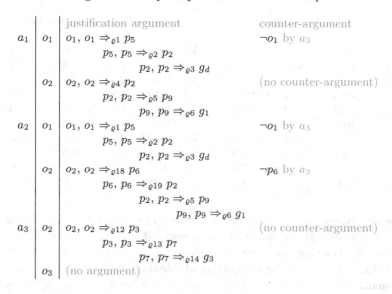

| | | justification argument | counter-argument |
|---|---|---|---|
| $a_1$ | $o_1$ | $o_1,\ o_1 \Rightarrow_{\varrho 1} p_5$ | $\neg o_1$ by $a_3$ |
| | | $p_5,\ p_5 \Rightarrow_{\varrho 2} p_2$ | |
| | | $p_2,\ p_2 \Rightarrow_{\varrho 3} g_d$ | |
| | $o_2$ | $o_2,\ o_2 \Rightarrow_{\varrho 4} p_2$ | (no counter-argument) |
| | | $p_2,\ p_2 \Rightarrow_{\varrho 5} p_9$ | |
| | | $p_9,\ p_9 \Rightarrow_{\varrho 6} g_1$ | |
| $a_2$ | $o_1$ | $o_1,\ o_1 \Rightarrow_{\varrho 1} p_5$ | $\neg o_1$ by $a_3$ |
| | | $p_5,\ p_5 \Rightarrow_{\varrho 2} p_2$ | |
| | | $p_2,\ p_2 \Rightarrow_{\varrho 3} g_d$ | |
| | $o_2$ | $o_2,\ o_2 \Rightarrow_{\varrho 18} p_6$ | $\neg p_6$ by $a_3$ |
| | | $p_6,\ p_6 \Rightarrow_{\varrho 19} p_2$ | |
| | | $p_2,\ p_2 \Rightarrow_{\varrho 5} p_9$ | |
| | | $p_9,\ p_9 \Rightarrow_{\varrho 6} g_1$ | |
| $a_3$ | $o_2$ | $o_2,\ o_2 \Rightarrow_{\varrho 12} p_3$ | (no counter-argument) |
| | | $p_3,\ p_3 \Rightarrow_{\varrho 13} p_7$ | |
| | | $p_7,\ p_7 \Rightarrow_{\varrho 14} g_3$ | |
| | $o_3$ | (no argument) | |

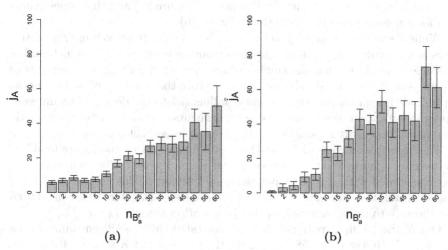

**Fig. 2.** Average (countered) option justification percentages $j_\mathcal{A}$ and $\bar{j}_\mathcal{A}$ (with standard errors of the mean) with $n_{B_a^r} \in \{1, \ldots, 25\}$

## 5.2   Experimental Validation of Scenario Generation

The scenario generation method is controlled by a large number of input parameters. To investigate which input parameter settings within a reasonable range (see Table 4) produce interesting dialogues a software experiment was performed. Scenarios were generated repeatedly, with a total of a 1000, with random

**Table 6.** Input parameters and their influence on $j_A$ and $\bar{j}_A$

| | option justification $j_A$ | | | | countered option justification $\bar{j}_A$ | | | |
|---|---|---|---|---|---|---|---|---|
| | $\beta$ | $t$ | $P$ | ideal | $\beta$ | $t$ | $P$ | ideal |
| $l$ | −0.51 | −28.66 | < 0.001 | 5 | −0.05 | −1.65 | < 0.1 | 4 |
| $n_{B_a^r}$ | 0.43 | 23.99 | < 0.001 | 60 | 0.53 | 14.60 | < 0.001 | 45 |
| $n_{B_a^{\bar{r}}}$ | 0.21 | 12.29 | < 0.001 | 9 | −0.03 | −0.84 | NS | 3 |
| $n_{O_r}$ | −0.15 | −8.71 | < 0.001 | 3 | −0.16 | −5.31 | < 0.001 | 2 |
| $n_S$ | −0.12 | −6.72 | < 0.001 | 75 | −0.15 | −4.67 | < 0.001 | 35 |
| $n_{B_{\bar{f}}^o}$ | −0.04 | −2.09 | < 0.05 | 5 | 0.08 | 2.52 | < 0.05 | 6 |
| $n_R$ | −0.04 | −2.54 | < 0.05 | 5 | 0.10 | 3.32 | < 0.001 | 5 |
| $n_{G_a^{\bar{r}}}$ | −0.02 | −0.96 | NS | 2 | 0.05 | 1.67 | < 0.1 | 3 |
| $n_A$ | 0.01 | 0.47 | NS | 4 | 0.37 | 12.26 | < 0.001 | 6 |
| $n_{G_r}$ | −0.01 | −0.43 | NS | 2 | −0.04 | −1.44 | NS | 3 |

parameter settings and the two metrics $j_A$ and $\bar{j}_A$ are applied to see if the agent's options in the scenario are justified and countered justified.

To visualize the effect an input parameter can have Figure 2 shows the (countered) option justification for the number of role-originating beliefs $n_{B_a^r}$ allocated to an agent. Clearly the more beliefs are assigned to an agent the higher chances are that it can form arguments for its options (Figure 2a) and that other agents can form a counter-argument to that (Figure 2b).

While the effects on individual parameters can already be seen in graphs, this does not provide a full insight into the dynamics between the parameters. For example, it might be that the number of roles has no effect unless the number of agents is high (or low). It is important to capture the interplay of parameters as so to find the parameters that are most influential to the degree of (countered) option justification. When performing experiments that make use of the scenario generation process it is possible to adjust those important parameters.

The input parameters with the strongest influence on $j_A$ and $\bar{j}_A$ are found by performing a multiple linear regression analysis on the set of 2000 scenarios that were generated with random input parameter settings. This creates a model of the data and, in a stepwise fashion, determines the parameters that contributed significantly to the (countered) option justification metrics $j_A$ and $\bar{j}_A$.

Out of the 10 input parameters 7 have a statistically significant influence on $j_A$, with $F(10, 1989) = 158.7$, $P < 0.001$ and adjusted R-squared 0.44. This means that 44% of the variance in $j_A$ can be explained from the 7 input parameters. For $\bar{j}_A$ 8 parameters have a statistically significant influence, with $F(10, 768) = 42.94$, $P < 0.001$ and adjusted R-squared 0.35, that is, explaining 35% of the variation in $\bar{j}_A$. Table 6 shows the input parameters with significant influence ordered by the amount of influence (standard beta coefficient), $t$ and $P$ values (probability values, where non-significant parameters are labelled NP).

Different interesting results can be derived from the statistical analysis. Foremost, when experimenting with the deliberation system and scenario generation process of this paper the length of rule chains $l$ is the first parameter that should be varied when a differing degree of option justification $j_A$ is to be tested. The bigger $l$ is, the smaller $j_A$ will be, in line with the intuition that it increases belief disparity. On the other hand, if focus of an experiment is on countering proposals the number of agents $n_A$ should be varied instead, since that will have most influence on $\bar{j}_A$. Unsurprisingly the number of role-originating beliefs $n_{B_a^r}$ has a high influence on both $j_A$ and $\bar{j}_A$, since a larger number of beliefs from an agent's role will increase the chance of ending op with all rules for a chain or the right negated beliefs for a chain respectively. Moreover, it has an even bigger influence on $\bar{j}_A$ than on $j_A$, visualized by the steeper slope in Figure 2.

The most influential parameters have been established, but not yet the parameter setting that gives the most interesting dialogues, that is, that maximizes $j_A$ and $\bar{j}_A$. This often will be the starting point when experimenting since it offers the agents scenarios with most chances of proposing options and countering those. The parameter setting that maximizes one of the metrics will be called the ideal setting and can be found using the regression model defined above. As the model predicts precisely (with $P < 0.001$) the outcome of $j_A$ or $\bar{j}_A$ it can also be used to find the maximal value. A sufficiently large data set ($N = 2000$) is produced for both metrics and maximal values are found. The parameter values that produce these maximal values are shown in Table 6 and yield $j_A = 66\%$ and $\bar{j}_A = 99\%$. Hence, with the ideal settings for $j_A$ the agents will be able to propose roughly half of their options while with the ideal values for $\bar{j}_A$ the agents can counter essentially all options that are justified. Future work will study how a single ideal setting for combined measures of interestingness can be established.

# 6    Conclusion

A methodology has been proposed to model a scenario generation process for argumentation-enabled deliberation dialogues. The contribution is twofold. First, the state of the art in preparation of experiments for argumentation-based dialogues has been advanced. A scenario generation process for deliberation is proposed that is the first to the authors' knowledge that allows for structured argumentation and through this supporting the full dynamics of the underlying argumentation problem. Secondly, it is shown how an experimental analysis helps to evaluate the quality of the scenario generation process by identifying the most influential input parameters and giving the ideal parameter settings that maximize the interestingness of scenarios.

The method as proposed in this paper, as well as the specific system described, is used in a larger project to make the uses of argumentation in multiagent systems concrete. It has allowed us to experimentally analyse the uses of argumentation in realistic scenarios by testing a variety of strategies for argumentative and non-arguing agents as well as identify specific scenarios in which argumentation is more (or less) suited.

**Acknowledgments.** This research was supported by the Netherlands Organisation for Scientific Research (NWO) under project number 612.066.823.

# References

1. Black, E., Bentley, K.: An Empirical Study of a Deliberation Dialogue System. In: Modgil, S., Oren, N., Toni, F. (eds.) TAFA 2011. LNCS, vol. 7132, pp. 132–146. Springer, Heidelberg (2012)
2. Dung, P.M.: On the acceptability of arguments and its fundamental role in non-monotonic reasoning, logic programming and n-person games. Artificial Intelligence 77(2), 321–357 (1995)
3. Karunatillake, N.C., Jennings, N.R., Rahwan, I., McBurney, P.: Dialogue games that agents play within a society. Artificial Intelligence 173(9-10), 935–981 (2009)
4. Kok, E.M., Meyer, J.-J.C., Prakken, H., Vreeswijk, G.A.W.: A Formal Argumentation Framework for Deliberation Dialogues. In: McBurney, P., Rahwan, I., Parsons, S. (eds.) ArgMAS 2010. LNCS, vol. 6614, pp. 31–48. Springer, Heidelberg (2011)
5. McBurney, P., Hitchcock, D., Parsons, S.: The eightfold way of deliberation dialogue. International Journal of Intelligent Systems 22(1), 95–132 (2007)
6. Ontañón, S., Plaza, E.: Multiagent Inductive Learning: an Argumentation-based Approach. In: Proceedings of the 27th International Conference on Machine Learning, Haifa, Israel, vol. (2), pp. 839–846 (2010)
7. Paglieri, F., Castelfranchi, C.: Why argue? Towards a cost-benefit analysis of argumentation. Argument and Computation 1(1), 71–91 (2010)
8. Pasquier, P., Hollands, R., Rahwan, I., Dignum, F., Sonenberg, L.: An empirical study of interest-based negotiation. Autonomous Agents and Multi-Agent Systems 22(2), 249–288 (2010)
9. Prakken, H.: An abstract framework for argumentation with structured arguments. Argument and Computation 1(2), 93–124 (2010)
10. Rahwan, I.: Guest editorial: Argumentation in multi-agent systems. Autonomous Agents and Multi-Agent Systems 11(2), 115–125 (2005)
11. Rao, A., Georgeff, M.: Modeling rational agents within a BDI-architecture. In: Proceedings of the 2nd International Conference on Principles of Knowledge Representation and Reasoning, pp. 473–484. Morgan Kaufmann (1991)
12. Walton, D.N., Krabbe, E.C.W.: Commitment in dialogue: Basic concepts of interpersonal reasoning. State University of New York Press, New York (1995)

# What Are Models for?

Peter McBurney

Department of Informatics, King's College London, London WC2R 2LS, UK

**Abstract.** In this paper I discuss some of the purposes and functions of building models, particularly agent-based models, and present a comprehensive list of these purposes and functions. Careful thought and attention is needed when modeling domains containing intelligent entities, which is usually the case for agent modeling. Reflection on the challenges involved in such domains leads me to propose the construction of meta-models, which are models of the relationship between an intended model of the domain and the entities in the domain, when the entities may have access to the intended model or its outputs. Agent-based computing approaches provide disciplined means of specifying, designing, developing and evaluating such meta-models.

## 1 Introduction

What are models for? Most users and developers of models, in my experience, seem to assume the answer to this question is obvious and thus never raise it. In fact, modeling has many potential purposes, and some of these may conflict with one another. Criticism of modeling efforts or the outputs of those efforts may arise because of mis-perception of the aims and purposes of the modeling activity. Agent-based modeling is usually undertaken for domains having autonomous entities, whether living or organizational, and these entities may also be intelligent. In such cases, a model may exert an influence on the domain being modeled, because the entities in the domain may have, or may seek to have, models of their own. I discuss some of these issues in this paper, starting with the issues of representation and prediction of some real world domain. Many of my reflections apply to any type of modeling, not just agent-based modeling and not even just computer simulation modeling; they also apply to both models developed for business and public policy decisions as well as models for research purposes.

## 2 Representational and Predictive Functions

### 2.1 Models and Reality

Most modelers when asked what models are for are likely to answer that they are intended to represent some real phenomenon, some portion of reality. Following Rosen [1] and Hughes [2], we might understand the relationship between the model and reality by means of a sequence of relationships between reality and models:[1]

---

[1] The three process labels are due to Hughes [2].

M. Cossentino et al. (Eds.): EUMAS 2011, LNAI 7541, pp. 175–188, 2012.
© Springer-Verlag Berlin Heidelberg 2012

- *Denotation* is the process by which the model (let us call it $M1$) is developed in order to represent some portion of reality (called $R1$).
- *Demonstration* is the working-out or working-through of the model, finding the consequences of the initial states or assumptions either deductively or otherwise, so that we move from some initial model state $M1$ to some consequential state or collection of model outputs, $M2$.
- *Interpretation* is the process of inference from the model consequences $M2$ back to the reality intended to be modeled, perhaps back to an inferred or consequential state of reality, called $R2$.

Demonstration could be undertaken in many different ways: deductive mathematical consequence; physical motions, as in a wind-tunnel or in an orrery (a physical model of planetary relationships and motions); or the flow of communicative interactions between individual agents in a multi-agent model of a society. These various mechanisms are referred to as the *internal dynamics* of the model by Hughes [2]. Morgan [3] argues that such dynamics are typically set going by something external to the model, such as the asking of a *"What if"* question. When run, the model's internal dynamics lead it to some resulting state or to the generation of outputs or consequences, as properties of the model. The modeler then uses these model properties to infer conclusions about the real domain that the model was intended to represent. Such inference from the conclusions or consequences generated by the model back to the reality may be contested. In mainstream economic theory, for example, inference from non-deductive models has usually been regarded as problematic, as discussed in [4,5]. One consequence of this view in mainstream economics has been that research drawing on agent-based models has had great difficulty being published.[2] But since all modeling involves abstraction from reality, even deductive inference is only valid if certain governing assumptions about those aspects of reality abstracted away hold true. In past work [7], we identified 12 inference steps necessary to validly draw conclusions about human carcinogenicity of chemicals based on experimental evidence, of which only one step was statistical inference (i.e., inductive inference). Any inference from a mathematical model using deductive internal dynamics back to reality would require similar contextual inference steps for validity of the interpretation stage.

Robert Rosen understood this fact through the use of a category theoretic model of the modeling process [1]. The three successive processes — denotation, followed by demonstration, followed by interpretation — that connect real state $R1$ to real state $R2$ are only valid if the indirect path they construct between $R1$ and $R2$ via $M1$ and $M2$ mirrors some alternative direct path between $R1$ and $R2$. In other words, modeling the domain will only produce valid inference if the successive stages of denotation, demonstration, and interpretation mirror (in some domain-specific sense) the development of the real phenomenon when it transitions from $R1$ to $R2$.

What exactly does it mean *"to mirror"*? In an influential article in 1953 [8], the economist Milton Friedman argued that models aimed at prediction only need to predict well. They do not need to, and indeed may not be able to, describe the world in state

---

[2] According to [6], only 8 out of 43,000 recent papers in the top twenty journals in Economics drew upon multi-agent models or computational economics.

$R1$, nor even the actual physical or social processes that take the world from state $R1$ to state $R2$. In other words, a model may have good predictive properties without having good representational or explanatory properties. Newton's theory of gravity, for example, predicted the motion of the planets in solar orbit without providing any (or any reasonable) explanation for gravity. Friedman's famous example also involved Newton: a good player of billiards may be able, based on experience and intuition, predict the likely motion of a billiard ball without any knowledge, let alone any use, of Newton's three laws of motion. Whether or not we accept Friedman's argument depends to a large extent on what we believe a model is for: is it essentially to predict the world or only to represent or explain it?

The game theorist and economist, Ariel Rubinstein, has said that his main purpose in creating models is to better understand and to sharpen his intuitions about the real phenomenon being modeled [9]. How does a model help in understanding? In a series of papers, Mary Morgan and colleagues [3,10,11,12,13,14] have argued that models in economics are idealizations or abstractions of aspects of reality which enable the creation of worlds parallel to the real world. By altering the underlying assumptions or by exploring the internal mechanisms of the model, the modeler is able to explore alternatives to the real world by, for example, asking *What if?* questions, considering counter-factual assumptions, or pursuing alternative development paths. Thus, both the world represented *by* the model and the world *of* the model can be explored. In this view of modeling, Morgan argues, models themselves are not best understood as passive recipients of exploration, but as active participants in the creation of knowledge [3]: by their physical, mathematical, or computational nature, models resist some uses and they facilitate others.

Another issue for representation is that most models typically denote multiple real phenomena, not one particular phenomenon or one state of reality. Newton's equations of motion, although developed with the planets of Earth's solar system in mind, in fact constitute a class of distinct models, and only some (perhaps even only one) denote the actual planets of our Solar system. To model the particular solar system we find ourselves in, various variables, called parameters, need to be instantiated with particular values. This process of instantiation of parameter values so as to match a particular reality is called *model calibration*. The idea that modeling is a process of creating classes of models has been explored in economics by John Sutton [15]. An example of this class-of-models approach is the model of diffusion of agent-software technologies across business networks given in [16]. A related view, due to Trygve Haavelmo [17] and Marcel Boumans [18], is that a model can be seen as an experimental design, and the data used for calibration comprises one experimental outcome of it. Running the model with different input parameters or initial values generates additional experimental outcomes.

Calibration of models and assessment of model predictions assumes that we have some way to measure those aspects of reality that our model purports to represent. This can be problematic, for various reasons. In the case of economic and social domains, the aspects of reality used for calibration or model prediction may be social artefacts: most macro-economic variables (e.g., inflation rates, unemployment levels, etc) do not exist in nature, and are themselves socially-constructed entities. Often their construction is a long and technical process, itself drawing on theories or models of the phenomena in question, and subject to debate and contestation along the way. There are many different operationalizations of the variable called the *supply of money*, for example, and so a modeler may have considerable freedom of choice in calibrating or assessing his or her model against monetary reality. A related issue is the use of *stylized facts* for model calibration and assessment: these are generalizations of reality, also usually developed or mediated through some theory. In economics, the "fact" that *an increase in price leads to a fall in aggregate demand* is an example: in any particular market at any particular time, aggregate demand may or may not fall when price rises, for any number of reasons. So many are the exceptions to this particular "fact" that economists even have a name for the exceptions to it, which are called Giffen Goods. In calibrating or assessing the predictions of a model against stylized facts, a modeler is not using a model to represent reality, but using a model to represent another model of reality.

A further issue with model calibration and assessment arises in theoretical physics and elsewhere: we may have no independent access to the reality intended to be represented by the model other than via the model itself. String theory, for example, seeks to model reality by positing a number of additional spatial dimensions to the three which we humans have experience of. Since we do not have access to these dimensions we cannot independently calibrate string theoretic models against them, nor assess any predictions arising from our models about them.[3] It would seem to me that this situation makes absurd any claims that mathematics is *"unreasonably effective"* in modeling scientific phenomena [20], since how we could tell? Our only way to assess the effectiveness or otherwise of mathematical models of physics is via more mathematics.[4] Likewise, marketing models seeking to predict future consumer purchase intentions can not be calibrated independently of the models themselves, since there are no facts of the matter to assess the model against.

## 2.2 Intelligent Entities

For the social and policy sciences, the real phenomena represented by a model usually include human individuals or organizations. These entities may be intelligent and may thus act in anticipation of future events.[5] Indeed, models of human societies or human activities may well seek to represent entities — for example, economic agents — who themselves have models of their environment, and who may use these models to guide their actions. What should the modeler assume about the models being used by the entities being modeled? This is a question which most agent-based modelers will face at some point, because agent-based models seek to represent entities in some real domain as separate individuals. One very strange answer to this question is given by a branch of economics, so-called *Rational Expectations Theory*, which assumes, firstly, that all

---

[3] Perhaps this explains why, at the time of writing, String Theory and M-theory models have yet to generate a single empirically-testable prediction after nearly four decades and thousands of person-years of development [19].

[4] I owe this insight to Stephen Reye.

[5] Focusing mainly on biological and ecological domains, Rosen called such phenomena *anticipatory systems* [1].

economic actors in the model have access to an identical model themselves, and, secondly, that this identical model is the very model being constructed by the modeler. This recursive theory, due originally to economist John Muth [21], has become influential in mainstream economics.[6] To anyone outside mainstream economics, however, these two assumptions are simply bizarre.

Another issue for models of intelligent entities is that the model, or even the fact of modeling, may influence the behavior of the real entities. The most famous example is the Black-Scholes-Merton model of options pricing [23,24]. Prior to the development of this model, trade in options and similar derivative financial products was limited because potential traders were not able to coherently price such products, and there was no agreed theoretical basis for determining such prices. Black and Scholes, and separately Merton, proposed a family of models for options pricing which then led to an explosion in trading of these. To develop their models, the modelers needed to make assumptions about how traders would behave in such marketplaces. Once the models were available, traders, having available no other guide to their behavior, adopted the behaviors assumed by the modelers. Borrowing a term from the philosophy of language for utterances which bring about changes in the world [25], sociologists of economics have called such modeling activities, *performative* [26]: they create the very reality they purport to describe.

Other examples in Economics involve the use of economic game theory to design auction mechanisms, particularly for complex domains such as the combinatorial auctions of PCS radio-frequency spectrum in the USA from 1994 onwards by the US Federal Communications Commission [27,28]. Here one can see the models acting as blueprints for the behaviors of the participants, facilitating some behaviors and precluding others.

Game theory also features in another primary instance of models being performative: the development of western military strategy for nuclear weapons. Game theory models of nuclear warfare provided strategists with the language and conceptual frameworks to identify and explore alternative actions and their likely consequences in this domain [29,30]. One weakness with a game-theoretic view of some interaction is that the actions and strategies suggested by the theory rely on all the participants believing they are playing the same "game", and believing that the other participants also believe this of one another. Philip Mirowski even speculates that in the late 1950s, the USA feared that the leaders of the USSR were not playing the same game as they were, and so American

---

[6] An interesting question for sociologists of economics is why this theory became influential. One possible explanation is that these assumptions may lead the resulting models to be mathematically tractable more often than do more realistic assumptions. Another possible explanation is that rational expectations theory justifies a particular (conservative) position regarding public policy: any macro-economic policy action will be undermined by pre-emptive, countervailing actions by intelligent economic actors able to second-guess the policy makers. Thus, in this view, it is better for a policy-maker to do nothing than for policies to be subverted pre-emptively. As economist George Stigler once suggested [22], in the market for economic theories, as in any other market, the suppliers of theories produce the theories demanded by those potential consumers of theories who have the money to pay for them; perhaps, then, it should not be surprising that mainstream economic theory has tended to provide support for government policies that favour rich and powerful interests.

political and military leaders embarked on a campaign to persuade the Soviet Union to adopt game theory for nuclear strategy also[7] [30].

## 2.3   Models and Public Policy

Several features of the relationships between models and domains containing intelligent entities have significant consequences for public policy development and implementation. Two important such features, both related to perfomativity of models, are those of self-fulfilling and self-denying prophecies.[8] If everyone in some system believes that all the others in the system will act in a certain way, each person may then act pre-emptively or in mitigation such that the forecasted behaviour is, or is not, brought about. For example, if there are two alternative routes between two towns, and the majority of drivers hear a radio forecast of heavy traffic on the first route, they may all choose instead to take the second route, thus leading to congestion on the second and lighter traffic on the first; the forecast would therefore be self-denying. Alternatively, if the experience of drivers is such that they tend to dis-believe radio forecasts they hear, then the majority may choose the first route, thus fulfilling the forecast.

As would be expected, these issues become important in matters of public policy, particularly where governments or regulators, by their announcements or their words, communicate forecasts to citizens. In Britain in March 2012, drivers of tankers carrying petrol to service stations indicated that they may stage a strike the following month. A Government minister then announced that car-owners should ensure, in anticipation of any strike, that their petrol tanks were full, an announcement that led to mass and immediate panic buying of petrol. There was thus soon a shortage of petrol caused solely by the widespread and erroneous belief that a petrol shortage was imminent. The fact that panic buying led to garages selling out of petrol of course confirmed public beliefs of an impending shortage.[9]

Because of incidents such as this, most western Governments are very careful about what they announce to their citizens, how they announce it, and when, regarding matters of public health, food safety or national security. Such careful consideration is not uniform across all public policy areas, however. Within economics, there is a widespread belief that the more information is widely known to economic agents, the better will be their economic decision-making, and the better the functioning of the economy as a whole. This belief has led most western central banks to release full information about their decision-making processes for deciding policy on interest rates and on other monetary policy instruments; the Bank of England, for example, openly publishes the minutes of the meetings of its Monetary Policy Committee (albeit with a short delay after each meeting). Clearly, the economic actors concerned with decisions about central bank interest rates are (or, are assumed to be) better informed, and possibly more deliberative

---

[7] US leaders seem to have done so by stating publicly that game theory was *not* useful for nuclear strategy, as a form of reverse psychology.

[8] These terms were coined by sociologist Robert K. Merton in 1948 [31], who was, interestingly, the father of Robert C. Merton, co-developer of options pricing theory [24].

[9] Funder [32] presents another example, from the last days of the German Democratic Republic in 1988-1989.

decision-makers, than are members of the general public concerned with mad-cow disease or similar health scares. But, as far as I am aware, there is no over-arching theory or model of the relationships between model and domain for public policy domains comprising intelligent, purposeful entities that suggests information should be publicly released by governments in the case of economic domains, and not publicly released in the case of health or security domains. Both these contrasting public policies (release all information readily versus release only limited information carefully) seem to be based merely on implicit, untested assumptions about model-domain relationships and the impacts of additional information on participant behaviours.

## 3  Mensatic and Epideictic Functions

In addition to representation and prediction, models also serve several other functions in use. Here I discuss two functions which are usually either overlooked or implicit. In their list of three primary roles of business models, for example, Baden-Fuller and Morgan [33] appear to overlook both these roles of models.

The first I term the **mensatic** function, from the Latin word for table, *mensa*. Here the model acts as a vehicle to identify interested stakeholders and to bring them together, around a common metaphorical table. Models for forecasting demand can serve this function internally within companies and with interested outsiders, such as distribution partners [34]. For potential new ventures, particularly those in high-technology industries, business models and plans serve this function with investors and with other potential stakeholders, such as regulators and suppliers. Doganova and Eyquem-Renault present a case study of a potential high-technology start-up in France, describing this mensatic role in detail [35]. In matters of public policy, too, models can act to bring stakeholders together and to help co-ordinate their beliefs and actions. In formulating public health policies for dealing with malaria in developing countries, for instance, epidemiological models can act to co-ordinate the actions of the many stakeholders who need to participate for effective strategy formulation and execution: medical personnel, public health officials, national, regional and local government officials, community and religious leaders, foreign aid donors, international agencies, pharmaceutical companies, and suppliers of other treatment materials. Policy development and planning requires the co-ordination of actions between these various stakeholders in order to design and execute co-ordinated campaigns against the disease [36].

By bringing stakeholders "to the table", models also serve as the basis for identifying, and potentially deciding, trade-offs in public policy. In complex policy domains such as public health or environmental risk assessment, the potential consequences, costs or benefits of decisions may be experienced differentially by different people or groups within a society, and thus identification of these becomes a major part of public policy formulation [37]. Policy decisions in these domains usually involve complex multi-attribute trade-offs, and, here too, both the making of policy and the forging of a wide public consensus benefit from having different stakeholders discuss and compare decision alternatives [38]. Within western public policy, these deliberative decision processes are probably most finely developed for environmental risk assessment decisions [39,40] and in land-use planning decisions [41].

The mensatic role of models is particularly important for decisions made by multiple people or teams, such as those for major public policy domains. Even for the trading decisions of a private hedge fund, decisions may involve competitors and other outsiders, with the model playing a central role, as Hardie and Mackenize have shown [42]. For economic and marketplace domains, sociologist Michel Callon has called models *market devices*, because they help to engineer, to bring into being, the associated marketplace [43].

Models may also serve an **epideictic** function. Epideictic reasoning involves inference from the form or the style of an argument, rather than from its content only. In an example due to William Rehg [44], suppose you seek advice from two different doctors about treatment for a serious medical condition. One doctor, let us call her Dr X, says that there are three possible courses of treatment. She labels these courses, A, B and C, and then proceeds to walk you methodically through each course – what separate basic procedures are involved, in what order, with what what likely consequences and side effects, and with what costs and durations, what chances of success or failure, and what survival rates. She finishes this methodical exposition by summing up each treatment, with pithy statements such as, *"Course A is the cheapest and most proven. Course B is an experimental treatment, which makes it higher risk, but it may be the most effective. Course C . . . "*, etc.

The other doctor, lets call him Dr Y, in contrast talks in a manner which is apparently lacking all structure. He begins a long, discursive narrative about the many different basic procedures possible, not in any particular order, jumping back and forth between these as he focuses first on the costs of procedures, then switching to their durations, then back again to a discussion of costs, then on to some expected side effects, with tangential discussions about the history of the experimental tests undertaken on one of the procedures, and also about the architect who built the hospital, etc, etc. And he does all this without any indication that some basic procedures are part of larger courses of treatment, or that they are even linked in any way, and speaking without using any patient-friendly labeling or summarizing of the decision-options.

Which doctor would you choose to treat you? If this description was all that you knew, then Doctor X would appear to be the much better organized of the two doctors. Most of us would have more confidence being treated by a doctor who sounds better-organized, who appears to know what he or she was doing, compared to a doctor who sounds disorganized. More importantly, it is also evident that Doctor X knows how to structure what she knows into a coherent whole, into a form which makes her knowledge easier to transmit to others, easier for a patient to understand, and which also facilitates the subsequent decision-making by the patient. We generally have more confidence in the underlying knowledge and expertise of people able to explain their knowledge and expertise well, than in those who cannot, and usually this confidence is justified.

If we reasoned this way, we would be choosing between the two doctors on the basis of their different rhetorical styles: we would be judging the contents of their arguments (in this case, the content is their ability to provide us with effective treatment) on the basis of the styles of their arguments. Such reasoning processes, which use an argument's form to assess its content, are called epideictic, as are arguments which draw attention to their own style.

Since the advent of spreadsheet software applications, business plans for new ventures or new products almost invariably contain a model of the business and of the marketplace in which it will exist. Such business plans and models are often out-of-date very quickly, particularly in turbulent or high-technology markets, or depend on unverifiable conjectures about which there are no facts of the matter (such as future consumer purchase intentions or the reactions of competitors). Investors and other stakeholders, such as distribution partners or suppliers, assessing plans for new business ventures know all this. The function of such business plans and models is not to model or to predict or to control reality accurately, since these goals in any case would usually be impossible. Rather, the function of these models is to force intending new venture managers to engage in structured and rigorous thinking about the domain, and to provide a means by which potential investors in the venture can probe this thinking. By challenging the prior assumptions, the internal dynamics, or the interpretation of the model, potential investors can assess the depth and rigor of the thinking of the management, as well as as assessing managers' flexibility and adaptability in recognizing and responding to changes in the market environment. Investors and other stakeholders thus typically engage in a stress-test of managers' beliefs and plans — contesting the assumptions and reasoning of the business plan; being unreasonable in questions and challenges; prodding and poking and provoking the management team to see how well and how quickly they can respond, in real time, without preparation. In all of this, a decision on the substance of the investment is being made from evidence about the form, of how well the management team responds to such stress testing. This is perfectly rational, given the absence of any other basis on which to make a decision and given our imperfect knowledge of the future. Thus, the business model becomes a vehicle by which potential investors and other stakeholders may assess the capabilities of the management team; the model serves, in other words, an epideictic function.

## 4    A List of Reasons for Modeling

Several authors have proposed lists of reasons for undertaking modeling, or lists of potential functions of models: Rubinstein [9] lists four reasons for undertaking economic modeling; Bailer-Jones [45] lists five functions of models in science; Epstein [46] lists 17 reasons to build explicit models;[10] and Baden-Fuller and Morgan [33] present three functions of models in business domains. Each of these lists has omissions. Seeking a comprehensive list of reasons for constructing models, I have drawn on these four lists as well as the the reflections above, to create the following list:

**1. To understand natural reality:** To better understand some real phenomena or existing system. This is perhaps the most commonly perceived purpose of modeling, in the sciences and the social sciences.

**2. To predict natural reality:** To predict (some properties of) some real phenomena or existing system. As discussed above, a model aiming to predict some domain may be

---

[10] Epstein's reasons are at multiple levels of granularity, and some of his reasons are the consequences of modeling rather than reasons for doing so, at least for honest modelers, e.g., *"Challenge the robustness of prevailing theory through peturbations"* and *"Expose prevailing wisdom as incompatible with available data"*. He also numbers only 16 of the 17 reasons.

successful without aiding our understanding of the domain at all. For many modeling activities, calibration and prediction are problematic, and so predictive capability may not always be possible as a means of model assessment.

**3. To control natural reality:** To manage or control (some properties of) some real phenomena or existing system.

**4. To understand an existing human model or artefact:** To better understand a model of some real phenomena or existing system. Arguably, most of economic theorizing and modeling falls into this category, and Rubinsteins preferred purpose is this type [9].

**5. To predict an existing human model or artefact:** To predict (some properties of) a model of some real phenomena or existing system.

**6. To understand, predict or control a future human model or artefact:** To better understand, predict or manage some intended (not-yet-existing) artificial system, so to guide its design and development. Understanding a system that does not yet exist is qualitatively different to understanding an existing domain or system, because the possibility of calibration is absent and because the model may act to define the limits and possibilities of subsequent design actions on the artificial system. The use of speech act theory (a model of natural human language) for the design of artificial machine-to-machine languages, or the use of economic game theory (a mathematical model of a stylized conceptual model of particular micro-economic realities) for the design of online auction sites are examples here. The modeling activity can even be performative, helping to create the reality it may purport to describe, as in the case of the Black-Scholes-Merton model of options pricing discussed above.

**7. As a locus for discussion:** To provide a locus for discussion between relevant stakeholders in some business or public policy domain, a function I termed, *mensatic*. Most large-scale business planning models have this purpose within companies, particularly when multiple partners are involved. Likewise, models of major public policy issues, such as epidemics, often have this function. In many complex domains, such as those in public health, models provide a means to tame the complexity of the domain. Modeling thus enables stakeholders to jointly explore relevant concepts, data, system dynamics, policy options, and the assessment of potential consequences of policy options, in a structured and shared way.

**8. To resolve trade-offs:** To provide a means for identification, articulation and potentially resolution of alternative action options, alternative trade-offs, and their consequences in some business or public policy domain; examples include health risk assessment of chemicals or new products by environmental protection agencies, and models of disease epidemics deployed by government health authorities.

**9. To structure thinking:** To enable rigorous, structured and justified thinking about the assumptions and their relationships to one another in modeling some domain. Business planning models usually serve this purpose. They may be used to inform actions, both to eliminate or mitigate potential negative consequences and to enhance potential positive consequences, as in retroflexive decision making [47].

**10. To train people:** Models can provide expedited and deliberately-focused experiences of reality, which is why flight simulators are used to train airplane pilots. Market games and marketing models are now commonplace in companies for training of marketing, sales and advertising staff.

**11. To assess the modelers:** To enable a means of assessment of managerial competencies of the people undertaking the modeling activity. This is the *epideictic* function of modeling, where the model itself is a vehicle to enable interested stakeholders to learn about and assess the assumptions, the reasoning processes, and the future action plans of the people doing the modeling. As mentioned above, business plans and models for new ventures are almost always used in this way by potential investors and business partners to assess the management team of new ventures, and to decide whether or not to participate in the venture.

**12. To play:** As a means of play, to enable the exercise of human intelligence, ingenuity and creativity, in developing and exploring the properties of models themselves. This purpose is true of that human activity known as doing pure mathematics, and perhaps of most of that academic activity known as doing mathematical economics.

# 5   Conclusions

The list of reasons for modeling given in this paper shows the diversity of functions of models, particularly when models are created not merely for research, but to support decision-making in business or in public policy. The brief discussion at the end of Section 2.3 about the varying views across different public policy domains on the question of what model information should be available to the entities being modeled, points to the need for the development of meta-models for any model of an important domain. Imagine we seek to model a target domain, $X$. A meta-model $M$ would include the intended model of the domain, let us call it Model $A$, together with a representation (another model, $B$) of the domain $X$. The key purpose of the meta-model is to better understand (and possibly also to predict and to control) the relationships between Model $A$ and the real intelligent entities inside domain $X$. Depending on the granularity of our model $A$, then we may be able to assume that model $B$ is in fact the same model as model $A$. Likewise, the real entities inside $X$ may be assumed themselves to have access to model $A$ or to model $B$. As with any model, constructing the meta-model $M$ will allow us to explore *"What if?"* questions, such as alternative policies regarding the release of information arising from model $A$ to the intelligent entities inside domain $X$. Indeed, we could even explore the consequences of allowing the entities inside $X$ to have access to our meta-model $M$.

Constructing such a meta-model in any particular domain will not necessarily be straightforward and will require careful thinking and analysis. Because of the recursiveness involved, the thought and analysis required is similar to that used in counterespionage, as described, for example, in [48]. Fortunately, we in the multi-agent systems community have several well-developed techniques for undertaking such meta-modeling: proven methodologies for agent-oriented software engineering, such as *Gaia* [49], and detailed, comprehensive techniques for the careful analysis of dynamic knowledge and belief, such as those in [50]. Arguably, all we currently lack is a good theoretical understanding of joint action, and how it occurs among a group of autonomous agents.

**Acknowledgments.** This paper arose from an invited talk at the ninth *European Work-shop on Multi-Agent Systems (EUMAS 2011)* held in Maastricht, The Netherlands, in November 2011. I thank the organizers for their invitations to speak at EUMAS and to write this paper for the post-proceedings volume. A later version of the talk was given to the 2012 workshop of the *European Working Group on Decision Support Systems (EWG-DSS)*, held in Liverpool, UK, in April 2012. I thank the EWG-DSS organizers for their invitation to speak there, and I am grateful to the audiences of both these talks for their interesting questions and comments. My understanding of the epistemological and pragmatic issues surrounding modeling has benefited greatly from discussions over many years with a large number of people, including Robert Bartels, Martin Chapman, Neill Haine, Tony Hawkins, Benjamin Herd, Peter Lewis, Robert Marks, Marian McEwin, David Midgley, Tim Miller, Lin Padgham, Simon Parsons, the late Ray Paton, Steve Phelps, Stephen Reye, John Roberts, Edward Robinson, Elizabeth Sklar, Elizabeth Sonenberg, Robert Stratton, Nassim Taleb, and the late Ted Wheelwright. The views expressed here, along with any mistakes or omissions, are my own.

# References

1. Rosen, R.: Anticipatory Systems: Philosophical, Mathematical and Methodological Foundations. Pergamon Press, Oxford (1985)
2. Hughes, R.I.G.: Models and representation. Philosophy of Science 64(suppl.), S325–S336 (1997)
3. Morgan, M.S.: Models, stories and the economic world. Journal of Economic Methodology 8(3), 361–384 (2001)
4. Marks, R.E.: Validating simulation models: a general framework and four applied examples. Journal of Computational Economics 30(3), 265–290 (2007)
5. Midgley, D.F., Marks, R.E., Kunchamwar, D.: Building and assurance of agent-based models: an example and challenge to the field. Journal of Business Research 60(8), 884–893 (2007)
6. Leombruni, R., Richiardi, M.: Why are economists sceptical about agent-based simulations? Physica A 355, 103–109 (2005)
7. McBurney, P., Parsons, S.: Dialectical argumentation for reasoning about chemical carcinogenicity. Logic Journal of the IGPL 9(2), 191–203 (2001)
8. Friedman, M.: The methodology of positive economics. In: Friedman, M. (ed.) Essays in Positive Economics, pp. 3–43. University of Chicago Press, Chicago (1953)
9. Rubinstein, A.: Modeling Bounded Rationality. MIT Press, Cambridge (1998)
10. Morgan, M.S., Morrison, M.: Models as Mediators. Cambridge University Press, Cambridge (1999)
11. Morgan, M.S.: Symposium on *Marshall's Tendencies*: How models help economists to know. Economics and Philosophy 18, 5–16 (2002)
12. Morgan, M.S.: Imagination and imaging in model building. Philosophy of Science 71, 753–766 (2004)
13. Morgan, M.S.: 1: Modelling as a method of enquiry. Cambridge University Press (2009)
14. Morgan, M.S., Knuuttila, T.: Models and Modelling in Economics (2008)
15. Sutton, J.: Marshall's Tendencies: What can economists know? MIT Press, Cambridge (2000)
16. McKean, J., Shorter, H., Luck, M., McBurney, P., Willmott, S.: Technology diffusion: the case of agent technologies. Autonomous Agents and Multi-Agent Systems 17(3), 372–396 (2008)

17. Haavelmo, T.: The probability approach in econometrics. Econometrica 12(suppl.), 1–115 (1944)
18. Boumans, M.: How Economists Model the World to Numbers. Routledge, London (2005)
19. Smolin, L.: The Trouble With Physics: The Rise of String Theory, the Fall of a Science, and What Comes Next. Houghton Mifflin, New York City (2006)
20. Wigner, E.P.: The unreasonable effectiveness of mathematics in the natural sciences. Communications on Pure and Applied Mathematics 13, 1–14 (1960)
21. Muth, J.F.: Rational expectations and the theory of price movements. Econometrica 29(3), 315–335 (1961)
22. Stigler, G.J.: Do Economists matter? Southern Economic Journal 42(3), 347–354 (1976)
23. Black, F., Scholes, M.: The pricing of options and corporate liabilities. Journal of Political Economy 81(3), 637–654 (1973)
24. Merton, R.C.: Theory of rational option pricing. Bell Journal of Economics and Management Science 4(1), 141–183 (1973)
25. Austin, J.L.: How To Do Things with Words. Oxford University Press, Oxford (1962)
26. MacKenzie, D.A.: An equation and its worlds: *Bricolage*, exemplars, disunity and performativity in financial economics. Social Studies of Science 33, 831–868 (2003)
27. Alexandrova, A.: Connecting economic models to the real world: game theory and the FCC. Philosophy of the Social Sciences 36, 173–192 (2006)
28. Nik-Khah, E.: Designs on the Mechanism: Economics and the FCC Auctions. Ph.D., University of Notre Dame, Notre Dame, Indiana, USA (December 2005)
29. Kahn, H.: On Thermonuclear War, 2nd edn. Princeton University Press, Princeton (1961); First edition published 1960
30. Mirowski, P.: Machine Dreams: Economics Becomes a Cyborg Science. Cambridge University Press, Cambridge (2002)
31. Merton, R.K.: Social Theory and Social Structure. Free Press, New York City (1968)
32. Funder, A.: Stasiland: True Stories from Behind the Berlin Wall. Granta Books, London (2003)
33. Baden-Fuller, C., Morgan, M.S.: Business models as models. Long Range Planning 43, 156–171 (2010)
34. McBurney, P., Parsons, S., Green, J.: Forecasting demand for new telecommunications services: an introduction. Telematics and Informatics 19(3), 225–249 (2002)
35. Doganova, L., Eyquem-Renault, M.: What do business models do? innovation devices in technology entrepreneurship. Research Policy 38, 1559–1570 (2009)
36. The malERA Consultative Group on Modeling: A research agenda for malaria eradication: modeling. PLoS Medicine 8(1), e1000403 (2011)
37. Page, T.: A generic view of toxic chemicals and similar risks. Ecology Law Quarterly 7(2), 207–244 (1978)
38. Fiorino, D.J.: Environmental risk and democratic process: a critical review. Columbia Journal of Environmental Law 14, 501–547 (1989)
39. Graham, J.D., Rhomberg, L.: How risks are identified and assessed. Annals of the American Academy of Political and Social Science 545, 15–24 (1996)
40. Graham, J.D., Wiener, J.B. (eds.): Risk Verus Risk: Trade-offs in Protecting Health and the Environment. Harvard University Press, Cambridge (1995)
41. Forester, J.: The Deliberative Practitioner: Encouraging Participatory Planning Processes. MIT Press, Cambridge (1999)
42. Hardie, I., MacKenzie, D.: Assembling an economic actor: the *agencement* of a hedge fund. The Sociological Review 55(1), 57–80 (2007)
43. Muniesa, F., Millo, Y., Callon, M.: An introduction to market devices. The Sociological Review 55, 1–12 (2007)

44. Rehg, W.: Reason and rhetoric in Habermas's Theory of Argumentation. In: Jost, W., Hyde, M.J. (eds.) Rhetoric and Hermeneutics in Our Time: A Reader, pp. 358–377. Yale University Press, New Haven (1997)
45. Bailer-Jones, D.M.: When scientific models represent. International Studies in the Philosophy of Science 17(1), 59–74 (2003)
46. Epstein, J.M.: Why model? Keynote address to the Second World Congress on Social Simulation. George Mason University, USA (2008)
47. Wohlrapp, H.: A new light on non-deductive argumentation schemes. Argumentation 12, 341–350 (1998)
48. Bagley, T.H.: Spy Wars: Moles, Mysteries and Deadly Games. Yale University Press, New Haven (2007)
49. Wooldridge, M.J., Jennings, N.R., Kinny, D.: The Gaia methodology for agent-oriented analysis and design. Autonomous Agents and Multi-Agent Systems 3(3), 285–312 (2000)
50. Ditmarsch, H., Hoek, W., Kooi, B.: Dynamic Epistemic Logic. Synthese Library, vol. 337. Springer, Berlin (2007)

# QUERYPOMDP: POMDP-Based Communication in Multiagent Systems*

Francisco S. Melo[1], Matthijs T.J. Spaan[2], and Stefan J. Witwicki[1]

[1] INESC-ID/Instituto Superior Técnico
2780-990 Porto Salvo, Portugal
{fmelo,witwicki}@inesc-id.pt
[2] Delft University of Technology
2628 CD, Delft, The Netherlands
m.t.j.spaan@tudelft.nl

**Abstract.** Decentralized Partially Observable Markov Decision Processes (Dec-POMDPs) provide powerful modeling tools for multiagent decision-making in the face of uncertainty, but solving these models comes at a very high computational cost. Two avenues for side-stepping the computational burden can be identified: structured interactions between agents and intra-agent communication. In this paper, we focus on the interplay between these concepts, namely how sparse interactions impact the communication needs. A key insight is that in domains with local interactions the amount of communication necessary for successful joint behavior can be heavily reduced, due to the limited influence between agents. We exploit this insight by deriving local POMDP models that optimize each agent's communication behavior. Our experimental results show that our approach successfully exploits sparse interactions: we can effectively identify the situations in which it is beneficial to communicate, as well as trade off the cost of communication with overall task performance.

## 1 Introduction

Decentralized Partially Observable Markov Decision Processes (Dec-POMDPs) provide powerful modeling tools for multiagent decision-making with limited sensing capabilities in stochastic environments. However, the prohibitive computational cost required to compute an optimal decision rule renders them intractable except for the smallest of problems.[1] In the literature, two avenues for side-stepping the computational burden can be identified: *localized interactions between agents*—where the actions of each agent depend on the other agents only in specific, localized situations [1–7]—and *intra-agent communication*—where agents

---

* This work was funded in part by Fundação para a Ciência e a Tecnologia (INESC-ID multiannual funding) through the PIDDAC Program funds and the project CMU-PT/SIA/0023/2009 under the Carnegie Mellon-Portugal Program. M.S. is funded by the FP7 Marie Curie Actions Individual Fellowship #275217 (FP7-PEOPLE-2010-IEF).

[1] Dec-MDPs are known to be NEXP-complete even in 2-agent scenarios.

are able to communicate with one another so as to partly mitigate the impact of partial observability [8–15]. In this paper, we focus on the *interplay* between these concepts, namely how sparse interactions impact the communication needs.

A key insight is that in domains with local interactions the amount of communication necessary for successful joint behavior can be heavily reduced, due to the limited influence between agents. Several previous works have implicitly relied on this observation, exploring sparse interactions by having agents share information locally [5, 7, 11, 16, 17]. In this work, we explicitly reason about the benefits of communication/information sharing in scenarios with sparse interactions. Sparse interactions enable, to some extent, decoupling the decision-process of the different agents. We leverage such decoupling to derive local models that optimize each agent's communication behavior, allowing it to overcome partial observability in those situations where decoupled decisions are not possible.

We provide a new way of optimizing communication by proposing a model in which agents need to plan about when to query other agents' local states, which we call QUERYPOMDP. We observe that to execute optimal joint policies in fully observable scenarios—policies which can be computed efficiently—agents will generally need to reason about the state of other agents. However, in scenarios where interactions are sparse, this need will be greatly reduced. Our approach thus relies on the interplay between sparse interactions and their impact on the communication needs for executing fully observable policies. Our agents construct a local POMDP model of the environment from the fully observable joint policy of all other agents. Solving this POMDP model allows the agent not only to determine how to solve the task at hand but also to determine when to query the local state of the environment. Our approach thus allows the agents to explicitly reason about communication, without incurring in the prohibitive computational cost of Dec-POMDP models that include communication [18]. Furthermore, in contrast to many methods in the literature [11, 14], QUERYPOMDP can properly handle noisy communication channels, and does not require strong independence assumptions [19]. Our empirical analysis on benchmark problems demonstrates the efficacy of QUERYPOMDP in balancing communication costs with coordination benefits.

The remainder of this work is organized as follows. First, Section 2 briefly introduces the relevant background regarding Dec-POMDP models, followed by a motivating example which is presented in Section 3. Section 4 describes our proposed model for state querying, and how it can be solved for multiple agents. Experiments are presented in Section 5, followed by a discussion of related research in Section 6. Finally, Section 7 concludes and describes future work.

## 2    Background

We start by reviewing *Decentralized Partially Observable Markov Decision Processes* (Dec-POMDPs) and related decision theoretic models. An $N$-agent Dec-POMDP $\mathcal{M}$ can be specified as a tuple $\mathcal{M} = (N, \mathcal{X}, (\mathcal{A}_k), (\mathcal{Z}_k), \mathsf{P}, (\mathsf{O}_k), r, \gamma)$, where:

- $\mathcal{X}$ is the joint state-space;
- $\mathcal{A} = \times_{i=1}^{N} \mathcal{A}_i$ is the set of joint actions, with each $\mathcal{A}_i$ the individual action set for agent $i$, $i = 1, \ldots, N$;
- Each $\mathcal{Z}_i$, $i = 1, \ldots, N$, represents the set of possible local observations for agent $i$;
- $\mathsf{P}(y \mid x, a)$ represents the transition probabilities from joint state $x$ to joint state $y$ when the joint action $a$ is taken;
- Each $\mathsf{O}_i(z_i \mid x, a)$, $i = 1, \ldots, N$, represents the probability of agent $i$ making the local observation $z_i$ when the joint state is $x$ and the last joint action taken was $a$;
- $r(x, a)$ represents the expected reward received by all agents for taking the joint action $a$ in joint state $x$;
- The scalar $\gamma$ is a discount factor.

An $N$-agent *Decentralized Markov decision process* (Dec-MDP) is a particular class of Dec-POMDP in which the state is *jointly fully observable*. Formally this can be translated into the following condition: for every joint observation $z \in \mathcal{Z}$, with $\mathcal{Z} = \times_{i=1}^{N} \mathcal{Z}_i$, there is a state $x \in \mathcal{X}$ such that $\mathbb{P}\left[X(t) = x \mid Z(t) = z\right] = 1$, where $X(t)$ is the joint state of the process at time $t$ and $Z(t)$ the corresponding joint observation. Although apparently simpler, optimally solving of a Dec-MDP is in the same complexity class as optimally solving a Dec-POMDP. A *partially observable Markov decision process* (POMDP) is a 1-agent Dec-POMDP and a *Markov decision process* (MDP) is a 1-agent Dec-MDP. Finally, an *N-agent multiagent MDP* (MMDP) is an $N$-agent Dec-MDP that is *fully observable*, i.e., for every individual observation $z_i \in \mathcal{Z}_i$ there is a state $x \in \mathcal{X}$ such that $\mathbb{P}\left[X(t) = x \mid Z_i(t) = z_i\right] = 1$.

In this partially observable multiagent setting, an individual (non-Markov) policy for agent $i$ is a mapping $\pi_i : \mathcal{H}_i \longrightarrow \Delta(\mathcal{A}_i)$, where $\Delta(\mathcal{A}_i)$ is the space of probability distributions over $\mathcal{A}_i$, and $\mathcal{H}_i$ is the set of all possible finite histories for agent $i$. The purpose of all agents is to determine a joint policy $\pi$ that maximizes the total sum of discounted rewards. In other words, considering a distinguished initial state $x^0 \in \mathcal{X}$ that is assumed common knowledge among all agents, the goal of the agents is to maximize

$$V^\pi = \mathbb{E}_\pi \left[ \sum_{t=0}^{\infty} \gamma^t r\big(X(t), A(t)\big) \mid X(0) = x^0 \right]. \tag{1}$$

For a more detailed introduction to Dec-POMDPs and related models see, for example, [20].

## 3   A Motivating Example

Multi-robot systems constitute a primary motivation for our work and provide a natural example of the class of problems considered herein. In multi-robot systems, interaction among robots is naturally limited by the robot's physical

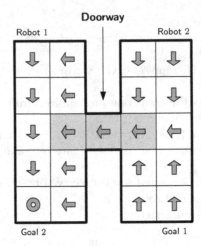

**Fig. 1.** H-Environment, where two robots need to interact only around the narrow doorway to reach their corresponding goals. The shaded arrows correspond to a possible policy for Robot 2 in the absence of Robot 1.

boundaries (workspace, communication range, etc.) and limited perception capabilities. It is therefore natural to subdivide the overall task into smaller tasks that each robot can execute either autonomously or as part of a small group. Moreover, besides being embedded in a physical environment, robots typically have a way of communicating among themselves.

We motivate our ideas in a simple navigation scenario, depicted in Fig. 1. In this scenario, two robots (Robot 1 and Robot 2) must navigate to their corresponding goal states (marked as Goals 1 and 2). At the same time, they must avoid colliding in the narrow doorway (the central state), since it leads to a large penalty. Each robot has 4 possible actions (namely "Move North", "Move South", "Move East" and "Move West") that move the robot in the corresponding direction. The motion of one robot does not depend on the position or action of the other robot except in the doorway: if the robots collide in the doorway, then their actions have an increasing failure probability. Complicating matters, initially each robot starts uniformly at random in one of the 10 locations on its side of the doorway.

In a fully observable situation, the agents will move toward their respective goals. When reaching the doorway, if the other robot is also close to the doorway one of the two will stop so that the other can safely traverse.[2] It will then resume its trajectory to its goal.

In order for the agents to actually execute the policy just described, they only need to reason about the state of the other agent when reaching the darker area in their starting side of the environment. And then, once one robot is in the doorway, it can just proceed toward its goal, independently of the state of the other robot. Moreover, even if the robots are generally unable to observe the position

---

[2] Which one stops is determined by the joint policy they adopt.

of the other robot, but they are able to *query it*, they can reasonably assume that the other robot will behave more or less as in the fully observable scenario. This observation is the departing point for the model and approach proposed in this paper and described in the continuation.

## 4    A Model for State Querying

We depart from an $N$-agent Dec-MDP model, and address the problem of when communication can be beneficial to improve the performance in such a model. For the purposes of our study, we momentarily focus on the decision processes of all except one agent, which we refer to as agent $k$. Unlike other communication-based approaches to Dec-MDPs (e.g., [11]), we adopt a relatively general communication model, in which the messages received by an agent are taken as part of its local (noisy) observation. Also, messages received by agent $k$ depend on explicit information-querying actions executed by $k$.

Throughout this section, we represent the (finite) state-space of the Dec-MDP as a set $\mathcal{X}$ and assume that it can be factorized as $\mathcal{X} = \mathcal{X}_k \times \mathcal{X}_{-k}$, where the elements $x_k \in \mathcal{X}_k$ correspond to agent $k$'s local state. The state at time $t$, $X(t)$, is thus a pair $\langle X_k(t), X_{-k}(t) \rangle$. We also assume that the observations of each agent do not depend on the actions of the remaining agents, *i.e.*,

$$\mathbb{P}\left[Z_i(t) = z_i \mid X(t), A(t)\right] = \mathbb{P}\left[Z_i(t) = z_i \mid X(t), A_i(t)\right],$$

for all $i = 1, \ldots, N$. Therefore, we can simply write the observation probabilities as $O_i(z_i \mid x, a_i), i = 1, \ldots, N$.

### 4.1    Query Actions and Resulting Observations

For the purpose of allowing our agent to reason about communication, we assume that each agent has the ability to *query* the other agents for their local state information. In order to make this explicit, we differentiate between *communication actions* and the remaining actions—henceforth referred as *primitive actions*, and write the set of individual actions for agent $k$ as the cartesian product of the set of communication actions, $\mathcal{A}_k^C$, and the set of primitive actions, $\mathcal{A}_k^P$, *i.e.*, $\mathcal{A}_k = \mathcal{A}_k^C \times \mathcal{A}_k^P$. We also assume that transition probabilities are independent of the communication actions,

$$P(y \mid x, \langle a_{-k}, (a_k^C, a_k^P) \rangle) = P(y \mid x, \langle a_{-k}, (b_k^C, a_k^P) \rangle)$$

for any $x, y \in \mathcal{X}$, $a_{-k} \in \mathcal{A}_{-k}$, $a_k^P \in \mathcal{A}_k^P$ and $a_k^C, b_k^C \in \mathcal{A}_k^C$.

We also differentiate between *communication observations*—*i.e.*, observations that result from communication actions—and *primitive observations*, that do not depend on the communication actions. Formally, we write the set of individual observations for agent $k$ as the cartesian product of the set of communication observations, $\mathcal{Z}_k^C$, and primitive observations, $\mathcal{Z}_k^P$, *i.e.*, $\mathcal{Z}_k = \mathcal{Z}_k^C \times \mathcal{Z}_k^P$. Communication observations correspond to either the local state of other agents or

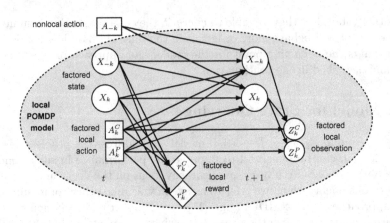

**Fig. 2.** The factored decision model, from agent $k$'s perspective

the null observation, $0$, *i.e.*, $\mathcal{Z}_k^C = \mathcal{X}_{-k} \cup \{0\}$. Moreover, we consider that communication observations do not depend on primitive actions, and that primitive observations do not depend on communication actions. This means that we can decouple the observation probabilities as

$$O_k\big((z_k^C, z_k^P) \mid x, (a_k^C, a_k^P)\big) = O_k^C(z_k^C \mid x, a_k^C)O_k^P(z_k^P \mid x, a_k^P),$$

where

$$O_k^C(z_k^C \mid x, a_k^C) = \mathbb{P}\left[Z_k^C(t) = z_k^C \mid X(t) = x, A_k^C(t) = a_k^C\right]$$
$$O_k^P(z_k^P \mid x, a_k^P) = \mathbb{P}\left[Z_k^P(t) = z_k^P \mid X(t) = x, A_k^P(t) = a_k^P\right].$$

Finally, we assume that the reward function can also be decomposed as the sum of two components. The first component, denoted $r^C$, concerns the *cost of communication* and is independent on the primitive actions of agent $k$ and on the actions of the other agents. The second component, denoted as $r^P$ corresponds to the "regular" (or domain-level) reward defining the overall goal of the agents. It is assumed independent of the communication actions of agent $k$. Formally, if $a = \langle a_{-k}, a_k \rangle$ and $a_k = (a_k^C, a_k^P)$, this means that the reward $r$ can be written as

$$r(x, a) = r^P(x, \langle a_{-k}, a_k^P \rangle) + r^C(x, a_k^C). \tag{2}$$

Figure 2 depicts a dynamic Bayesian network that summarizes all above considerations.

Following the discussion in Section 3, and for the purpose of its planning process, agent $k$ will treat all remaining agents as if they follow a Markov policy, $\pi_{-k}$, that corresponds to the optimal policy for the underlying MMDP. This policy, being Markovian, depends only on the state of the system at time $t$, $X(t)$, *i.e.*,

$$\mathbb{P}\left[A_{-k}(t) = a_{-k} \mid H(t)\right] = \mathbb{P}\left[A_{-k}(t) = a_{-k} \mid X(t) = x\right] = \pi_{-k}(x, a_{-k}), \tag{3}$$

where $A_{-k}(t)$ denotes the action taken by all agents other than $k$ at time $t$, $H(t)$ denotes the whole history of the process up to time $t$ and $a_{-k} \in \mathcal{A}_{-k}$. From this perspective, the decision process for agent $k$ can be modeled as a (single-agent) POMDP that we describe in the next section.

## 4.2  POMDP Model for a Single Agent

Let $\mathcal{M} = (N, \mathcal{X}, (\mathcal{A}_k), (\mathcal{Z}_k), \mathsf{P}, (\mathsf{O}_k), r, \gamma)$ be a Dec-MDP as described above. Let $\pi_{-k}$ denote the (state-dependent) joint MMDP policy for all agents other than $k$. We can now denote the single-agent POMDP model for agent $k$ as a tuple $\mathcal{M}_k = (\mathcal{X}, \mathcal{A}_k, \mathcal{Z}_k, \mathsf{P}_k, \mathsf{O}_k, r_k, \gamma)$, where:

- $\mathcal{X}$ corresponds to the original Dec-MDP state-space.
- $\mathcal{A}_k$ is the individual action-space for agent $k$.
- $\mathcal{Z}_k$ is the individual observation-space for agent $k$.
- $\mathsf{P}_k$ are the transition probabilities obtained from the original transition probabilities. In particular, given an action $a_k = (a_k^C, a_k^P)$, we have

$$\mathsf{P}_k(y \mid x, a_k) = \sum_{a_{-k} \in \mathcal{A}_{-k}} \pi_{-k}(x, a_{-k}) \mathsf{P}(y \mid x, \langle a_{-k}, a_k^P \rangle).$$

- $\mathsf{O}_k$ are the observation probabilities for agent $k$, that match the original Dec-MDP observation probabilities. In particular, given an action $a_k = (a_k^C, a_k^P)$, we have

$$\mathsf{O}_k(z_k \mid x, a_k) = \mathsf{O}_k^C(z_k^C \mid x, a_k^C) \mathsf{O}_k^P(z_k^P \mid x, a_k^P), \tag{4}$$

where $z_k = (z_k^C, z_k^P)$.

- $r_k$ is the reward function obtained from the original Dec-MDP reward function after averaging over the other agents' policy, $\pi_{-k}$, i.e.,

$$r_k(x, a_k) = \sum_{a_{-k} \in \mathcal{A}_{-k}} \pi_{-k}(x, a_{-k}) r(x, \langle a_{-k}, a_k \rangle).$$

Given this POMDP model, we can use standard POMDP solution techniques to explore the trade-off between the costs and benefits of communication for agent $k$.

## 4.3  Results for the H-Environment Example

Continuing the example of Section 3, the application of our model allows us to better understand under which circumstances the benefits of using communication compensate for its costs. For this purpose, we fix the policy of Agent 2 as shown in Fig. 1, which corresponds one possible joint MMDP policy for this environment. As explained above, given such a policy we can construct a POMDP from the point of view of Agent 1, in which it can query Agent 2's states at any time step, at a particular communication cost. For illustration purposes, the initial state of Agent 2 is selected randomly on the right half of the environment.

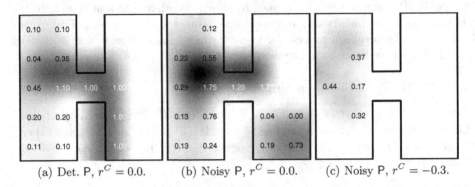

(a) Det. P, $r^C = 0.0$.      (b) Noisy P, $r^C = 0.0$.      (c) Noisy P, $r^C = -0.3$.

**Fig. 3.** Results for the H-environment. (a)-(c) Query frequency in each state for Agent 1, varying in deterministic (Det. P) or noisy (Noisy P) transitions and communication cost.

We test several experimental conditions that include the presence or absence of transition noise and different costs for the communication actions.

We examine in which states Agent 1 queries Agent 2's state. When communication is free (Figs. 3(a) and (b)), Agent 1 queries in all the states it passes through.[3] With a communication cost of 0.3 (Fig. 3(c)), however, it only queries when near to and left of the doorway. In these states it is crucial to know Agent 2's location to avoid potential collisions, an intuition that is exploited automatically by our model. The use of a POMDP model in this context ensures that the agent explicitly reasons about information gathering which, in our setting, translates in weighting the benefits of communication in terms of the overall task against the costs associated with it.

### 4.4   Computing Policies for Multiple Agents

In the previous section we proposed using a POMDP model to compute the policy for one agent $k$, treating all other agents as if they were following the optimal joint policy for the underlying MMDP. Given this POMDP model for agent $k$ we can compute the corresponding optimal policy using any preferred POMDP solution technique. We use this approach to better understand the communication needs of one agent in a simple multiagent navigation scenario, and to determine in which situations the cost of communication outweighs its value.

We now want to extend these ideas and actually compute the policy for *all* agents in the Dec-MDP. The idea of using POMDP models to plan in multiagent scenarios has been previously explored in the Dec-POMDP literature [21, 22]. The general difficulty with these approaches arises from the fact that each agent has only a local observation of the joint state of the world. This implies that,

---

[3] We note that, due to the transition noise, an agent can remain in the same state more than one consecutive time-step, and hence the values > 1.

when planning for agent $k$, the POMDP model necessary to properly capture the behavior of all agents other than $k$ can either be prohibitively large, require agent $k$ to reason about how the other agents reason about agent $k$'s state, leading to infinitely nested beliefs, or both [21, 22].

In our approach, we rely on the intuition discussed in Section 3, according to which the use of *active communication* allied with *sparse interactions* may actually alleviate the difficulties associated with planning in multiagent systems with partial observability. We plan for each agent $k$ while treating all other agents as if following the *optimal joint MMDP policy*. In scenarios where interactions are sparse, the general behavior of the agents is expected to roughly follow the MMDP policy, as discussed in Section 3 and in those situations where coordination is necessary, agents can resort to communication, but weighting the benefits of such communication with the associated costs.

Several previous works have already studied the benefits of exploiting communication and structured interactions separately (see, for example, [5, 6, 8]).[4] The novelty in our approach lies precisely on the fact that we can explicitly exploit the interplay between these two aspects (communication and sparse interactions) to attain efficient planning in multiagent problems. Section 5 describes the application of our approach in several navigation scenarios of different dimensions. Our results empirically show that our approach is indeed able to make effective use of communication and attain a performance that indeed approaches that observed in fully observable settings.

## 5    Experiments

In this section we illustrate the application of our method to several navigation scenarios from the POMDP and Dec-POMDP literature. We use robot navigation scenarios (Fig. 4), since our model is particularly suited for modeling multi-robot problems. Furthermore, results can be easily visualized and interpreted in this class of problems.

**Experimental Setup.** In each of the test scenarios, each of two (identical) robots departs from one of the locations marked with a dot, and must reach the state marked with a circle that is furthest from its initial state. Each robot has 4 actions that move the robot in one of the four possible direction with probability 0.8 and fail with probability 0.2, plus a fifth "NoOp" action.

All agents have full local state observability. The shaded regions correspond to areas inside of which the agents are able to successfully communicate, *i.e.*, when an agent queries another agent, it incurs a cost of $-0.1$ and successfully observes the local state of the queried agent with a probability of 0.8. With a probability of 0.2 it receives no observation about the state of the other. In the white cells, an agent is never able to perceive the state of the other, but still incurs a penalty of $-0.1$ if it attempts to communicate. In other words, the agents can always

---

[4] We refer to Section 6 for a detailed discussion of related approaches.

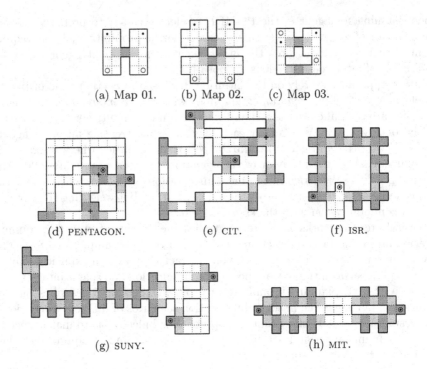

(a) Map 01.     (b) Map 02.     (c) Map 03.

(d) PENTAGON.     (e) CIT.     (f) ISR.

(g) SUNY.     (h) MIT.

**Fig. 4.** Environments used in the experiments

attempt to communicate, incurring in a penalty of $-0.1$ ($r^C(x) = -0.1$ for all $x \in \mathcal{X}$), but only in the shaded areas does communication succeed (with high probability). The darker cells correspond to states where the agents receive a penalty of $-20$ when standing there simultaneously, in which case the rate of action failure is also increased to $0.4$ for both agents. When an agent reaches its goal position, it receives a reward of 10 and moves to a rewardless absorbing state. Throughout the experiments, we used $\gamma = 0.95$.

For each of the test scenarios, following the approach in Section 4, we compute the optimal MMDP joint policy that we use to determine a POMDP model describing the decision process for each individual agent. This POMDP is then solved using the PERSEUS approximate solver [23]. We test our QUERYPOMDP policy for 100 independent trials of 250 steps each and measure the obtained performance in terms of total discounted reward. We also test the performance of other sets of agents that communicate at different (but fixed) frequencies (see Table 1(a)):

– "NEVER COMM" agents *never communicate*. These agents observe only their local state, and each follows the optimal policy for the underlying single-agent MDP obtained by disregarding the other agent in the environment;
– "ALWAYS COMM" agents *communicate at every time-step*, incurring the corresponding penalty. As QUERYPOMDP agents, they are subject to

**Table 1.** (a) Main differences between the groups of agents used. (b) Total discounted reward for each set of agents in each of the test-scenarios. Entries in *italic* in the same column are not statistically different.

(a) Different methods used.

| Agents | Comm. Freq. | Succ. Comm. | Failed Comm. |
|---|---|---|---|
| QUERYPOMDP | Variable | POMDP | POMDP |
| NEVER COMM | Never | – | Indiv. MDP |
| ALWAYS COMM | 1 step | MMDP | Indiv. MDP |
| COMM $k = 2$ | 2 steps | MMDP | Indiv. MDP |
| COMM $k = 3$ | 3 steps | MMDP | Indiv. MDP |
| COMM $k = 4$ | 4 steps | MMDP | Indiv. MDP |

(b) Experimental results.

| Environment | Map 1 | Map 2 | Map 3 | CIT | ISR | MIT | PENT. | SUNY |
|---|---|---|---|---|---|---|---|---|
| # States | 441 | 1,296 | 400 | 4,900 | 1,849 | 2,401 | 2,704 | 5,476 |
| QUERYPOMDP | 5.132 | 3.598 | 6.156 | *5.260* | *6.755* | *2.964* | 6.444 | *5.328* |
| NEVER COMM | −1.834 | 0.900 | 1.917 | *5.306* | 6.663 | *2.959* | 5.641 | *5.283* |
| ALWAYS COMM | 1.961 | 2.248 | 3.276 | 3.286 | 4.779 | 1.116 | 5.038 | 3.297 |
| COMM $k = 2$ | −0.069 | 1.097 | 3.001 | 4.306 | 5.839 | 2.141 | 5.578 | 4.294 |
| COMM $k = 3$ | −0.127 | 1.707 | 1.564 | 4.666 | 6.114 | 2.426 | 5.246 | 4.646 |
| COMM $k = 4$ | −0.785 | 1.289 | 3.295 | 4.324 | 5.760 | 2.106 | 5.448 | 4.317 |
| MMDP | 5.787 | 5.253 | 6.608 | *5.305* | *6.817* | 3.182 | 7.606 | *5.297* |

communication errors/limitations and, as such, are not always able to perceive the state of the other agent. When communication fails, the agent observes only its local state and adopts the individual MDP policy. When communication succeeds, it adopts the underlying MMDP policy.

– "COMM $k = 2, 3, 4$" agents query the state of the other agent every $k$ steps. Except for the different communication frequency, they are otherwise similar to "ALWAYS COMM" agents.

Comparisons between these different agents will allow us to analyze (i) the impact that communication costs can have on performance, if communication is not optimized; and (ii) the impact that communication can have in mitigating partial observability. As discussed ahead, direct comparison against other methods such as the one in [11] is not very informative, as these do not trade-off communication costs with task performance.

**Results and Discussion.** The performance of the 6 agent groups in terms of total discounted reward is summarized in Table 1(b). As a reference against which to assess the quality of our computed policy we also provide the results for the MMDP optimal policy in the different environments, providing a performance upper bound. The QUERYPOMDP approach performs very favorably, outperforming all other policies and coming close to the MMDP upper bound in several of the tested scenarios.

The results in Table 1(b) prompt several interesting observations. First, comparing the performance of the MMDP policy against that of the group that never communicates provides an important indication of how critical coordination is in a given scenario. NEVERCOMM agents act individually, disregarding the existence of other agents in the environment. In environments where coordination is critical, NEVERCOMM agents will perform poorly. MMDP agents, on the other hand, always act in a perfectly coordinated manner, in which coordination does not come at a cost. In an environment where little coordination is needed, the difference between these two groups is going to be small. In contrast, scenarios that require significant coordination will cause the performance of the two groups to significantly differ.

From Table 1(b), we can see that coordination is critical in the smaller environments (Maps 1-3). In the larger environments, such as CIT, MIT and SUNY, coordination is less critical. The results in the smaller environments illustrate the impact of effective communication in mitigating the effects of partial observability. Our method is actually able to attain a performance very close to that of the MMDP agents, even paying for communication. Additionally, our approach uses communication efficiently, since the performance of all other communicating agents is significantly inferior. In contrast, in CIT, MIT and SUNY, non-communicating agents actually attain optimal performance. The difference in performance to the communicating groups can be explained by the communication penalty. Again, in these scenarios, our approach is able to manage communication needs, as it performs similarly to non-communicating agents.

A second observation is that the MMDP performance is an upper bound on the optimal Dec-MDP performance. This means that in those scenarios where our approach performs close to or as well as the MMDP group, we can immediately conclude that it is also performing close to or as well as the optimal Dec-MDP policy. A general comparison of the performance of our method against that of the MMDP group indicates that our method, if not optimal, must be very close to optimal in most scenarios tested. This, in turn, indicates that approximating the behavior of our agents with that of MMDP agents does provide a solid basis for planning.

We also applied our approach to a benchmark problem from the Dec-POMDP literature, namely the firefighting problem with 3 houses and 3 fire levels [24]. In this scenario, the QUERYPOMDP agents are allowed to communicate at a cost, but no observation results out of it, since there is no communication in the original problem. Allowing for no shared information among agents renders our version of the firefighting problem effectively equivalent to the original problem and thus enables a meaningful comparison between the two methods.

Applying our method in the firefighting problem provides useful insights into two important aspects of our method. First, on the trade-off between communication costs and benefits, our method should figure out that communication is

**Table 2.** Results of QUERYPOMDP in the Firefighting problem [24]

| Problem | Dimension | QUERYPOMDP | Optimal |
|---|---|---|---|
| Firefighters [24] | 432 | −7.679 | −7.176 |

useless in this setting and effectively not use it. Second, concerning the general applicability of our method, the results should shed some light on whether the proposed approximation provides meaningful information in scenarios with local interactions sense, *i.e.*, if each agent, by assuming the other agents to behave according to the MMDP policy, are still able to make good decisions.

The performance of our approach is summarized in Table 2, corresponding to the total reward obtained over a 6-step run, averaged over 1,000 independent Monte Carlo trials. For comparison, we also provide the optimal value for the 6-step horizon, reported in [25]. As expected, the QUERYPOMDP agents learn not to use communication. Moreover, although the firefighting problem does not strictly adhere to the setting considered in this paper, it still exhibits some level of independence that our approach is successfully able to leverage—the difference in obtained performance is statistically not significant.

Summarizing, our results show that, in scenarios with sparse interactions like the ones analyzed, our agents behave approximately as MMDP agents, effectively using communication to mitigate the effects of partial observability.

# 6    Related Work

In the Dec-POMDP literature, early approaches introduced the idea of transition and reward independence as forms of simplified interactions [26]. Further examples of models with sparse interactions include *interaction-driven Markov games* (IDMGs) [5,17], *distributed POMDPs with coordination locales* [7], *transition-decoupled POMDPs* [6], *factored Dec-POMDPs* [4], and models relying on event-driven interactions [3,27].

Our representation is closest to IDMGs [5], which leverage independence between different agents in a Dec-POMDP to decouple the decision process in significant portions of the joint state-space. In those situations in which agents interact, IDMGs rely on communication to bring down the the computational complexity of the joint decision process. The use of communication to overcome partial observability sets this approach apart from other approaches that also exploit local interactions. However, communication is assumed to *always* take place and to be error-free [5]. In our case, we add explicit query actions to the agents action repertoires, enabling them to ask another agent's state, under environment-specific constraints. For instance, two robots may only be able to share information when they are physically close. We further assume that communication is not error-free and comes at a cost that must be considered.

Explicit communication in multiagent planning was already addressed in [18], where the proposed Com-MTDP model allows agents to explicitly reason about communication in Dec-POMDP scenarios. However, being a generalization of Dec-POMDPs, it shares the discouraging computational complexity of the latter model. The actual process of communication has been investigated in [28]. Roth et al. [11] propose to exploit a factored Dec-MDP model and policy representation, in which agents query other agents' local states when this knowledge is required for choosing their local actions. Although this work already seeks to optimize communication, this optimization is conducted parallel with the underlying decision process. Therefore, the cost of communication does not directly translate in the agent's task performance, as in our proposed approach, rendering the tradeoff between communication costs and benefits unclear. Another closely related work is that of Wu et al. [14] where communication is used as a means to decrease the planning complexity in Dec-POMDP models. Like in our proposed approach, this work considers that communication may not always be available. However, unlike our approach, this work does not consider explicitly optimization of communication. Finally, Mostafa and Lesser [16] do optimize communication, while considering the presence of communication limitations. However, this optimization is also conducted parallel with the underlying decision process, without directly impacting in the agent's task performance. Also, none of the aforementioned methods considers noisy communication channels.

A key point in our approach is that, although we use the MMDP policy in our planning, its computation is significantly more efficient than computing a centralized policy for the actual partially observable decision problem. The fact that we plan individually for each agent is somewhat related to several works that use round-robin policy optimization to individually optimize the policy of different agents in Dec-POMDP settings. One of the early examples is the JESP algorithm [21], which also models agents individually as POMDPs, but does not use communication. Round-robin policy optimization has been used to learn communication primitives in Dec-POMDPs whose base models are transition and observation independent [12], but which are coupled through the communication actions agents can choose to execute. In that case, however, agents have to learn when sending a particular message will be beneficial for team performance, which is far from trivial given that the policy of the receiving agent does not exploit the information provided by incoming messages. In our case, however, agents can opt to query other agents' states, and it is much easier to determine when doing so improves performance. Secondly, we consider a much richer model where agents also "physically" influence each other, instead of only through communication.

## 7   Conclusions

In this paper, we analyzed the interplay between sparse interactions and communication in multiagent planning. We observed that, in scenarios where interactions among agents are sparse (i.e., intra-agent action coordination is only infrequently necessary), the distributed execution of an MMDP policy seldom requires full-state information. As such, if each agent is (individually) allowed to query other agents for their local state information when necessary, it may be possible to partly mitigate partial state observability and leverage more efficient planning approaches.

Relying on this insight, we proposed the use of a POMDP model to analyze the communication needs of an agent in a Dec-MDP scenario where the interaction between the agents is sparse. Our model accommodates communication costs and failures—the agent must explicitly reason about these factors in its decision process. QUERYPOMDP allows agents to optimize communication, explicitly trading-off its costs with its benefits in terms of the underlying task.

We used our approach to optimize communication in the simple scenario of Fig. 1, where our approach was successfully able to capture the intuition that the fundamental states for coordination are those around the doorway. We further explored the usefulness of this approach in computing policies for larger and more general Dec-MDPs. We built POMDP models for each agent by considering the other agents to behave as if in an MMDP, and use the obtained POMDP optimal policies. Our results show that our agents are able to effectively using communication to mitigate the effects of partial observability, behaving approximately as MMDP agents. One important avenue of future work is to generalize these techniques beyond Dec-MDPs, to scenarios in which agents can query other agents' observations instead of states.

# References

1. Allen, M., Zilberstein, S.: Agent influence as a predictor of difficulty for decentralized problem-solving. In: Proc. 22nd AAAI Conf. Artificial Intelligence, pp. 688–693 (2007)
2. Becker, R., Zilberstein, S., Lesser, V., Goldman, C.: Transition-independent decentralized Markov decision processes. In: Proc. Int. Conf. Auton. Agents and Multiagent Systems, pp. 41–48 (2003)
3. Becker, R., Lesser, V., Zilberstein, S.: Decentralized Markov decision processes with event-driven interactions. In: Proc. Int. Conf. Auton. Agents and Multiagent Systems, pp. 302–309 (2004)
4. Oliehoek, F., Spaan, M., Whiteson, S., Vlassis, N.: Exploiting locality of interaction in factored Dec-POMDPs. In: Proc. Int. Conf. Auton. Agents and Multiagent Systems (2008)
5. Spaan, M., Melo, F.: Interaction-driven Markov games for decentralized multiagent planning under uncertainty. In: Proc. Int. Conf. Auton. Agents and Multiagent Systems, pp. 525–532 (2008)
6. Witwicki, S., Durfee, E.: Influence-based policy abstraction for weakly-coupled Dec-POMDPs. In: Int. Conf. Automated Planning and Scheduling (2010)
7. Varakantham, P., Kwak, J., Taylor, M., Marecki, J., Scerri, P., Tambe, M.: Exploiting coordination locales in distributed POMDPs via social model shaping. In: Proc. 19th Int. Conf. Automated Planning and Scheduling, pp. 313–320 (2009)
8. Goldman, C., Zilberstein, S.: Optimizing information exchange in cooperative multiagent systems. In: Proc. 2nd Int. Conf. Autonomous Agents and Multiagent Systems, pp. 137–144 (2003)
9. Goldman, C., Zilberstein, S.: Communication-based decomposition mechanisms for decentralized MDPs. J. Artificial Intelligence Res. 32, 169–202 (2008)

10. Roth, M., Simmons, R., Veloso, M.: Decentralized communication strategies for coordinated multiagent policies. In: Multi-Robot Systems: From Swarms to Intelligent Automata, pp. 93–106 (2005)
11. Roth, M., Simmons, R., Veloso, M.: Exploiting factored representations for decentralized execution in multiagent teams. In: Proc. Int. Conf. Auton. Agents and Multiagent Systems, pp. 469–475 (2007)
12. Spaan, M., Gordon, G., Vlassis, N.: Decentralized planning under uncertainty for teams of communicating agents. In: Proc. Int. Conf. Auton. Agents and Multiagent Systems (2006)
13. Tasaki, M., Yabu, Y., Iwanari, Y., Yokoo, M., Tambe, M., Marecki, J., Varakantham, P.: Introducing communication in Dis-POMDPs with locality of interaction. In: IEEE/WIC/ACM Int. Conf. Web Intelligence and Intelligent Agent Technology, vol. 2, pp. 169–175 (2008)
14. Wu, F., Zilberstein, S., Chen, X.: Multi-agent online planning with communication. In: Proc. Int. Conf. Automated Planning and Scheduling, pp. 321–329 (2009)
15. Xuan, P., Lesser, V., Zilberstein, S.: Communication decisions in multiagent cooperation: Model and experiments. In: Proc. 5th Int. Conf. Autonomous Agents, pp. 616–623 (2001)
16. Mostafa, H., Lesser, V.: Offline planning for communication by exploiting structured interactions in decentralized MDPs. In: IEEE/WIC/ACM Int. Conf. Web Intelligence and Intelligent Agent Technology, pp. 193–200 (2009)
17. Melo, F., Veloso, M.: Decentralized MDPs with sparse interactions. Artificial Intelligence 175(11), 1757–1789 (2011)
18. Pynadath, D., Tambe, M.: The communicative multiagent team decision problem: Analyzing teamwork theories and models. J. Artificial Intelligence Res. 16, 389–423 (2002)
19. Becker, R., Carlin, A., Lesser, V., Zilberstein, S.: Analyzing myopic approaches for multi-agent communications. Computational Intelligence 25(1), 31–50 (2009)
20. Seuken, S., Zilberstein, S.: Formal models and algorithms for decentralized decision making under uncertainty. Auton. Agents and Multi-Agent Systems (2008)
21. Nair, R., Tambe, M., Yokoo, M., Pynadath, D., Marsella, S.: Taming decentralized POMDPs: Towards efficient policy computation for multiagent settings. In: Proc. 18th Int. Joint Conf. Artificial Intelligence, pp. 705–711 (2003)
22. Doshi, P., Gmytrasiewicz, P.: On the difficulty of achieving equilibrium in interactive POMDPs. In: Proc. 21st AAAI Conf. Artificial Intelligence, pp. 1131–1136 (2006)
23. Spaan, M.T.J., Vlassis, N.: Perseus: Randomized point-based value iteration for POMDPs. J. Artificial Intelligence Res. 24, 195–220 (2005)
24. Oliehoek, F., Spaan, M., Vlassis, N.: Optimal and approximate Q-value functions for decentralized POMDPs. J. Artificial Intelligence Res. 32, 289–353 (2008)
25. Spaan, M., Oliehoek, F., Amato, C.: Scaling up optimal heuristic search in Dec-POMDPs via incremental expansion. In: Proc. Int. Joint Conf. Artificial Intelligence, pp. 2027–2032 (2011)
26. Becker, R., Zilberstein, S., Lesser, V., Goldman, C.: Solving transition independent decentralized Markov decision processes. J. Artificial Intelligence Res. 22, 423–455 (2004)
27. Mostafa, H., Lesser, V.: A compact mathematical formulation for problems with structured agent interactions. In: Proc. AAMAS MSDM Workshop (2011)
28. Goldmann, C., Allen, M., Zilberstein, S.: Learning to communicate in a decentralized environment. J. Auton. Agents and Multiagent Systems 15(1), 47–90 (2007)

# A Multi-agent Based Governance of Machine-to-Machine Systems

Camille Persson[1,2], Gauthier Picard[2], Fano Ramparany[1], and Olivier Boissier[2]

[1] Orange Labs Network and Carrier, TECH/MATIS, Grenoble, France
firstname.lastname@orange.com
[2] Fayol Institute, Ecole des Mines de Saint-Etienne, France
lastname@emse.fr

**Abstract.** In *Machine-to-Machine (M2M)* systems, multiple devices (sensors, actuators), situated in the physical world, interact together to provide data to added value services. In the *SensCity* project, the proposed M2M infrastructure, to support cityscale application, must be able to support the increase in the number of services and applications that are deployed on it. It is thus necessary to share the infrastructure use dynamically between them. In this paper, we propose the use of multi-agent technologies to define an adaptive and agile layer to govern and adapt the M2M infrastructure to the different applications using it. We illustrate our proposal within a smart parking management application.

## 1 Introduction

The next generation of cities are getting smarter by providing automated services to improve the life of their citizens (e.g. optimized garbage collection, smart metering, traffic redirection and parking management). These added value services build what we call *Machine-to-Machine (M2M)* systems, i.e. a network of smart devices –sensors and actuators– interacting with each other without human intervention (see Fig. 1).

Recent improvements in low-power wireless technologies [15] enable wireless devices to be connected to the Internet with a low deployment cost and a long lifespan –20 years expected. Such developments allow applications to be immersed in the real world and to directly act on the environment. When looking at the deployment of such

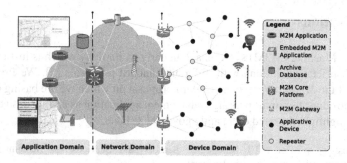

**Fig. 1.** An end-to-end M2M architecture [6]

M. Cossentino et al. (Eds.): EUMAS 2011, LNAI 7541, pp. 205–220, 2012.
© Springer-Verlag Berlin Heidelberg 2012

systems, stakeholders are involved in different areas: application providers, constrained devices constructors, LLNs radio experts and telecommunication operators. However, the building of such *vertical* solutions on a city scale is too expensive and not flexible enough. There is a growing need and interest for M2M infrastructures that provide *horizontal* integration and sharing of devices between stakeholders [1].

This paper considers the practical use case issued from the SensCity[1] project, which aims at providing an M2M platform for deploying multiple smart city services. This platform makes possible to connect heterogeneous wireless devices to a GPRS gateway using Wavenis –long range, energy efficient radio technology. As for the application, standard access to the devices is provided via web services.

In order to be deployed on a city scale and used by different applications, such an infrastructure is faced with a multi-faceted problem of scalability [7] in terms of size, heterogeneity, topology, etc.To tackle this problem, an agile governance is required to conciliate both "vertical" and "horizontal" concerns. Such a governance system should adapt to the different requirements of the M2M applications deployed on such an infrastructure so that the whole system scales.

Given the complexity and inherent decentralization of the infrastructure, we propose the use of multi-agent technologies to define this governance layer on top of the M2M infrastructure. We used a newborn multi-agent oriented programming framework called JaCaMo[2] to implement it. In order to obtain an agile governance, the governance strategy is defined as an explicit organization specification, using the $MOISE$ framework [9], part of the JaCaMo platform. Thanks to the explicit and agent-readable specifications, agents are able to reason about the governance of the system to change and adapt it to the evolution of the system. The proposed multi-agent governance is illustrated by a smart parking management application.

Section 2 motivates our approach with a description of the M2M infrastructure and the smart parking application that we consider in this paper. Based on this applicative context, we describe the multi-agent governance layer deployed on top of the M2M components (Section 3). We then focus, in Section 4, on the definition of the governance strategy stressing how it can be dynamically adapted by agents. The application of this governance applied to the smart parking management use case is described in Section 5. Then, Section 6 discusses the proposed approach and compares it to related works. Finally, Section 7 concludes this paper and considers the perspectives for future work.

## 2    Motivations

Machine to Machine (M2M) systems are an early technology which is just raising out of fully proprietary solutions with different standard proposals [6]. We first give an overview of the *M2M architecture* standard proposal on which we are basing our work. We then introduce the smart parking management application as an illustrative example where we highlight the need of an agile governance layer.

---

[1] The SensCity project (FUI Minalogic) Sensors and Services for Sustainable Cities: http://www.senscity-grenoble.com/

[2] http://www.jacamo.sourceforge.net

## 2.1 Machine-to-Machine Architecture

The M2M Technical Committee of the European Telecommunications Standards Institute (ETSI) is defining standards for M2M infrastructure. The scope of these standards cover communication from the devices to the applications, through gateways and a core platform. As shown in the latest version of ETSI's specification draft [6], the M2M architecture is divided into three domains (cf. Fig. 1): *Device*, *Network* and *Application*.

The Device Domain is composed of applicative devices –*sensors* and *actuators*– and repeaters communicating in a Wireless Sensor and Actuator Network (WSAN) linked to a gateway. The WSAN groups several devices communicating together. Devices can embed several sensors and actuators, or none of them. *Repeaters* are placed to extend the coverage managed by a *gateway*. It manages one or several WSANs, security and device authentication and can also manage quick reaction to sensed events generating commands to devices. The *gateway* sends/receives messages to/from the *platform* via broadband access. Thus it also belongs to the *Network Domain*. The *core platform* is involved in both the *Network Domain* and the *Application Domain*, as shown with the synthesis of the functionalities of this platform in Table 1. On one hand, it is responsible for network communications with other platforms. On the other hand, it gives the *application* –managing business logic– transparent access to the devices and stores the messages (see *ETSI M2M Functional Specification* [6] for further details).

**Table 1.** M2M core platform's functionalities [6]

|  | Network Domain |  | Application Domain |
|---|---|---|---|
| REM | Remote Entity Management | AE | Application Enablement |
| GC | Generic Communication | CB | Compensation Brokerage |
| RAR | Reachability Addressing and Repository | TM | Transaction Management |
| CS | Communication Selection | HDR | History Data Retention |
| IP | Interworking Proxy |  |  |
| SEC |  | Security |  |

## 2.2 Use Case Scenario: A Smart Parking Management

In order to be deployed at a city scale and used by different client applications, a *vertical solution* as a whole cannot be used since it is too expensive and not flexible enough. Installing *horizontal integration* solution is of growing interest in order to share devices between different stakeholders [1]. To this aim, agility is required for conciliating different requirements.

In the following, let's consider a Smart Parking System where car detectors are used for monitoring parking places. The collected data are used and shared between, at least, two applications: Car Guidance, City Monitoring. When a car parks in or leaves the place, the event is notified through the M2M infrastructure: a message is 1. sent to the gateway (Device Domain) which 2. authenticates and 3. forwards it to the M2M platform (Network Domain) where 4a. it is stored and 4b. notified to subscriber applications (Application Domain), which in turn 5. retrieve the message. Applications can also send commands to the devices using the reverse path to act on the environment, e.g. to raise a parking post to reserve a place.

The *Car Guidance* application helps drivers to find a parking place directly and close to their destination following their preferences, reducing traffic flow and pollution[3]. To do this, it needs to monitor the places within an area around the destination when the driver is getting close to this area. In the case of reservable parking places, the application can send a message to actuate a parking post for the user.

The *City Monitoring* application is used by city services (eg. police) to monitor no-parking places. It requires alerts to be sent when a place is occupied during a nonstationary time with a variable priority (e.g. water access for firemen has priority over garage doors).

As sending messages consumes a lot of energy, due to several applications sharing the same devices with heterogeneous requirements, it raises issues such as scalability and energy consumption. Furthermore, other applications, using other devices, will share the same infrastructure –the platform and the gateways– generating traffic and resource management issues.

In this context, an agile governance is required to define how the resources –devices, servers, network– should be used. Each *vertical* requirements can be specified by a *Service Level Agreement (SLA)* contract between an *application*, the *shared infrastructure* (i.e. servers, gateways and repeaters) and a set of *devices*. The governance layer concerns both the *vertical* infrastructure –i.e. interactions between an application and devices– and the *horizontal* infrastructure –i.e. sharing the resources between different applications. The goal of this paper is to propose a multi-agent based governance model to manage the shared M2M infrastructure.

## 3    Overview of the Multi-agent Governance

Given the different requirements and motivations expressed in the previous section, this section describes the multi-agent approach used to define the M2M governance, describe by Fig. 2. To clearly separate the different concerns that arise in such applications, we have chosen a multi-agent oriented programming approach which is supported by the JaCaMo[4] [18] framework. This multi-agent oriented programming framework allows the development of MAS taking into account three different programming dimensions, namely *agent*, *environment*, and *organization*.

JaCaMo is built upon the synergistic integration of three existing agent-based technologies: *(i)* Jason [4], *(ii)* Moise [9], and *(iii)* CArtAgO[19]. A JaCaMo multi-agent system (i.e., a software system programmed in JaCaMo) is given by a multi-agent organization programmed in Moise, organizing autonomous agents programmed in Jason, working in shared distributed artifact-based environments programmed in CArtAgO. JaCaMo integrates these three platforms by defining a semantic link among concepts of the different programming dimensions at the meta-model and programming levels, in order to obtain a uniform and consistent programming model aimed at simplifying the combination of those dimensions when programming multi-agent systems.

---

[3] Parking search is estimated to be from 5% to 10% of traffic and represented a total waste of 70 millions hours for a cost of 600 millions in France [13] (2005).

[4] http://www.jacamo.sourceforge.net

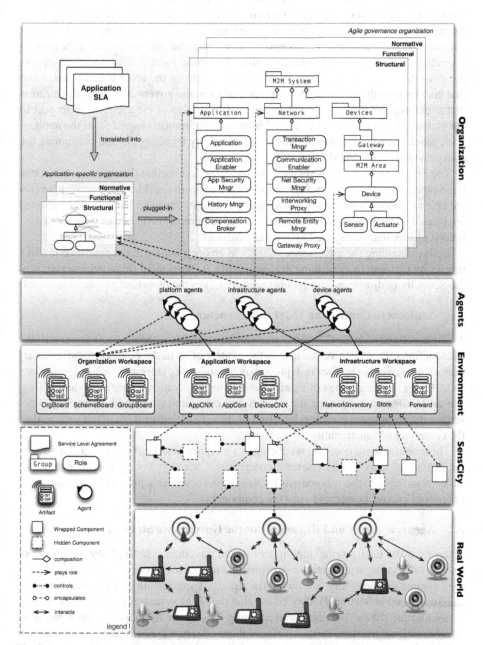

**Fig. 2.** On top of the *SensCity Core Platform*, the multi-agent based governance layer architecture is as follows: *artifacts* encapsulate the components to allow the *agents* to control the platform by applying the SLAs strategy defined by an *organization* following the ETSI recommendations

These three dimensions are used to define the governance layer deployed on top of the M2M infrastructure (cf. Fig. 2) aiming at governing its use by the different applications: (*i*) artifacts encapsulate the infrastructure components and provide the agents with the necessary actions and perceptions to monitor and control the use of these components, (*ii*) agents are the reasoning entities that make local decisions with respect to the governance taking into account their partial view on the infrastructure status and that cooperate with the other agents participating in the governance, (*iii*) organization that structures and regulates the autonomous functioning of the agents with respect to the global governance strategy defined from the requirements issued from the applications providing added value services in the smart city by acting on and consuming the data provided by the M2M infrastructure.

The organization limits the place of the possible actions that the agents can execute, letting them decide locally and autonomously. Thanks to the MoIsE framework, agents are able to reason about the organization and decide to change it when it is not adapted anymore to the current state of the governance requirements (e.g. high number of violations greater than authorized by the SLA contract).

Before detailing the governance strategy as an organization in the next section (Section 4), we first start by describing the use of artifacts (Section 3.1) to monitor and control the SensCity platform and the agents (Section 3.2) of the proposed governance model.

### 3.1 Artifacts to Control the M2M Infrastructure

Artifacts defined with the CArtAgO platform are used to encapsulate components of the M2M infrastructure to give the agents the control of it. In the context of the *SensCity* project, the governance layer is deployed on top the core platform which is divided into an *USP* part to manage the notifications sent to the applications, their rights and billing, and an *UCCP* part to manage the devices and communications with them. Fig. 3 describes the component-based architecture of these two platforms. Artifacts encapsulate the components' functionality.

These artifacts are used to give the agents a representation of the system to govern. An artifact monitors one or several components' activity: the agents are notified of statuses and calls to the components by signals and observable properties. The artifact's operations enable the agents to use the component.

### 3.2 Agents to Apply and Reason about the Governance Strategy

Agents are the decision-making entities of the governance layer. They adopt one or several roles in the organization corresponding to the part of the governance for which they assume responsibility. Following the strategy specification given by the organization (described in Section 4), they ensure that the M2M system is functioning correctly by monitoring the infrastructure and adapting it using the artifacts. For example, if an agent notices an overload on the platform, it can interrupt the calls to its components in order to filter the calls and redirect some of them to another platform.

Agents implements the governance policies. They can reason about the strategy definition and evaluate it with respect to the M2M system's functioning. They can adapt either the M2M infrastructure using the artifacts or redefine the strategy by proposing new organizational specifications.

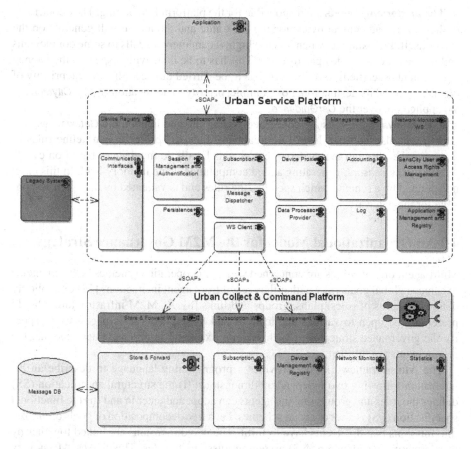

**Fig. 3.** The *SensCity's core platform* component-based architecture divided into an *USP* part communicating with applications and an *UCCP* part communicating with the gateways and devices

As the different parts of the M2M infrastructure should be handled differently, different kinds of agents have been identified: *appAg*, *platformAg*, *gwAg* and *deviceAg*.

**The *appAg* agents** ensure the requirements fulfilment from the application point of view. Thus, this type of agent regulates the commands and requests sent by an application to the devices and check the notifications it receives. To perform this regulation, an AppAg is able to intercept messages by using the *AppCNXArt* artifact to control them and validate the transmission.

**Similarly, the *deviceAg* agents** control the usage of the devices specified by the SLA, by using encapsulation artifacts such as *DeviceCNXArt*, to ensure that the devices perform their obligations. The agent can evaluate the load of a device by the number of roles it has adopted, and so make smarter use of the device (e.g. combine two messages at once, or skip messages if not necessary). The main goal of such an agent is to make the device's life as long as possible. It negotiates the requirements in this aim and can eventually give priority to one contract over another.

The *platformAg* **agents** are responsible for the platform functioning. They contribute to the contract agreement by evaluating the traffic and the load it will generate on the server itself. For example, when it is too high, it can intercept calls to some components and redirect them to a delegated server. This has to be done with respect to the latency requirements specified, so redirection has to be carried out according to the priority of the message and its destination. For example, priority to notifications to the *CityMonitoring* application over the *CarGuidance*.

The *gatewayAg* **agents** are concerned with traffic and load on the *Gateway*, as *platformAg*, but also with the local rule treatment. Indeed, *application* can define rules to generate –i.e. through the *gateway*– commands locally to the devices based on events sensed by the *sensors*, generating added computational and memory load. In this case, it is defined by a scheme which specifies the rules and is validated by the agent responsible for the gateway.

# 4 An Organizational Model for the M2M Governance Strategy

Multi-agent organizations are concerned with the cooperation schemes between agents to achieve global goals [8] whether they result from agent interactions [17] or explicitly defined in terms of roles, plans, groups and links [8]. As M2M infrastructures should preferably be open to various applications and stakeholders, it is necessary to specify the governance strategies of such systems explicitly in order to guarantee that the requirements are fulfilled.

The MOISE framework [10] provides a programming language to describe an organization following two independent dimensions: (i) the structural specification (SS) defines the roles and groups that the agents can adopt and enter in and (ii) the functional specification (FS) is a set of social schemes, i.e. a tree decomposition of goals organized into missions that the agents have to fulfil. The two dimensions are linked together by the normative specification (NS) assigning missions to roles. This makes MOISE very suitable for the definition of a flexible governance strategy since we can envision to change either the SS, the FS or the NS without changing the other ones.

The organizational specification describes the governance objectives with respect to both *vertical* and *horizontal* concerns. In fact, as the infrastructure is shared by several heterogeneous applications and devices, the governance strategy must take into account the "horizontal" issues. Hence, a main frame defines the *horizontal* aspects which are extended for each *vertical* applicative requirements.

This section describes the organization corresponding to the M2M Organizational Specification (OS) for the governance strategy of the M2M architecture as described in Section 2 and highlights the key points for reorganization. This specification can be understood by the agents, so they can govern the M2M system based on it. Furthermore, they can reason about it to choose whether to follow it or not and then to adapt it to the situation.

## 4.1 Structural Specification

Fig. 4 shows the structural specification of the M2M OS. On one side it specifies the *horizontal* structure of an M2M architecture (within the M2M System group) and on the

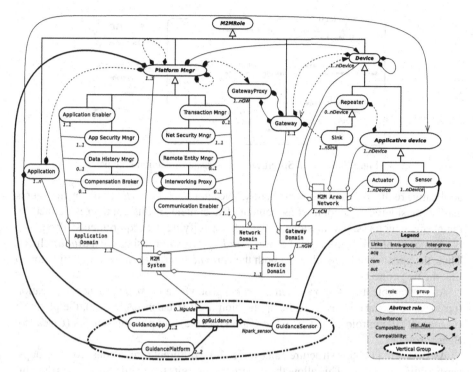

**Fig. 4.** Structural Specification for an M2M system and its extension for a "vertical" application (Car Guidance)

other side it defines one or several *vertical* groups (e.g. gpGuidance group). The agents can adopt one or several roles –depending on compatibility and cardinalities– to declare explicitly which part of the governed system they assume the responsibility of.

The *horizontal* part is composed of three groups corresponding to the M2M architecture described in Section 2.1: (i) the Device Domain group, (ii) the Network Domain group and (iii) the Application Domain group. This specification maps the functionalities of these different domains into roles.

The *Gateway* and *Gateway Proxy* roles are made compatible to allow agents to play both roles at the same time in the Device Domain and Network Domain groups respectively.

Each functionality of the M2M Core Platform is defined as a role in the Application Domain group –*Application Enabler, Application Security Manager, Data History Manager, Compensation Broker*– or in the Network Domain group –*Remote Entity Manager, Network Security Manager, Communication Enabler, Interworking Proxy*. All these roles inherit from the abstract *Platform Manager* role to make global the property of compatibility between any of these roles and to also express the communication link.

Finally, the *Application* role is responsible for performing the business logic by sending commands to the devices and by retrieving the collected data.

The *vertical* part is composed of specific groups which represent a contract between an application, the devices, the platforms and gateways. In particular, such a group expresses the application needs in terms of parts of the M2M system to be involved in the

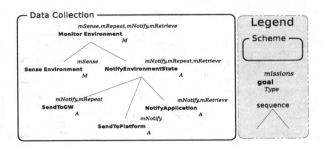

**Fig. 5.** Functional Specification: the Data Collection scheme

applicative realization and their cardinality. The adoption of a *vertical* role by the agents can be considered as a contract agreement. The content of this contract is defined by the norms which assigns missions to the roles specifying the requirements. The group is composed of roles linked to the *horizontal* specification using *compatibility* links. Thus, the agents can be involved in both the *vertical* and the *horizontal* organization to link the two concerns.

As an example, Fig. 4 shows such a *vertical* group for a *Parking Guidance* application (gpGuidance group). It involves the application itself (*GuidanceApp* role), the platform (*GuidancePlatform* role), a gateway (*GuidanceGW* role) and parking sensors (*Guidance-Sensor* role).

As shown in [11] this structure can evolve along different dimensions (roles, groups, cardinalities, links...). This allow the governance to suits to the infrastructure's dynamics. As an example, if more agents are needed to manage a part of the M2M system, the cardinality of the corresponding roles can be increased.

### 4.2 Functional Specification

The functional specification describes coordination schemes by means of goals to be globally satisfied by the agents in the organization. It gives the agents a comprehensive understanding of the system's functioning but it does not tell them how to achieve these goals: the agents are free to decide which actions to perform to satisfy the goals they are committed to. The following describes one of the social schemes that we have defined for *vertical* data collection.

The scheme in Fig. 5 describes the goals to collect data from sensors. The root goal (*Monitor Environment*), is a maintenance goal which is satisfied sequentially by (i) sensing the environment (*SenseEnvironment*) and (ii) notifying the subscribed applications the environment's state (*NotifyEnvironmentState*). The first sub-goal is accomplished in the context of the the the *mSense* mission. The notification can be made either after each time something is sensed or after reporting several measures at once. It is an achievement goal satisfied by the following sub-goal sequence: (i) send to the gateway (*SendToGW*), (ii) send to the platform (*SendToPlatform*) and (iii) notify applications the sensed value (*NotifyApplication*).

Let's notice that the figure does not express the whole specification. In particular, each mission is qualified by the minimum and maximum number of agents to commit to; goals can be parameterized when instantiating the scheme. Agents can customize a scheme for a particular application or for special situations. For example, different areas of the city could be monitored differently depending on the traffic, the time of day or the user demand, then the agents can fine-tune these values to adapt the scheme to the situation in order to avoid unuseful message transmissions.

### 4.3 Normative Specification

Norms delimit the actions that are allowed in the system. In $\mathcal{M}$OISE a norm assigns a mission to a role, following a deontic relation when a condition is satisfied and specifies a finite time in which to fulfil it. Thus, it provides a flexible way of assigning tasks to the agents.

Table 2 summarizes a part of the norms used for the M2M system corresponding to the data collection scheme. Agents playing *Sensor* roles must sense the environment (*mSense* mission). This mission consists of sensing the environment either regularly (norm $n_{01}$), or at each change (norm $n_{02}$). In any case, Sensor agents must commit to the mSense mission (norm $n_{03}$).

Agents are free to decide whether to follow or violate these norms. It can be regulated by reinforcement or punishment to encourage them to follow the norms. But it also provides a way to detect irrelevant specifications: an agent might violate a norm because it is impossible to satisfy a goal. Then agents should either redefine the norm –e.g. modify the condition, relax the deontic relation– or the scheme itself –e.g. delete a goal or add an alternative to it; define a sequence to make the goal reachable.

**Table 2.** Normative specification for an M2M system

| Id | Condition | Role | Rel. | Mission | TTF |
|---|---|---|---|---|---|
| $n_{01}$ | $scheduled(sensing\_time)$ | *Sensor* | perm | *mSense* | $t_{sense}$ |
| $n_{02}$ | $occurred(event)$ | *Sensor* | perm | *mSense* | $t_{sense}$ |
| $n_{03}$ | $n_{01} \vee n_{02}$ | *Sensor* | obl | *mSense* | $t_{sense}$ |
| $n_{04}$ | $changed(sensed\_value)$ $\wedge is\_critical(situation)$ | *Sensor* | obl | *mNotify* | $t_{send}$ |
| $n_{05}$ | $t_{last\_msg} \geq msg\_period$ $\vee is\_full(buffer)$ | *Sensor* | obl | *mNotify* | $t_{send}$ |
| $n_{06}$ | $on\_receive(msg)$ | *Repeater* | obl | *mRepeat* | $t_{repeat}$ |
| $n_{07}$ | $on\_receive(msg)$ $\wedge is\_authenticated(msg)$ | *Gateway* | perm | *mNotify* | $t_{notify}$ |

......... ...

## 5   Application: Smart Parking Management with the SensCity Platform

This section describes the application of the governance model presented in Sections 3 and 4 to the scenario described in Section 2.2. It consists of an extension of the based organization by new roles, linked to the generic ones, grouped in a specific group that is responsible for specific schemes and ruled by specific norms.

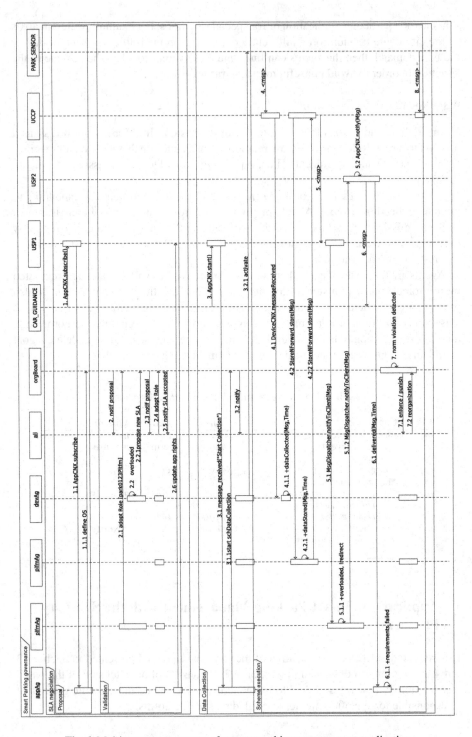

**Fig. 6.** Multi-agent governance of a smart parking management application

In the smart parking scenario the *CarGuidance* and *CityMonitoring* applications are governed by *appAg* agents while the *CarDetector*, *ParkingPost* devices are controlled by *deviceAg* agents. Each of the SensCity sub-platforms (*USP* and *UCCP* are controlled by a *platformAg* agent). In order to simplify and reduce the applicative description, no *Gateway* is considered here.

The following scenario is illustrated by the Fig. 6 sequence diagram in which the agents are the underlined participants, the *all* participant represents all the agents involved in the collaboration scheme, the *OrgBoard* artifact represents the organizational specification and controls, and *CAR_GUIDANCE*, *USP1*, *USP2*, *UCCP* and *PARK_SENSOR* represent elements of the M2M infrastructure, encapsulated by artifacts.

The first step consists of negotiating the SLA defined by a set of norms that manage the application-specific roles and missions. The SLA definition is done following the norm negociation cycle principle [3]: (i) a social scheme template is parameterized following the application needs, (ii) social norms define the SLAs for these goals and (iii) acceptance is achieved by role adoption. When the *CAR_GUIDANCE* application asks (1) the *USP1* platform for a subscription to a set of $N_{park\_sensors}$ devices, the *appAg* agent intercepts (1.1) the call and formulates the requirements as an organizational specification (1.1.1): a gpGuidance group composed of the *GuidanceApp*, *GuidancePlatform* (with cardinality 2) and *GuidanceSensor* (with cardinality $N_{park\_sensors}$) roles, a parameterized Data Collection scheme and norms corresponding to the application's requirements. All of the agents concerned are notified of the proposal (2). The agents can validate the SLA proposal by adopting one or several roles in the organization (2.1). But if they estimate that the proposal is not affordable, e.g. a resource will be overloaded (2.2), they can propose a new specification (2.2.1). This new proposal is communicated again (2.3) and the same process occurs until all of the agents validate the SLA by adopting the roles (2.4). Then the *appAg* will update the application's rights in the *USP1* platform.

Then the *CAR_GUIDANCE* application can start the subscription (3) which will be handled (3.1) by the *appAg* by starting the Data Collection scheme (3.1.1). The agents are notified of goals to achieve defined by the norms (3.2), so the *deviceAg* agents activate the *PARK_SENSOR* devices they are responsible for (3.2.1). When messages are received by the *UCCP* platform (4), the *deviceAg* makes sure that it meets the requirements (4.1, 4.1.1).

The *UCCP*'s StoreNForward component is encapsulated by an artifact, so a *platformAg* agent can regulate and validate the message's storage (4.2, 4.2.1, 4.2.2) before it is transmitted to the *USP1* platform (5). There, a *platformAg* agent interrupts the *MessageDispatcher* component (5.1) because it is overloaded (5.1.1) and decides to redirect it to the *USP2* platform (5.1.2) which transfers the message to the application (5.2, 6). This is notified to the *appAg* agent (6.1) which considers the requirements as not satisfied (6.1.1).

The norm violation (7) can be handled either by reinforcement and punishment mechanisms (7.1) applied to the agents and/or by a reorganization process (7.2) based on the analysis of the system's failures by the agents.

# 6    Related Work and Discussion

M2M is a promising paradigm and is the topic of several works. For instance, the SEN-SEI project[5] uses a virtual representation called "WSAN Islands" which provides the sensor value of the physical device and can be fed by predictive agents to reduce communications to sensors. Our work goes a step further since SENSEI doesn't yet provide any governance structure to control its components' behavior.

Some of them propose a governance structure. For instance, an agent-based approach is used by the US Ocean Observatories Initiatives to build an Ocean Observatories Initiative Cyberinfrastructure [5] to monitor the oceans with a marine sensor platform. It defines an infrastructure for an M2M server composed of six service networks interacting together following predefined interaction scenarios. The AAMSRT framework [14] gives another multi-agent approach for managing sensor re-targeting on satellites. Yet, both of these models use a static organizational model even if the second one is based on agents negotiating their commitment to missions.

Our paper proposes a template for an end-to-end M2M architecture. The openness and the heterogeneity of applicative requirements made necessary to ensure agility to the specifications by the means of organizational adaptations. For example, the *sensing_time* and $t_{sense}$ values in norm $n_{01}$ are specific to the applicative needs and the type of sensor. Agents can adapt the *OS* by extending the existing organization as a generic framework: new norms specific to applicative requirements, involving new roles extending existing ones to fulfil specific goals.

Moreover, as the *OS* is explicit and understandable for the agents, they can reason about it in order to improve the system's performances. For example, faced to a scalability issue, role cardinalities could be increased to enable some functionalities and components of the platform to be delegated to several agents. In contrast, security issues could lead to more atomicity by lowering role cardinalities.

Nevertheless, such a reorganization raises several issues: while self-organizing MAS's are more adaptive and robust, they might not converge in a stable organization [16]. Furthermore, the (re)organizational cost [12] must be taken into account to decide when to adapt. Another issue is to define who manages the reorganization: dedicated agents applying the organizational policy [11] or the applicative agents directly as in the AMAS [2] theory? While the former solution suffers robustness and scalability, the latter raises trust management issues. A possibility would be balancing between agents adapting locally based on their perception and dedicated agents for definitive organizational changes.

A contribution of our work is the explicitly expression of the *vertical* and *horizontal* concerns as different part of the organization. This model simplifies the analyze and reorganization process as the agent can clearly identify which part of the specification doesn't suit. Nevertheless, modifying a part of the organization raises issues with respect to the organization's integrity and consistency. For example, what does an agent is supposed to do when it is fulfilling a mission but the cardinality has just decreased in the *OS*? And what are the side effects?

---

[5] SENSEI (Integrating the Physical with the Digital World of the Network of the Future), EU ICT FP7, http://www.sensei-project.eu/

Hence, a solution is to stop the organization, update its definition and restart the groups and schemes. However, this approach is not satisfying neither as maintenance goals make difficult to define the time to stop a scheme. Furthermore, goals might have been modified so it is not possible to save all the schemes' states to restore them.

Therefore, a step further would be to split the model into several organizations: one for the *horizontal* concerns and one for each *vertical* application requirements. This would lead to several small organizations easier to analyze and adapt separately. Then agents will be able to reason in term of organization involvement in order to adapt the priority of one application's requirements or the horizontal objectives. Yet, much work have to be done to specify *extra-organization* links and constraints.

## 7 Conclusion and Further Work

Through a smart parking management application, this paper has presented a multi-agent architecture for an agile governance of Machine-to-Machine systems. The governance system is implemented using the JaCaMo framework in order to separate the different governance layers: CArtAgO artifacts are used to monitor and handle the M2M infrastructure, Jason agents applies the governance strategy and reason about the governance objectives which are specified as a Moise organization.

This governance model takes into account both the *vertical* application requirements and the shared infrastructure *horizontal* concerns, following the latest recommendations of the ETSI [6]. Furthermore, in order to meet scalability requirements, it highlights several key elements for adapting the structural, functional and normative specifications.

An other step in our work will focus on exploring reorganization aspects following two directions: (i) a behavioural specification to enable agents to adapt the organization directly and (ii) the definition of new roles dedicated to organization monitoring and reorganization processes to control the reorganization. Furthermore, while splitting the *horizontal* and the *vertical* concerns into several organization, it would be necessary to define *heuristics* to prioritize an organization over an other one.

In the meantime, the proposed organization, agents and artifacts will be deployed in an M2M infrastructure as a demonstrator in order to test and validate this model under real conditions.

## References

1. Barkai, J.: Keynote speech – how to design your business (and products) for machine to machine communication. In: Connected World Conference (2008),
   http://www.connectedworldmag.com/conference/
   index.php?q=2008-Presentations
2. Bernon, C., Camps, V., Gleizes, M.P., Picard, G.: Engineering Self-Adaptive Multi-Agent Systems: the ADELFE Methodology, ch. 7, pp. 172–202. Idea Group Publishing (2005)
3. Boella, G., Van Der Torre, L.: Norm negociation in mutltiagent systems. International Journal of Cooperative Information Systems 16(1), 97–122 (2007)
4. Bordini, R., Hübner, J., Wooldridge, M.: Programming Multi-Agent Systems in AgentSpeak Using Jason. John Wiley & Sons, Ltd. (2007)

5. Chave, A., Arrott, M., Farcas, C., Farcas, E., Krueger, I., Meisinger, M., Orcutt, J., Vernon, F., Peach, C., Schofield, O., Kleinert, J.: Cyberinfrastructure for the US Ocean Observatories Initiative: Enabling interactive observation in the ocean. In: Oceans 2009-Europe, pp. 1–10 (May 2009)

6. ETSI: Tech. Spec. 102 690 V<0.13.3>, Machine-to-Machine communications – Functional architecture (July 2011)

7. Firesmith, D.: Profiling Systems Using the Defining Characteristics of Systems of Systems (SoS). Techreport, Software Engineer Institute, Pittsburgh, Pennsylvania (2010)

8. Horling, B., Lesser, V.: A survey of multi-agent organizational paradigms. The Knowledge Engineering Review 19(04), 281–316 (2005)

9. Hübner, J.F., Sichman, J.S., Boissier, O.: Developing Organised Multi-Agent Systems Using the MOISE+ Model: Programming Issues at the System and Agent Levels. Agent-Oriented Software Engineering 1(3/4), 370–395 (2007)

10. Hübner, J.F., Sichman, J.S., Boissier, O.: A Model for the Structural, Functional, and Deontic Specification of Organizations in Multiagent Systems. In: Bittencourt, G., Ramalho, G.L. (eds.) SBIA 2002. LNCS (LNAI), vol. 2507, pp. 118–128. Springer, Heidelberg (2002)

11. Hübner, J.F., Sichman, J.S., Boissier, O.: Using the MOISE+ for a Cooperative Framework of MAS Reorganisation. In: Bazzan, A.L.C., Labidi, S. (eds.) SBIA 2004. LNCS (LNAI), vol. 3171, pp. 506–515. Springer, Heidelberg (2004)

12. Kota, R., Gibbins, N., Jennings, N.: Decentralised Approaches for Self-Adaptation in Agent Organisations. ACM Transactions on Autonomous and Adaptive Systems, 1–36 (2011)

13. Lefauconnier, A., Gantelet, E.: Parking place search: strategies, associated nuisances, parking management issues in france. Tech. rep., SARECO, Paris, France (2005) (in French), http://www.sareco.fr/Publications/Temps_de_recherche.pdf

14. Levy, R., Chen, W., Lyell, M.: Software agent-based framework supporting autonomous and collaborative sensor utilization. In: Proc. of 8th Int. Conf. on Autonomous Agents and Multiagent Systems (AAMAS 2009), pp. 93–100 (May 2009)

15. Ma, X., Luo, W.: The Analysis of 6LowPAN Technology. In: IEEE Pacific-Asia Workshop on Computational Intelligence and Industrial Application, vol. 1, pp. 963–966. IEEE Com. Soc. (December 2008)

16. Picard, G., Hübner, J.F., Boissier, O., Gleizes, M.P.: Reorganisation and Self-organisation in Multi-Agent Systems. In: 1st International Workshop on Organizational Modeling, ORGMOD 2009, pp. 66–80 (June 2009)

17. Picard, G., Mellouli, S., Gleizes, M.-P.: Techniques for Multi-agent System Reorganization. In: Dikenelli, O., Gleizes, M.-P., Ricci, A. (eds.) ESAW 2005. LNCS (LNAI), vol. 3963, pp. 142–152. Springer, Heidelberg (2006)

18. Piunti, M., Boissier, O., Hübner, J.F., Ricci, A.: Embodied Organizations: a unifying perspective in programming Agents, Organizations and Environments. In: COIN10@MALLOW, pp. 98–114. Springer (September 2010)

19. Ricci, A., Piunti, M., Viroli, M., Omicini, A.: Environment programming in cartago. In: Bordini, R.H., Dastani, M., Dix, J., El Fallah-Seghrouchni, A. (eds.) Multi-Agent Programming: Languages, Platforms and Applications, vol. 2, pp. 259–288. Springer (2009)

# A Proposal of Process Fragment Definition and Documentation

Valeria Seidita[1], Massimo Cossentino[2], and Antonio Chella[1]

[1] Dipartimento di Ingegneria Chimica Gestionale Informatica Meccanica
Università degli Studi di Palermo, Italy
{seidita,chella}@dinfo.unipa.it
[2] Istituto di Reti e Calcolo ad Alte Prestazioni, Consiglio Nazionale delle
Ricerche - ICAR/CNR Palermo, Italy
cossentino@pa.icar.cnr.it

**Abstract.** This paper focuses on the field of Situational Method Engineering (SME) for the construction of agent-oriented design processes. Whatever SME approach a method designer wants to use, he has to manage two main elements: the (method or process) fragment and the repository where it is stored. Specific fragment definition and documentation are fundamental during these activities, for new process composition, and for the consequent system design activities. This paper aims at illustrating a proposal of fragment definition and documentation. This proposal is aimed to be an input for the IEEE FIPA Design Process Documentation and Fragmentation working group and, as regards our own research work, this is the ideal completion of the methodological practices prescribed in the PRoDe approach for new processes composition.

## 1   Introduction

The work presented in this paper starts and is based on what we have done during the latest years towards the definition of the best way to create ad-hoc agent oriented design processes. The development of a multi agent system always requires great efforts in learning and using an existing design process.

It has been said and heard several times that it does not exist one design process (or also a methodology or a method) to develop systems able to solve every kind of problems and that there is the need for creating techniques and tools for a designer to develop an ad-hoc design process prior to use it on the base of his own needs [11][20][19].

In order to solve this problem and to give means for one to develop an agent system using the "right" design process, we adopted the (Situational) Method Engineering approach and we started from pointing out what we intend for design process. (Situational) Method Engineering [8][2][11][15] provides tools and techniques for creating design processes by reusing portion of existing ones, called *method fragment*, stored in a repository, the *method base*.

In [4] the main elements of an agent-oriented design process have been identified, they fundamentally ground on three of the main elements a designer always

M. Cossentino et al. (Eds.): EUMAS 2011, LNAI 7541, pp. 221–237, 2012.
© Springer-Verlag Berlin Heidelberg 2012

meets during design, they refer to the *stakeholders* that perform *activities* in order to produce *design results* (also labelled *work products or artefacts*).

The key idea of our approach is that this core triad has to be augmented by another important element: the *system metamodel*. This concern, also deduced from the MDE [16] approach, led to the consideration that producing design results, is nothing else but instantiating elements from a (meta-)model.

The system metamodel is the fundamental element to be considered following the (Situational) Method Engineering approach, PRoDe (the Process for designing Design Processes), we have recently created [17]. In PRoDe the creation of design processes can be done by following specific phases from analysis to implementation. The system metamodel contains the set of constructs that will satisfy the system requirements.

A lot of existing (Situational) Method Engineering approaches exist [7][14][12] [9][1], they are developed around three main phases: the *process requirements analysis*, the *process fragments selection* and the *process fragment assembly*. The principal aim of SME is to manage the *method fragment*.

Nowadays, there are a lot of definitions of method fragment in the research on (Situational) Method Engineering. We claim that none of them can be universally applied. Different (Situational) Method Engineering approaches own different notion of method fragment and as a consequence they use proprietary repositories. Actually, this reason and the lack of a unique fragment interface severely limit the availability of repositories.

In this paper we focus on the process fragment definition and documentation by identifying its main elements and following a twofold aim: reuse, in terms of providing all the information for supporting the selection and assembly phases, and reuse in a more general design point of view, hence providing information useful to designers. During system development, designer needs guidelines on the portion of work described in the fragment and how to produce the related artefacts. So the main notion, we deal with, is the System Metamodel that represents the major improvement to the work proposed in [17].

Our aim is to give a definition aiming at well documenting the process fragment. We pursue a twofold objective: 1) using the fragment at the system design time and 2) reusing in storage and assembly, in so doing we lay the foundations for establishing a standard definition of fragment and the related standard documentation. This work is the natural prosecution of the work done by the authors within the IEEE FIPA Design Process Documentation and Fragmentation working group that already resulted in the standard way of documenting design processes [10].

In the following sections the definition and a template for documentation of process fragment will be shown together with an example of documentation.

## 2   Background and Motivation

During the latest years the fact that the projects' features and organization specificities greatly influence the software development methods has become evident. Besides the more the software systems become complex the more this fact becomes urgent. The consequence is that it does not exist a unique development method that could fit every kind of needs organizations could present and that can be used for engineering every kind of software systems.

In this scenario it is increasing the need for techniques allowing organizations to create and then to use their own development method(s). Specific development methods could take into account the kind of problems the organization is devoted to solve and the characteristics they present in terms of designers/developers skills, known and used tools and so on.

The discipline of Method Engineering has faced this problem and some important results has been reached. The Method Engineering has been defined by Brinkkemper et al. [2] as "the engineering discipline to design, construct and adapt methods, techniques and tools for the development of information systems ". Method engineering aims to accomplish two different scopes: the first is to create situation specific methods for meeting organizational features and represent a sort of choice list, the second is to produce the so called method "on the fly". Hence the system development implies and starts with the definition of development methods that fit specific project situations (this is the matter of a sub-area of Method Engineering (ME), the Situational Method Engineering (SME) [11]).

The best and quickest way to develop situation specific methods is reusing existing ones. For these purposes (S)ME prescribes to break down existing methods into "components" that may be stored in a repository. These components may be retrieved (analyzed and then selected) from the repository in order to be composed/assembled in a new method fitting project/organization needs. They can also be used as they are or adapted in order to best fit specific needs or in order to facilitate the composition of the process.

Still open issues are: the definition of the components and their granularity, how they have to be selected from the repository and how they can be assembled.

In the past the authors developed an approach for new design processes composition (PRoDe [17]) that entails the aforementioned "component" namely the *Process Fragment* and also the *System Metamodel*.

The **Process Fragment** is a portion of design process adequately created and structured for being reused during the composition and enactment of new design processes both in the field of agent oriented software engineering and in other ones (model driven engineering-based approaches are preferred fields of application for the proposed definition).

The **System Metamodel** is the definition of constructs needed for creating system models.

It is our belief that during the enactment of the methods one (or more) process role refers, more or less knowingly, to the metamodel in order to produce work products where instances of a set of metamodel constructs are managed (more details about this argument can be found in [10]).

Managing process fragments is the main aim of PRoDe, it covers the three main phases of SME, the process requirement analysis and the definition of process fragment, the selection and then the assembly. Because of our conviction about the importance of the system metamodel in all the design activities, it has a central role in PRoDe.

The first activity in the PRoDe approach entails a set of steps that, starting from the process requirements, are able to produce the system metamodel or in any case a first draft of it. PRoDe is iterative, the new design process, after a first enactment, might be modified/enhanced due to test results and new requirements identification. As regard selection and assembly the PRoDe approach provides a well defined set of activities for identifying and retrieving fragments from repository basing on some considerations made on the system metamodel [17]. The PRoDe activities, as well as other SME approach activities, are also highly grounded on the SME fundamental element, the *Process Fragment* (or method fragment or chunk or simply fragment - however it is named by different researchers), and obviously on the repository aimed at storing it. In order to apply a SME approach in the most fruitful way, a well done definition and documentation of process fragment is useful for properly storing, selecting and assembling new design processes whatever SME approach one wants to follow.

The process fragment definition together with the specific SME process (see for instance [17]) used for retrieving and composing fragments may notably influence how the repository is conceived and constructed. We try to not take this chance by using the definition we propose in the following section.

## 3   The Process Fragment Definition

Figure 1 represents all the elements composing a Process Fragment. It contains all the elements useful for representing and documenting the fragment under the process, product and reuse point of view; the proposed fragment documentation template, that will be presented in the following section, slavishly follows the proposed representation, its elements and their definitions.

The root element, the *Process Fragment*, has been generally extracted from an existing design process, therefore an important information to be stored in the repository is the *Design Process* the fragment refers to. This serves for the designer to set the application context and the particular features the fragment would exhibit. The *Process Fragment* can be of three different levels of granularity: *phase*, *composed* and *atomic*, each of them is related to the quantity of work to be done and to the complexity of the produced outcome.

— A *phase (process) fragment* delivers a set of work products belonging to the same design abstraction level of the design flow. Such a work product may belong to any of the cited work product types. An example of phase-level work product may be a system analysis document; it is composed of several work products (diagrams, text documents, . . . ) all belonging to the same design abstraction level (system analysis).

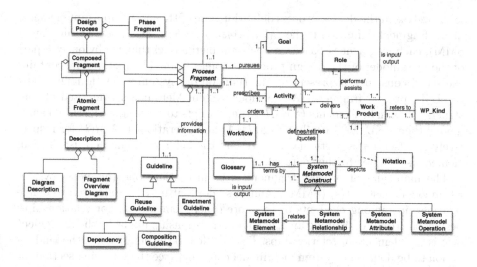

**Fig. 1.** The Process Fragment View

- A *composed (process) fragment* delivers a work product (or a set of instances of the same work product). Such a work product may belong to any of the cited work product types.
- An *atomic (process) fragment* delivers a portion of a work product and/or a set of system model constructs (in terms of their instantiation or refinement). A portion of a work product is here intended never to be a whole work product; in other words, atomic fragments never deliver entire work products.

The process fragment prescribes some activities to do, each of them is a portion of work that has to be performed by one or more stakeholders (*Roles*).

Activity delivers *Work Products*, where the results of design activities are drawn by using a specific *Notation* and each work product is developed under the responsibility of one role. The notation to be used greatly influences the flow of work to be done for producing a work product and for this reason a fragment has to be supplied with a set of *Guidelines*. As regards the process and product perspective of the fragment the *Enactment Guidelines* provides all the elements, description and so on, for applying the workflow prescribed in the fragment.

It is not mandatory to follow a specific notation, the same kind of diagram (for instance a structural one) may be expressed by using different notations without significant differences in the resulting expressiveness. Moreover, different kinds (*WP_Kind*) of work products can be delivered. We identified two main work product kinds: graphical and textual, the former when an activity results in a diagram, the second when designers produce textual documents. Finally a work product can be of composite kind if it is a composition of the previous said kinds, for instance a document with a diagram and the text explaining it (more details can be found in [18]).

As well as in the design process definition, one of the most important elements in the fragment definition is the *(Multi-Agent) System Metamodel* (Multi-Agent SMM); each fragment is based on a system metamodel that is obviously a part of the metamodel of the design process it comes from. The metamodel contains the set of constructs representing the (portion of) system to be designed using a specific process fragment. We consider System Metamodel composed of constructs that can be elements (*SMME* - the concepts to be designed), relationships among them (*SMMR*), attributes (*SMMA*) and operations (*SMMO*) for respectively representing a particular feature and the behavioral characteristics of an element (see [6] for further details).

The main aim of process fragment is to instantiate one (or more) system metamodel construct(s) (SMMC) and in so doing it may be requested to define relationships among elements or to quote other elements and/or relationships; besides the result of defining an element or a relationship might be the refinement of existing elements or relationships. This fact led to the definition of the kinds of action to be done on a system metamodel construct (see the following section for details). Finally SMMC has a definition to be listed in a glossary; the definition is mainly useful during selection when the method designer wants know which kind of metamodel construct better fits with the metamodel construct s/he is dealing with.

Until now we explored the process and product part of the fragment through a set of elements that has to be necessarily present in the fragment documentation, now let us quickly focus on the elements that principally deal with the reuse aspect of the fragment: *Goal*, and *Dependency* guidelines. The fragment goal is the objective the process part of the fragment wants to pursue and it is to be used during fragment selection from the repository. For this reason it is related to the new design process requirements, in other words, a goal describes the contribution a fragment may give to the accomplishment of some design process requirements.

The dependency guideline aims at describing specific constraints, if they exist, for the fragment to be composed with other ones, for instance, there can be fragments dealing with system metamodel elements that are very specific to particular application domains, in this case it should be possible that such fragments can be composed with fragments coming from the same classes of design processes.

It is important noting that the way the work has to be performed inside one fragment may slightly change depending on the notation of the work product produced; if the result has to be a graphical work product the activity and the related guidelines are different if we want to use two different notations. Since the fragment aims at designing a specific system metamodel construct, we can consider the fragment itself independent from the specific notation. The same result can be obtained by producing different work products in different notations.

In the following table we give the detailed definition of all the elements composing a process fragment:

**Table 1.** Process Fragment Elements Definitions

| Term | Definition |
| --- | --- |
| Design Process | It is the design process from which the fragment has been extracted. |
| Phase | A specification of the fragment position in the design workflow. Usually referring to a taxonomy (i.e. Requirements elicitation, Analysis, Design, etc.) |
| Goal | The process-oriented objective of the fragment. |
| Activity | A portion of work assignable to a performer (role). An activity may be atomic (sometimes addressed as Action) or composed by other activities. |
| Work Product | The resulting product of the work done in the fragment; it can be realized in different ways (diagram, text,..) also depending on the specific adopted notation. |
| WP_Kind | Represents the specific kind one work product can be; it strictly depends on the means the adopted notation provides. One work product can be: Structured or Free text, Structural, Behavioural or Composite |
| Notation | Each deliverable can be drawn by using a specific notation. Concepts dealt by the fragment have to find a mapping in the notation. Notation usually includes a metamodel and a set of pictorial prescriptions used to represent the instantiation of metamodel elements. |
| Role | The stakeholder performing the work in the process and responsible of producing a work product (or a part of it). Usually referring to a taxonomy (i.e. System Analyst, Test Designer, etc.) |
| System Metamodel Construct | (abstract class) The concept the fragment deals with, for instance a fragment aiming at defining the system requirements has to define and to identify the concept of requirements. Each metamodel construct has to be defined during, at least, one portion of process work and has to appear in at least one work product. |
| System Metamodel Element | It is an entity of the metamodel that is instantiable into an entity of the system model. Examples of System Metamodel Elements (SMME) are: classes, use cases,.... |
| System Metamodel Relationship | It is the construct used for representing the existence of a relationship between two (or more) instances of SMMEs. For instance, the aggregation relationship among two instances of a SMME class is an instance of the SMMR association. |
| System Metamodel Attribute | It is a particular kind of elements used for adding properties to SMMEs. *An SMMA is a structural feature and it relates an instance of the class to a value or collection of values of the type of the attribute.* [21]. The attributes type is a SMME. |
| System Metamodel Operation | It is a behavioral feature of a classifier that specifies the name, type, parameters, and constraints for invoking an associated behavior [21]. |
| Glossary | A list of definitions for the system metamodel constructs. |
| Description | It is the textual and pictural description of the fragment; it provides a bird-eye on the whole process the fragments comes from and the fragment overview in terms of tasks to be performed, roles and work product kind to be delivered. |

**Table 1.** (*Continued*)

| Term | Definition |
|---|---|
| Composition Guideline | A set of guidelines for assembling/composing the fragments with others. This may include notational specifications, and constraints (also addressing issues like platform to be used for system implementation and application area) |
| Dependency | The description of specific dependencies of this fragment from other ones; it is useful for composition. |
| Enactment Guideline | The description of how to perform the prescribed activity. This may include best practices and specific techniques for achieving the expected results. |

# 4   The Process Fragment Documentation

The document used for the Process Fragment description is made of six main sections (the template is shown in Figure 2), each of them refers to one (or a set of) element(s) of the Process Fragment representation (see Figure 1). Three sections deals with the three main elements a design process is composed of, as we stated in section 2, they are: *Stakeholders*, *Workflow* and *Deliverable*, hence the description of who performs the work to be done and how, in order to deliver an artefact of the system model.

The *Stakeholders* have to be simply described through the name and the description of the activities (the work) their are responsible for. They are named Role in compliance with SPEM 2.0 [13].

The *Workflow* section serves for documenting all that regards the structure of the portion of work to be done in the process fragment. It covers the set of procedural rules for sequencing design activities and documents/artefacts exchanged among Roles in order to produce the main output of the fragment.

The concept of workflow we had in mind when we created this document template is the one introduced by [22], it is structured by work breakdown elements that give us the possibility to represent portion of design work at every level of granularity, hence we can represent phases, activities and tasks.

The Workflow description is made with one SPEM 2.0 activity diagram that represents the portion of work related to the role performing it and all the needed input and output documents. Each work breakdown element is completed with a textual description of information such as the name, the kind e.g. if it is a task, an activity or other else, the description and the roles involved in the work. Besides the list of all the input and output system metamodel constructs and the list of all the input and output work products are needed in order to have means for analyzing the process fragment, also automatically, during the selection and assembly phase when a new design process is being creating.

The *Deliverable* section is made of two main parts, the first deals with the truly description of the document kinds to be produced in order to provide guidelines for producing them and the second handles the relationships of the work product with the constructs of the system metamodel here managed. So in

```
1. Fragment Description
    1.1. Fragment Goal
    1.2. Fragment Granularity
        1.2.1. Composing fragments
    1.3. Fragment Origin
        1.3.1. The Process Lifecycle
    1.4. Fragment Overview
2. System metamodel
    2.1. Definition of System metamodel elements
    2.2. Definition of System metamodel relationships
    2.3. Definition of System metamodel attributes
    2.4. Definition of System metamodel operations
        2.4.1. Fragment Input/Output in Terms of System Metamodel Constructs
        2.4.2. Definition of input system metamodel constructs
3. Stakeholders
    3.1. Role 1
4. Workflow
    4.1. Workflow description
    4.2. Work Break Down Elements description
    4.3. Work Break Down Elements' input/output in terms of system metamodel constructs
    4.4. Fragment's Input/Output in terms of Work Product
5. Deliverables
    5.1. Document name
        5.1.1. Deliverable notation
        5.1.2. Deliverable content in terms of system metamodel constructs
6. Guidelines
    6.1. Enactment Guidelines
    6.2. Reuse Guidelines
        6.2.1. Composition
        6.2.2. Dependency Relationship with other fragments
7. Glossary
8. References
```

**Fig. 2.** Process Fragment Document Template

the first part of the section the description on how to produce the work product and an example on the specific notation used are given.

This part of the document aims at exhaustively providing all the information for the designer to produce the deliverables. In the second part of this section the said relationships are represented in a particular kind of diagram that the authors created by extending SPEM 2.0 [6], namely the *work product content diagram*.

The word *content* let us understand that this diagram aims at having a complete and detailed view on the elements managed during the production of the work product. Exactly this diagram collects all the system metamodel constructs that are managed during the enactment of the process fragment and are also reported in the work product, hence the design process input constructs that are not reported in the work product are not shown in this diagram.

Input constructs are used by designer for the analysis and for reasoning about the system to be produced. In the content diagram we also report information about the type of design actions made on each construct.

One specific design action is made on each metamodel construct and it is useful for catching various information about the fragment and the resulting work product. The list of possible design actions has been identified by analyzing the way of working of designer; we used for that a lot of agent oriented design processes under the hypothesis that each work product production aims at instantiating at least one metamodel construct.

Instantiating means defining one or more instances of metamodel construct that have to be represented in the work product following one specific notation. Often, during the definition of one construct designer needs to consider other constructs already defined in other process fragment and/or to report them in the work product he is producing. Another frequent situation is when designer relates one instance of one construct to another one, for instance a generalization among classes, in this case he defines a relationship.

Finally designer could need to refine constructs by adding information or features to an already defined one, in this case he defines attributes and/or operations for that construct. Therefore the possible design actions to be made on system metamodel constructs are:

- **define**, instantiation of construct (element, relationship, attribute and operation), the label used is **D** for all construct except for the relationship in which case it is **R**,
- **quote**, reporting a construct in the work product, the labels used are **Q**, **QR**, **QA** and **QO** respectively for element, relationship, attribute and operation. Quotation also introduces relationship, hence dependency, with other work products.

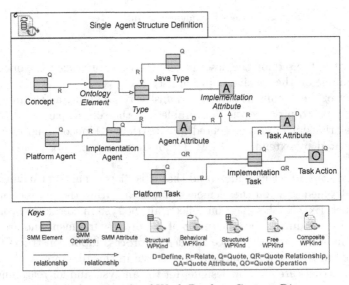

**Fig. 3.** An example of Work Product Content Diagram

In Figure 3 an example of work product content diagram is given, it represents the outcome of the Single Agent Structure Definition process fragment extracted from PASSI [3]; here we can see that the aim of this process fragment is to produce a work product where the Implementation Agent and Implementation Task are respectively refined by adding the Agent Attribute and the Task Attribute, hence these latter are defined whereas the former are quoted and related with them. Besides, in order to define the Agent Attribute and the Task Attribute, Concept and Java Type have to be quoted. Finally the work product prescribes to also report the Task Action and the Platform Agent that are consequently quoted. It is worth noting that the notational symbol used for System Metamodel Construct (SMMC) is not used for system metamodel relationship, even if we understand that this is not stylistically correct from a notational point of view we prefer to maintain that for reducing the complexity of producing and reading this kind of diagrams. Besides there can be more than one relationship among instances of the same constructs and this is shown by the number close to the R label. This kind of diagram let designer to easily identify all the system metamodel constructs the fragment is devoted to manage.

Another notational element that can be seen in this diagram and that is largely used in all the SPEM 2.0 diagrams of the fragment documentation is the Work Product Kind. Briefly, we needed to represent different kinds of work product so we extended SPEM in order to include the following kinds[1]:

- Behavioural, it is a graphical kind of work product and is used to represent the dynamic aspect of the system (for instance a sequence diagram representing the flow of messages among agents along time);
- Structural, it is also a graphical kind of work product and is used for representing the static aspect of the system, for instance a UML class diagram;
- Structured, it is a text document ruled by a particular template or grammar, for instance a table or a code document;
- Free, it a document freely written in natural language;
- Composite, this work product can be made by composing the previous work product kinds, for instance a diagram with a portion of text used for its description.

The main aim of the section on Deliverables is to provide, among the others, some kind of guidelines for producing the work product. Another kind of guidelines has to be documented in the *Guidelines* section, here there are two types of guidelines, the *enactment* and the *reuse*. The enactment guideline provides a textual description on how to carry out the work in the fragment by referring and describing in details how to manage the system metamodel constructs of the fragment.

The aim of the reuse guidelines is very different, they are directed to the reuse possibility of the fragment thus providing suggestions for composing the fragment with other ones and the dependencies from other fragments. Reuse guidelines supplies another view on the dependencies of the fragment already

---

[1] Definitions reported from our previous work on the matter in [18].

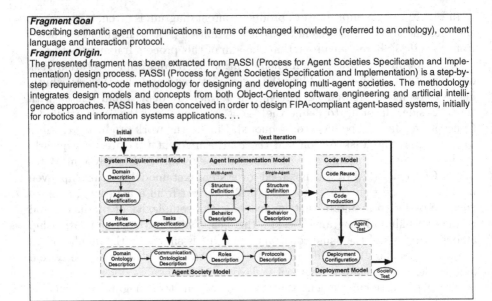

**Fig. 4.** A Portion of the COD Fragment Document - The Fragment Description

visible in the workflow description by means of the input work products and in the content diagram by means of the quoted elements so as in all the tables describing input and output constructs of the fragment.

What we consider the key concept of our approach to SME for representing design process in general and process fragment in particular, the *System Metamodel*, is documented in the second section on the proposed template. The attention paid to the System Metamodel, how it is conceived and it is composed of is the most important improvement the authors give to the previous fragment definition made in [17]. The section on metamodels includes a class diagram for representing the Complete System Metamodel of the fragment and the definition of each SMM Construct together with, when applicable, a statechart describing its different states while managed by the designer during the application of the fragment. An example reported from the Communication Ontological Description (COD) process fragment is shown later in Figure 5 (consider that this and the following figures are extracted from the COD documentation so other figures are present with different numeration). Then all the input/output system metamodel constructs are listed in a table where a distinction is made between the constructs to be designed and the ones to be quoted.

The first section regards the *Fragment Description* that includes: the *goal*, the *granularity*, the *origin* of the fragment and an *overview* on the fragment. The description of the fragment *goal* aims to provide the reader with a quick understanding of the goal pursued by the process fragment using a simple sentence like, for instance, "the aim of this fragment is collecting requirements",

**System metamodel**

The portion of metamodel of this fragment is:

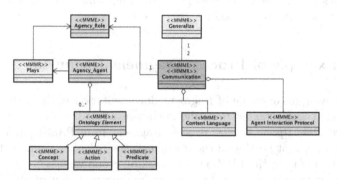

**Figure a.** The fragment System metamodel

This fragment refers to the MAS meta-model adopted in PASSI and contributes to define and describe the elements reported in Figure a.

***Definition of System metamodel elements.***

This fragment underpins the following model elements:

**Agency_Agent** - an autonomous entity capable of pursuing an objective through its autonomous decisions, actions and social relationships. It is capable of performing actions in the environment it lives; it can communicate directly with other agents, typically using an Agent Communication Language; it possesses resources of its own; it is capable of perceiving its environment; it has a (partial) representation of this environment in form of an instantiation of the domain ontology (knowledge); it can offer services; it can play several, different (and sometimes concurrent or mutually exclusive) agency_roles.

Each agent may be refined by adding knowledge items necessary to store/manage communication contents. The Agency_agent statechart is:

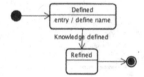

Description of the Agency_Agent states:

*Defined*: An Agency_Agent is in this state once it is instantiated in the system model. The agent's unique name has to be defined.

*Refined*: An Agency_Agent moves in this state once its knowledge chunks are defined.

**Fig. 5.** A Portion of the COD Fragment Document - The System Metamodel

possibly relating the description to common-sense in software engineering. The goal serves mainly in giving a mean for the method designer to select the right fragment for his purposes.

As regard the granularity, it establishes the length of the work done in the fragment and in some way the complexity of the fragment in terms of work product. As already said there can be three kinds of fragment: *phase*, *composed* and *atomic* (see also Figure 1).

Finally *Glossary* and *References* completes the documentation by providing useful description of the most important terms used in the fragment and a list of references for improving knowledge on the fragment, above all on the origin, the application context and so on.

## 5    An Example of Process Fragment Document

In the following an example of fragment documentation is given through a set of figures that we extracted from the document related to the *Communication Ontological Descritpion - COD* process fragment from PASSI [3]. Each figure represents a relevant portion of the document, the complete version of this fragment can be found in the FIPA DPDF working group website[2].

Looking at the fragment outline, it can be seen that first of all we focus on the fragment presentation through its goal and its origin, in so doing we reach a twofold objective, letting the designer have a quick idea on the focus and the domain in which the fragment might work and allowing a sort of automatic or semiautomatic selection of the fragment. Figure 4 shows the fragment goal, it is described in a very concise textual form that puts in evidence the main elements the fragment will deal with, for instance it can be noticed the words

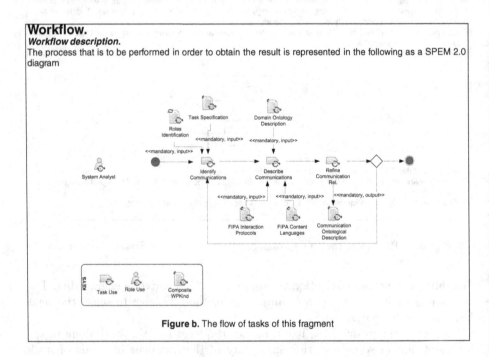

**Workflow.**
*Workflow description.*
The process that is to be performed in order to obtain the result is represented in the following as a SPEM 2.0 diagram

**Figure b.** The flow of tasks of this fragment

**Fig. 6.** A Portion of the COD Fragment Document - The Workflow Description

---

[2] http://www.pa.icar.cnr.it/cossentino/fipa-dpdf-wg/docs.htm

**Example.**

In Figure c, the PurchaseManager agent starts a communication (see QueryForAdvice association class) with the PurchaseAdvisor agent. The communication contains the Course ontology, the Query protocol and the RDF language. This means that the PurchaseManager wants to perform a speech act based on the FIPA query protocol in order to ask the PurchaseAdvisor advice on how to purchase (supplier, number of stocks, number of items per each, purchase-money) provided the Course information.

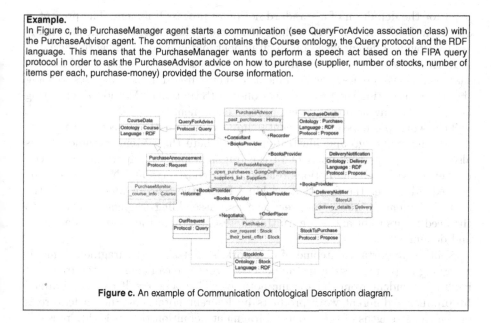

**Figure c.** An example of Communication Ontological Description diagram.

**Fig. 7.** A Portion of the COD Fragment Document - An Example of the Produced WP

*agent communication, knowledge* and *protocol*. It is to be hoped that this part of the document were compiled using words focussing on the fragment scope. Figure 4 also shows a portion of the section dedicated to the design process the fragment has been extracted from, the importance of this early discussion has been already said.

As well as a design process, each process fragment is based on a MAS metamodel composed of elements and relationships; the fragment document has to explore this issue and to show all the elements type to be defined/quoted/related in the fragment. Figure 5 shows the COD document section about System metamodel. As already said the process fragment description, and documentation, is principally aimed at showing the process and product part of the fragment for easily identifying the way in which it can be reused. Figure 6 refers to the fragment description section and details the inputs, the outputs and the fragment workflow through a SPEM 2.0 activity diagram.

The fragment document continues with an example and the explanation on how to produce the work product (see Figure 7) and with a set of composition guidelines and dependency relationships.

# 6    Conclusions and Remarks

In this paper we presented the process fragment definition and the documentation template we use in our work. After a long experience done on the construction of design processes we realized that this template is an optimum starting

point for the definition of a standard notion of process fragment. The presented
document has been conceived with both a textual and a diagrammatic part in order to provide different views on the fragment and in order to allow the designer
to retrieve the most useful information for his own needs in a quick and also visual fashion. We created the document for being used for two purposes: reusing
the fragment during the process creation in a (Situational) Method Engineering
fashion and using it during design process enactment.

This work presents a fundamental improvement with respect to the work
done some years ago and illustrated in [17], here the system metamodel was
also considered as a component of the fragment but its importance has been
now enriched by all the notions related to its constructs and how they can be
defined. Moreover the fact that within PRoDe the System Metamodel is the
central element for retrieving, selecting and assembling fragments have led to
the need for its right and more fruitful representation in the fragment definition
and documentation.

Another important outcome of our work is that since the fragment aims at
designing a specific system metamodel construct, we can consider the fragment
itself independent from the specific notation. The same result can be obtained
by producing different work products in different notations. Such a feature is
one of the strengths of the proposed fragment definition that is highly reusable
and composable being mainly oriented to the metamodel construct it is aimed
to define; for instance a fragment that delivers UML based work products can
be easily composed to another fragment delivering free textual work product, it
is only important that the two have a matching set of input/output metamodel
constructs. This fact overcomes the problem of interfaces among fragment and
the problem, until now present, of having all fragments producing work products
with the same notation; at worst we could create design processes where different
parts have different notations but also this problem can be overcame by using a
CAPE (Computer Aided Process Engineering) tool able to instantiate the right
CASE tool for managing the enactment of the newly created design process. An
example of such CAPE tool is Metameth, a prototype that we developed in the
past in our laboratory [5].

**Acknowledgment.** This work has been partially supported by the EU project
FP7-Humanobs.

# References

1. Brinkkemper, S., Saeki, M., Harmsen, F.: Meta-modelling based assembly techniques for situational method engineering. Information Systems 24, 24 (1999)
2. Brinkkemper, S., Welke, R.J., Lyytinen, K.: Method Engineering: Principles of
   Method Construction and Tool Support. Springer (1996)
3. Cossentino, M.: From requirements to code with the PASSI methodology. In: Agent
   Oriented Methodologies, ch. IV, pp. 79–106. Idea Group Publishing, Hershey (2005)

4. Cossentino, M., Gaglio, S., Garro, A., Seidita, V.: Method fragments for agent design methodologies: from standardisation to research. International Journal of Agent-Oriented Software Engineering (IJAOSE) 1(1), 91–121 (2007)
5. Cossentino, M., Sabatucci, L., Seidita, V.: A collaborative tool for designing and enacting design processes. In: Proceedings of the 2009 ACM Symposium on Applied Computing, SAC 2009, pp. 715–721. ACM, New York (2009)
6. Cossentino, M., Seidita, V.: Metamodeling: Representing and modeling system knowledge in design processes. Technical Report 11-02, Technical Report ICAR-CNR (July 29, 2011)
7. Gupta, D., Prakash, N.: Engineering Methods from Method Requirements Specifications. Requirements Engineering 6(3), 135–160 (2001)
8. Harmsen, A.F., Brinkkemper, S., Oei, H.: Situational method engineering for information system projects. In: Methods and Associated Tools for the Information Systems Life Cycle, Proceedings of the IFIP WG8. 1 Working Conference CRISí 1994, pp. 169–194 (1994)
9. Henderson-Sellers, B.: Method engineering: Theory and practice. In: Karagiannis, D., Mayr, H.C. (eds.) Information Systems Technology and its Applications, pp. 13–23 (2006)
10. IEEE Foundation for Intelligent Physical Agents. Design Process Documentation Template, Document number XC00097A-Experimental (2011)
11. Kumar, K., Welke, R.J.: Methodology engineering: a proposal for situation-specific methodology construction. In: Challenges and Strategies for Research in Systems Development, pp. 257–269 (1992)
12. Mirbel, I., Ralyté, J.: Situational method engineering: combining assembly-based and roadmap-driven approaches. Requirements Engineering 11(1), 58–78 (2006)
13. OMG. Object Management Group. Software & Software Process Engineering Metamodel. version 2.0. Document number: formal/2008-04-01 (2008)
14. Ralyté, J.: Towards situational methods for information systems development: engineering reusable method chunks. In: Procs. 13th Int. Conf. on Information Systems Development. Advances in Theory, Practice and Education, pp. 271–282 (2004)
15. Saeki, M.: Software specification & design methods and method engineering. International Journal of Software Engineering and Knowledge Engineering (1994)
16. Schmidt, D.C.: Model-driven engineering. Computer 39(2), 25–31 (2006)
17. Seidita, V., Cossentino, M., Hilaire, V., Gaud, N., Galland, S., Koukam, A., Gaglio, S.: The metamodel: a starting point for design processes construction. International Journal of Software Engineering and Knowledge Engineering 20(4), 575–608 (2010)
18. Seidita, V., Cossentino, M., Gaglio, S.: Using and Extending the SPEM Specifications to Represent Agent Oriented Methodologies. In: Luck, M., Gomez-Sanz, J.J. (eds.) AOSE 2008. LNCS, vol. 5386, pp. 46–59. Springer, Heidelberg (2009)
19. Slooten, K., Brinkkemper, S.: A method engineering approach to information systems development. In: Proceedings of the IFIP WG8. 1 Working Conference on Information System Development Process, pp. 167–186. North-Holland Publishing Co. (1993)
20. ter Hofstede, A.H.M., Verhoef, T.F.: On the feasibility of situational method engineering. Information Systems 22(6/7), 401–422 (1997)
21. UMLR-Revision-Taskforce. Omg uml specification v. 2.2. Object Management Group (2009)
22. WfMC. The workflow management coalition (2005), http://www.wfmc.org

# Recognizing Internal States of Other Agents to Anticipate and Coordinate Interactions

Filipo Studzinski Perotto

Constructivist Artificial Intelligence Research Group, Toulouse, France
`filipo.perotto@ufrgs.br`

**Abstract.** In multi-agent systems, anticipating the behavior of other agents constitutes a difficult problem. In this paper we present the case where a cognitive agent is inserted into an unknown environment composed of different kinds of other objects and agents; our cognitive agent needs to incrementally learn a model of the environment dynamics, doing it only from its interaction experience; the learned model can then be used to define a policy of actions. It is relatively easy to do so when the agent interacts with static objects, with simple mobile objects, or with trivial reactive agents; however, when the agent deals with other complex agents that may change their behaviors according to some non-directly observable internal properties (like emotional or intentional states), the construction of a model becomes significantly harder. The complete system can be described as a *Factored and Partially Observable Markov Decision Process* (FPOMDP); our agent implements the *Constructivist Anticipatory Learning Mechanism* (CALM) algorithm, and the experiment (called *mept*) shows that the induction of non-observable variables enable the agent to learn a deterministic model of most of the system events (if it represents a well-structured universe), allowing it to anticipate other agents actions and to adapt to them, even if some interactions appear as non-deterministic in a first sight.

**Keywords:** Factored Partially Observable MDPs, Anticipatory Learning Mechanisms, Model-Based RL, Constructivist Artificial Intelligence, Agent Intersubjectivity.

## 1 Introduction

Trying to escape from AI classic (and simple) maze problems toward more sophisticated (and therefore more complex and realistic) agent-based universes, we are led to consider some complicating conditions: (a) the situatedness of the agent, which is immersed into an unknown universe, interacting with it through limited sensors and effectors, without any holistic perspective of the complete environment state, and (b) without any *a priori* model of the world dynamics, which forces it to incrementally discover the effect of its actions on the system in an on-line experimental way; to make matters worse, the universe where the agent is immersed can be populated by different kinds of objects and entities,

M. Cossentino et al. (Eds.): EUMAS 2011, LNAI 7541, pp. 238–258, 2012.
© Springer-Verlag Berlin Heidelberg 2012

including (c) other complex agents, and in this case, the task of learning a predictive model becomes considerably harder.

We are especially concerned with the problem of discovering the existence of other agents' internal variables, which can be useful to understand their behavior. Our cognitive agent needs to incrementally learn a model of its environment dynamics, and the interaction with other agents represents an important part of it. It is relatively easy to construct a model when the agent interacts with static objects, with simple mobile objects, or with trivial reactive agents; however, when dealing with other complex agents which may change their behaviors according to some non-directly observable internal properties (like emotional or intentional states), the construction of a model becomes significantly harder. The difficulty increases because the reaction of each agent can seem like a non-deterministic behavior from the point of view of our agent, regarding the information provided by the perceptive elements of the situation.

We can suggest at least two points of interest addressed by this paper: the first one is about concept creation, the second one is about agent inter-subjectivity. The capability to develop new abstract concepts have always been a central point in most philosophical and psychological theories concerned with cognitive issues; the possibility of constructing high-level elements to understand the experienced reality has often been pointed as an important capability that enables the human being to deal and adapt itself to a so complex and dynamical environment as the real world [31], [37]. In contrast to the kind of approach usually adopted in AI, which easily slip into the strategy of treating exceptions and lack of information by using probabilistic methods, many cognitive scientists insist that the human mind tries to accommodate the disturbing events observed in the reality by improving the mental model with new levels of abstraction, new representational elements, and new concepts. Moreover, the intricate problem of dealing with other complex agents has also been studied by cognitive science for some time, from psychology to neuroscience, suggesting that the human being has developed the capability to attribute mental states to the others, in order to represent their beliefs, desires and intentions, and so being able to understand their behavior [1], [3], [14].

In this paper, we use the *Constructivist Anticipatory Learning Mechanism* (CALM), defined in [35], to solve the *mept* problem, where a cognitive agent is inserted into an environment constituted of other objects and also of some other agents, which are non-cognitive in the sense that they do not learn anything, but that are similar to our agent in terms of structure and possible behaviors. CALM is able to build a descriptive model of the system where the agent is immersed, inducting, from the experience, the structure of a factored and partially observable Markov Decision Process (FPOMDP). Some positive results have been achieved due to the use of 4 integrated strategies [35], [33], [34]: (a) the mechanism takes advantage of the situated condition presented by the agent, constructing a description of the regularities of the system relatively to the own agent's point of view, which allows to set a good behavior policy without the necessity of "mapping" the entire environment; (b) the learning process is anchored on the construction of an anticipatory model of the world, what could be more efficient and more powerful than traditional *model free* reinforcement learning methods, that directly learn a policy; (c) the mechanism uses some heuristics designed to *well-structured universes*, where conditional dependencies between variables exist in a limited scale, and where most of the phenomena can be described in a deterministic way, even if the system as a whole is not, representing what we call a partially deterministic environment; this characteristic seems to be widely common in real world problems; (d) the mechanism is prepared to discover the existence of hidden or non-observable properties of the universe, which cannot be directly perceived by the agent sensors, but that can explain some observed phenomena. This last characteristic is fundamental to solve the main challenge presented in this article because it enables our agent to discover the existence of internal states in other agents, which is necessary to understand their behavior and then to anticipate it. Further discussion about situatedness can be found in [50], [4], [47].

Thus, the basic idea concerning this paper is to describe the CALM mechanism, proposed in [35], presenting its features, and placing it into the *Markov Decision Process* (MDP) framework panorama. The discussion is supported, on the one hand, by these introductory philosophical conjectures, and on the other hand, by the *mept* experiment, which creates a multi-agent scenario, where our agent needs to induce the existence of internal variables to the other agents. In this way, the paper presents some positive results in both theoretical and practical aspects. Following the paper, section 2 overviews the MDP framework, section 3 describes the CALM learning mechanism, section 4 introduces the experiment and shows the acquired results, and section 5 concludes the paper, arguing that the discover and induction of hidden properties of the system can be a promising strategy to model other agents internal states.

## 2  Markov Decision Process Framework

*Markov Decision Process* (MDP) and its extensions constitute a quite popular framework, largely used for modeling *decision-making* and *planning* problems. An MDP is typically represented as a discrete stochastic state machine; at each time cycle the machine is in some state $s$; the agent interacts with the process by choosing some action $a$ to carry out; then, the machine changes into a new state $s'$, and gives the agent a corresponding reward $r$; a transition function $\delta$ defines the way the machine changes according to $s$ and $a$. Solving an MDP is finding the optimal (or near-optimal) policy of actions in order to maximize the rewards received by the agent over time. When the MDP parameters are completely known, including the reward and the transition functions, it can be mathematically solved by *dynamic programming* (DP) methods. When these functions are unknown, the MDP can be solved by *reinforcement learning* (RL) methods, designed to learn a policy of actions on-line (at the same time the agent interacts with the system), by incrementally estimating the utility of state-actions pairs and then by mapping states to actions [48].

## 2.1   The Classic MDP

Markov Decision Process first appeared (in the form we know) in the late 1950s [5], [24], reaching a concrete popularity in the AI research community from the 1990s [39]. Currently the MDP framework is widely used in the domains of *Automated Control*, *Decision-Theoretic Planning* [7], and *Reinforcement Learning* [16]. A "standard MDP" represents a system through the discretization and enumeration of its state space, similar to a *state machine* in which the transition function can be non-deterministic. The flow of an MDP (the transition between states) depends only on the system current state and on the action taken by the agent at the time. After acting, the agent receives a reward signal, which can be positive or negative if certain particular transitions occur.

However, for a wide range of complex (including real world) problems, the complete information about the exact state of the environment is not available. This kind of problem is often represented as a *Partially Observable Markov Decision Process* (POMDP) [28]. The idea of representing non-observable elements in a MDP is not new [2], [44], but became popular with the revived interest on the framework, occurred in the 1990s [10], [29], [28]. The POMDP provides an elegant mathematical framework for modeling complex decision and planning problems in stochastic domains in which the system states are observable only indirectly, via a set of imperfect, incomplete or noisy perceptions. In a POMDP, the set of observations is different from the set of states, but related to them by an observation function $\omega$; the underlying system state $s$ cannot be directly perceived by the agent, which has access only to an observation $o$. The POMDP is more powerful than the MDP in terms of modeling (i.e. a larger set of problems can be described by a POMDP than by an MDP), but the methods for solving them are computationally even more expensive, and thus applicable in practice only to simple problems [21], [30], [40].

The main bottleneck about the use of MDPs or POMDPs is that representing complex universes implies an exponential growing-up on the represented state space, and the problem quickly becomes intractable. Fortunately, most of real-world problems are quite well-structured; many large MDPs have significant internal structure, and can be modeled compactly if the structure is exploited in the representation; the factorization of states is an approach to do so [9]. In the factored representation, a state is implicitly described by an assignment to some set of state variables. Thus, the complete state space enumeration is avoided, and the system can be described referring directly to its properties. The factorization of states enables to represent the system in a very compact way, even if the corresponding MDP is exponentially large [19], [41]. When the structure of the *Factored Markov Decision Process* (FMDP) is completely described, some known algorithms can be applied to find good policies in a quite efficient way [19]. However, the research concerning the discovery of the structure of an underlying system from incomplete observation is still incipient [13], [12].

## 2.2    Factored and Partially Observable MDP

The classic MDP model can be extended to include both factorization of states and partial observation, then composing a *Factored Partially Observable Markov Decision Process* (FPOMDP). In order to be factored, the atomic elements of the non-factored representation will be decomposed and replaced by a combined set of elements. The description of a given state s in the original model will be decomposed in a set $\{x_1, x_2, ... x_n\}$ in the extended model; a given action $a$ becomes a set $\{c_1, c_2, ... c_m\}$; the monolithic reward signal $r$ becomes $\{r_1, r_2, ... r_k\}$; and the transition function $\delta$ is replaced by a set of transformation functions $\{T_1, T_2, ... T_n\}$.

A FPOMDP ([18], [20], [38], [40], [42], [12]) can be formally defined as a 4-tuple $\{X, C, R, T\}$. The finite non-empty set of system properties or variables $X = \{X_1, X_2, ... X_n\}$ is divided into two subsets, $X = P \cup H$, where the subset $P = \{P_1, P_2, ... P_k\}$ represents the observable properties (those that can be accessed through the agent sensory perception), and the subset $H = \{H_{k+1}, H_{k+2}, ... H_n\}$ represents the hidden or non-observable properties; each property $X_i$ is associated to a specified domain, which defines the values the property can assume. $C = \{C_1, C_2, ... C_m\}$ represents the controllable variables, composing the agent actions, $R = \{R_1, R_2, ... R_k\}$ is the set of (factored) reward functions, in the form of normal probability distributions $R_i : P_i \rightarrow N(\mu_i, \sigma_i^2)$, and $T = \{T_1, T_2, ... T_n\}$ is the set of transformation functions, as $T_i : X \times C \rightarrow \Pi(X_i)$, defining the system dynamics. Each transformation function can be represented as a *Dynamic Bayesien Network* (DBN) [11], which is an acyclic, oriented, two-layers graph; the first layer nodes represent the environment situation in time $t_i$ and the second layer nodes represent the next state in time $t_{i+1}$ [9]. A stationary policy $\pi$ is a mapping $X \rightarrow C$ where $\pi(x)$ defines the action to be taken in a given situation. The agent must learn a policy that optimizes the cumulative rewards received over a potentially infinite time horizon. Typically, the solution $\pi^*$ is the policy that maximizes the expected discounted reward sum, as indicated in the classical Bellman optimality equation [5], here adapted to our FPOMDP notation.

$$V^\pi(x) = R(x) + max_c \left[ \gamma . \sum P(x', x, c).V^\pi(x') \right] \tag{1}$$

In this paper, we consider the case where the agent does not have an *a priori* model of the universe where it is situated (i.e. it does not have any idea about the transformation function), and this condition forces it to be endowed with some capacity of learning, in order to be able to adapt itself to the system. Even if there is a large research community studying model-free methods (that directly learn a policy of actions), in this work we adopt a model-based method, through which the agent must learn a descriptive and predictive model of the world, and so define a behavior strategy based on it. Learning a predictive model is often referred as learning the structure of the problem, which is an important research objective into the MDP framework community [13], as well as in related approaches like *Induction of Decision Trees and Decision Graphs* [23], *Bayesian Networks* [32], [17] and *Influence Diagrams* [25].

In this way, when the agent is immersed in a system represented as a FPOMDP, the complete task for its anticipatory learning mechanism is both to create a model of the transformation function, and to define an optimal (or sufficiently good) policy of actions, in order to establish a behavioral strategy; a given policy of actions $\pi : X \rightarrow C$ defines the behavior to be taken in each given situation. Some algorithms create stochastic policies, and in this case the action to take is defined by a probability. Degris and Sigaud [12] present a good overview of the use of this representation in artificial intelligence, referring several related algorithms designed to learn and solve factored FMDPs and FPOMDPs, including both the algorithms designed to calculate the policy given the model [9], [8], [20], [38], [26], [45], [18], [42], [41] and the algorithms designed to discover the structure of the system [13], [12],[46], [27].

## 3   Anticipatory Learning Mechanism

Anticipatory learning mechanisms refer to methods, algorithms, processes, machines, or any particular system that enables an autonomous agent to create an anticipatory model of the world in which it is situated. An anticipatory model of the world (also called predictive environmental model, or forward model) is an organized set of knowledge allowing inferring the events that are likely to happen [36]. When immersed in a complex universe, an agent (natural or artificial) needs to be able to compose its actions with the other forces and movements of the environment. In most cases, the only way to do so is by understanding what is happening, and thus by anticipating what will (most likely) happen next. A predictive model can be very useful as a tool to guide the behavior; the agent has a perception of the current state of the world, and it decides what actions to perform according to the expectations it has about the way the situation will probably change. The necessity of being endowed with an anticipatory learning mechanism is more evident when the agent is fully situated and completely autonomous; that means, when the agent is by itself, interacting with an unknown, dynamic, and complex world, through limited sensors and effectors, which give it only a local point of view of the state of the universe and only partial control over it. Realistic scenarios can only be successfully faced by an agent capable of discovering the regularities that govern the universe, understanding the causes and the consequences of the phenomena, identifying the forces that influence the observed changes, and mastering the impact of its own actions over the ongoing events.

### 3.1   CALM

The *Constructivist Anticipatory Learning Mechanism* (CALM), detailed in [35], is a mechanism developed to enable an agent to learn the structure of an unknown environment where it is situated, trough observation and experimentation, creating an anticipatory model of the world, which will be represented as an FPOMDP. It is inspired on the theory of the human intelligence described by [37]. CALM learning process is *active* and *incremental*: the agent needs to choose between alternative actions *online*, and learn the world model as well as the policy at the same time it actuates. There is no separated previous training time; the agent has a single uninterrupted interactive experience into the system, quite similarly to real life problems; it needs performing and learning at the same time. The task is composed by two parts: first, building a world model, i.e. to induce a structure which represents the dynamics of the system (composed by agent-environment interactions). Second, to establish a behavioral policy, i.e. to define the actions to do at each possible different state of the system, in order to increase the estimated rewards received over time.

The task becomes harder because the environment is only partially observable, from the point of view of the agent, constituting an FPOMDP. In this case, the agent has perceptive information from a subset of sensory variables, but the system dynamics depends also on another subset of hidden variables. To be able to create a consistent world model, the agent needs, beyond discover the regularities of the phenomena, also discover the existence of non-observable variables that are important to understand the system evolution. In other words, learning a model of the world is more than describing the environment dynamics (the rules that can explain and anticipate the observed transformations), it is also discovering the existence of hidden properties (once they influence the evolution of the observable ones), and finally find a way to deduce the values of these hidden properties. The system as a whole is in fact a FPOMDP, but CALM is designed to discover the existence of non-observable properties, integrating them in its anticipatory model, and in this way CALM can induce a structure to represent the dynamics of the system in a form of a FMDP (if the agent can successfully discover and describe the hidden properties of the FPOMDP which it is dealing with, then the world becomes treatable as a FMDP because the hidden variables become known). There are some algorithms able to efficiently calculate the optimal (or near-optimal) policy, when the FMDP is given [19]. The algorithm to calculate the policy of actions used by CALM is similar to the one presented by [13]. On the other hand, the main challenge is to discover the structure of the problem based on the on-line observation, and CALM do it using representations and strategies inspired on [15].

**Representing Predictive Knowledge by Schemas.** CALM tries to reconstruct, by experience, each system transformation function $T_i$, representing it by an anticipatory tree; each anticipatory tree is composed by pieces of predictive knowledge called schemas; each *schema* represents some perceived regularity occurring in the environment (some regular event checked by the agent during its interaction with the world) by associating context (sensory and abstract), actions and expected results (anticipations).

A schema is composed by three vectors, $\Xi = \{context \wedge action \rightarrow result\}$, denoting a kind of predictive rule. The *context vector* has their elements linked both with the agent sensors and with the abstract variables; these abstract variables are represented by (mentally created) *synthetic elements* not linked to any sensor but referring to non-sensory properties of the universe, which the existence is induced by the mechanism. The *action vector* is linked with the agent effectors. Context and action vectors can represent sets of equivalent situations or actions, by generalization. The *result vector* represents the value expected for the context in the next time, after executing the given action in the given context. Each element vector can assume any value in a discrete interval defined by the respective variable domain.

Some elements in these vectors can undertake an "undefined value". For example, an element linked with a binary sensor must have one of three values: true, false or undefined, represented respectively by the symbols $\{1, 0, \#\}$. The undefined value generalizes the schema because it allows to ignore some properties to represent a set of situations. The learning process happens through the refinement of the set of schemas. After each experienced situation, CALM updates a generalized episodic memory, and then it checks if the result (context perceived at the instant following the action) is in conformity to the expected result of the activated schema. If the anticipation fails, the error between the result and the expectation serves as parameter to correct the model. The context and action vectors are gradually specialized by differentiation, adding each time a new relevant feature to identify more precisely the situation class.

The use of undefined values makes possible the construction of an *anticipatory tree*. Each node in that tree is a schema, and relations of generalization and specialization guide its topology (quite similar to decision trees or discrimination trees). The root node represents the most generalized situation, which has the context and action vectors completely undefined. Adding one level in the tree is to specialize one generalized element, creating a branch where the undefined value is replaced by the different possible defined values. This specialization occurs either in the context vector or in the action vector. In this way, CALM divides the state space according to the different expected results, grouping contexts and actions with its respective transformations. The tree evolves during the agent's life, and it is used by the agent, even if until under construction, to take its decisions, and in consequence, to define its behavior. The structure of the schemas and an example of their organization as an anticipatory tree are presented in Figure 1.

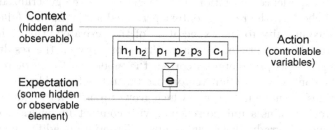

**Fig. 1.** The anticipatory tree; each node is a schema composed of three vectors: context, action and expected result; the leaf nodes are decider schemas

The context in which the agent is at a given moment (perceived through its sensors) is applied in the tree, exciting all the schemas that have a compatible context vector. This process defines a set of excited schemas, each one suggesting a different action to do in the given situation. CALM will choose one to activate, performing the defined action through the agent's effectors. The algorithm always chooses the compatible schema that has the most specific context, called decider schema, which is the leaf of a differentiated branch. This decision is taken based on the calculated utility of each possible choice. There are two kinds of utility: the first one estimates the discounted sum of rewards in the future following the policy, the second one measures the exploration benefits. The utility value used to take the decision depends on the circumstantial agent strategy (exploiting or exploring). The mechanism has also a kind of generalized episodic memory, which represents (in a compact form) the specific and real situations experimented in the past, preserving the necessary information to correctly constructs the tree.

## 3.2  Anticipatory Tree Construction

The learning process happens through the refinement of the set of schemas. At each given moment in the time, the set of schemas of our agent, gradually constructed by the mechanism, is supposed to be coherent with all the past experience, describing in a organized way the regular phenomena observed during the interaction with the universe. To do so, the mechanism must have a memory of the past situations, but this memory cannot be neither too much precise (because remembering all the experienced episodes would require a nonviable amount of space) nor too much simple (because the lack of information makes impossible to revise the model in case of contradiction with new disequilibrating observations). The implementation of a feasible episodic memory is not evident; it can be very expensive if we try to stock too much information coming from the sensory flow; however, using some strong but well chosen restrictions (like limiting dependency analysis between variables), and using a generalized and structured representation of the past experience, it becomes computationally viable.

After each experienced situation, CALM actualizes the generalized episodic memory and checks if the result (context perceived at the instant following the action) is in conformity to the expectation of the activated schema in the anticipatory tree. If the anticipation fails, the error between the result and the expectation serves as parameter to correct the model. In the anticipatory tree topology, the context and action vectors are taken together. This concatenated vector identifies the node in the tree, which grows up using a top-down strategy: the initial tree contains a unique schema, with completely generalized context and action, and it is gradually specialized by differentiation, adding new relevant features to identify more precisely the category of equivalent situations, which implies the creation of new branches in the tree where the context and action vectors are each time more defined. In well-structured universes, there is a shorter way starting with an empty vector and searching for the probably small set of features relevant to distinguish the important situations, than starting with a full vector and having to waste energy eliminating a lot of useless elements. Selecting the good set of relevant features to represent some given concept is a well known problem in AI, and the solution is not easy, even by approximated approaches. To do it, CALM adopts a forward greedy selection [6], using the data registered in the generalized episodic memory.

The expected result vector can be seen as a label in each decider schema, anticipating how the world changes when the schema is activated. Initially all different expectations are considered as different classes, and they are gradually generalized and integrated with others. The agent has two alternatives when the expectation fails. In a way to make the knowledge compatible with the experience, the first alternative is to try to divide the scope of the schema, creating new schemas, with more specialized contexts. Sometimes it is not possible and then the schema expectation is reduced. In the expected result vector, # means that the element is not deterministically predictable. Another symbols can be used to represent some special situations, in order to reduce the number of schemas; it is the case of the symbol '=', used to indicate that the value of the expected element will not be changed.

Three basic methods compose the CALM learning function, namely: *differentiation*, *adjustment*, and *integration*. Differentiation is a necessary mechanism because a schema responsible for a context too general can hardly make precise anticipations. If a general schema does not work well, the mechanism divides it into new schemas, differentiating them by some element of the context or action vector. In fact, the differentiation method takes an unstable decider schema and changes it into a two level sub-tree. The parent schema in this sub-tree preserves the context of the original schema. The children, which are the new decider schemas, have their context vectors a little bit more specialized than their parent. They attribute a value to some undefined element, dividing the scope of the original schema. Each one of these new deciders engages itself in a part of the domain. In this way, the previous correct knowledge remains preserved, distributed in the new schemas, and the discordant situation is isolated and treated only in its specific context. Differentiation is the method responsible to make the anticipatory tree grows up. Each level of the tree represents the introduction of some new constraint. The algorithm needs to choose what will be the differentiator element, and it could be from either the context vector or the action vector. This differentiator needs to separate the situation responsible for the disequilibrium from the others, and the algorithm chooses it by calculating the information gain, and considering a limited (parametrized) range of interdependencies between variables. Figure 2 illustrates the differentiation process.

When some schema fails and it is not possible to differentiate it in any way, then CALM executes the adjustment method. This method reduces the expectations of an unstable decider schema in order to make it reliable again. The algorithm simply compares the activated schema's expectation and the real result perceived by the agent after the application of the schema, setting the incompatible

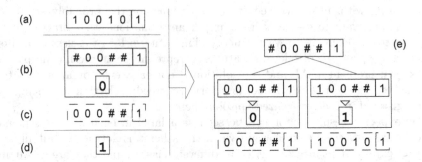

**Fig. 2.** Differentiation method example; (a) some real experimented situation (with five variables) and executed action (one variable); (b) activated schema (with compatible context and action); (c) associated episodic memory (representation of real situations where the scheme has been activated, in this case representing no interdependencies between variables); (d) real observed result, after the execution of the action; (e) sub-tree generated by differentiation, in order to compensate the divergence observed between expectation and result

expectation elements to the undefined value ('#'). The adjustment method changes the schema expectation (and consequently the anticipation predicted by the schema). Successive adjustments can reveal some unnecessary differentiations. Figure 3 illustrates that.

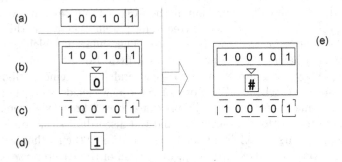

**Fig. 3.** Adjustment method example; (a) some real experimented situation and action; (b) activated schema; (c) related episodic memory; (d) real observed result; (e) schema expectation reduction after adjustment

In this way, the schema expectation can change (and consequently the class of the situation represented by the schema), and the tree maintenance mechanism needs to be able to reorganize the tree when this change occurs. Therefore, successive adjustments in the expectations of various schemas can reveal unnecessary differentiations. When CALM finds a group of schemas with similar expectations to approach different contexts, the integration method comes

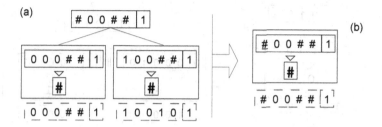

**Fig. 4.** Integration method; (a) sub-tree after some adjust; (b) an integrated schema substitutes the sub-tree

into action, trying to join these schemas by searching for some unnecessary common differentiator element, and eliminating it. The method operates as shown in figure 4.

### 3.3  Dealing with the Unobservable

When CALM reduces the expectation of a given schema by adjustment, it supposes that there is no deterministic regularity following the represented situation in relation to these incoherent elements, and the related transformation is unpredictable. However, sometimes a prediction error could be explained by considering the existence of some abstract or hidden property in the environment, which could be useful to differentiate an ambiguous situation, but which is not directly perceived by the agent sensors. So, before adjusting, CALM supposes the existence of a non-sensory property into the environment, which will be represented as a synthetic element. When a new synthetic element is created, it is included as a new term in the context and expectation vectors of the schemas. Synthetic elements suppose the existence of something beyond the sensory perception, which can be useful to explain non-equilibrated situations. They have the function of amplifying the differentiation possibilities.

In this way, when dealing with partially observable environments, CALM has two additional challenges: (a) inferring the existence of unobservable properties, which it will represent by synthetic elements, and (b) including these new elements into its predictive model. A good strategy to do this task is looking at the historical information. In the case where the POMDP is completely deterministic, it is possible to find sufficient little pieces of history to distinguish and identify all the underlying states [22], and we suppose that it is similar when the POMDP in non-deterministic but well structured.

CALM introduces a method called *abstract differentiation*. When a schema fails in its prediction, and when it is not possible to differentiate it by the current set of considered properties, then a new boolean synthetic element is created, enlarging the context and expectation vectors. Immediately, this element is used to differentiate the incoherent situation from the others. The method attributes

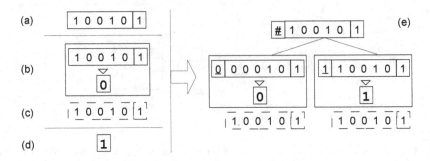

**Fig. 5.** Synthetic element creation method; (e) incremented context and expectation vectors, and differentiation using synthetic element

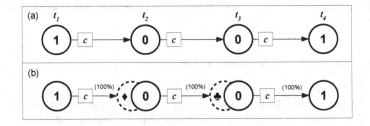

**Fig. 6.** Predicting the dynamics of a non-observable property; in (a) a real experienced sequence; in (b) the use of a synthetic element to explain the logic behind the observed transformations

arbitrary values to this element in each differentiated schema. These values represent the presence or absence of some non-observable condition, necessary to determine the correct prediction in the given situation. The method is illustrated in figure 5, where the new elements are represented by card suites.

Once a synthetic element is created, it can be used in next differentiations. A new synthetic element will be created only if the existing ones are already saturated. To avoid the problem of creating infinite new synthetic elements, CALM can do it only until a determined limit, after which it considers that the problematic anticipation is not deterministically predictable, undefining the expectation in the related schemas by adjustment.

The synthetic element is not associated to any sensory perception. Consequently, its value cannot be observed. This fact can place the agent in ambiguous situations, where it does not know whether some relevant but not observable condition (represented by this element) is present or absent. Initially, the value of a synthetic element is verified *a posteriori* (i.e. after the execution of the action in an ambiguous situation). Once the action is executed and the following result is verified, then the agent can rewind and deduce what was the situation really faced in the past instant (disambiguated). Discovering the value of a synthetic element after the circumstance where this information was needed can seem useless, but in fact, this delayed deduction gives information to another method called *abstract anticipation*. If the non-observable property represented by this synthetic element has a regular dynamics, then the mechanism can propagate the deduced value back to the schema activated in the immediate previous instant. The deduced synthetic element value will be included as a new anticipation in the previous activated schema. Figure 6 shows how this new element can be included in the predictive model.

## 4   Experiment

The CALM mechanism has already been used to successfully solve problems such as *flip*, which is also used by [43] and [22], and *wepp*, which is an interesting RL situated problem. CALM is able to solve both of them by creating new synthetic elements to represent underlying states of the problem [35], [33], [34]. In this paper, we introduce an experiment that we call *mept* (acronym to the actions that the agent can do: move, eat, play, touch).

In the *mept* experiment, the agent is inserted into a two-dimensional environment (like a "grid") where it should learn how to interact with other agents and objects that can be found during its life. Our agent needs to create a policy of actions in a way to optimize its feelings (internal rewards). When it is hungry, it feels good by eating some food (which is an object that can be sometimes found in the environment, among other uneatable objects like stones). Agents and objects can be differentiated by observable features, it means that our agent can sensorially distinguish what is the "thing" with which it is interacting. However, both food and stone have the same appearance, and in this way, to discover if the object is either food or stone, the agent needs to experiment, it means, the agent needs to explicitly interact with the environment in order to take more information about the situation, for example, tapping the object to listen what sound it makes.

When our agent is happy, it founds pleasure by playing with another agent. However, the other agents also have internal emotional states; when another agent is angry, any tentative to play with results in an aggression, which causes a disagreeable painful sensation to our agent. Playing is enjoyable and safe only if both agents are happy, or at least if the other agent is not angry (and then, not aggressive), but these emotional states are internal to each agent, and cannot be directly perceived. With such configuration, our agent will need to create new synthetic elements to be able to distinguish what is food and what is stone, and to distinguish who are aggressive and who are peaceable.

At each time step, our agent can execute one of 4 actions: *move, eat, play* or *tap*. Moving itself is a good strategy to scape from other aggressive agents, but it is also the action that changes the context, allowing the agent to search for different contexts. The agent does not control precisely the movement it does; the action of moving itself causes a random rotation followed by a position changing to an adjacent cell. Eating is the good choice when the agent is hungry and it is in front of some food at the same time, action that ceases the bad sensation caused by hungry. Playing is the good action to be carried out when the agent is happy and in frontal contact with another non-aggressive agent. Tapping is the action that serves to interacting with other objects without compromise; doing it, the agent is able to identify the solution to some ambiguous situations; for example, tapping stones or tapping food provokes different kinds of sound effects; the same for another agents, that react to a tap with a growl when angry, and with a laugh when happy.

The agent has two limited external perceptions, both focused on the cell that is directly in front of it; the sense of *vision* allows it to see if the place before him contains an object, an agent, or nothing; the sense of *hearing* permits to listen the sounds coming from there. The agent's body has 5 internal properties, corresponding to 5 equivalent internal perceptions: *pain, anger, hungry, happiness,* and *pleasure.* Pleasure occurs always when the agent plays with another agent, independently of the other agent internal state (which is quite selfish). However, as we know, our agent can get punched if the other agent is angry, and in this case pain takes place. When our agent feels pain and hungry at the same time, it becomes angry too. Initially the agent does not know anything about the environment or about its own sensations. It does not distinguish the situations, and also does not know what consequences its actions imply.

The problem becomes interesting because playing can provoke both positive and negative rewards, the same for eating, that is an interesting behavior only in certain situations; it depends on the context where the action is executed, which is not fully observable by sensors. This is the model that CALM needs to learn by itself before establishing the behavior policy. Figures 7 to 10 show some of the anticipatory trees created by the mechanism after stabilization.

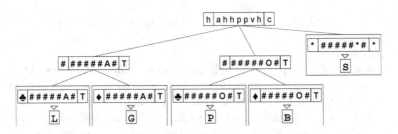

**Fig. 7.** Anticipatory tree for hearing; the only action that provokes sound is tapping (T), it is different depending on the mood of the tapped agent (happy or angry); if the action is other (*) than tapping, then no sound is produced

Figure 5 shows the evolution of the mean reward comparing the CALM solution with a random agent, and with two classic *Q-Learning* [49] implementations: the first one non-situated (the agent has the vision of the entire environment as flat state space), and the second one with equivalent (situated) inputs than CALM.

The non-situated implementation of Q-Learning algorithm (Classic Q) takes much more time to start drawing a convergence curve than the others, and in

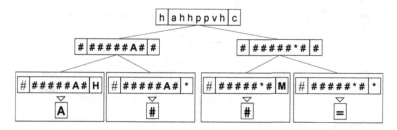

**Fig. 8.** Anticipatory tree for vision; when the agent taps (T) another agent (A), it verifies the permanence of this other agent in its visual field, which means that tapping an agent makes it stay in the same place; however, no other actions (*) executed in front of an agent (A) can prevents it to leave its position, and so the prediction is undefined (#); the same for moving itself (M), which causes a situation changing and the unpredictability of the visual field for the next instant; in all of the other cases the vision stays unchanged

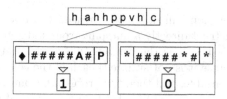

**Fig. 9.** Anticipatory tree for pleasure; playing with a peaceable (◊) agent (A) is pleasant, and it is the only known way to reach this feeling

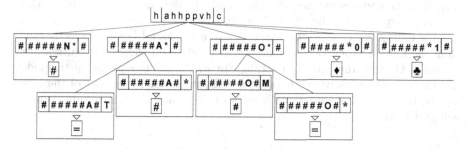

**Fig. 10.** Hidden element anticipatory tree; this element allows identifying whether an object is food or stone, and whether an agent is angry or not; CALM abstract anticipation method allows modeling the dynamics of this variable, even if t is not directly observable by direct sensory perception; the perception of the noise (1) is the result that enables the discovering of the value of this hidden property; the visual perception of an object (O), or the fact of tapping (T) another agent (A), also permit to know that the hidden element does not change

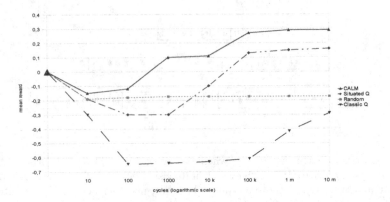

**Fig. 11.** Evolution of mean reward in a typical execution of the mept problem, considering four different agent solutions: CALM, situated Q-Learning, Random, and Classic Q-Learning; the scenario is a 25x25 grid, where 10% of the cells are stones and 5% are food, in the presence of 10 other agents

fact, the expected solution will never be reached; it is due to the fact that Q-Learning tries to construct directly a mapping from states to actions (a policy), but the state space is taken as the combination of the state variables; in this implementation (because it is not situated) each of the cells in the environment compose a different variable, and then the problem becomes quickly big; by the same cause, the agent becomes vulnerable to the growing of the board (the grid dimensions imply directly in the complexity of the problem).

The CALM solution converges much earlier than Q-Learning, even taken in its situated version, and CALM found a better solution also; it is due to the fact that CALM quickly constructs a model to predict the environment dynamics, including the non-observable properties in the model, and so it is able to define a good policy sooner. The "pause" in the convergence that can be seen in the graphic indicates two moments: first, the solution found before correctly modeling the hidden properties as synthetic elements, and then, the solution after having it. On the other side, Q-Learning stays attached to a probabilistic model, and in this case, without the information about the internal states of the other agents, trying to play with them becomes unsafe, and the Q-Learning solution will prefer do not do it.

## 5    Conclusions

The CALM mechanism, presented in [35], can provide autonomous adaptive capability to an agent, because it is able to incrementally construct knowledge to represent the deterministic regularities observed during its interaction with the system, even in partially deterministic and partially observable environments. CALM can deal with the incomplete observation trough the induction and prediction of hidden properties, represented by synthetic elements, thus it is able to overpass the limit of sensory perception, constructing more abstract terms to represent the system, and to describe its dynamics in more complex levels. CALM can be very efficient to construct a model in non-deterministic environments if they are well structured. In other words, if the most part of transformations are in fact deterministic relatively to the underlying partially observable properties, and if the interdependence between variables are limited to a small range. Several problems found in the real world present these characteristics.

This paper presented a new experiment (*mept*) which, even if simple, introduces a new challenge to the agent : learning the regularities in the interaction with other complex agents. We have successful demonstrate that the CALM mechanism is able to create an anticipatory model of the other agents' behaviors when certain conditions are satisfied. The next step in this way could be to insert several cognitive agents like CALM in the same scenario; it means, agents that change our own internal model and policy of action, and in this way, agents that present non-stationary behaviors; the difficulty for one agent to model the other agents in this kind of condition would be even harder.

We believe that the same strategy can be adapted to several kinds of classification tasks, where a previous database of samples are available. In this case, the algorithm learns to classify new instances based on a model created from a training set of instances that have been properly labeled with the correct classes. This task is similar to several real world problems actually solved with the computer aim, such as e-mail filtering, diagnostic systems, recommendation systems, decision support systems, and so on.

# References

1. Astington, J.W., Harris, P.L., Olson, D.R. (eds.): Developing Theories of Mind. Cambridge University Press, Cambridge (1988)
2. Astrom, K.J.: Optimal Control of Markov Decision Processes with Incomplete State Estimation. Journal of Mathematical Analysis and Applications 10, 174–205 (1965)
3. Bateson, G.: Steps to an Ecology of Mind: Collected Essays in Anthropology, Psychiatry, Evolution, and Epistemology. University of Chicago Press (1972)
4. Beer, R.D.: A dynamical systems perspective on agent-environment interactions. Artificial Intelligence 72, 173–215 (1995)
5. Bellman, R.: A Markovian Decision Process. Journal of Mathematics and Mechanics 6 (1957)
6. Blum, A.L., Langley, P.: Selection of relevant features and examples in machine learning. Artificial Intelligence 97, 245–271 (1997)
7. Blythe, J.: Decision-Theoretic Planning. AI Magazine 20(2), 37–54 (1999)
8. Boutilier, C., Poole, D.: Computing optimal policies for partially observable decision processes using compact representations. In: Proceedings of the 13th National Conference on Artificial Intelligence, AAAI, OR, USA, vol. 2, pp. 1168–1175. AAAI Press, Portland (1996)
9. Boutilier, C., Dearden, R., Goldszmidt, M.: Stochastic dynamic programming with factored representations. Artificial Intelligence 121(1-2), 49–107 (2000)

10. Chrisman, L.: Reinforcement Learning with Perceptual Aliasing: the perceptual distinctions approach. In: Proceedings of the 10th National Conference on Artificial Intelligence, AAAI, San Jose, CA, USA, pp. 183–188. AAAI Press (1992)
11. Dean, T., Kanazawa, K.: A model for reasoning about persistence and causation. Comp. Intel. 5(3), 142–150 (1989)
12. Degris, T., Sigaud, O.: Factored Markov Decision Processes. In: Buffet, O., Sigaud, O. (eds.) Markov Decision Processes in Artificial Intelligence. Loria, Vandoeuvre-lès-Nancy (2010)
13. Degris, T., Sigaud, O., Wuillemin, P.-H.: Learning the Structure of Factored Markov Decision Processes in Reinforcement Learning Problems. In: Proceedings of the 23rd International Conference on Machine Learning, ICML, pp. 257–264. ACM, Pittsburgh (2006)
14. Dennett, D.: The Intentional Stance. MIT Press, Cambridge (1987)
15. Drescher, G.: Made-Up Minds: a constructivist approach to artificial intelligence. MIT Press, Cambridge (1991)
16. Feinberg, E.A., Shwartz, A.: Handbook of Markov Decision Processes: methods and applications. Kluwer, Norwell (2002)
17. Friedman, N., Koller, D.: Being Bayesian about Network Structure: a bayesian approach to structure discovery in bayesian networks. Machine Learning 50(1-2), 95–125 (2003)
18. Guestrin, C., Koller, D., Parr, R.: Solving Factored POMDPs with Linear Value Functions. In: Proceedings of the Workshop on Planning under Uncertainty and Incomplete Information, Seattle, WA, pp. 67–75 (2001)
19. Guestrin, C., Koller, D., Parr, R., Venkataraman, S.: Efficient Solution Algorithms for Factored MDPs. Journal of Artificial Intelligence Research 19, 399–468 (2003)
20. Hansen, E.A., Feng, Z.: Dynamic programming for POMDPs using a factored state representation. In: Proceedings of the 5th International Conference on Artificial Intelligence, Planning and Scheduling, AIPS, Breckenridge, CO, USA, pp. 130–139. AAAI Press (2000)
21. Hauskrecht, M.: Value-function approximations for partially observable Markov decision processes. Journal of Artificial Intelligence Research 13, 33–94 (2000)
22. Holmes, M., Isbell, C.: Looping Suffix Tree-Based Inference of Partially Observable Hidden State. In: Proceedings of the 23rd International Conference on Machine Learning, ICML, pp. 409–416. ACM, Pittsburgh (2006)
23. Jensen, F.B., Graven-Nielsen, T.: Bayesian Networks and Decision Graphs, 2nd edn. Springer (2007)
24. Howard, R.A.: Dynamic Programming and Markov Processes. MIT Press, Cambridge (1960)
25. Howard, R.A., Matheson, J.E.: Influence Diagrams. In: The Principles and Applications of Decision Analysis, pp. 720–762 (1981)
26. Hoey, J., St-Aubin, R., Hu, A.J., Boutilier, C.: SPUDD: Stochastic Planning Using Decision Diagrams. In: Proceedings of the 15th International Conference on Uncertainty in Artificial Intelligence, UAI, Stockholm, Sweden. Morgan Kaufmann, San Francisco (1999)
27. Jonsson, A., Barto, A.: A Causal Approach to Hierarchical Decomposition of Factored MDPs. In: Proceedings of the 22nd International Conference on Machine Learning, ICML, Bonn, Germany, pp. 401–408. ACM (2005)
28. Kaelbling, L.P., Littman, M.L., Cassandra, A.R.: Planning and acting in partially observable stochastic domains. Artificial Intelligence 101, 99–134 (1998)

29. Kaelbling, L.P., Littman, M.L., Cassandra, A.R.: Acting optimally in partially observable stochastic domains. In: Proceedings of the 12th National Conference on Artificial Intelligence, AAAI, Seattle, WA, USA, pp. 1023–1028. AAAI Press (1994)
30. Meuleau, N., Kim, K.-E., Kaelbling, L.P., Cassandra, A.R.: Solving POMDPs by Searching the Space of Finite Policies. In: Proceedings of the 15th International Conference on Uncertainty in Artificial Intelligence, UAI, Stockholm, Sweden, pp. 427–443. Morgan Kaufmann, San Francisco (1999)
31. Murphy, G.L.: The big book of concepts. MIT Press, Cambridge (2002)
32. Pearl, J.: Causality: models of reasoning and inference. Cambridge University Press (2000)
33. Perotto, F.S., Álvares, L.O.: Incremental Inductive Learning in a Constructivist Agent. In: Proceedings of the Research and Development in Intelligent Systems XXIII, SGAI 2006, pp. 129–144. Springer, London (2007)
34. Perotto, F.S., Álvares, L.O., Buisson, J.-C.: Constructivist Anticipatory Learning Mechanism (CALM): Dealing with Partially Deterministic and Partially Observable Environments. In: Proceedings of the 7th International Conference on Epigenetic Robotics, Piscataway, NJ, USA, pp. 117–127. Lund University Cognitive Studies, New Jersey (2007)
35. Perotto, F.S.: Un Mécanisme Constructiviste d'Apprentissage Automatique d'Anticipations pour des Agents Artificiels Situés. PhD Thesis. INP, Toulouse, France (2010) (in French)
36. Perotto, F.S.: Anticipatory Learning Mechanisms. In: Seel, N.M. (ed.) Encyclopedia of the Sciences of Learning. Springer, Heidelberg (2012)
37. Piaget, J.: La Psychologie de l'Intelligence. Armand Colin, Paris (1947)
38. Poupart, P., Boutilier, C.: VDCBPI: an approximate scalable algorithm for large scale POMDPs. In: Proceedings of the 17th Advances in Neural Information Processing Systems, NIPS, Vancouver, Canada, pp. 1081–1088. MIT Press, Cambridge (2004)
39. Puterman, M.L.: Markov Decision Processes: discrete stochastic dynamic programming. Wiley, New York (1994)
40. Shani, G., Brafman, R.I., Shimony, S.E.: Model-Based Online Learning of POMDPs. In: Gama, J., Camacho, R., Brazdil, P.B., Jorge, A.M., Torgo, L. (eds.) ECML 2005. LNCS (LNAI), vol. 3720, pp. 353–364. Springer, Heidelberg (2005)
41. Shani, G., Poupart, P., Brafman, R.I., Shimony, S.E.: Efficient ADD Operations for Point-Based Algorithms. In: Proceedings of the 8th International Conference on Automated Planning and Scheduling, ICAPS, Sydney, Australia, pp. 330–337. AAAI Press (2008)
42. Sim, H.S., Kim, K.-E., Kim, J.H., Chang, D.-S., Koo, M.-W.: Symbolic Heuristic Search Value Iteration for Factored POMDPs. In: Proceedings of the 23rd National Conference on Artificial Intelligence, AAAI, Chicago, IL, USA, pp. 1088–1093. AAAI Press (2008)
43. Singh, S., Littman, M., Jong, N., Pardoe, D., Stone, P.: Learning Predictive State Representations. In: Proceedings of the 20th International Conference on Machine Learning, ICML, Washington, DC, USA, pp. 712–719. AAAI Press (2003)
44. Smallwood, R.D., Sondik, E.J.: The optimal control of partially observable Markov decision processes over a finite horizon. Operations Research, Informs 21, 1071–1088 (1973)

45. St-Aubin, R., Hoey, J., Boutilier, C.: APRICODD: Approximate policy construction using decision diagrams. In: Proceedings of the 12th Advances in Neural Information Processing Systems, NIPS, Denver, CO, USA. MIT Press, Cambridge (2000)
46. Strehl, A.L., Diuk, C., Littman, M.L.: Efficient Structure Learning in Factored-State MDPs. In: Proceedings of the 22nd National Conference on Artificial Intelligence, AAAI, Vancouver, Canada, pp. 645–650. AAAI Press (2007)
47. Suchman, L.A.: Plans and Situated Actions. Cambridge University Press (1987)
48. Sutton, R.S., Barto, A.G.: Reinforcement Learning: an introduction. MIT Press (1998)
49. Watkins, C.J.C.H., Dayan, P.: Q-learning. Machine Learning 8(3), 279–292 (1992)
50. Wilson, R., Clark, A.: How to Situate Cognition: Letting Nature Take its Course. In: Aydede, M., Robbins, P. (eds.) Cambridge Handbook of Situated Cognition. Cambridge University Press, New York (2008)

# Author Index